W9-AWC-313

A Whole Different Ball Game

The Inside
Story of
Baseball's
New Deal

Marvin Miller

Preface by Studs Terkel

Introduction by Bill James

A FIRESIDE BOOK
Published by Simon & Schuster
New York London Toronto Sydney Tokyo Singapore

F

FIRESIDE
Simon & Schuster Building
Rockefeller Center
1230 Avenue of the Americas
New York, New York, 10020

Copyright © 1991 by Marvin Miller
All rights reserved
including the right of reproduction
in whole or in part in any form.
First Fireside Edition 1992
Published by arrangement with Carol Publishing Group.
FIRESIDE and colophon are registered trademarks
of Simon & Schuster Inc.
Manufactured in the United States of America

10 9 8 7 6 5 4 3 2 1 Pbk.

Library of Congress Cataloging in Publication Data
Miller, Marvin, date.
    A whole different ball game : the sport and business of baseball /
Marvin Miller.—1st Fireside ed.
        p.   cm.
    "A Fireside book."
    Includes index.
    1. Baseball—United States—Finance—History.   2. Trade-unions—
Baseball players—United States—History.   I. Title.
    GV880.M57   1991
    338.4'7796357—dc20   91-42121
                                                                               CIP

ISBN: 0-671-76942-1 Pbk.

To
Terry

Contents

Foreword

by STUDS TERKEL

WHEN I WAS YOUNG AND EASY, Carl Hubbell was the nonpareil of southpaws. When he took the mound, no matter whom he faced, it was money in the bank for the Giants. He was their meal ticket. The fans came to see him, not Horace Stoneham, the proprietor.

Yet years and wars and floods later, when ballplayers had formed a union and had discovered something hitherto foreign to them—security—an embittered old man, Carl Hubbell, held forth from his front porch. He dreamed of the good old days and damned the union, remembering the generosity of "Mr. Stoneham." He had forgotten that *he* had been Mr. Stoneham's meal ticket.

Perhaps it was natural for an elderly man, who had been the most skilled of craftsmen, to feel this way. What he had received in wages was pitiful when contrasted to the "stratospheric" salaries of today's ballplayers, some of whom couldn't carry his scuffed mitt. He had forgotten the twilight years of so many of his colleagues, pensionless and penniless. Twilight comes early for these athletes, four to five years being the average career in the big leagues. Today, one of seventy who sign a contract makes it to the majors. No matter how disparate their skills, they're still the best at their trade.

Steve Hamilton, a relief pitcher of recent years, as thoughtful as he was well traveled, put it most succinctly. "There's a great to-do about our salaries. But no one questions the income of the six hundred top lawyers or top insurance men—the kind who own ball clubs. I've always wondered about that."

It is surprising that more of us haven't wondered about that, too. Who provides us more delight and surcease from our daily trials, top ballplayers or top insurance men? Or top accountants, whom Hamilton might have included among the Mister Misters.

This is by way of introducing this revealing memoir that tells us about more than baseball. Though it's about ballplayers and owners, it's about a powerful myth, destroyed. It's about thralldom and independence. In short, it's an exhilarating work.

Marvin Miller, the founding executive director of the Major League Baseball Players Association, came along and not only changed the rules of the game but brought an end to the age of innocence: for some of our finest athletes, it was a liberating experience. They discovered that "union" was not a dirty word. They discovered a sense of community. One of the most moving aspects of this book concerns ballplayers, including the stars, fighting not only for themselves, but for the old-timers as well and for the kids yet to come. In these days, when union-busting is the fashion of the day, and mean-spiritedness the new religion, this is pretty thrilling stuff.

Marvin Miller, I suspect, is the most effective union organizer since John L. Lewis. Though the times may be out of joint for trade unionism, though "scab" is no longer a dirty word in too many quarters, something remarkable has happened to our pro athletes: they have discovered where the body is buried, who gets what and who earns what he gets. And it began with the baseball players.

It hasn't been easy. Miller's story is something of a saga. He and the few bold players who backed him were battling a myth: baseball is a sport, not a business, and thus not subject to antitrust laws. That was a 1922 Supreme Court decision, written by, of all jurists, Oliver Wendell Holmes. An "advisor" to the ballplayers, in the pre-Miller days, advised them they were the luckiest men on earth, being paid for playing a kid's game. A lot of fans still believe it.

So did the ballplayers in 1966, when the union came into being. At the beginning of spring training, when Miller hit the camps and met the players for the first time, the vote of the first four clubs was 102 to 17 against him. The remaining sixteen teams voted 472 to 34 in his favor. Who said pro athletes aren't fast learners?

The year 1981 was, of course, the watershed year. It was the year of the strike engineered and provoked by the owners and drum-majored by the ineffable Bowie Kuhn. The arrogance of the owners, who had apparently forgotten what century this was, was reminiscent of General Bullmoose on a bad day. As you'll discover in these pages, there were hilarious moments worthy of W. C. Fields. The owners blew it, the players won. In their triumph, they discovered that Mister Mister was not that bright. That, too, was a liberating experience.

Despite the fears, so long extant, that a players' union would destroy the game, it's healthier than ever, especially for the owners. Attendance records are shattered; TV revenue runs into multimillions; and the teams, despite free agency (or perhaps because of it), are better balanced.

Perhaps there is a metaphor here. I hope a lot of fans read this book. It's a pip of an eye-opener.

Introduction

by Bill James

If baseball ever buys itself a mountain and starts carving faces in it, one of the first men to go up is sure to be Marvin Miller. (Let's see...who else would be in the group? Babe Ruth, Branch Rickey, Jackie Robinson, Judge Landis...That's four already, five with Marvin. Maybe they can buy *Kenesaw* Mountain and get an extra one that way.)

To be put in stone is a terrible fate to wish upon the living, let alone a living labor leader. Twenty years ago sportswriters used to describe everything said by Marvin Miller as a "demand," and everything done by the union as though the entire thing was an extension of his ego: "Marvin Miller met with his executive board in Manhattan this morning and demanded coffee and a danish."

I am always surprised by how easily arrogance can be passed off as humility, in the real and confusing world, and how often humility will be mistaken for arrogance. Miller's battle was not for himself, but for what he saw as being right, the right of the players to control their own careers and participate in the enormous

• xiii •

wealth generated by major league baseball. He worked hard to keep the spotlight off himself and on the issues, on the absurdity of the status quo—but the simple fact that so little was known about *him,* as a man, enabled his opponents to paint onto him whatever image they chose. He courted enemies among the wealthy and powerful and became the target of their animus. Because he attacked the settled issues of power, it was easy to portray him as arrogant. Because he was so effective, it was easy to portray him as powerful. The irony of Miller's greatness is that he became larger than life by trying hard not to be, by trying simply to slip into the role he had created for himself.

I think this book is, in a sense, Marvin Miller's effort to get down off Rushmore, to walk and talk among us, not as a figurehead, still revered and still hated these many years later, but as a human being. He certainly hasn't lost his faith in the justness of the cause for which he fought, but he remembered Charlie Finley not merely as an adversary, but as a *guy*—sometimes comical and normally patronizing, but human. He remembers Bill Veeck as we all do, fondly, and seems genuinely unaware that beside his own footprint in the history of the game, that of Bill Veeck is tiny and temporary—cute, but not lasting.

To many people the labor situation in baseball today seems bizarre and distorted, but, then, many things would seem bizarre and distorted if cut off from their history. The economics of baseball today still seem bizarre to many of us because we grew up in an age when a few rich and powerful men, using propaganda and the press, were able to steel their idea of The Natural Order of Things. Their idea, carefully designed for our comfort, still echoes in our subconscious, banging off what is and creating the notion that something must be amiss in a world of such large dollar signs.

The passionate beliefs of a generation ago have withered into postures of economic convenience, advocated now by men who could work as well for one camp as for the other if the offer was right. Bowie Kuhn wrote an autobiography a few years ago, *Hardball,* subtitled "Ten Years Behind the Curve." Okay, so it wasn't; it could have been. I recommend that book as a companion to this one. From 1966 to this moment, the owners have been just behind the curve, always trying to get the players to accept today the offer that would have been acceptable yesterday and generous a couple of weeks ago. Marvin prods a little gentle humor out of the fact that Bowie, ten years out of baseball, is still trying to protect the owners' pocketbooks—but he himself, almost ten years away from the titles and trappings of power, still believes fervently in the positions he advocated so brilliantly years ago. He *developed* those positions; they are his natural children, while Kuhn merely adopted arguments which had been around for generations and attempted to convert them from public justifications into a viable defense.

And that is what makes Miller special to the history of the game, that he was the man who saw the absurdity inherent in The Natural Order of Things and took the trouble to expose it. While the economics of baseball today are bizarre to many of us, Miller was the first to see that the economics of baseball twenty-five years ago were bizarre in their own way. Miller was able, by the sheer logical force of the arguments he developed, to shatter an existing structure grown heavy with the weight of time. Anyone can see in retrospect the absurdities that Miller exposed, but what many people fail to see is that there is something quite improbable in the story of Marvin Miller himself.

Acknowledgments

Writing, as many who have attempted it would agree, tends to be a lonely occupation. I fully expected the writing of this book would be no exception. But the encouragement, support, and solid help of so many people, offered and enthusiastically accepted, made it more like a team effort than a lonely solo.

Foremost among those who were responsible for this happy state of affairs is Allen Barra, who assisted me throughout. As a columnist for *The Village Voice,* a contributor to numerous magazines, and a book reviewer, Allen Barra unmistakably established his professionalism and talent as a writer. Additionally, working with him revealed to me his unflagging energy, total dependability, and delightful sense of humor—much-needed qualities that I greatly appreciated. His contributions to this book were significant from start to finish and of inestimable value. I am truly grateful.

I am especially indebted also to my wife, Terry, an original and talented writer in her own right, whose contributions to this book were major. Her patience and support through all the difficult periods were, of course, important. Her concrete help in organizing and recrafting material, editing and rewriting, constructive reading of manuscripts, intelligent suggestions, and key reminders were so worthy and vital as to far exceed anything that I or any husband had a right to expect. My appreciation is deep.

It would not be possible to construct a complete list of all those who were helpful in the making of this book. But, with apologies to any whom I may inadvertently overlook, I want to acknowledge the contributions of the individuals listed below and express my thanks to them. Their efforts, large or small, were meaningful to me: My daughter, Susan Miller, my son, Peter Miller, Hank Aaron, Jonelle Barra, Red Barber, Jim Bouton, Lucille Cohen, Bud Collins, Donald J. Davidson, Jesus Diaz, Don Fehr, Bob Friedman, Joe Glickman, Jerry Holtzman, Reggie Jackson, Bill James, Chuck Korr, Andy Lachow, Dick Moss, Gene Orza, Jim Quinn, Milton Scofield, Nan Scofield, Steve Schragis, Tom Seaver, Studs Terkel, Jay Topkis, Cynthia Trapp, Allan J. Wilson.

The foregoing acknowledgments are to those people whose encouragement and efforts were related to the writing and completion of *A Whole Different Ball Game.* The book itself is based on my career, and I want to acknowledge my debt to the literally thousands of people (including those in the labor movement who preceded me) whose activities and knowledge and intelligence and good will were responsible for whatever we jointly achieved. I wish to thank all those men and women with whom I worked in government and in the Steelworkers Union, and, most of all, the major league ballplayers throughout all those years when we worked together to bring into being a whole different ball game.

A Whole Different Ball Game

1...

To Baseball

IF YOU ARE ELECTED executive director of the Major League Baseball Players Association, your general counsel will be Richard Nixon."

Robin Roberts paused, flexed the fingers of his powerful right hand, and waited for my response.

He had spoken clearly, but I couldn't believe my ears.

"*Richard Nixon?*" I asked in surprise. "The ex–Vice President?"

Roberts nodded. Looking at me expectantly were Jim Bunning (Phillies) and Harvey Kuenn (Cubs), two other members of the screening committee of the Players Association. Had they not been so earnest, I would have laughed.

Work shoulder to shoulder with Tricky Dick? After twenty-five years in labor relations—on the side of labor—I could scarcely think of anyone I would have liked less to work with. For despite his attempt to put himself across as a populist, Richard M. Nixon, by background, experience, and ambition, was more attuned to the owners of baseball, some of whom he knew personally, than to players. That Roberts would even mention his name showed how little the players knew about labor relations. Or about me.

It was shortly before Christmas in 1965, and I was sitting in an actuary's office in Cleveland, talking to three earnest but naive ballplayers about becoming head of their union, an organization with little autonomy and less money. At the time, I was forty-eight, the chief economist and assistant to the president of the Steelworkers Union, and a member of President Lyndon B. Johnson's National Labor-Management Panel. I had had two terrific job offers in the last month—one from Harvard University, the other from the Carnegie Endowment for International Peace—but I kept thinking about the job in baseball.

Two weeks before, I had been in San Francisco for a meeting of the Kaiser Steel Long-Range Sharing Plan Committee. I was the plan's principal author and a member of the committee, which had developed a new approach to achieving industrial peace. As I rode the elevator down to the hotel's conference room early in the morning, the chairman of the committee, Dr. George W. Taylor, stepped in. When I had worked at the War Labor Board in Philadelphia during World War II, Taylor had been the board's national chairman in Washington. He taught economics and was a dean at the Wharton School in the University of Pennsylvania and had been a labor advisor to almost every President from Herbert Hoover to LBJ.

As the doors to the elevator closed, Taylor asked, "Do you know Robin Roberts?"

That struck me as an odd question. Anyone who knew baseball knew Robin Roberts. He had pitched for fourteen seasons in Philadelphia and had recently been traded from Baltimore to Houston. He had won twenty games six times, including one remarkable season in which he had gone 28–7 for a last-place team. Some called it the best season any pitcher ever had. "Not personally," I said, "but I certainly know who he is."

"Roberts called me last week," Taylor said quickly. "He's heading a committee that's looking for someone to revive the players' union, someone adept at dealing with management and contracts and especially with pension plans. The union has been around for a while, but it can't do much because the owners control it. He asked me to recommend some names. The first person I thought of was you. Interested?"

"I don't know," I said. As I spoke, my mind flashed to some of Roberts's career highlights, including the masterful game he pitched against the Yankees in the 1950 World Series, allowing just one run through nine innings—and losing when Joe DiMaggio hit a home run in the tenth. What the hell, I thought. It wouldn't hurt to find out more about it. "Sounds interesting," I continued. "I'll certainly talk to him."

As we left the elevator, Taylor said he would call Roberts as soon as he could. Within an hour he had arranged for me to meet the players who were screening candidates. The meeting would be in Cleveland in two weeks' time.

I hadn't agreed to the interview simply because Taylor asked me. The fight for the presidency of the Steelworkers Union in 1964 and 1965 had split the organization. Subsequent collective bargaining negotiations in the basic steel industry had regressed to a standstill, and LBJ had intervened in the summer of 1965, dragging both sides to Washington for eight days and eight nights of ballbusting bargaining—the most stressful sessions in my sixteen years with the Steelworkers Union. Somewhat worn down by the events of the last two years and disgusted with the in-house politicking that had followed the election struggle, I had come, in my mind, to a fork in the road: One well-worn path returned to Pittsburgh, the other veered to academia. Now a third had appeared, leading to baseball: It was, as Robert Frost has said, the road less traveled. Actually, it was a road that hadn't been traveled at all.

When I returned to Pittsburgh from San Francisco, I began boning up on baseball in preparation for my meeting with the ballplayers. Considering that major league players represented the very top of their profession, salaries were bad—no, not just bad: pitiful. During the past twenty years, a period of rampant inflation, the major league minimum had gone from *$5,000* to *$6,000* a year. The average salary was a paltry $19,000, and since World War II, only superstars like Ted Williams, Stan Musial, Joe DiMaggio, Willie Mays, and Mickey Mantle had reached the unofficial maximum of $100,000. When Pirates slugger Ralph Kiner (the man with the second-highest home run to at-bats percentage in baseball history) asked for a raise, the team's general manager, Branch Rickey, summed up the owners' attitude with his reply: "We finished last with you; we could have finished last without you!" Of course, Rickey neglected to mention how many fewer tickets he would have sold without Kiner.

Stated simply, players had no rights. The few who had tried to stand up to the owners of baseball had been squashed. In 1946, New York Giants outfielder Danny Gardella had been blacklisted from the big leagues by Commissioner A. B. "Happy" Chandler for "defecting" to a newly created Mexican League. In the 1950s Yankee minor leaguer George Toolson, who wanted out of the Bombers' talent-rich organization, challenged the game's inviolate reserve rule, which, in effect, *bound him to one club for life.* Toolson's suit went all the way to the U.S. Supreme Court, where he lost in 1953 by the lopsided margin of seven to two. The court affirmed Justice Oliver Wendell Holmes's 1922 decision that baseball was "sport not trade" and so was not subject to federal antitrust laws. (As I write this, it still isn't.)

Several men had tried (and failed) to help the players to obtain improved working conditions. In 1946, Robert F. Murphy, a lawyer who had worked for the National Labor Relations Board, tried to form the American Baseball Guild. Ridiculed mercilessly by the press and infiltrated (with the support of Happy Chandler) by spies, the union quickly folded. Another lawyer, J. Norman Lewis,* served as a part-time legal advisor to the players, but by the spring of 1959 the owners had had enough and urged (*read:* told) the player reps to fire him.† Not long after his dismissal, management persuaded the player reps to accept another part-time advisor, Robert Cannon, a Milwaukee circuit court judge who, to paraphrase Will Rogers, never met an owner he didn't like. Cannon continually reminded the players that they were the

---

*Fed up with the existing pension plan, Ralph Kiner (Pirates) and Allie Reynolds (Yankees), the player reps of their respective leagues, hired Lewis in 1953 to help in the upcoming negotiations. It was a move that outraged the owners.

†Club officials dominated the selection of player reps in the 1940s and 1950s. Subsequently, the players on each team elected a club player representative, and these representatives, in each league, elected a league player rep.

luckiest men alive to be paid to play ball, even saying, without a trace of irony, that baseball had the "finest relationship between players and management in the history of the sport."

Tired of Cannon's patronizing ways and worried about the upcoming pension negotiations, the players formed a search committee in the winter of 1965 to find a full-time executive director and establish a Players Association in New York City— something Robin Roberts had lobbied for as early as 1960. (The closest thing to headquarters they had was a filing cabinet in the office of a players' licensing agent named Frank Scott.)

Oddly enough, I soon learned, Cannon was also under consideration for the job of full-time executive director of the Players Association, along with Chub Feeney, the vice president of the San Francisco Giants; John Gabel, a Cleveland actuary for the players' benefit plan; the great former Tigers slugger Hank Greenberg; and perhaps the best-known ex-pitcher, Bob Feller. "Rapid Robert" had a small business in Cleveland and was campaigning for the position like a man possessed, wooing everyone in sight until he became a big-league pest.

Which brings us back to the actuary's office in Cleveland in 1965. During the meeting, Roberts acted as spokesman, Bunning asked some questions, and Kuenn mostly listened. The fourth member of the committee, Pittsburgh pitcher Bob Friend, wasn't there. In response to my questions about working conditions, Bunning said that playing fields and locker rooms were often lousy, even dangerous, the travel schedule brutal, and the season much too long. The players hadn't received a raise when the schedule was increased from 154 to 162 games.* However, unlike most steelworkers their age, the players were *most* concerned about the pension plan. Every player, it seemed, knew of a former big leaguer who was out of the game and out of work, with nothing to show for a career of training, playing ball, and traveling except some memories.

And as the meeting went on, I found that if I didn't bring up other issues, Roberts would talk about the pension plan to the exclusion of anything else. Strange as this seemed, I was being told

---

*This happened in the American League in 1961, one year later in the National League.

that as far as most players were concerned, the pension was practically the sole purpose of the association. The first pension plan, it seems, was established in 1947—thanks to the competitive threat of the Mexican League as well as Murphy's American Baseball Guild. The next pension agreement was negotiated in 1954 by J. Norman Lewis, assisted by Kiner and Allie Reynolds. It provided that the plan was to be funded by 60 percent of the radio and television proceeds of the All-Star Game and World Series and 60 percent of the net gate of the All-Star Game. These proceeds amounted to about $2,500,000 a year by 1966.

Roberts's biggest fear was that the owners would scrap the "60–40" formula when the current pension plan expired on March 31, 1967. Rumor had it, he said, that Dodgers owner Walter O'Malley—the craftiest businessman in baseball—anticipated much larger television contracts on the horizon and didn't want the Association to get 60 percent (or any percentage) for the players. Roberts also didn't like the fact that the players weren't getting a cent from the network Game of the Week package, a deal that had been negotiated after the current pension agreement was signed. Roberts said: "I think the owners are undervaluing the World Series and All-Star deals, which they have to share with us, and jacking up the price for the Game of the Week, which they keep for themselves." (As it turned out, Roberts's fears were justified; the players were getting screwed.)

Talk eventually turned to the proposed budget for the Players Association. Earlier in the selection process, the players had asked Judge Cannon (who fully expected to be offered the job) how much it would take to operate the Association. The obsequious judge met with the owners, who agreed to draw the money from the All-Star Game, and decided on an annual budget of $150,000—$50,000 of which was targeted for the executive director's salary. When Roberts told me this, I swallowed hard. Twice. The Taft-Hartley Act, which has governed labor relations since 1947, strictly forbids financing a union with management's money. For the moment, however, I remained silent.

The interview was now into its third hour. The more Roberts talked, the more I felt that there was potential for making improvements for the players. Until, that is, he began talking about the process for selecting the executive director.

"In the past two weeks," Roberts said, "we've talked to a lot of your present and former colleagues, and you come out with high marks. I really think you're the man for the job. But we have to be realistic. This committee has to come up with at least four or five candidates. The player representatives will pick one and he'll be subject to a vote by all the players.* But here's the rub. Most players are conservative. They don't know anything about unions. In fact, to many, especially guys from small towns down south, 'union' is a dirty word. The best way to combat this is to have a dual ticket, with you as director and a noted conservative as general counsel."

That's when he dropped the name of Richard M. Nixon.

I sat there stunned, feeling like a rube on "Candid Camera." Being a generation older than Roberts, I probably had a completely different perspective on Nixon. I had met him during the steel strike in 1959, when then Vice President Nixon called top union officials to the White House to mediate the dispute (Eisenhower was ill). But I had known, long before that brief meeting, that Nixon represented everything I loathed in American political life. To me, he was "Tricky Dick," the neophyte congressional candidate from California who won election by slandering his opponent, Jerry Voorhis. I knew him as the senatorial candidate who weaseled into office using rotten red-scare tactics against Congresswoman Helen Gahagan Douglas; as Ike's running mate who had almost been tossed from the ticket when it was discovered he had received improper campaign funding from California oil moguls; as the phoney making the sickening "Checkers" speech that saved his vice-presidential bid; and finally, and perhaps most important, as a politician who consistently supported antiunion legislation. Clearly, Nixon was not *my* first choice as a running mate!

"Sorry," I said instantly. "It won't work."

Roberts frowned. "Why not?"

I thought, Where do I start? I took a deep breath. "First off," I said, "Nixon is an owners' man. He has no background whatsoever in representing employees and wouldn't know the difference

---

*The vote, I later learned, included coaches, trainers, and managers as well as the players.

between a pension plan and a pitcher's mound. If you want the Players Association to have any autonomy, he's the exact opposite of what you're looking for. And second, he won't be around that long. He's going to run for President again."

Roberts, Bunning, and Kuenn looked baffled. Bunning said, "How do you know?"

"Nixon's been crisscrossing the country since 1962," I said, "appearing at Republican fund-raisers, piling up political capital. It's common knowledge that he's pushing hard for the nomination in 1968."

No one said anything. I had blown it, I realized, and started to get up to leave. Still, I felt compelled to offer one last comment. "Look, you haven't asked for it, but let me give you some advice. If you were a large union with a big staff, you could afford to have some varying viewpoints, but this is, as unions go, a tiny organization. And you *can't* have that kind of incompatibility in a union with just two professionals. Whoever you finally get as director, let him pick his own counsel."

I shook hands all around and left.

On my way home I thought about what had just happened. It was quite obvious that the players I had just met had a very different value system than I had. But what disturbed me most was that they had not understood that Nixon was, by temperament, background, experience, and ambition, closely attuned to wealthy and powerful interests, and that if you were to rank all the people in the country in terms of their fitness to be a union counsel, Richard Nixon might be at the very bottom of the ranking!

When I got home, I greeted my family with a terse summary of a meeting that had lasted well over three hours. "I blew it," I said. "Forget about going back to New York."

As events would show, I was right about Nixon.

2 . . .

Brooklyn, U.S.A.

Brooklyn. The name elicits laughter (as do Podunk, Walla Walla, Cucamonga, and Hicksville), but it evokes memories of baseball. Brooklyn and the Dodgers—affectionately called "dem Bums." Brooklyn and Ebbets Field, home of those Boys of Summer. Several decades after I left Brooklyn, that connection still seemed to provide a shorthand explanation for certain events in my life.

When I was elected executive director of the Players Association in 1966, I was asked repeatedly by reporters (and numerous others) how it had happened that I moved from being the chief economist and assistant to the president of the Steelworkers Union, one of the largest and most prestigious of American unions, to becoming head of the first legitimate union in the history of baseball (and in organized sports). The true answer was far too complex for such interviews. But, early on, I discovered an indirect answer, which seemed to enlighten the inquiring re-

• 11 •

porters. "I grew up in Brooklyn," I said, "not far from Ebbets Field."

Heads nodded. No further explanation was required. No one had to ask if I had been a baseball fan as a kid. No questions had to be posed about my interest in the new job. They wrote: "The new executive director of the Major League Baseball Players Association grew up in Brooklyn, not far from Ebbets Field." That said it all.

It was true, of course. My parents had bought a modest, semidetached single-family house in the Flatbush section of Brooklyn in 1917, shortly before my first birthday. And yes, I was one of the countless kids who felt intimately connected to the fortunes of the Dodgers. Like most of my friends, I could recite the vital statistics of every Dodger—and of most of their competition too.

My father, Alexander Miller, was an ardent baseball fan as well, but of the hated New York Giants. He sold ladies' coats on the outskirts of Chinatown in lower Manhattan and had to work weekends and holidays. There were no night games then, but he managed to introduce me to Ebbets Field, taking me to the ballpark through my early years whenever he could. But only after school closed for the summer. My mother, Gertrude Wald Miller, a teacher in the New York City school system, wouldn't tolerate my playing hooky. My Uncle Sid, who had no sons, took me to Dodgers games more often—often coming up with box seats— even though he lived in New Jersey and rooted for the Yankees. More important, Uncle Sid gave me my first wheels—a shiny black bike—and convinced my overprotective father that I had the know-how to skillfully operate a bike despite the growing number of cars on the streets.

My father was a kind man, liked by everyone who knew him. It was clear to me, even as a small boy, that there was no meanness in him. He was generous, taking great pleasure in spending money on those around him even though he spent little on himself. When I visited him at work, we would walk through the Bowery (where virtually all the homeless hung out), around Chinatown and along the streets of the Lower East Side, where he had been raised. My father always had an ample supply of coins in his pocket, and he passed them out to his regular "customers" and to anyone else who asked. On these lunchtime walks, he exchanged greetings with residents, shopkeepers, and restaurant owners in English (his first language), Yiddish (the tongue my Russian-born grandfather usually spoke at home), or rudimentary Chinese (which he had picked up after working near Chinatown for decades).

Shopping for a coat or suit with my father was always an adventure. He knew all about fabrics and tailoring (his father had been a tailor), and his prowess at negotiating the best price for a suit or overcoat was Hall of Fame material. My father would make disparaging comments to the storekeeper (though not *too* disparaging) on the fabric, the workmanship, the extent of the alterations, and anything else he could think of in order to drive down the price. Having already tried on nineteen coats, I would have to wait impatiently—coyly concealing how much I liked the new garment—while the two of them scrutinized every seam, sleeve, and stitch. At times, my father would abruptly break off negotiations and we would walk out. Invariably, the store owner would follow. Negotiations would resume on the street—with a subtle shift in bargaining power—and the deal would be completed, an agreement reached that was satisfying to both of them.

My father may have been the first (and one of the few) small 'd' democrats in my life. Usually my father didn't leave for work until ten A.M., hours after my mother had gone. In those days the ashes from the coal furnaces that heated the homes were placed in tall metal cans and dragged to the edge of the street. These heavy cans were then emptied into special Sanitation Department trucks once or twice a week. The trucks were manned by three workers: a driver, usually white, and two men who did the lifting, usually black. Throughout the winter my father would invite the crew into our home to warm up. When he had liquor (this was during Prohibition), he served them a drink (usually Four Roses or Canadian Club). When he didn't have liquor, he served hot coffee. With these burly, soot-stained men, my father displayed an easy camaraderie. My mother objected, when she finally found out, not because of bigotry or even snobbery but because she was disturbed by the ashes on the furniture. And being a lot more frugal than my father, she complained about the cost of the liquor.

Like most father-son relationships, ours was complicated. The difference in our views on religion was a serious problem. Alexander Miller was an Orthodox Jew. From a very early age I felt estranged from his beliefs. Initially, I bowed to his edict and went to Hebrew school four days a week (after a full day of public school). But when I turned ten, I stopped going. Because I loved my father, it was difficult to disobey him, but I felt as strongly about the issue as he did. Principle aside (and perhaps more important), I hated losing out on the free time after school. That was recreation time—the punchball and handball games in the schoolyard, the stickball and touch football games in the street, and the baseball games and football scrimmages on the sandlots.

As my thirteenth birthday approached I became aware of an impending crisis—my bar mitzvah. My mother, who had not opposed me in my rejection of Hebrew school, came up with a compromise solution: a private tutor, three nights a week for the six months leading up to my thirteenth birthday. This cram course enabled me to learn enough Hebrew to conduct myself creditably at the bar mitzvah ceremony, but this rift with my father never completely healed.

Another problem between my father and me traced to a birthing injury to my right shoulder. I will never know the trauma felt by my parents, or whether they felt guilty—no matter how unjustified such feelings would have been. My birth was a difficult one and required the use of instruments. Whether the doctor needed assistance which wasn't available, I don't know, but in the delivery, a nerve, or nerves, in my right shoulder were irreparably damaged. The injury wasn't noticeable immediately, but when I started crawling, it was quite apparent that I was putting all my weight on my left arm and shoulder. Those years must have been the worst for my parents. For years they tried all sorts of treatments to relieve the condition—by therapists, by mechanical massage, and much more. Most of this I've blocked out.

When they finally accepted that this condition was permanent, the worst was over. I made the necessary adjustments, compensating in ways that I wasn't aware of until much later. The disability itself was not something viewed as major. The primary problem was that I couldn't raise my right arm above shoulder level normally. I could (and can) raise it by using my left arm to guide it or by doing it in one fairly rapid, continuous motion, as in tossing a tennis ball up before hitting a serve.

I don't remember setting out to prove that the disability was no big deal, but I did, nonetheless. My mother was a very important help. From day one, she stressed that I was expected to do anything that everyone else could do, and to do it even better. There would be failures along the way, she said, but I should never use my arm as an excuse. And she gave me tasks that a less purposeful, less determined parent might not have assigned: shoveling coal to stoke the furnace, maneuvering the waist-high cans of ashes from the basement out to the street in front of the house, clearing the walk of snow and ice, and so forth. It was only much later that I realized that she had, almost exclusively, selected "two-handed" jobs for me, instead of "one-handed" chores like painting the kitchen stools or the front stoop.

Gertrude Miller was a woman who believed in setting high standards. It was the way she lived her own life. She taught elementary school for forty-five years, with time out for the births of her two kids: myself and my younger sister, Thelma. Born in New York in 1890, in what became known as the Yorkville section of Manhattan, my mother was one of ten children and the youngest of six daughters. I never knew her Hungarian parents or even heard much about them, but I do know that they raised their daughters as strong women. Considering that my mother and her sisters came of age in the early 1900s, it was unusual that four of the women were "do-it-all" career types: Two started businesses and maintained them along with marriages and children for most of their lives. This was, remember, half a century before Betty Friedan and Molly Yard.

Academically, she set even higher standards. When I showed an interest in reading, at about the age of three and a half, my mother began to teach me regularly, and by the time I was four I could read and write my name and address, stuff like that. I also knew my multiplication tables, so when I was five, my mother enrolled me in the first grade even though the minimum age was six. She had prepared me well. Soon I was "skipped" to the second grade, and I was not even six. (Not to boast; this practice was rather common in the New York schools back then.) Anyhow, by the time I entered my freshman year at James Madison High School, I was only eleven. The year was 1929. Before the year was out, the stock market crashed, and in the years that followed, a deep, worldwide depression set in and changed people's lives dramatically. The Depression taught me a great deal about the nature of our society. It tested to an extreme degree the ties that bound families; it almost certainly led to my decision to study economics; it was the backdrop which led to my first professional job, working with the unemployed; it led to a sequence of events which found my father on a picket line for the first time in his life; and it definitely led to my enduring interest in the trade union movement.

My father's attitude toward my physical condition was exactly the opposite of my mother's, and he made no attempt to hide it. He didn't consider me competent to handle physical chores of any kind, and wanted me to avoid games, even running. Luckily, my father's interventions were limited by his long working hours. Still, he would embarrass the hell out of me when he called out to me during a game of touch football to be careful, not to run so fast, to watch out for cars, and when, on occasion, he admonished other kids for playing too rough with me.

Our neighborhood in Flatbush was probably fairly typical of most middle-class areas at that time, but there seemed to be an unusual number of boys, perhaps as many as fifty on our street alone. Regardless of the season, there was never a lull in the sports action. There was an unwritten ladder one climbed, from peewee substitute to novice regular to established veteran, and, finally, to a leadership position of coach and teacher to the youngest kids. Through the years I became a better-than-average athlete, and not just on the street and sandlots. After our street was paved, I was a roller-skate hockey regular; I also (over my father's objections) skated on ice at an early age. Later, I began entering amateur speed-skating races at the Brooklyn Ice Palace and winning medals. At Brighton Beach Baths on Coney Island I played a game called hand tennis on an abbreviated tennis court without a racket, twice reaching the finals of the singles tournament. Still later, at Miami University (Ohio), I was the four-wall handball champ in singles and coholder of the doubles title two years in a row. I was a southpaw pitcher on the intramural baseball team and was the school's table tennis champion. I even worked out with the boxing team, holding my own with the welterweights. Much later, in Pittsburgh, at age thirty-six, I started playing tennis and won several local tournaments, but was never able to advance beyond the first couple of rounds of the Western Pennsylvania championship tournaments.

None of this was world class, of course, but to my father, it was a signal accomplishment. He was indescribably happy when he discovered I was able to compete successfully. For a long time I gave my mother full credit for bringing about the healthy development of a child who began life with an apparent problem. And surely her intelligent, disciplined, and loving approach went a long way toward that end. But so did the fierce competition of my friends and neighbors and the ample opportunity I had to play every sport imaginable. And there was my persistent need to show my father that, despite his worries, I really could excel. I wanted him to know that my arm injury, which had plagued *him* so, didn't hinder *me* at all.

Psychologists say that a child's personality is formed by the age of six. It's very difficult, and perhaps impossible, to unravel the separate threads which make up your life and from them determine a credible cause-and-effect that explains how you came to be the person you are. Obviously, genetics, early childhood training, and the environment shape your basic personality. There are, however, other crucial influences which shape you later in life. For me, such influences are unmistakable.

In 1936 I met a seventeen-year-old Brooklyn College student. She was bright and beautiful and (even though she didn't agree with much of what I said) politically aware. Two years later, at nineteen, she graduated from college. We were married the following year. In the fifty-one years since then, Theresa Morgenstern Miller—Terry to all but her immediate family—has personified femininity and strength.

In the first twenty-seven years of our marriage we lived and worked in New York (several times), Washington, D.C. (three times), in Philadelphia, and in Pittsburgh before resettling in New York in 1966. Our son, Peter, was born in Philadelphia on V-J Day in 1945, and our daughter, Susan, was born on Long Island in 1949. After Susan began school, Terry resumed her education, receiving her Ph.D. in 1961 from the University of Pittsburgh. She worked at Pittsburgh's Child Guidance Center as a clinical psychologist, then on an experimental project on team teaching, and as a lecturer at Carnegie Institute of Technology (now Carnegie-Mellon). Upon returning to New York, she worked at a number of institutions. When she retired in 1980, she was an associate professor at the City University of New York. She is, in her seventy-first year, still a beautiful, active, energetic woman, ever alert to an intellectual challenge. One includes learning Japanese, in part, I think, to be able to communicate with our six-year-old grandson, Neil, who lives in Tokyo with Peter and Yuko, our daughter-in-law.

Time, place, people. These were the influences that pushed me to build the first solid, democratic union of professional athletes—the organization that created a whole different ball game.

Not bad for a skinny kid from Brooklyn.

3 . . .

Making It to the Majors

NOT SO FAST. I did not jump directly from Brooklyn, U.S.A., child of the Depression, to leadership of the baseball players' union. At the time Robin Roberts appeared on my horizon, I was in my sixteenth year with the Steelworkers Union. Hired after a brief interview by Philip Murray, I began as a staff economist in 1950. Within ten years I had become the union's chief economist, a key advisor, and assistant to the president of the third largest union in America.

Before I arrived at the Steelworkers Union, I had been more or less meandering about my life, not remaining in any place for more than three years. At the National War Labor Board during World War II I received an advanced education in labor-management problems and the resolution of disputes. The WLB had been given unprecedented authority to adjudicate union-management disputes as a quid pro quo for the labor movement's pledge to forego strikes and industry's agreement not to lock workers out for the duration of the war. The experience I gained as a hearing officer for the WLB, dealing with almost every type of disputed issue, in a wide variety of industries, could not have been duplicated anywhere or at any other time.

Earlier, when I worked for the New York City Department of Welfare, I had become an active member of a union that exerted a powerful influence on the way I viewed the world, the State, County and Municipal Workers of America (SCMWA), CIO. If the War Labor Board provided my advanced education in labor matters, the SCMWA earlier had given me a fundamental, basic training as a union member, active in the operation of a local union.

It was at the Steelworkers Union that I was able to put it all together and use my previous training to the utmost. I became an experienced negotiator, adept at making practical application of my background and training as an economist, and, after a time, I was recognized as a negotiator who provided imaginative solutions to complex problems.

There was a good fit between my personality and my background and what needed to be done at that time in steel and other industries within the union's jurisdiction. *That* was the most important part of the work for me. The job didn't pay particularly well, but there were other rewards, in addition to the challenge of the work. There was appreciation within the union and recognition by the public for the work I did, and there were encounters with the movers and shakers of society, with steel company executives, like Henry Kaiser, with unionists, like Philip Murray and Arthur Goldberg (later a Supreme Court justice), and with Presidents, past, prospective, or current (Nixon, Kennedy, Johnson) since almost every basic steel dispute eventually was settled in the White House. (Later, when I was with the baseball players' union, I added Reagan to my list; I was invited to one of Nancy's Just Say No meetings.)

Telling of my life and work in the Steelworkers Union would take a complete book in itself. Instead, I hope to touch on only those aspects which were most interesting and most relevant to the life and work in major league baseball which followed in the next several decades.

When the war ended in August 1945, it meant, of course, that the remaining days of all the government's war agencies, including the War Labor Board, were numbered. V-J Day was a glorious day for the country, and, for me, it meant even more. On that day Terry gave birth to our first child, Peter Daniel. The happiness and excitement over the beginning of fatherhood and the ending of World War II at the same time were overwhelming. A sense of concern about the future, however, was to creep in shortly as the rumors of the termination of the War Labor Board gained increasing credibility. The no-strike, no-lockout pledges, effective only during the war, were terminated. The postwar disputes and major strikes throughout the country, involving millions of workers, began before the year was out and were in full swing in early 1946. The WLB went "out of business" at the end of 1945; unions and employers were on their own for the first time in three years.

Over the next few years I remained in labor relations work: as a commissioner of conciliation in the Labor Department's U.S. Conciliation Service; as an organizer-researcher-negotiator for the International Association of Machinists; and, for a brief period, in a similar capacity for the New York region of the United Automobile Workers.

In July 1949 our second child was born, and to our delight was a daughter—Susan Toni. I was thirty-two years old, and, with the family now numbering four, I gave more thought to the need for stable, career-type employment. In early 1950 an opportunity arose. I received a call from a former colleague at the War Labor Board. Otis Brubaker, who had become the research director of the Steelworkers Union, said he had an opening for a staff economist. I flew to Pittsburgh for an interview with Philip Murray, president of the United Steelworkers of America and of the Congress of Industrial Organizations (CIO). After leading the successful drive to organize the steel industry, Murray had become the union's first president in 1941.

One of the most powerful labor leaders of his time, in person Murray was quiet and gentle, almost shy, nothing like the fiery leader I had read about and heard on the radio. He even sounded different. When he spoke in public, Murray's Scottish burr was pronounced. Sitting across from him in his office in February 1950, I found his accent to be as mild as a spring day, with barely a trace of the old country. Murray had rubbed elbows with Roosevelt and Wilkie and Truman, with John L. Lewis and Robert A. Taft, with Henry Wallace and Sidney Hillman, but leaning back in his chair he seemed as uncomfortable as someone in a dentist's chair. He didn't seem to know what to say to me. Otis Brubaker was also there, and we struggled to make conversation, but Murray mostly listened, asked almost no questions. After about twenty minutes, he commented that he thought I was well qualified. "You know," Murray said, "some unions don't consider the research department to be all that important, but I don't feel that way. I think a staff economist is a very responsible position, and I want you to understand that." I told him I agreed and appreciated his feeling. There followed another uncomfortable silence, the three of us like strangers in a stuck elevator.

Finally, Murray asked, "When can you come to work?"

I was a bit taken aback. "Well, I'd have to give notice to my present employer, and find a place to live in Pittsburgh," I answered, thinking about my daughter, who was just seven months old. "I guess I can start in a few weeks."

Murray looked at his calendar. "March first okay?"

I nodded. "Fine." We stood up and shook hands.

Phil Murray was exactly twice my age when I met him. His air of gentleness and quiet dignity was so different from that of his mentor, John L. Lewis, president of the United Mineworkers Union, whom Murray had served as vice president for twenty-two years. John L. was dignified, too, but in a very different way. I never got to know John L., yet I can never forget him, with his shaggy lionlike mane of black hair, the thick, bushy eyebrows. He was the most impressive speaker I've ever heard. This was a time when individuals wrote their own speeches; Lewis's bore the stamp of Shakespeare and the King James Bible, and they were delivered with the ferocity of an itinerant preacher. Never will I forget his statement to President Franklin Delano Roosevelt when FDR took a position of neutrality toward the bitter auto strike at Ford's River Rouge plant in 1939 ("a plague on both your houses," said FDR.) Lewis lashed out at FDR: "It ill behooves one who has supped at labor's table"—the UMW alone had contributed $500,000 to FDR's 1936 campaign—"and who has been sheltered in labor's house to curse with equal fervor and fine impartiality both labor and its adversaries when they become locked in deadly embrace." Lewis then came out in support of the Republican candidate, Wendell Willkie, in the 1940 presidential race.

So different from John L. Lewis was Philip Murray that when Murray died in November 1952, at the age of sixty-six, shortly after Dwight Eisenhower defeated Adlai Stevenson, some said Murray preferred death to a Republican administration.

After Murray's death, David J. McDonald, who had been the secretary-treasurer, was appointed president. McDonald had been Murray's protégé, starting out as his private secretary in 1923 with the UMW. Tall and handsome, McDonald looked more like a leading man than the stereotypical labor leader. (He had, in fact, once considered an acting career.) His good looks and his fondness for associating with those who were socially elite made him increasingly suspect as a trade unionist. He was perceived as a "Hollywood" type, a man who lived in unbecoming affluence. He was portrayed by the press as a tuxedo unionist, while his counterpart in the Auto Workers Union, Walter Reuther, was presented as a humble person who peeled his own oranges instead of breakfasting in stylish hotel restaurants during union conventions. Nevertheless, McDonald's home in Pittsburgh was modest, and his labor credentials were authentic. He was the son of a steelworker, born on a day that his father was out on strike; and he was fond of saying, "I was born with a union spoon in my mouth." Although McDonald lacked the appearance of a strong trade unionist, he was aware of his areas of deficiency and he knew enough to turn to the people who could fill in for him. During his administration of the union some of the most stunning advances in wages, supplementary benefits, pensions, and working conditions took place.

But that did not stop a growing disaffection with his leadership, something which was to lead me to think about making a career change. In 1964 a palace revolt erupted. The secretary-treasurer of the union, Iorwith W. Abel, challenged McDonald for the top position. His campaign attracted the support of most of the district directors, elected officials who had grown increasingly discontented with the diminished role they played during contract negotiations. They resented the reliance on professionals like David Feller, Ben Fisher, and me (and others), and felt themselves shut out of the process. Abel capitalized on this during his campaign. At one point he distributed pictures of McDonald at a black-tie reception at the White House. Meanwhile, his supporters issued a leaflet attacking the so-called technicians—the economists, lawyers, pension and arbitration experts—many of whom happened to be Jewish. It was a subtly vicious appeal to anti-Semitism. When I pointed this out to Abe, he promised the leaflets would never appear again. And they didn't.

McDonald was counting on his incumbency and on efforts to smear Abel as a "sell-out" artist. Both men had advised me not to take an active part in the struggle—I hadn't intended to—and it was morale-boosting to know that each was concerned that I remain regardless of the election results, but I was saddened to see the union split down the middle the way it was, and I felt that the animosities might never be healed.

While this internecine warfare was going on, a new steel agreement with the industry was awaiting negotiation. Negotiations began seven months before the old contract expired. Both McDonald and Abel were on the negotiating committee, and they weren't speaking to each other. The industry had no idea which of the two would be the next president, and they feared that this stalemate would prevent the reaching of an agreement. There could be a strike by default. It was a mess.

The election, held in February 1965, resulted in a victory for I. W. Abel by a very narrow margin. In the U.S. McDonald had a tiny lead, but in Canada Abel carried the vote by an unbelievably lopsided margin. Not surprisingly, all three Canadian directors were Abel supporters. Abel nosed out McDonald by roughly 2 percent of the vote—fewer than 10,000 votes.

We still had an industrywide contract to negotiate. For several days, however, McDonald considered filing an appeal. The campaign had put him deep in personal debt, and the appeal, which would have had to be paid for out of his pocket, would have been costly. Furthermore, it would have prevented his applying for his pension and left him without income for an indefinite period. He decided to complete his term and retire. Shortly afterward, he sold his home in Pittsburgh and moved to Palm Springs, California.

As soon as Abel was elected, rumors started circulating that I would be fired. After all, McDonald had appointed me as his assistant. I knew my job was secure, but the newspapers didn't.

When the stories appeared I began receiving job offers. Right after the inauguration on May 1, Abel made it official. He wanted me to continue in all my capacities—as chief economist, as assistant to the president, and as a member of the basic steel negotiating committee.

We were back in negotiations the next day—minus McDonald and Howard Hague, defeated for reelection as vice president, and David Feller, who had resigned as associate general counsel after Abel's victory. There were only two months until the contract expired. After all the turmoil we were miles apart. But even with Abel installed in office, we progressed at a snail's pace. Negotiations, which are always difficult, were brutal.

When talk of a strike surfaced, the government started sniffing around. The Vietnam war, now going full force, had become a cancer that threatened to consume LBJ's administration. A nationwide steel strike was one of his nightmares. Johnson sent in Bill Simkin, the director of the Federal Mediation and Conciliation Service. Simkin made no headway. Secretary of Labor Bill Wirtz showed up next. It was, as Yogi Berra said, "déjà vu all over again."

The June deadline was roughly a week away when Johnson called Abel. Before you could say Lady Bird, we were streaking to Washington, D.C., aboard Air Force One. From Andrews Air Force Base an army helicopter whisked both sets of negotiators to the edge of the White House lawn. It was only a 150-yard walk from the landing pad to the Rose Garden, but we were stuffed into two separate stretch limos (one for each side) and hustled to the Oval Office.

And so began our eight days and eight nights with Lyndon Baines Johnson. The President greeted us in the Cabinet Room with a rah-rah speech, informing us that Wirtz would act as his liaison during negotiations. Then Wirtz escorted us next door to the old Executive Office Building, to a room half below ground. It was stifling hot and humid in Washington at the time, and the air-conditioning units in the room were broken—or so we were told. I learned later that the "broken air conditioner" was an old trick from Johnson's Texas days—the thinking being that if both sides had to negotiate in a sauna, a settlement would be reached much faster. Johnson also didn't want us to go out to lunch, opting to order in stale (and sometimes soggy) sandwiches instead.

Johnson's energy level throughout the ordeal was nothing short of amazing. He was like a manic-depressive in the manic stage. He greeted us enthusiastically each morning, usually around seven-thirty, urging us to settle "the damn thing" as fast as possible. His pep talks reminded me of a big ol' football coach rallying his troops at halftime. He peppered Wirtz with bulletins throughout the day. And each night, sometimes as late as one A.M., he popped in to wish us good night and set an early morning hour as the time for reconvening. His boundless energy was spectacular, considering that he was getting very little sleep and that this was very much a "hands-on" President of the United States with the weight of the daily operations of his office, the Vietnam War, the basic steel dispute, and who knew what else pressing on him.

As one day slipped imperceptibly into the next, Wirtz showed more signs of strain than anybody. He was keeping the same hours as we were, after having just finished mediating a settlement in a tough tugboat dispute in New York, *and* he was getting harangued by Johnson day and night. The poor guy looked like a dazed sentry on the downside of fifty cups of coffee. His job, which involved communicating detailed bargaining points back and forth to each side, became an uphill struggle. One day I explained several new wrinkles in the pension-plan proposals to him. He carefully wrote down everything I said, nodding wearily after each point. Then he shuffled off to present the information to the other side. He walked out the door, stopped, turned to me, and said, "Marvin, I've forgotten what you just told me."

"Bill," I said, slightly stunned, "you took notes."

"Oh, yeah," he whispered, pausing to scan the room through bloodshot eyes. "I don't know what I did with them."

I helped him search through his pockets. When we found the notes, I had to explain entire points to him all over again.

Around day five, Johnson, who was growing increasingly impatient, showed up in midafternoon to say he wanted to meet the union alone. "I got to tell you," he said tiredly in his thick Texas drawl, "you might not like to hear it, but I gotta tell you where I was last night after you men left. I was down in the War Room around two in the morning poring over the maps, thinking about the decisions I got to make overseas. I gotta send my boys and my planes on all these bombing raids and I'm getting reports about the body bags piling up on the San Francisco docks and I tell you all this because we just can't have a stoppage. We got too many lives depending on it."

When he finally finished, the room was eerily silent. Much to my surprise, Abel spoke up. "We're aware there's a war going on, Mr. President, but we here have a responsibility for the safety, health, and welfare of our workers. I appreciate your position, but you didn't say anything in your remarks about how unreasonable the position of the steel industry has been during these negotiations. We'll settle this thing when industry begins bargaining in good faith. But we won't cheat our members either." LBJ listened intently, but did not reply.

As the week wore on, we got closer and closer to a settlement. Before we reached a tentative agreement, however, the furnaces were already being banked in anticipation of a strike. To understand the enormity of this action, you need to know that steel furnaces must be cooled slowly, over several days; otherwise they crack and collapse. Banked furnaces are effectively taken out of production. So a shutdown costs a company tens of millions of dollars in lost production.

No sooner did Johnson get word of a settlement than both sides were escorted directly to the Fish Room, right near the Oval Office.

R. Conrad Cooper, the vice president of labor relations for U.S. Steel, was desperate to call corporate headquarters and tell them to stop the shutdown. When we got to the Fish Room, Cooper snatched up a telephone to make his call. The line was dead.

He walked across the room, ripped open the door, and just about smacked into two armed marines. Cooper demanded to know: "What's wrong with this phone?"

"Sorry, sir," one said. "Instructions are no telephone calls!"

Tall, well-built, and very dignified, Cooper, who was mostly bald, looked a little like Mr. Clean without the earring. At first, he couldn't comprehend what they were telling him. "I have some *urgent* calls to make," he insisted.

"Sorry, sir," the marines said in stereo. "No word is to leak until the President can see you all at once."

With that they shut the door. Cooper stood in disbelief. Then it hit him: Johnson wanted to announce the settlement. He probably was saving the announcement for the six o'clock news, almost an hour away. The thought turned Cooper white. "That bastard!" he muttered, referring to Johnson. "The furnaces are going down while we sit here! That SOB is going to cost us millions and millions of dollars! There's no reason for this!" He was apoplectic. Finally, seeing there was nothing he could do, he quieted down. About fifteen minutes later, the door opened and we were told, "The President will see you now in the Oval Office."

There were two couches lined up opposite each other, and Johnson had a chair at the head. While LBJ congratulated us on a "marvelous" settlement, Cooper tried in vain to get Johnson's attention. I went over the suggested press release for several minutes and made some changes, and when that was finished, Johnson called for a telephone.

"Get me Lady Bird!" he told the White House operator loudly. "Hello, Bird. You'll never guess who I have lined up here. I got the whole steel industry and the Steelworkers Union, and there's not going to be a strike!" Sitting to the left of LBJ was Cooper, looking like a man who had just watched his house burn to the ground. A staunch Republican, Cooper couldn't stand Johnson in the first place. And now this goddamn Democrat was refusing to let him make a phone call that could save the industry a fortune.

Without warning, Johnson said, "Hey, Bird, wait a minute, I want you to say hello to Coop," and he thrust the phone at Cooper. "Say something to Lady Bird," he said, smiling. I would have given anything for a camera to capture the look on Cooper's face. He'd never met Mrs. Johnson and never wanted to, while less than two feet away the President of the United States was beaming like Bert Parks. Fighting back the rage, a livid Cooper mumbled something and handed the phone back to Johnson.

LBJ then shouted into the phone, "Now, Bird, I want you to say something to Abe." Abel, who didn't like the delay any more than Cooper, at least knew Mrs. Johnson, and he chatted with her for a few minutes.

By this time, it was nearing six o'clock. "Now," Johnson said, "we're going down to announce the settlement to the press. I want Coop and Abe to stand with me at the podium." Dutifully, Abel and Cooper stood on either side of the President as Johnson made the announcement, happily noting that at this very moment the furnaces were going to be relit. Standing behind the trio, I envisioned Cooper going berserk and strangling the President before a national television audience.

The press conference lasted just a few minutes, and we were free. Almost. Next we were escorted back to the Oval Office for photos, and then we were ushered out to the Rose Garden for *more* pictures. Finally, word came that Johnson was heading to Texas, and we were all asked to go out to say good-bye to him. By this time, Wirtz looked like he was ready for the grave. Johnson said: "Bill, I don't want you to desert these people. Help them out with travel arrangements, ya hear." Finally, much to everyone's relief, Johnson dashed into the waiting helicopter and vanished, like Superman, up, up, and away.

It was a far cry from my first visit to the White House in 1963. The Taft-Hartley Act, which gave the President the ability to impose an eighty-day injunction in a dispute affecting national health and safety, also contained a provision allowing him to set up a twelve-person labor-management advisory panel. Truman and Eisenhower hadn't used it. President Kennedy did.

I was appointed one of the six labor members of the panel in the summer of 1963. We had our first meeting with Kennedy in June. When the President entered the Cabinet Room, there were about twenty-five people standing around the room, in small groups, talking to each other. Twelve of us were the newly appointed panel members; he had not met any of us. Kennedy moved around the room, shaking hands. A few minutes later we were asked to be seated, and we sat around the cabinet table in random fashion. The President then proceeded to address us individually by name and offered a comment indicating he knew about our work. When he reached me, for example, he spoke about my work on the Kaiser Steel Long-Range Sharing Plan, asked several insightful questions, offered a compliment, and moved on to the next panel member. It was quite impressive. He had no notes; we wore no name tags.

For the next half hour Kennedy spoke intelligently about some of the current labor issues being discussed in academic circles. It was all very promising. Five months later, he was killed in Dallas. JFK's reputation among liberal people has always puzzled me a bit; his aggressiveness in getting us involved in a near disaster in Cuba and a genuine disaster in Vietnam would have been, and was condemned in, say, a Richard Nixon. Nonetheless, I think he understood the need for strong unions and the importance of collective bargaining better than most Presidents.

My last visit to the White House, in 1982, was very different. A few weeks before I retired from the Players Association, Kenneth Moffett, the executive director–elect, and I attended a conference with various athletes and their representatives about a new antidrug policy. This time we were led to assigned seats in the Cabinet Room, and President Ronald Reagan and the First Lady circled the table shaking hands. The Reagans sat in front of a blackboard filled with charts and statistics, which I figured would be used by some official from the Drug Enforcement Agency after the President had made a few introductory statements. But when Reagan pulled out his now-famous three-by-five index cards, I thought, "Wow, I guess he's going to get into the guts of this." Wrong! He started reading a prepared welcoming statement that a ten-year-old could have mouthed off the top of his head. All I could do was recall my first visit to the White House and how impressed I had been with the intelligence and preparation of the extremely well informed John F. Kennedy. What a contrast to this second-rate actor—and I don't mean second-rate *movie* actor, since I had long since forgotten he had ever been in movies—who couldn't shoo a cow from the middle of the road without cue cards. "So," I thought, "this is what the country has come to." Not quite, but it was the direction in which it was moving.

In any event, after eight hectic days with LBJ in 1965, my life remained chaotic. I was so busy throughout the summer that I barely had time to think. There were countless details to be worked out on the steel settlement; there were contracts to be negotiated in aluminum and can manufacturing; there were meetings of the Kaiser Committee, and on and on. During this whirlwind activity I accepted an invitation from John Dunlop, an economics professor at Harvard and one of the three public members of the Kaiser Committee, to speak to a graduate seminar on labor relations.

After the seminar, Dunlop and Derek Bok (the future president of Harvard) and I got together for a drink. They, of course, had heard the rumors about my supposed departure, which they mentioned hesitantly before asking if I would be interested in a position as a visiting professor at Harvard. The term, they said, was open, anywhere from one to three years. The offer was quite attractive: a good salary (more than I was making at the Steelworkers), an excellent (portable) pension, an eight-and-a-half-month work year, some writing on labor relations matters of my choice, and as much or as little teaching of graduate students as I wanted. And Dunlop, who knew me quite well, said, "We just built new tennis courts which you could use whenever you want." At the time, I was so tired, so worn out from the previous two years of nonstop stress and strain that I almost agreed on the spot.

I promised I would think about it.

I had also had an inquiry from the Carnegie Endowment for International Peace. They had a large grant for a multiyear study that they wanted me to direct. Their hypothesis was that government had a lot to learn about the art of negotiation and could profit from the experience of veteran labor negotiators in resolving international disputes. I came to New York for an interview. But the position seemed like a loosely structured academic exercise. I passed.

Soon after the Harvard offer, George Taylor asked me to call Robin Roberts. Terry and I talked and talked about what I should do. My son, Peter, was all for my taking the Harvard job. I had my doubts. Sure, I was tired now, but could I adjust after so many years as an activist to a more sedate life-style? More important, I thought, the opportunity in baseball would never come again. The Players Association was a totally ineffective organization, and anything I did would be an improvement, and a big one. Other academic opportunities would likely be available down the road. And, if truth be told, the chance to lead an organization after years of toiling in the background was quite attractive.

During all the turmoil at the union caused by Abel's candidacy, various people had asked me, quite casually, "Did you ever think of running for office?" I had. There's a real practical way I could do this, I thought. Traditionally, the position of secretary-treasurer of the Steelworkers Union was a stepping-stone to the presidency. For a while I considered speaking to McDonald and asking him to put me on his ticket as a candidate for secretary-treasurer, in his campaign against Abel.

One day, I said to my wife, "What would you say if someday I ran for president of the Steelworkers?"

She hated the idea. Or, to be more accurate, she was scared to death, thinking, no doubt, about the attempted assassination in 1948 of Walter Reuther, president of the United Auto Workers, who was nearly killed at home by a bullet through a window that shattered his arm.

I reassured her that her fears were groundless.

She thought the potential for violence was greater than I admitted. And she might have been right. In my mind, I would have made significant changes. Suppose a future president of the USW wasn't a traditional leader; suppose he was somebody who felt that the labor movement needed reform from top to bottom, who felt the labor movement had sold out the workers by not forming a Labor Party. That type of president would anger quite a few powerful people.

The more I thought about it, the more attractive the idea became. Of course, all this took place only in my head. I never did approach McDonald, and he picked a district director from Kentucky named, fittingly enough, Al Whitehouse, who was defeated in the election along with McDonald and Hague.

I don't know what different path I would have taken had the opportunity in baseball not presented itself. Would I have stayed with the Steelworkers or given it up for the Ivy League? I do know that the more I thought about the Players Association, the more I figured I could make a difference. I loved baseball, and I loved a good fight, and, in my mind, ballplayers were among the most exploited workers in America.

4...

Take Me Out to the Players Association

AFTER THE INTERVIEW with Robin Roberts, Harvey Kuenn, and Jim Bunning, I found my mind drifting back to bits and pieces of our conversation. I had accepted that I wouldn't be pursuing the job in baseball, but I kept thinking about it nonetheless. Several days after the interview, Roberts called, essentially to see how adamant I was about serving with Nixon.

I said, "Very."

"Well," he said, "I'd like to go forward with your name anyway and see what happens. We can rethink this general counsel setup."

I agreed, reluctantly, and gave him a written summary of my background to present to the player representatives at a meeting in New York in January. I planned to be in Puerto Rico at the annual meeting of the National Academy of Arbitrators. It was agreed that I would call him from San Juan to find out the result.

When I phoned, Mrs. Roberts answered. "Robbie isn't in," she said, "but he left a message. He's terribly sorry, but Cannon received a plurality of the votes." So that was it.

• 33 •

Upon my return to Pittsburgh, Roberts called. Apparently, the night before the election, Bob Friend—a good pitcher and a better Republican—did a major-league PR job on the player reps to get his man, Robert Cannon, elected.

I thanked Roberts for the explanation and wished him well.

Ten days later, Roberts called again. "Things have changed," he said excitedly. "Cannon has pissed off a number of player reps by demanding additional conditions. Some of the reps didn't like him in the first place, and Bob Friend is no longer backing him. Without Friend's support, Cannon is through. The reps are going to meet and start the selection process all over."

"I'm no longer a candidate," I said coldly. "Friend, who didn't even bother to come to the meeting in Cleveland, apparently was in control of the selection process all the way. He had the whole deal wrapped up in his mind. Now you're saying that Friend has second thoughts. I never met him, and I don't know what he's thinking, and I don't want to go through this again."

For the next few days, Roberts called every day. He was either desperate or persuaded, deep down, that I wanted the job. Finally he asked, "Would it help if Friend called you himself?"

"Probably not," I said.

"I've told him you're much more qualified for the job than Cannon, and he's kicking himself for not listening to me. I'm sure he'd do all he could to get you elected."

I said, without making a commitment, "Let him call."

The phone rang an hour later. It was Friend. "Cannon misled me," he said. "I'd known him a long time and felt that he was more familiar with the players' problems because he'd been our legal advisor for the past six years, but I made a mistake. I hope you'll reconsider."

I told him I wanted to think about it. Two days later, I called him back. "If the players elect me," I said, "I'll accept the job."

Not long after that call from Friend, I received another, from the American League player rep, Bob Allison. A tall, powerfully built outfielder for the Minnesota Twins, Allison had been Rookie of the Year with the Washington Senators in 1959. In 1963, he hit 35 home runs and led the league with 99 runs scored. He finished with 256 career home runs.

Allison was giving me the results of the meeting with the player reps, but I could barely hear what he was saying. It sounded as if he were calling from the middle of a Shriners convention. "Several reps abstained," he shouted, "but the vote was unanimously in favor of selecting you as head of the Association." He told me I would have to visit the spring training camps as soon as possible in order to gain the approval of the players, managers, coaches, and trainers.

Time was tight. Most clubs broke camp by April 2, and here it was early March. In order to meet with all twenty clubs I would have to travel to training camps in Florida, California, and Arizona.

Allison congratulated me. Again, I had trouble hearing him. "What's all that noise?"

He said: "That's the press."

"The press?"

"Well," he said, "we just had a press conference and announced the results of the election."

"Election?" I said. "Bob, this is only a *nomination*. It's subject to a vote of all the players."

"I know."

"You know?" I said, dumbfounded. "Not only is my nomination subject to a vote, but I haven't said anything to anyone at the Steelworkers Union." I pictured I. W. Abel, the Steelworkers president, opening his morning paper to learn that his trusty assistant had a new job.

"Oh," he said, "I guess we shouldn't have done it this way."

That was not the last time I would be dismayed by the inexperience of this group that I was expected to lead.

The next day, Sunday, March 6, the *New York Times* carried a brief story headed "Ballplayers Group Hires Union Official," but in Pittsburgh the story made the front page. By afternoon I was inundated with calls from friends, colleagues, and relatives congratulating me on a new job, which, of course, I didn't have. Real estate agents, inquiring about the availability of our house, called nonstop. (The housing market in Pittsburgh was tight, and according to the story, I was bound for the Big Apple, my bags all but packed.) During one of the few moments the phone was free, I tried—unsuccessfully—to reach I. W. Abel. That evening my family took refuge at a restaurant and we pondered my predicament.

On Monday morning I went straight to Abel's office. He's fishing in South America, his secretary informed me, his whereabouts unknown. She did, however, know when he was scheduled to land in Miami. She gave me the number of his connecting flight to Los Angeles for a meeting of the Kaiser Committee, on which we both served.

I contacted the vice president and the secretary-treasurer of the USW, told them what was happening—they had already read all about it—and arranged to take three weeks' vacation. Before flying south, I sent each player representative a copy of another *New York Times* article, titled "Creative Labor Man to Go to Bat for Ballplayers." It described my background and had a picture of me, so at least the players would recognize me when I showed up. There were, however, two errors in the story: one, that Judge Cannon served on an unpaid basis (he was paid $15,000 a year while he served as a full-time judge in Milwaukee); and two, that I played a fierce game of tennis. I enjoy tennis, but I'm no pit bull.

Next, I met with Frank Scott in Fort Lauderdale. Scott, in effect, was administrative assistant to Judge Cannon and handled various chores for the Players Association. He knew the teams' schedules and could help me arrange to meet with them. We worked out an itinerary and sent telegrams to twenty player reps informing them when I would be at each training camp. That night, Frank Scott and I went out to dinner (at the dog track) with Bob Friend, Whitey Ford, and their wives. The next afternoon, I boarded a flight to Los Angeles and arranged to be seated next to I. W. Abel.

When I brought Abel up to date on the baseball saga, a stern look crossed his lined face. He remained silent, contemplating what I had just said. During the Depression, he had worked in a brickyard firing a kiln at sixteen cents an hour, twelve hours a day, seven days a week. In the mid-1930s, he began organizing the mills; during one year, he led forty-two wildcat walkouts. "You really want to do this?" Abel asked finally.

"I have my doubts, Abe"—most of his acquaintances called him Abe—"but there's an awful lot about this I don't understand."

He nodded. "The whole thing sounds crazy to me. You've been

with the Steelworkers for sixteen years. You're the chief economist, assistant to the president. You're highly respected in this organization. Why would you want to leave?"

"It's a challenge," I said. "I'm going to kick myself if I don't give it a try." That was so, but it wasn't the whole truth. When, one year earlier, Abel won the bitterly contested fight for president of the Steelworkers Union over the far more flamboyant David McDonald, everything changed for the worse, including staff relationships, the effectiveness of the union, and the nature of negotiations with the industry.

Abel wasn't pleased at my leaving. "I don't think you should do this. But if you're decided, I wish you the best." I knew Abel pretty well, and it seemed to me he hadn't said everything that was on his mind. But he changed the subject, and for the rest of the flight we discussed the forthcoming Kaiser Committee meeting.

There were only nine people on the Kaiser Committee— George Taylor, the chairman; John Dunlop, of Harvard; David Cole, a nationally known arbitrator (the three public members); Edgar Kaiser, the president of Kaiser Steel; Abel; and myself among them—but there were many aides and assistants also in attendance. The conference room was crowded and noisy, but as soon as I walked in, the hubbub stopped. Apparently they had been discussing front-page stories in the morning newspapers. The *Los Angeles Times* and the *Los Angeles Herald Examiner*, spread out on the conference table, contained stories about yours truly. Evidently, Buck Rodgers, California's regular catcher, Jimmy Piersall, and several other Angels, such as Jack Sanford, Lew Burdette, and Joe Adcock, had sounded off against my selection. I was flabbergasted. Rodgers was the Angels' player rep—part of what amounted to an executive board which had nominated me by unanimous vote. Now, the day before I was to go to Palm Springs to meet with the team, he was making antiunion statements as if I were going to demand extra pay for extra-inning games or insist that lineups be based on seniority.

After the morning session of the Kaiser Committee, I decided to go out to lunch by myself to think. I suspected that this was a smear campaign organized by the owners. Why else would I be lynched before I showed up at the first meeting? It just didn't make sense. Later, I learned that Cannon was behind the campaign.*

After lunch, I sat by myself in a little park within the hotel complex. I had been there a few minutes when Abel strolled up, sat down, and asked: "Is this Rodgers crazy? He's supposed to be endorsing you to the players, not running you down. Don't they have a sense of responsibility here?"

"I don't understand any of this," I said, feeling discouraged.

"Don't be a fool. This is a setup. It's gotta be. I thought this sounded crazy on the plane, and I think it's nuts now."

I said, "I'm going to go through with these meetings with the players and I'll see how the vote goes."

Abel studied me through his gold-rimmed glasses. "Listen," he said, "I don't think you should open yourself up to this. These players don't seem to have any idea of what a union is. But if you really want to do it, do it with the assurance that any time you change your mind, I'll welcome you back."

Well, that's all I had to hear. It was the second time in a year that Abel had backed me. By the time I returned to the conference room, I was thinking about Buck Rodgers, Jimmy Piersall, and the rest of the California Angels. Tomorrow would be my first real test in baseball.

ON THE WAY to Palm Springs, I kept thinking about my warm welcome to baseball. One headline read "Buck Rodgers Says, 'We Don't Want Any Labor Boss in Baseball.'" Center fielder Jimmy Piersall claimed Robin Roberts "railroaded" Miller into the position (whatever that meant). First baseman Joe Adcock said, "Pro sports has no place for unions," and pitchers Jack Sanford and Lew Burdette rounded out the dissonant Angel chorus with similar comments. Players at other training camps—third basemen Ron Santo of the Cubs and Eddie Mathews of the Braves, and first baseman Ron Fairly of the Dodgers (and the club's player rep)—echoed the sentiments. As far as I could tell, no shortstop,

---

*Ironically, in just a few months, Judge Cannon would be subject to a protest demonstration. A Roman Catholic priest led the NAACP in picketing Cannon's house in suburban Milwaukee because of his membership in a men's organization that specifically excluded nonwhites.

second baseman, or right fielder found me offensive, so you couldn't field an All-Star team with players who didn't want me, but that was small comfort.

Though the people I would be representing were far better off than workers in any other union, representing them looked to be a tough job. Despite the complex problems in the steel industry and the burdensome size of the union (1,250,000 members), at least the rank and file had a strong union consciousness. If a steelworker was improperly laid off, you didn't have to tell him to come to the union to file a grievance; nor did you have to explain to a veteran steelworker how important union solidarity was to his welfare.

Not so in baseball. Players were not only ignorant about unions, they were positively hostile to the idea: They didn't know what a union was, but they knew they didn't want one. There was a reason for this attitude. From time immemorial, the baseball powers-that-be force-fed the players propaganda: The commissioner (although appointed and paid by the owners) represented the players; players were privileged to be paid to play a kid's game; and (the biggest fairy tale of all) baseball was not a business and, in any case, was unprofitable for the owners.

Remember, many people in the workplace don't develop a union consciousness until they've had some work experience. After they've had a few rough years, maybe been cheated and mistreated and made some mistakes, they begin to see the value of a union. This scenario, of course, would exclude 99.9 percent of all ballplayers, most of whom are signed right out of high school. Which is not to say that ballplayers didn't have bad experiences in organized baseball. Players continually griped about the schedule, the rotten playing conditions, the poor medical treatment, and the macho tradition of playing hurt: How many pitchers saw their careers go down the drain after logging three hundred–plus innings a year? But ballplayers simply didn't know how to voice such complaints—there was no place to go.

The research that I had done—and I had done a lot in the months preceding my first spring training trip—shocked me. Picture an industry where about a third of the employees are black or Latino. And suppose from the time you began hiring these minorities (Jackie Robinson) to the time you finally hired one black manager (Frank Robinson), thirty-five years have elapsed. You might think that such an industry would have to mount some kind of defense in the face of such shocking figures. Especially when one discrimination case after another was being brought in other industries with similar violations. But in 1966, major league baseball was as lawless, in its own way, as Dodge City in 1876. Antitrust laws, laws against discrimination, health and safety laws, simply didn't apply, because they weren't enforced by the courts or by federal, state, or local authorities. Was it any wonder that the buttoned-down baseball establishment was arrogant? If no one holds you accountable, you think that no one can.

Part-time advisor J. Norman Lewis (1954–60) and the ever-unctuous Judge Robert Cannon (1960–66) told the players that they lived in the best of all possible worlds. Cannon endorsed the owners' increase in the schedule from 154 to 162 games without an increase in pay for the players, accepting instead a few dollars a day more in meal money for them. The expanded schedule angered baseball purists, but it put additional millions of dollars each year in the owners' pockets.

Even Robin Roberts, one of the most enlightened of the players, had a naive view of the role the Players Association was to play. Roberts's number-one priority was the pension, which he felt was being inadequately administered by Charlie Segar, secretary to Commissioner William "Spike" Eckert. Of course, the pension should *never* have been administered out of the commissioner's office, but Roberts had had no problem with that because he did not understand the commissioner's tie to the owners. In fact, when the search committee arrived at the idea of creating an independent office for the Players Association, they went to the commissioner to talk about how it would be financed. Imagine John L. Lewis going to the chief executive officer of U.S. Steel to ask for help in financing an independent Steelworkers Union!

Another example of Roberts's concern for the owners' sensibilities occurred the morning after Bob Allison of the Twins told me the player reps had approved my selection as executive director. Robin phoned early Sunday morning while I was half-awake. "You may not know this," he said, sounding as nervous as a pitcher on Opening Day, "but ballplayers don't wear mustaches."

As far as I could recall, Frenchy Bordagaray, a Brooklyn Dodger in the 1930s and 1940s, had been the last player to wear one, shaving only after he had been threatened by management. "I'm aware of that," I said, fingering the modest growth on my upper lip.

"It's probably not the best thing for your image," he said apologetically.

Now I was awake. "Robbie, this is 1966. Take a look at the young people in the stands wearing long hair, beards, and mustaches. I'm not going to shave a mustache I've had since I was seventeen because of some management hang-up." (In just a few years, Charles Finley, owner of the Oakland A's, was encouraging his players to grow long hair, sideburns, and handlebar mustaches, and paying three hundred dollars per face in an attempt to evoke a Gay Nineties look.)

It was the first and last time the subject came up, but as I sped by the San Bernardino Mountains, it reminded me how far behind the times the players really were. Before the first meeting in Cleveland I had read through the pension plan, the Uniform Player's Contract, and the Major League Rules and discovered a number of things, including that this highly touted pension was a contributory plan with inadequate benefits. (The Steelworkers Union had abolished employee contributions to pension plans in steel in 1949.)

The Uniform Player's Contract was just as bad. It had obviously been drafted by the owners' lawyers—no document that had been *negotiated* could ever have been so one-sided. It reminded me of a form lease drawn up by an association of landlords and handed to prospective tenants for signature. But I did find some very interesting provisions, one of which was Paragraph 10a. The first time I read it, I did a double take. What I had been told—and what the *players believed*—was that once a player signed his first contract, he no longer had control over his career. But the plain words of this section of the contract, as I read it, gave a club a one-year option on a player's services after his contract expired. *Nothing more.* It provided that if a club and player did not agree on a new contract to replace the one that had terminated, the club could renew the old contract for *one additional year*.

If someone had asked me what the reserve rule meant the day George Taylor mentioned Robin Roberts to me, I would have replied, "It means that a player cannot choose to leave the club that first signs him." I didn't know its origins, how it evolved, or anything about the labyrinth of interlocking rules. That came much later. But like most baseball fans I had been aware of previous attempts by players to gain the freedoms other people take for granted, such as the right to leave an employer and find a different job. I also knew, without being familiar with the details, that no one had been successful in combating the baseball monopoly which, although it used such outlawed tactics as blacklisting, had never been curtailed, either by the United States Supreme Court, the Congress, or the Justice Department in any administration, Republican or Democratic, or by any state or local government. The Supreme Court started the whitewash of the baseball monopoly with its 1922 opinion, written by Oliver Wendell Holmes, that baseball was not subject to federal antitrust laws. (No such exemption ever existed, either in the Sherman or Clayton antitrust laws.) Simply put, Justice Holmes declared baseball is a sport, a series of exhibition games, not in interstate commerce! Thirty-one years later, in 1953, the high court continued its improbable exemption for baseball's monopoly, as it would do a third time, nineteen years later in 1972.

When I left Los Angeles, I had all the confidence of a condemned man, but by the time I arrived in Palm Springs, I was eager to face the challenge ahead. My immediate problem was quite different. I had no hotel reservation, and it looked like my best bet that Saturday evening was a park bench: There wasn't a vacant room to be had within forty miles. The union rep who had driven me from Los Angeles suggested I call David McDonald, who had retired to Palm Springs after losing the 1964 election. I hadn't spoken to McDonald in almost a year, but when I called, he gladly offered to put me up for the night, though he and his wife, Rosemary, were on their way to a dinner party. Not only did they make me feel right at home, they even gave me the keys to Rosemary's car so I could get to the ballpark early the next morning for my meeting with Bob Rodgers and the Angels' players.

After they left, I sat down at the McDonalds' writing table to prepare what I was going to say to the Angels. I couldn't help but reflect on my good fortune. In the span of eight hours, two archrivals—Abel and McDonald—men who really disliked each other, had gone out of their way to help me. Now, of course, I was on my own. Since my first contact with Roberts, I'd been attacked by players publicly and been subjected to intensive press coverage, more so in the last few weeks than during my sixteen years with the Steelworkers. I would learn that the media coverage of five hundred players in major league baseball far exceeded the ink spent on even a lengthy steel strike of five hundred thousand workers that affected the entire economy. Roberts had warned me to expect resistance among the players, but I also suspected that the owners had had a hand in stirring up opposition. Baseball's owners had had their way too long to accept any loss of control to a union without a struggle. And I hadn't even met any of the owners!

After several hours, I called it quits. Tomorrow would be a long day. Before meeting the Angels, I had an eight A.M. breakfast scheduled with player rep Buck "We Don't Want Any Labor Boss in Baseball" Rodgers. I could hardly wait.

When you meet a man who has publicly bashed you in the newspaper, how do you greet him? "Buck! Loved your piece in the *Examiner!*" Or do you say: "Did you mean 'labor boss' in a bad way or a good way!"

At six-foot-two and 190 pounds, Rodgers was a tall, trim, handsome man—not at all like the square-built, barrel-chested, broken-nosed catchers I grew up watching, backstops like Hank DeBerry, Al Lopez, Ernie Lombardi, and Gabby Hartnett. In 1962, Rodgers had been a rookie with promise; now he was having problems, finishing the 1965 season with a career-low batting average of .209. David McDonald, who had been angered by Rodgers's comments in the paper, was prompted to sneer, "Rodgers can't even hit his weight"—a slight exaggeration.

As we shook hands I could tell Rodgers was ill at ease. We ordered breakfast, dispensed with the small talk, and got down to business. "I don't get it," I said, lifting a copy of the paper with his offending quotes. "You supported my nomination. Why the sudden outburst of criticism? We hadn't even met."

Rodgers wasn't just uncomfortable, he was embarrassed. "After your nomination," he said, playing with the omelet on his plate, "a handful of players—friends of Cannon's—told me it would be a mistake to support a labor man. Then Cannon began campaigning around here. He said you'd bring racketeering and goon squads to baseball."

I had suspected the owners of slandering me; this was the first I'd heard about Cannon's smear campaign. Although I should have suspected it from the wording of the petition, allegedly written by players, printed in the *Los Angeles Herald Examiner*: "Our feeling is that [the new director of the Players Association] should have a *legal* background that the owners [*sic*] can respect." Like maybe a judge? And the most telling line: "We have progressed a great deal in the past few years and we think this relationship between the owners and the players should continue."

"The pro-Cannon players put a lot of pressure on me," Rodgers continued. (A more perceptive or intelligent man would have said, "The players in management's pocket put a lot of pressure on me.") "Then the newspaper guys started hounding me. And I guess I said some things I shouldn't have," he said, literally wiping egg from his face. "You should know that a lot of people out here agree with Cannon and are helping him."

It was an explanation. Not a wholly satisfying one, but better than nothing. I later was told by some of Rodgers's teammates that he had left out a few facts; namely, that Cannon had reproduced five hundred copies of his petition for mailing to all the players and that club officials had picked up the tab.

There seemed little point in being angry with Rodgers for his role in the situation. He was a member of the executive board that had nominated me, and I had the right to expect a little more support from him, but he was being subjected to a lot of pressure. And he was a twenty-seven-year-old player coming off a bad season, looking for a measure of job security in a cutthroat profession. But I needn't have worried about Buck Rodgers. He retired in 1969 after nine seasons with the Angels. He was rewarded with a coaching job in the majors, then managed in the minors; and in 1981 he managed the Milwaukee Brewers to the second-half title of the strike-shortened season, the first time the Brewers made the playoffs. Rodgers resurfaced as skipper of the Expos in 1985, a post he holds today.

After breakfast we made our way to the Angels clubhouse, which was crowded with the forty-man spring training roster. Before I said anything, Rodgers went around asking the younger players if they were "on the plan." To qualify for the pension plan a player had to have at least sixty days of major league service. Those that didn't were asked to leave. That's how intertwined the pension and the Players Association were.

After a quick introduction I talked for perhaps twenty minutes about my background and experience, the origin of the Players Association, the relationship between its being dominated by the owners and its ineffectiveness, and the nature of a real union as a united voice of its members. I spoke briefly about baseball as an extremely profitable business—which would become even more so with the growth of television—and I stressed the need for players to take an active part in order to make their organization an effective one. I also touched on the reserve rules by questioning the need for such restrictive controls over players—controls which did not exist in any industry other than sports.

The players' reaction was hard to gauge. Actually, there seemed to be no reaction. So I switched gears and brought up the players' number-one concern—the pension. "I've been told that players feel that you have a great pension plan. I disagree. In some ways it was a landmark, but because of inflation you are actually worse off in 1966 in terms of benefits than you were in 1947 when it was established."

A few eyebrows lifted around the room.

"In determining the value of a pension plan you must project to when you are fifty, sixty, or older, when you will be drawing benefits. Unless a monthly retirement benefit is adjusted regularly to reflect higher living costs, it's unlikely to be enough to buy a full tank of gas in thirty years." I pressed on, discussing some of the other grossly inadequate provisions in the plan.

The silent Angels slowly came to life, though no one stumbling upon us would have mistaken the gathering for a revival meeting. Part of the problem was that no one had ever encouraged the players to think independently or critically about their situation. I tried to impress on them that unions were far more democratic than they had been led to believe and that, in any case, the effectiveness of their organization depended on them, on their input.

I had started out by promising that I would leave ample time for questions, comments, discussion. When I paused to do so, an uneasy silence and a sea of blank stares filled the room. "This is *your* organization," I stressed, sounding, I realized, a little like a schoolmaster. "I want you to feel free to ask anything you want. If I don't have the answers, I'm not embarrassed to say 'I don't know,' and then I'll go out and find the answers."

Finally, Jimmy Piersall spoke up and asked the question on everyone's mind. "Are you going to have the ballplayers go out on strike?" The word "strike" was like a gong sounding and couldn't have had any less resonance. It was the owners' worst nightmare. And most (if not all) players felt the same way. Three years earlier, Bob Friend had summed up this paranoia best in a piece he penned in the *Sporting News*: "It would destroy baseball if fans were exposed to the spectacle of someone like Stan Musial picketing a ballpark." But there was more. The national press had been following the running feud between Jimmy Hoffa, president of the Teamsters, and George Meany, president of the AFL-CIO. Because of racketeering charges, the Teamsters had been purged from the ranks of the AFL-CIO. Just a few days earlier, Meany had been quoted as stating (incorrectly) that ballplayers were independent contractors and did not need unions. Hoffa shot back that it was about time for the players to organize and affiliate with the Teamsters. Baseball's power brokers were spreading the rumor that my election, in some inexplicable way, would bring the Teamsters Union into baseball. Warren Giles, president of the National League, peddled this line to numerous players in his league, and Joe Reichler, of the commissioner's office, spread some choice rumors in the American League. Incredibly, there were squads of management personnel preceding me into every training camp, warning the players that my election would spell the end of baseball. It was quite a welcome.

I decided to answer Piersall in a baseball framework. "When a player feels that a contract offer is less than he deserves, the only recourse he has is to hold out—in other words, he withholds, or threatens to withhold, his services. What is a strike but a withholding of services? The only difference is that *individual* holdouts are ignored and ineffective—even if your name is Joe DiMaggio or Sandy Koufax. But unified group action can never be ignored. A strike is a weapon that sometimes must be used, but only as a *last* resort, much like going to war.

"I want you to understand that this is going to be an adversarial relationship. A union is not a social club. A union is a restraint on what an employer can otherwise do. If you expect the owners to like me, to praise me, to compliment me, you'll be disappointed. In fact, if I'm elected and you find the owners telling you what a great guy I am, fire me! Don't hesitate, because it can't be that way if your director is doing his job. The owners loved Judge Cannon. Don't make the same mistake with your new executive director."

The meeting over, I left the clubhouse for the playing field. A compact man came up and introduced himself.

"Mr. Miller," he said, smiling, "I'm Tommy Lasorda. Tom Consiglio [a Steelworker colleague from Los Angeles] told me that you'd be here today. I came by to see if there was anything I could do for you." I never found out why a member of management was so friendly to me, but it was appreciated.

In 1966 Lasorda was managing Ogden in the Pioneer League, but he had been a southpaw pitcher for the Dodgers. He appeared in four games for the 1955 Dodgers—the first and only Brooklyn team to win a World Series. Lasorda never did get to enjoy the World Championship, having been sent back to the minors to make room for a Brooklyn-born "bonus baby" named Sanford Koufax.*

Lasorda and I talked about the attempt to create a bona fide union, he wished me luck, and I hurried off to return Rosemary McDonald's car and catch my flight to Phoenix. There I was scheduled to meet the San Francisco Giants and the Chicago Cubs.

As soon as the plane took off, I opened the newspaper. The lead story on the sports page detailed the continuing holdout of Koufax and Don Drysdale. In 1964 and again in 1965, the lefty-righty combo carried Los Angeles to World Series victories. In 1965, Koufax won twenty-six games, struck out 382, and won the Cy Young Award. His record of 70–18 over the last three years

---

*Lasorda did once fan twenty-five batters in a fifteen-inning game for the Schenectady Blue Jays, and he still holds the all-time International League record for career wins for the Montreal Royals.

gave him an unheard-of winning percentage of .795. Drysdale—60–45 during that same span—won twenty-three, seven of them shutouts, and fanned 210 batters in 1965.

Koufax was said to have been paid $70,000 in 1965, nowhere near the $130,000 per year paid to baseball's top-salaried star, San Francisco's Willie Mays. Koufax and Drysdale had grown tired of being played off against each other, come contract time, and had hired a lawyer to negotiate a package deal for them. A novel idea in 1966. Both were standing pat on their demand for a three-year deal that would bring them a total of $1 million. Drysdale was quoted as saying that there was "no reason to believe" they would play in 1966, and they were looking "to accept every reasonable offer" off the playing field because of the stalemate, including a movie scheduled to start in April. Dodgers owner Walter O'Malley's reply was: "I admire the boys' strategy and we can't do without them, even for a little while. . . . But we can't give in to them. There are too many agents hanging around Hollywood."* This was a reference to baseball's inflexible "policy" of refusing to deal with any agent.

Another off-the-field clash caught my attention. After thirteen seasons in Milwaukee, the Braves had accepted an offer to move to Atlanta. The state and city were suing major league baseball for approving the move, the first institutional challenge in forty-four years to the sport's immunity from antitrust laws. Of course, baseball claimed that the state court had no jurisdiction, citing its exemption from *federal* antitrust laws. One of baseball's attorneys in the case? Bowie Kuhn.

Staring out over the Arizona desert, I thought about Dodger southpaws Koufax and Lasorda: bonus baby versus minor league ham-and-egger. I thought back to those glorious 1955 Brooklyn Dodgers, to Walter O'Malley, the man who took baseball from Brooklyn, the first owner to say out loud that the game was a business he could operate as he chose. I thought about Milwaukee's attempt to hold on to its ball club. I had not yet met the lawyer named Kuhn, but he was someone I would get to know plenty well.

---

*Koufax and Drysdale settled for one-year contracts. The salary figures were not disclosed but were said to represent substantial increases, although far short of the players' proposed salaries.

GROWING UP in Brooklyn, I had a perfectly natural and healthy hatred of the New York Giants. I thought I was over it. After all, in 1958 both teams had moved out to the West Coast, and besides, I was no longer young or a Brooklynite. But sitting in the empty wooden bleachers in Phoenix as the San Francisco Giants took fielding practice, I felt stirrings of the old animosity from the days when Dazzy Vance, Lefty Clark,* Rube Bressler, Al Lopez—*my* team—did battle with Bill Terry, "Fat Freddie" Fitzsimmons, and Mel Ott—the *other* team—the "Jints." And the morning's meeting with the players had done little to improve my relationship with the club.

The *one* Giant that I could never dislike was just a line drive away, shagging flies under the scorching Arizona sun. In the field and on the bases, Willie Mays pranced around like a kid on the last day of school. Willie was Jackie Robinson with power, Ted Williams with wings, Joe DiMaggio without the emotional reserve. In 1951, he was the on-deck batter when Bobby Thomson hit his historic homer to win the pennant. Fourteen seasons later, he was thirty-four years old and still playing center field. He batted .317, drove in 112 runs, and led the National League with a career-high 52 homers. Had he not played his home games in Candlestick Park, he might well have broken Hack Wilson's league record of 56.

But I had no time for nostalgia. As in the previous day's meeting with California, the Giants had been as docile as does. Mostly silence, followed by a few hesitant questions. Now, mulling the last few days over, I had some serious questions of my own. Had Cannon and the owners completely brainwashed the players? What part were the managers playing? Was this trip a mere formality? After wax museum number two, it certainly seemed that way.

Horace Stoneham, the Giants' longtime owner, walked unsteadily toward me. In 1948 Stoneham stunned New York by hiring Leo Durocher to manage the Giants—a move not unlike Sitting Bull's joining forces with General Custer. Durocher despised the Giants, or so we had thought. He had been Brooklyn's slick-fielding shortstop, and later their surly field general, in-

*Also known as Watty Clark.

structing his troops to kick dirt at the umpires, curse enemy fans (especially at the Polo Grounds), and spike the opposition in retaliation for brushback pitches. One writer said Durocher was so thoroughly a Brooklyn product that he must have been spawned in the Navy Yard. When Dodger owner Branch Rickey decided he'd had enough of the Lip, Stoneham figured, why not?

Leo managed the Giants brilliantly. In 1948, he traded for Durocher-clone Eddie Stanky. In 1949, he brought up Monte Irvin and Hank Thompson, the first black players in Giants history, and reclaimed Sal "the Barber" Maglie from the Mexican League. And after calling up a slow-starting twenty-year-old rookie named Willie Mays in 1951 (and sticking with him through an 0-for-23 start), Durocher guided New York to one of the greatest comebacks in baseball history.

Stoneham plopped down beside me and introduced himself. "Is there any particular player you'd like to meet?" he asked.

I was floored. Not by the offer, but by Stoneham's breath—it had to be at least 80 proof. Stoneham had a reputation as a man who never met a drink he didn't like. In fact, after the Giants swept the Indians in the 1954 World Series (remembered best for Mays's miraculous over-the-shoulder grab of Vic Wertz's fly ball in the deepest part of the Polo Grounds), Durocher was toasted by a few of his Hollywood friends—Jack Benny, Danny Kaye, Groucho Marx, and George Jessel, to name a few. Danny Kaye's imitation of a highly inebriated Horace Stoneham brought down the house. (Let's not forget that Kaye was a lifelong Dodgers fan.) Of course, when Stoneham read about it in the paper, he didn't laugh. By the end of the 1955 season, Durocher was gone, good-bye. Still, I was surprised to discover that the man who had engineered New York's move to San Francisco was sauced at eleven o'clock in the morning.

"I've always admired Willie Mays," I said, studying Stoneham's flushed face.

Stoneham asked someone to get "the Captain." Mays's uniform was soaked through with sweat, and his handshake could have choked a firehose. I wanted Mays's views about the Players Association, but couldn't ask with Stoneham sitting there. Instead I congratulated Willie on winning his second MVP Award, and a few minutes later he was back on the field.

Stoneham stood with me while we watched the players work out. His conversation rambled like a tumbleweed in the desert. Had I been at a bar in downtown Phoenix, I would have smiled politely and moved off. I was racking my brains for a way to escape without seeming rude when Stoneham asked: "See that kid working out at third?" Not far from us, San Francisco's twenty-four-year-old third baseman, Jim Ray Hart, was taking infield practice. "Last season he hit .299 with 23 home runs and 96 RBIs."

"Good numbers," I said.

Scowling and hiccuping, Stoneham said: "If that man stays sober, we'll win the pennant." (Just for the record: In 1966 Hart hit .285 with 33 homers and 93 RBIs. The Giants finished second, one and a half games behind the Dodgers.)

I nodded gravely.

With that, Stoneham stumbled away.

If only Danny Kaye had been there.

Minutes later, Gary Schumacher, the Giants public relations man, joined me in the stands. Years earlier, Schumacher had been a sportswriter for several New York papers; I had read him as a young man.

"Rumor has it," he said, "that you were brought up in Brooklyn."

I nodded.

"Were you a Dodgers fan?"

He sounded like a maitre d' at the Four Seasons asking a bum if he had reservations.

"Sure," I said. "I spent hundreds of nickels taking the subway to Ebbets Field. I even remember reading your byline in the *Brooklyn Daily Eagle*."

Schumacher's subsequent challenge was as subtle as Stoneham's breath. "Well, if you were that big a fan, you should remember the teams in the 1930s."

Some things you never forget, even if they happened thirty-five to forty years ago. I paused only a moment. "Del Bissonette was at first, then Dolph Camilli, shortstop Glenn Wright, and at one time an aging Rabbit Maranville. In right, Babe Herman; he hit .393 in 1930. The center fielder was Johnny Frederick, and Rube Bressler played left. After fielding practice Bressler used to toss balls to us—the kids who hung out in the old left-field bleachers."

Schumacher looked surprised. But he came back with a question, "What about catcher?"

"Al Lopez was the regular," I said, "but Hank DeBerry caught when Dazzy Vance pitched."

"Pitchers?"

The guy was a masochist. "Dolf Luque, Lefty Clark, and Jumbo Jim Elliott."

With that I headed back to the motel to arrange a breakfast meeting in Scottsdale with player rep Larry Jackson of the Cubs, now managed by that old Brooklyn snapdog, Leo Durocher.

The Cubs were no different from the Giants, who were as apathetic as the Angels. I talked about improving the pension, increasing the salary structure, and modifying the reserve clause, and I attempted to get some input from the players in order to learn what they considered problems and what they would like to change. But the gospel according to the owners (the Papa-Knows-Best school of labor relations) was that this outsider was intent on defiling their sacred game. Cannon was one of their mouthpieces, several of the ass-kissing managers followed suit, and the players out west—even the player reps who had nominated me—complied.

This became clearer in Tucson during my meeting with the Cleveland Indians. Though the Indians were no more hostile during my actual presentation than the players in any other camp, when I asked for questions, Birdie Tebbetts, the Cleveland manager, brought out the heavy artillery. "How can the players be sure you're not a Communist?"

A catcher by trade, Tebbetts spent most of his playing days with the Tigers. In the 1950s, he managed the Reds; in 1963, he became Cleveland's skipper.

"A what?" I asked, not believing the question.

"Have you ever been investigated by the FBI?"

I tried to be patient. Perhaps Tebbetts had absorbed one too many foul tips in his playing days.

"Actually, I have," I said. "The FBI conducts security checks on all government employees. As I've already mentioned, I worked for several federal agencies before, during, and after World War II, and I'm currently a member of President Johnson's National Labor-Management Panel." Unable to hold my tongue, I asked: "Have *you* ever been given a security clearance?"

He didn't answer, but the abuse continued. As Tebbetts pressed on, I grew increasingly annoyed, and the rest of the Indians became restless. Our dialogue lasted about fifteen minutes, and it became obvious that there really was only one thing on his mind—to carry out an assignment to disrupt the meeting. His coaches, including George Strickland and Early Wynn, were just as obvious in their disparaging remarks.

I learned later that in his playing days Tebbetts had spoken up for the club owners against Robert Murphy, the man who began the American Baseball Guild on behalf of the players.

Finally, I interrupted another of Tebbetts's irrelevant questions by saying, "It's clear that all you want to do is sabotage this meeting. You've had your say, and you've taken up far too much of everyone's time. Now let the players have their meeting back."

To finish the story: A year later, I think it was, during spring training, I was down in Bradenton, Florida, with Dick Moss, a colleague from the Steelworkers whom I had named general counsel of the Players Association in January 1967. After our morning meeting with the players, Dick and I were sitting in the outfield bleachers soaking up the sounds of spring training. Making his way through the empty stands and heading toward us was a man intent on paying us a visit. He wasn't in uniform, and I didn't recognize him until he was close. It was Birdie Tebbetts.

Cleveland (87–75) had finished fifth in 1965, fifteen games behind the Minnesota Twins. The following season, Tebbetts directed the club to a 66–57 record, before they finally let him go. Currently, he was working as a scout. He asked a few questions about his pension. Then he said: "I really came out here to explain what happened at that meeting in Tucson. You probably know by now, but we were told to give you a hard time in that meeting." He didn't say where the instructions came from, though I suspected both Gabe Paul, president of the club, and AL President Joe Cronin.

I said I had guessed as much.

Birdie congratulated us on the job we were doing, especially the improvements in the pension. He wished us luck and moved on, sauntering across the field, walking among the supine players on the outfield grass. I saw Birdie once more, early in 1990, in Longboat Key, Florida. My wife and I were leaving a restaurant when he approached us. Birdie, still a scout at the age of seventy-seven, said: "I didn't want to let you leave without saying hello." We shook hands—two elderly men—and wished each other well.

With the western swing complete, I returned to Florida to meet the remaining sixteen clubs, sandwiching in a visit to Pittsburgh to finish negotiations with Alcoa and to touch base with my family. The first wave of votes had already been sent to Frank Scott, but it had been agreed that the results would not be made available until he had heard from all twenty clubs. I knew I hadn't made a big splash out west, but I would have been startled to discover that I hadn't even gotten my feet wet. The Angels rejected me, 25–6! I struck out in San Francisco, 27–0, with one abstention—said to be Willie Mays. I was ambushed by the Indians, 32–1, my lone vote coming from pitcher "Sudden Sam" McDowell. And I was mauled by Leo and the Cubs, 18–10. Out of the 119 players, coaches, managers, and trainers, *17* voted for me.

I can't be certain, but *had* I known the owners' back-alley tactics, including having the vote conducted by managers Bill Rigney (Angels), Herman Franks (Giants), Leo Durocher (Cubs), and Birdie Tebbetts (Indians), it's possible I would have taken I. W. Abel's advice and left the players to work themselves out of their one-hundred-year-old owner-dominated world. I'm not a quitter. Far from it. But the song lyrics "You gotta know when to hold 'em, know when to fold 'em" always made a lot of sense to me. I firmly believe that people can be swayed by ideas, by experience, and by example, but I also know that you cannot change an entire entrenched industry without widespread support. Had I known the vote in California and Arizona (102–17 against me), I very well might have concluded that my only potential allies—the players— had no stomach for a fight. Of course, as developments proved, I would've been very wrong.

I led off my trip to Florida with the Yankees in Fort Lauderdale. If there was one team in baseball that figured to be resistant to a union—to any change—I expected it to be the New York Yankees, baseball's version of the Ming Dynasty. After all, this was the team of which someone wrote: "Rooting for them was like rooting for U.S. Steel." Since 1950, the Bronx Bombers had been to the World Series eleven times, most recently in 1964. Maybe, I thought, finishing sixth in 1965 had raised their consciousness.

The night before the Yankee meeting, player rep Clete Boyer called to invite me to breakfast at his rented home. An excellent-fielding third baseman, Clete was the youngest of three brothers to play in the big leagues. His middle brother, Ken, a third baseman for St. Louis, won the National League MVP Award in 1964. The Boyer boys squared off in the World Series that season. Both homered, but the Cardinals won in a classic seven-game series. In 1965, the Yankees, after reaching the Series the year before, were crippled by injuries and faded to their worst finish in forty years. But the mood at spring training in 1966 was hopeful. For the Yanks, if not for me.

The meeting took place in the home locker room at Fort Lauderdale Stadium. The Yankees offered no great outpouring of support, but neither did they throw soiled sweat socks at me; actually, to my surprise, they *seemed* receptive. In discussing the reserve clause, I offered no concrete reforms, made no drastic statements, saying only that the few times the matter had been taken to court it seemed to me the judgment had been in error.

The initial reaction was blank. In fact, only one Yankee said anything. As you might guess, it was Jim Bouton, certainly one of the brighter, more alert, and more outgoing players. He said: "I think there would be a problem if the players could move from one team to the other. Wouldn't the wealthiest team get all the stars?"

Actually, with players having no freedom, a handful of the richest teams *had* been dominating the game for decades. "What would you say," I asked, "about a system which has produced one team that has won thirty pennants and twenty World Series in the past forty-five years?"

"You mean, like the Yankees," Bouton said, grinning. "Never thought about it like that."

That's because no one had ever raised the issue with the players before.

After the meeting, Joe Reichler, an assistant to Spike Eckert, came into the clubhouse. A former sportswriter, Reichler helped

Roy Campanella write his autobiography, *It's Good to Be Alive*, although the book he's best known for is *The Baseball Encyclopedia*. Reichler called me aside as if he had something very important to share. Leaning on the trainer's table, he said, "In order to be elected it's going to be very important to have the owners on your side."

"Uh-huh," I said, wondering if he, too, was about to suggest I shave my mustache and hire Nixon.

"Several of the owners are down here for spring training," he said. "You should invite them out for a drink."

"Well, Joe," I said, "I'm not antisocial, but I don't think that's the best thing for me to do at this point."

Reichler looked puzzled.

"I wouldn't refuse if an owner asked *me* out for a drink," I said, "but I don't think courting them is my job. I'm the newcomer to be welcomed or unwelcomed by the owners. So far, it's been the latter."

Reichler raised a disapproving eyebrow. "It's just a suggestion. But I do think you should at least contact John Galbreath. He is the chairman of the pension committee."

John W. Galbreath made his money in real estate and construction. He owned the Continental Can Building in New York, the U.S. Steel–Mellon Bank Building in Pittsburgh, and Darby Dan Farm, the stable that bred the 1963 Kentucky Derby winner, Chateaugay. Galbreath acquired the Pittsburgh Pirates in 1946. And he was about as hospitable to the idea of a union in baseball as he would have been to the horses in his stables forming an association. At the most recent cookout for players that he hosted each year at his Ohio farm, Galbreath had reportedly urged several of his players not to vote for me, saying a "labor boss" would ruin baseball. Months after my election, he wouldn't even acknowledge my presence in the same room.

I thanked Joe Reichler for his concern. As soon as he left, Boyer and Tom Tresh (without knowing what Reichler had said) came over to tell me what I already knew, "He's not to be trusted." Later, in *Ball Four*, Bouton wrote that his own mind was made up about me when Reichler ("the Commissioner's personal caddy") put his arm around him and solemnly warned him to be "very, very, very careful about this guy Miller."

Reichler and I would meet again, but never over cocktails.

The rest of the trip was a kaleidoscope of rental cars, motels, and speeches. A few moments stand out clearly in memory. After the first meeting with the Yankees in Fort Lauderdale, I met a sportswriter I had long admired. Red Smith had been a reporter in St. Louis and Philadelphia before becoming a syndicated columnist with the *New York Herald-Tribune*. What I especially liked about him (and what made him so different from other writers of his era such as Dick Young) was that he became *less* conservative as he got older. Over the years, Smith wrote more and more critically about baseball's power brokers. When Commissioner Happy Chandler suspended Brooklyn manager Leo Durocher for the entire 1947 season, Smith was critical. Chandler responded with an insult: Smith was trying to run him out of baseball; there was a high-stakes conspiracy in the works. Smith replied: "If I can get paid for thinking Happy Chandler has performed like a clown and a mountebank, then I want all that kind of money I can get. Ordinarily I have to work for mine." Another example: In the 1950s Red testified before a congressional subcommittee in favor of the reserve rule. He said, in effect, that baseball would be in chaos without it. Twenty-five years later he reversed his opinion, not only writing about his mistake, but strongly supporting the reforms which brought about free agency rights for the players.

Many of the sportswriters that I spoke to during spring training simply parroted management's line. Some called me "a business agent" or (the most frequent error, pronouncing the word as if it were a slur) "a lawyer." These guys shaped not only public opinion, but the players' opinions, too. I was mocked in print before I even had the job with facetious questions, such as "Will managers be forced to seek Mr. Miller's permission to yank a pitcher or send a utility man back to the minors?" Smith, however, was supportive and wished me well. During my years at the Players Association, he called many times, especially during the recurring crises. When he asked a question, I felt certain it was because he wanted to know the answer and that he would not ignore the facts that didn't fit a preconceived opinion. I didn't always feel the same way about other reporters who called.

At Orlando, the Twins' spring training facility, outfielder and player rep Bob Allison called again, this time asking if I would have dinner with him and owner Calvin Griffith. Calvin was the nephew of Clark "the Old Fox" Griffith, the former pitcher, manager, and longtime owner of the Washington Senators. As an owner, the Old Fox never seemed to have enough cash. In 1935, Griffith sold his All-Star player-manager Joe Cronin—the man who had led the club to the pennant in 1933 and who averaged 117 RBIs over five straight seasons—to Boston for $225,000. Cronin also happened to be Griffith's son-in-law.

I picked up more Griffith gossip in Bill Veeck's splendid autobiography, Veeck as in Wreck, a book I had been reading as I traveled from camp to camp. In 1948, Veeck attempted to pry two players—Early Wynn and Mickey Vernon—away from the obstinate owner. Veeck writes: "Griffith wouldn't deal with me. I kept after him constantly anyway, offering him bales of money, in addition to players, because I knew that Griffith did not have any great resistance to money. If I had been able to sit down alongside Griff and show him, say, $100,000 in cash, I had no doubt that—once he had been revived—he would have reached automatically for a pen."

Perhaps cheapness is genetically determined—at least in the Griffiths' case—because young Calvin was as tight with the dollar as Uncle Clark. One of the last owners to make his living entirely from baseball, Calvin was often accused of not going after big-time talent. Both the Senators and Twins were perennial cellar dwellers. For decades they had one of the lowest payrolls in baseball—and the most family members on the payroll.

I met Calvin Griffith, no longer a young man, and Bob Allison at the Twins' spring training headquarters, the Park Plaza Hotel. The evening began like a morticians' convention. Griffith brooded over his food, staring fixedly at a spot on the wall across the room. Allison fidgeted; I struggled to make conversation.

Suddenly Griffith put his drink down on the table, hard. "I want to know one thing," he said, glowering like Ted Williams just called out on strikes. "Are you going to negotiate each and every player's contract?"

I did a double take. "Do you mean, will I negotiate a collective bargaining agreement?"

"No!" he snorted. "Are you going to negotiate each player's individual salary?"

"No, it's not possible," I said simply. "The Players Association staff will consist of a general counsel, a secretary, and me. There's no way we could negotiate five hundred individual contracts each year."

A monumental look of relief crossed his doughy face, as he snatched up his fork and dug into his nearly untouched meal. All was right with *his* universe. But I don't think Bob Allison ever recovered from that meal—a short time later, he resigned as the American League and club player rep.

I had told Griffith the truth. But when the Players Association negotiated salary arbitration rights for players in the 1973 basic agreement, the Twins had more salary arbitrations than any other team in baseball (with Charles Finley's A's a close second). Griffith's cheapness was further showcased in 1979, during a speech at the Lions Club in Waseca, Minnesota. The owner bragged about how little he would pay Rod Carew, his seven-time batting champion, who had become a free agent at the end of the 1978 season and who was in contract negotiations. He essentially said that Carew was too dumb to know any better. Carew, a levelheaded gentleman and a legitimate superstar, ended his discussions with Griffith, angrily stating, "I don't want to be a nigger on that man's plantation." Soon after, he signed a five-year deal with the Angels.

Cocoa Beach, Astros training camp. Robin Roberts told me that he'd been getting postive feedback from many of the players. At age thirty-nine, Robin was preparing for what would be the last of his nineteen seasons in the major leagues. Compared to most of the players, Roberts was a visionary, but even he never truly accepted the idea that the union could strike if it had to. Like most players who came up before the midsixties, his main objective was to insure that the players' pension rights were protected. His aims were simple: He wanted the Players Association to be a more professional organization than it was; he saw it as a vehicle for improving the public image of the players and the game.

After I visited the four clubs out west, Robin, who had been monitoring the situation closely, kept reassuring me that things were going to be completely different in Florida. He said that he, Bob Friend, and Jim Bunning and a number of other players had been talking to players on each club about the importance of revitalizing the Players Association. He was, of course, right. Later, after reviewing that period, I concluded that Roberts knew the disastrous vote totals among the western clubs and was determined to keep the information from me because he was worried I might not persevere if I knew how the vote was going.

In the years that followed, I often pondered how different Roberts's career might have been had he played *after* the victories of the Players Association. If he hadn't been marooned in Philadelphia for fourteen years, on teams that could be charitably described as dreadful, he probably could have had thirty or even forty more wins and finished with, say, 320 instead of 286. Instead of finishing his career in Chicago, with a tenth-place club (Houston traded him to the Cubs during the 1966 season), he might have wound up on a pennant contender, even pitched in a few more World Series. And he might have made several million dollars. As it was, one of baseball's premier pitchers was paid a ridiculously low salary by the multimillion-dollar members of the Du Pont family who owned the Phillies in Roberts's glory days.

While waiting at the West Palm Beach Airport for my flight back to Pittsburgh, I called Frank Scott in New York. Scott reported that he had the votes of eighteen teams and expected the remaining two to respond in a day or so. (Some teams voted by secret ballot, some by a show of hands.) "I'll call you in Pittsburgh," he said, "with the final result."

I arrived home the Sunday before the Opening Day of the 1966 season, traditionally a Monday afternoon game in Cincinnati, the oldest major league franchise. Next day, Scott called. Florida had proved spectacularly more fertile ground than Cannon country. Out of a possible 506 votes, only 34 were noes. Five teams elected me unanimously, three cast just one negative vote. Six Boston Red Sox voted against me, as I later found out: Carl Yastrzemski, Reggie Smith, one other player, the manager, and two coaches. That was as bad as it got. Considering that on the sixteen teams in Florida there were 96 nonplayers (coaches, managers, and trainers) eligible to vote, the 34 negative votes led to a pleasing conclusion: Virtually all the players *and* almost two-thirds of the nonplayers had voted for me.

Without a doubt, I owed most of my success in the Florida voting to the sixteen player reps* and to Roberts and Friend. Despite tremendous pressure from their clubs to desert the union before it even got started, all of them supported me fully. None of them—unlike the four player reps out west (Buck Rodgers, Tom Haller, Larry Jackson, Max Alvis)—permitted a manager to conduct the vote or repudiated their earlier nominating vote or meekly accepted the coercion of their owners and managers, and each seemed genuinely eager to cooperate in winning the vote and winning it big! (Which explains a success rate of 93 percent.) In the years to come, many other players were vital to the success of the Players Association as crisis seemed to follow crisis; but to secure a union in baseball, where there had been a hundred years of failure, these men, at that beginning in 1966, were crucial. But for them, our infant organization would have been strangled in the crib—a thought that undoubtedly set some club owners to gnashing their teeth.

For myself, I think often of that first spring training trip—its problems, defeats, frustrations, and, finally, overwhelming victory. And in some ways, I think there was a small measure of poetic justice in the result. The hated Giants of my youth voted 27–0 against my candidacy; my beloved Dodgers unanimously backed me, 30–0; and the Pittsburgh Pirates, the club I had adopted as my own during the years with the Steelworkers, also provided overwhelming support, 31–0. (Who said vibes and body language don't count more than words or issues?) All told, the final vote was 489–136. Had I been less exhausted, I would have been overjoyed.

Although it's unlikely to happen, the players of today and tomorrow—with their seven-figure salaries, multiyear guaranteed contracts, salary arbitration and free-agency rights, six-figure pensions after retirement, and much, much more—should pause periodically in their busy lives and think about how it all came about, starting twenty-five years ago. In the process, they should

---

*Bob Allison, Frank Bolling, Clete Boyer, Jim Bunning, Johnny Edwards, Ron Fairly, Eddie Fisher, Bill Freehan, Dick Hall, Bob Lillis, Don Lock, Dave Morehead, Tim McCarver, Roy McMillan, Jim Pagliaroni, Wes Stock.

try to understand that those players who set in motion this revolution in baseball were paid, on average, about 2 percent of today's salaries; their minimum salary was 6 percent of the 1990 minimum, and the superstars were paid less than 3 percent of today's top salaries! In 1992, Roger Clemens and Dwight Gooden will be paid more than the total payroll of all the major league clubs combined ($9.5 million) when the players' union began in 1966. As another, more literary, Miller (Arthur) put it (in *Death of a Salesman*): "Attention must be paid."

5 ...

Cannon Country

THE PITTSBURGH NEWSPAPERS reported my election as head of the Players Association on April 12, 1966, two days before I turned forty-nine. The first to offer congratulations was ex-Steelworker president David McDonald, a serious baseball fan; the most effusive was the man who gave me my first bicycle, Uncle Sid "Give Those Baseball Bosses Hell!" Stern. Three days later, on April 15, Dick Moss bounded into my office and insisted that we go to Forbes Field to see the Pirates' home opener against St. Louis. Dick's love affair with the Pirates dated back to his days as a kid in Beaver Falls, Pennsylvania; Opening Day left him giddy.

Hope springs eternal on Opening Day, and the Pirates had especially high hopes going into the 1966 season. The Bucs had won ninety games in 1965 and finished five games behind Mays, McCovey, Marichal, and the rest of the Giants, and seven behind the Koufax-Drysdale Dodgers. The Pittsburgh right fielder, Roberto Clemente, led the National League in hitting at .329; Willie Stargell drove in 107 runs, and Vern Law and Bob Veale won seventeen games apiece. With newcomer Matty Alou joining regulars like Bill Mazeroski, Donn Clendenon, Stargell, and Clemente, the Pirates were considered the preseason favorites by many writers and players.

As we pushed through the Forbes Field turnstile, the ticket taker, who evidently recognized me from the picture in the paper, smiled and said, "This is the last time you'll have to pay for tickets, eh, Mr. Miller?"

It wasn't the time or place to discuss the issue, but I had already decided it would be best if I paid my own way into ballparks. While the act would be more symbolic than anything else, I didn't want to be beholden to the owners in any way. During my eighteen years with the Players Association I got in free only a few times: once as the guest of the Mets' Joan Payson and several times at the invitation of Mike Burke of the Yankees at Opening Day ceremonies.

The first glimpse of a baseball field after a dark and dreary winter in the concrete cityscape always gives me a thrill. But as I watched the Pirates hustle out onto the glistening manicured grass of Forbes Field that Friday afternoon, I realized this was not a throwback to my childhood at Ebbets Field. For me, baseball now was a whole different ball game.

My wife, Terry, had dug up some information in the Pittsburgh Public Library about America's Favorite Pastime, and it had me shaking my head. In June 1946, Robert Murphy, a volunteer organizer of a players' organization which he named the American Baseball Guild, called for the Pirates to strike before a night game at Forbes Field. The Bucs owner had refused to meet with Murphy and a committee of players to discuss working conditions. Baseball's newly elected commissioner, Happy Chandler, got wind of the plan from Pirate pitcher Rip Sewell (of the famed "blooper" pitch) and lined up a team of old-timers—including seventy-two-year-old Pirate Hall-of-Famer Honus Wagner—to substitute for the real ball club. Sewell announced he would scab (he didn't call himself that) and convinced other players not to strike. The players and the guild folded; Chandler happily rewarded Sewell with a gold watch. Several of the guild's lesser demands were met, but as Murphy said, "The players have been offered an apple, but they could have had an orchard."

But back to Opening Day. Cardinals ace Bob Gibson was blowing the Pirates away like ducks at a shooting gallery. Gibson pitched like twelve angry men, paralyzing Pittsburgh with his nasty curveball and hard, rising fastball. He also made three brilliant fielding plays en route to a complete-game victory, 9–2. Cardinals outfielders Curt Flood and Alex Johnson—two men with whom I would become quite familiar—also started the season with a bang: Flood went three for five and Johnson hit a two-run homer.

A few days after the game, Phillies right-hander Jim Bunning called. Robert Cannon was going to be making a speech in Pittsburgh at the end of April. He suggested I get together with Cannon "to iron out the details" of the contract Cannon had drafted for me.

Robert Cannon, too, was forty-nine years old in 1966. In 1965, while serving as "legal advisor" to the players, he had launched an unsuccessful bid to become commissioner of baseball—a move as incongruous as Walter Reuther, the head of the United Automobile Workers union, campaigning for the presidency of General Motors. As preposterous as this sounds, no one in baseball lifted an eyebrow. And he would have been the executive director of the Players Association were it not for his excessive last-minute demands.

Cannon was a tall, slender man, with close-cropped hair, an aquiline nose, and a tight, unsmiling mouth. At least he didn't smile during the forty-five minutes we spent together at the old Penn Sheraton Hotel in Pittsburgh. But I didn't smile much either, especially after reading the beginning of the contract he had drafted. The players had told me that my term of office would start July 1. Now I was reading that the contract didn't take effect until January 1, 1967, well after the pending pension negotiations with the owners were likely to have been concluded. I was also surprised to discover this was a two-year contract. The players had proposed, and I had accepted, a five-year deal.

In addition to salary, the contract provided $20,000 a year for "expenses," but did not require that the executive director account for how the money was spent, a very questionable provision. But I kept quiet and read on.

The strangest paragraph of all was labeled "Cancellation for Cause." Try this clause on for size: "If during the effective period of Agreement the said Miller is *charged* [my italics] with an act involving public ridicule or moral turpitude and the Players Association has reasonable grounds to believe it to be true, the Players Association on three days' notice to the said Marvin Miller may terminate this agreement."

"Charged?" "On three days' notice?" I thought this type of legal mumbo jumbo had gone out with the Salem witch trials. What exactly did it mean that I could lose my job by being *charged* with "public ridicule"? How exactly would "public ridicule" be measured? By a CBS–*New York Times* poll?

The "said Marvin Miller" took a deep breath and asked: "I don't understand this question of moral turpitude?" Just saying the phrase made me feel like a character out of a Charles Dickens novel. "What kind of depraved acts are you talking about?"

"It could be almost anything," Cannon replied matter-of-factly. "From being a hit-and-run driver to tax fraud."

"But it says 'charged,'" I said.

"Sure, if you're accused of breaking the law, the Players Association can terminate your contract. What are you so concerned about?" He looked puzzled. "It's for the players' protection."

I said, "I'm concerned about being innocent and nevertheless having my contract voided."

"You can always prove your innocence," he said.

Had Cannon gone to law school in Siberia? "Prove your innocence," I repeated. "Are you familiar with the phrase, 'innocent until proven guilty,' Judge?" I emphasized his title.

Cannon sat impassively. "What do you think it ought to say?"

I took that as a concession. "What does the player's contract say about this?"

Cannon shrugged.

"Let me check it out," I said. "I think it would be appropriate for me to have the same rights as the players."

He shrugged again. We parted without ordering coffee.

Of course, I couldn't accept the contract as it was. Dick Moss volunteered to give the contract the once-over before I called Robin Roberts and Jim Bunning. We made the following changes:

•I would start July 1, 1966—for a term of two and a half years.

•After submitting receipts, I would be reimbursed for reasonable expenses for job-related duties, but with a cap of $20,000 a year.

•As for moral turpitude, I borrowed from the player's contract: if I failed, refused, or neglected to conform to the standards of good citizenship, the Players Association could terminate my contract upon thirty days' written notice.

I yielded on the contract's length. Obviously, I preferred the five-year contract previously offered, but the players were being harangued by the owners for having selected me, and I didn't want to stir them up more than I had to. Besides, if they didn't want me after two and a half years, I wouldn't want to stay.

Roberts and Bunning readily accepted my changes. They hadn't noticed anything odd about having to prove my innocence, but they were enthusiastic about the provision requiring an accounting of all expenses, and they applauded my willingness to accept the shorter contract.

We soon had other worries. Lee MacPhail, Commissioner Eckert's deputy, told Cincinnati player rep Johnny Edwards that the players shouldn't have offered me a contract without a viable method of financing the Players Association. In essence, this was a veiled threat that the owners would renege on their commitment (and Commissioner Eckert's commitment) to provide $150,000 a year from All-Star Game funds for the Players Association.

Edwards, at six-foot-four and 220 pounds, was not easily intimidated—he would be Cincinnati's catcher until another Johnny named Bench came along in 1967. He told MacPhail that the players would choose whom they wanted.

As April turned into May, MacPhail's threat became a reality. It didn't matter that the $150,000 budget had been suggested by Cannon and approved by John Galbreath (Pirates) and Calvin Griffith (Twins) of the Pension Committee, Walter O'Malley (Dodgers) and Gabe Paul (Reds) of the Executive Council, Commissioner Eckert, and league presidents Joe Cronin (AL) and Warren Giles (NL). Nor did it matter that the $150,000 made up just 4 percent of the revenue from the All-Star Game. Baseball was making a biblical statement: "The Lords of Baseball give and the same Lords take away!"; that is, they give if they can handpick an owners' man to head the players' organization, but they take away if the players exercise their legal right to choose an experienced union man as their executive director. The point the owners made was not lost on the players. It was one of management's many major errors and a big lesson in the continuing education of players on the facts of life in the big leagues.

Ironically, the owners were doing the right thing for the wrong reason. They claimed the law prevented them from carrying out their commitment: The Taft-Hartley Act, they said, prohibited the payment of money by an employer to an employees' organization. Of course, the owners had cried neither Taft nor Hartley when they paid a yearly retainer to J. Norman Lewis and, later, Judge Robert Cannon and, as late as January 1966, approved the use of All-Star Game funds by the Players Association. And they had raised no objections when (apparently) Cannon was going to be approved as full-time executive director. Not until I was elected did they call down the letter of the law.

Actually, I was pleased. I realized much more clearly than they did that by citing Taft-Hartley, the owners had inadvertently acknowledged that baseball was an *industry* operating in interstate commerce (contrary to the Supreme Court's absurd ruling) and that the Players Association was a *labor organization*. The first point undermined baseball's long-cherished exemption from antitrust laws. The second gave further legitimacy to the Association. And by advancing this legal argument, the owners and their attorneys admitted for all to see that they had been violating the law for years.

But we were faced with a more pressing problem: How would the players finance their association? (Being right is one thing, but being right while trying to run a nearly bankrupt organization is another.) According to Robin Roberts and Jim Bunning, Commissioner William Eckert had proposed an unprecedented in-season meeting between the player reps, the owners, and the commissioner himself to address these very issues. I wasn't optimistic.

Weeks passed without any word on the date of this mythical meeting—I felt like a character in a Beckett play. By June 1, 1966, I was the executive director–elect, but I had no contract, and I had yet to find an apartment in New York—a task that seemed as daunting as cracking the reserve clause. Meanwhile, the press had been asking: Why were the owners pulling the plug on the players? When would Miller start? How would his office be financed?

I had an answer to that last question. The players' pension was a *contributory* plan, meaning employees and employers shared the costs, and it had been so since its inception in 1947. In the real world, most contributory plans had gone the way of the Edsel; the steel industry scrapped theirs in 1949. Yet baseball players contributed $344 each to the pension fund in addition to paying $50 in dues to the association. By switching to a *noncontributory* plan, the employer would fund the entire cost of a player's pension coverage, and he would no longer have to pay $344 for it. And if the players paid this sum to the Players Association as dues, we would, with the support of *most* of the players, have the $150,000 a year our fledgling operation needed. More important, the Players Association would be run autonomously. To make it work, each player would have only to sign a standard form authorizing the ball club to check off $344 a year from his salary and transfer it to the Players Association. The switch, incidentally, benefited the player in another way. He had been paying out $394 a year—$344 to the pension fund and $50 as dues—but the new figure involved only a $344 payment—as dues—and all of it would be tax deductible. Rather than discuss the details of this plan on the phone with the player reps, I decided to wait until we met in person.

The tougher sell, I knew, would be getting the owners to accept this new deal. I did call Commissioner Eckert, though, figuring that he might circulate my ideas among the owners. Eckert listened attentively, responding with uh-huhs and um-hums at the appropriate places. But when I hung up, I wasn't sure whether he was just being polite or perhaps hadn't understood what I was saying. I concluded: probably both.

Eight months earlier, William Dole Eckert (a.k.a. "Spike"), a fifty-seven-year-old retired U.S. Air Force general, had been the surprise choice to succeed Ford Frick as commissioner of baseball. The game's highest-paid player, Willie Mays, spoke for most baseball fans when he said: "Who's he?" A sportswriter at the *New*

York World-Telegram said, "My God, they've chosen the Unknown Soldier!" And *New York Daily News* columnist Dick Young declared: "The owners have laughed in the face of every fan who pays his buck at the ballpark. They have said they don't really need a commissioner at all."

While I hate to admit it in print, I agreed with Young. In the short time he'd been in office, Eckert seemed terribly over-matched by the job. If Frick was known as the "do-nothing" commissioner, then Eckert was the "know-nothing." (Some theorized that Frick had not retired but had been reincarnated.) Eckert knew almost nothing about baseball—either the game or the business. He had never been much of a fan. Though on second thought, he had a good excuse: Living in the nation's capital would have meant attending the Senators' games.

Shortly after my call to Eckert, Jim Bunning phoned. The long-awaited meeting was on: June 6 at the Biltmore Hotel in New York City. Bunning said I should expect an invitation shortly. Why hadn't Spike said anything about the meeting during our conversation? I suspected that if I were to wait for an invitation, I'd be back in the Beckett play. I called again.

Eckert's rationale for his silence was stunningly simple. "This is a meeting for baseball officials, Mr. Miller. Since you are not set to take office until July 1, you are not being invited."

I think that my answer, everything considered, was stunningly polite. "You are about to consider an important matter involving the Players Association, so important that, I am told, it is the first meeting ever held with all the player reps during a championship season. Why would you bar the executive director–elect from such an important meeting?"

"The commissioner," he said, referring to himself in the third person, "decides who will come to these meetings, and the commissioner has made that decision."

"Fine," I said, wondering if Eckert had just watched a rerun of *The Wizard of Oz*. "But please advise the commissioner that the only people in the room will be baseball officials. No players will attend your meeting!" This was no idle threat. The player reps were already outraged by Eckert's stall tactics and the owners' withdrawal of the money from the All-Star Game.

Two hours later, Eckert called. "It's highly irregular," he said, without a trace of apology, "but you are invited to the meeting."

With the exception of Pirates owner John Galbreath, the chairman of the Pension Committee, all the significant actors gathered in a large conference room at the Biltmore Hotel. Commissioner Eckert started the proceedings by reading from a prepared text, prattling on about the fine relationship between the player reps, the owners, and the commissioner. His fatuous remarks turned fictitious when he flatly denied the owners' prior commitment—a promise made to the players months before—to finance the new Players Association with proceeds from the All-Star Game. But he continued to insist that ownership cared for the players' best interests, patting them on the back with one hand and giving them the finger with the other.

After Eckert spoke, Paul Porter, the commissioner's Washington, D.C., counsel, took the floor. Porter was a distinguished attorney, a former New Dealer who had been appointed by Franklin D. Roosevelt to head the Office of Price Administration during the latter part of World War II. After the war, he joined a prestigious law firm, which became Arnold (of trustbusting fame), Porter and Fortas (later a Supreme Court justice). Ironically, this firm headed by liberals and trustbusters became the baseball monopoly's Washington counsel and advisor on legislative matters. This day, Porter was quite open—open enough to, in effect, negate Eckert's claim that there had been no commitment made to the players. Porter said that All-Star Game revenues were "owner money," that the Taft-Hartley Act made it illegal to transmit such money for the support of a labor union, and that he and other baseball attorneys had not "focused on" the Players Association as a union until "very recently." Porter even went on to take the blame for not having realized that the earlier commitment to use All-Star Game funds would have been illegal.

When Porter finished, I took one of the floor microphones. "First of all," I said, "there is a way to convert All-Star Game money from 'owner' money to 'player' money." Players, as everyone knew, were not paid for working in the All-Star Game, and their contracts did not require them to play. "This could be changed so that players are paid for their services, then they can do with the money as they choose." I went on to point out that the player reps couldn't help but notice that the owners had ignored the law when they thought that Cannon (who was in attendance) was going to be the executive director, had violated the law for years, but suddenly discovered the law when the players showed their independence by electing an experienced trade unionist.

The glowers around the room could have melted Mount Rushmore.

Eckert then made a few remarks about possibly solving the problem by converting the pension plan into a noncontributory one. He didn't explain it very well, nor did he say that I had given him the idea. (This was just as well. In the years to come, I discovered that in order to obtain acceptance of my ideas, I had often to make them seem to originate with the owners' representatives.)

Bob Carpenter, the owner of the Phillies and a member of the notoriously antiunion Du Pont family, jumped up. "Before we continue," he said, "I move that the players leave the room so we can discuss these issues." NL president Warren Giles said that would be useless since all twenty clubs weren't there to vote on it. "The owners can't discuss it," he said, "until we look into the legality of the proposal."

The National League player rep, Cincinnati catcher Johnny Edwards, stood up and pointed out that the owners' lawyers were, after all, in the room. Giles mumbled something about waiting until John Galbreath had been briefed. No manager buying time for a shelled starter ever stalled longer than the owners did. Finally Giants player rep Tom Haller (what is it about catchers?) cut through the rhetoric: "Mr. Commissioner," he said, staring directly at Eckert, "is it possible to get any of the owners to respond to Mr. Miller's proposal, which was made on behalf of the player reps?"

None did. Silence mingled with the acrid smell of cigar smoke. But the message was loud and clear. The current pension agreement didn't expire until April 1967; by delaying action today and tomorrow and for the next ten months, the owners hoped that the Players Association, bereft of any income, would go belly up. And the "said Marvin Miller" would vanish as had Robert Murphy twenty years earlier.

As the meeting dragged to a close, I urged that a decision be made as soon as possible. Eckert countered by insisting that *all* of the players vote on making the pension plan noncontributory. One of the most outspoken player reps, Eddie Fisher, the knuckle-ball reliever for the Chicago White Sox, lost control of his temper as he often lost control of his trademark pitch: "Not a single thing has been accomplished! We could have done what we did today through the mail. The player reps would like to know when our proposal will be considered. We have the authority to settle this matter with an agreement right now."

The commissioner hemmed and hawed some more, but Walter O'Malley and then Warren Giles pledged that the owners would sit down with me "as expeditiously as possible" to discuss the issues we had debated for most of the day. The meeting adjourned.

Fisher was wrong. We had actually accomplished a great deal. The Players Association had asserted its independence; I had proven I wasn't going to back down; and Eckert had put forth our idea as a way of financing the association. After we met the press, the player reps and I retired to another conference room.

The players were peeved. I said: "I know you feel betrayed—"

"Screwed!" Fisher interrupted. "There's no way the owners are going to hand over the one hundred fifty thou from the All-Star Game."

"Believe it or not," I said, "this 'screwing' will boomerang. The fact that the owners, league presidents, and commissioner have broken their word to you is an education all by itself. It will help you define what your organization is and help the players understand that the owners fear it and why." I then explained that if the owners had not reneged, we would still have had to find our own way of financing the players' organization, because the law really did forbid owner payments to unions and union officers. Finally, I told the reps (with Cannon still in attendance) that even the lack of funds would not scare me off. I'd report to work on July 1, signed contract or no!

The powwow at the Biltmore Hotel wasn't the only momentous event to occur on June 6. After the meeting, I joined Terry to look at yet another apartment in Manhattan. En route we passed a For Rent sign in the front window of a brand-new building in the Village. We slapped down a deposit (many times our housing costs in Pittsburgh) right then and there and went home to Pittsburgh.

Six days after the meeting at the Biltmore, Eddie Fisher, the top reliever (15–7) in the American League in 1965, was traded by Chicago to Baltimore for infielder Jerry Adair and minor league outfielder Johnny Riddle. (Just for the record: In 1966 Fisher appeared in a league-high 67 games with an ERA of 2.52.)

On June 21, fifty friends and co-workers from the Steelworkers, including the three new international officers, gathered for lunch to bid me farewell. We'd been together for sixteen years. A quarter century later, I think of Dodger broadcaster Vin Scully's comment to rookie pitcher Bob Welch before the 1980 All-Star Game: "The way a baseball career goes, you're just a blink of an eye away from going from an All-Star Game to an Old Timers Game." My years in the steel industry were important to me, but I felt I was making the right move. It's not often that a forty-nine-year-old veteran gets to play a new game.

A week later, Commissioner Eckert notified me that the owners had approved the shift to a noncontributory pension plan. No doubt the owners figured that the players, with no union experience, would not agree to use their former pension contribution to pay dues of $344 a year to a union with an unproven track record.

I planned to spend the ten days leading up to the All-Star Game in Frank Scott's office, poring over the records in the lone filing cabinet that belonged to the Players Association. I had barely begun when I received a phone call from the commissioner's office. The Executive Council would be meeting in Chicago to discuss the new television contract. I flew to Chicago the next day to attend that meeting.

At the June meeting in New York, I had been accompanied by Robin Roberts and the player reps. In Chicago I was alone. After the meeting, Jerome Holtzman, a sportswriter with the *Chicago Sun-Times* told me he had noted the contrast between owners like

Walter O'Malley and Bob Carpenter, multimillionaires accompanied by entourages of lawyers and aides, and me.

I bumped into baseball's *real* czar, Walter O'Malley, in the lobby. Surprisingly, he seemed pleased to see me. "David McDonald has told me a lot of good things about you," he said. O'Malley and McDonald had become friends after the ex–Steelworker president retired to Palm Springs. In fact, O'Malley had considered placing McDonald on the Dodgers' board of directors until he fell ill. "He tells me you're not a socialist."

A compliment, I assumed. "How'd that come up?" I asked.

"David told me that many of the liberal trade unionists are socialists. When he said you weren't, I was pleased. It means you understand why we're in business." He paused theatrically. "For profit."

"I favor profitable operations," I said. "Given the choice between negotiating with a destitute employer and one making tremendous profits, I'd pick the one with profits every time. When it comes to collective bargaining, bankrupt is a dirty word."

O'Malley beamed.

Soon after the meeting began, I understood why O'Malley was feeling so benevolent. With each new contract, television income was multiplying like the population of a third world country. Bowie Kuhn, the associate counsel for the National League, explained that, beginning in April 1967 and continuing for the next two years, the Executive Council would allot four million dollars a year to the pension plan. But Kuhn neglected to mention the 60–40 formula that existed under the old agreement. Sixty percent of the radio and television proceeds of the All-Star Game and World Series and 95 percent of the gate of the All-Star Game had belonged to the pension fund.*

"What are the figures for the TV package?" I asked.

"That's irrelevant," he said. "The 60–40 formula has been shelved."

It was clear that as the television deals grew more lucrative, the

---

*Originally only 60 percent of the gate receipts of the All-Star Game were allocated to the pension fund. When the number of All-Star Games was reduced from two to one each year, the pension fund's share of the gate receipts was increased to 95 percent and remained at that figure until 1967.

owners wanted more control over how the money was divvied up. They were offering a flat sum rather than a percentage. True, it was more dollars than the players had gotten the year before. But as television contracts continued to grow, the players' share would become a smaller piece of the whole pie.

I had been advised earlier that the commissioner had scheduled a press conference. I asked Eckert to stay behind for a few minutes as the meeting with the owners was coming to a close. I told him, as concisely as possible, that if he announced that the funding of the 1967 pension plan had been decided—with *no* collective bargaining having taken place—he and the owners would be violating the law. Eckert looked both puzzled and shocked. I urged him to talk to the lawyers and the owners before holding his press conference.

I thought to myself, maybe they'll catch on. The golden days of Robert Cannon and his rubber stamp were over. The owners would have to deal with their players by a new set of rules—the law.

Newspaper reports of Eckert's press conference indicated that he had heeded my warning.

BASEBALL'S STARS gathered for the 1966 All-Star Game at Busch Stadium in St. Louis. I had planned to fly to the game, but an airline strike canceled my flight from Pittsburgh, and I substituted a long, hot bus trip.

The day before the All-Star Game I met with the player reps. The meeting with the owners in Chicago on the application of television revenue to the next pension contract indicated clearly that the players were right: The owners intended to get rid of *any* formula that gave the players a claim on a share of the television revenue for their pension plan. I had reported this to the players, but I wanted to discuss the problem in detail with the player reps. As I saw it, the so-called 60–40 formula was not what it seemed to be. With no players or their representatives having any input into the periodic baseball negotiations with television networks, there was no way to verify the final figures. The players' pension plan was supposed to get 60 percent of the television and radio revenue from the All-Star Game and the World Series. Fine. That should be an easy calculation. What is the full amount agreed upon for those two jewels of major league baseball? Tell us the full amount, and we will know what 60 percent of it is. Easy, yes? No. Baseball negotiated television revenue for other features at the same time: a nationally televised game on Saturdays for a specified number of weeks and Monday night baseball throughout a major part of the season. How much did the 60–40 formula, applied to these games, produce for the players? Zero. They had never been part of the formula.

When a deal was made with a network, a total figure for all the rights was arrived at—but with no breakdown. The network had no interest in how baseball and the commissioner's office allocated the final figure: this many dollars for the World Series, and that many dollars for the Game of the Week, for example. So the door was open for arbitrary allocation by baseball officials, to the possible detriment of the players. If the World Series was under-valued, then the players' 60 percent would be short-changed. If the undervaluation was compensated for by an overvaluation of the games in which the players did not share, this arbitrary method let the owners pocket the difference. Some players had felt this to be true for quite a while. Additionally, the player representatives and their "advisors" had never been permitted to see the television contracts in order to verify the total payment for the rights!

Some preliminary research (Nielsen ratings and advertising rates for each segment of the television rights package) revealed that the players' fears were justified. The rights for the World Series and All-Star Game had been short-changed, on a relative basis, compared with the revenue allocated to the other nationally televised games. Worse, it was apparent that without the players' direct involvement in television negotiations, there was no way ever to make the 60–40 formula work in the players' best interests. Some players, however, and some observers from the sidelines, did not seem able to grasp that the old formula had outlived its usefulness. In clinging to the mythology that the pension plan itself was dependent upon the magic numbers, "60–40," legal theories were invented, such as the claim that the 1954 agreement, which first incorporated the formula, represented legal rights conferred in perpetuity. This was, of course, total nonsense, even though it had been put forward by a former legal "advisor" of the players and by a former Cleveland pitcher. When an agreement expires, it expires. The most recent funding agreement covering the pension plan contained the 60–40 formula, and it would expire March 31, 1967. The formula, like other longstanding practices, had value as a precedent, but its legal standing when we reached April 1 would be nil.

At that meeting of the player reps during the All-Star break, I began a discussion designed to clarify the situation. The owners, understandably, wanted to keep the lion's share of TV revenue, which, some of them foresaw, was likely to increase substantially in the years to come. They saw the 60–40 formula as a bar to keeping this bonanza for themselves. This all players understood. I said to the player reps: "What must also be understood is that the formula itself has large holes in it which could encourage fraud. In any case, what players are going to have to rely on is their own group strength to obtain adequate funds from the owners to finance a healthy and improving pension plan into the future."

Over time, the players understood this so well that in all the pension negotiations while I was the executive director—1967, 1969, 1972, 1973, 1976, and 1980—the Major League Baseball Players Benefit Plan received from the owners an amount each year which was never less, and in most years more, than the 60–40 formula would have produced from the TV revenue, which grew by leaps and bounds. It was the strength of the union, supported by its members, which produced the phenomenal growth of retirement and related benefits, and health-care provisions—not reliance on an outmoded formula which permitted cheating and which was subject to termination at intervals by the owners whenever they thought they could get away with it.

There was one item of personal business which I brought up. I did not have a signed contract. I had sold the house in Pittsburgh, made a large commitment on an apartment lease in New York, and Terry had quit her job as visiting professor of psychology at Carnegie-Mellon University. Somewhat reluctantly, I mentioned it to the players. I didn't want to seem like a mercenary, but, after all, my union experience had taught me, "No contract, no work." The room became quiet.

Then Cincinnati catcher Johnny Edwards spoke up. "This is

nonsense!" he said angrily. "Mr. Miller has been good enough to start working without a contract, but enough's enough. Let's show him we appreciate what he's already done. Give me a pen."

The redraft of Cannon's proposed contract had been distributed. Edwards signed, motioning to the American League player rep, Buck Rodgers, to do the same. The Angels catcher had bad-mouthed me to the press during spring training, but today he stepped to the center of the room and signed while White Sox reliever Bob Locker looked on and then signed as a witness. An outfielder and player rep of the Senators, Don Lock, and Roy McMillan, player rep of the Mets, also witnessed the signatures. It seemed to me a good omen that Locker and Lock were standing by. I felt confident the deal would be secure.

When time came for the All-Star Game to begin, the temperature hovered around 104 degrees; it seemed as if the artificial turf in Busch Stadium would melt. Starting pitchers Denny McLain and Sandy Koufax, flamethrowers both, were just adding to the heat. McLain was perfect over the first three innings. Koufax was almost as good, giving up only one run in the second inning on a misplayed fly ball and a wild pitch. By the fourth inning, I felt like Alec Guinness in *The Bridge on the River Kwai*. The heat was dropping fans like flies, and I decided to seek a brief refuge in the home team's air-conditioned clubhouse. Sandy Koufax sat off to the side of the deserted room, his left arm immersed in a tub of ice water. In uniform he had always looked slender to me, but his upper body was as chiseled as Rocky Marciano's. Koufax's upper left arm, however, looked more like Jersey Joe Walcott's face after Marciano knocked him out. It was as big as my thigh. I introduced myself. (Koufax and Don Drysdale, holdouts in the spring, had not been present at my meeting with the Dodger players during spring training.)

The appearance of his upper arm was alarming. Seeing the look on my face, Koufax reassured me: "Don't worry, Mr. Miller," he said, sweat still dripping down his face. "It always blows up like this after I pitch. This isn't bad at all. I only went three innings."

Koufax was always among the league leaders in complete games and innings pitched. From 1961 to 1966, the Brooklyn-born Dodger won 129 and lost 47, a winning percentage of .732. Only

Bob Gibson and Juan Marichal—at their best—could compare with Koufax in effectiveness. Koufax led the National League in ERA *five consecutive seasons*. In 1965 he struck out an amazing 382 hitters.

As I watched him ice his terribly swollen left arm, I was reminded of something that a player had said the day before at the meeting of the player reps: "The owners cut you because you don't produce a certain number of runs, but at the same time they make it tough for us to play well. Day games after a twinight doubleheader. You go out there twenty-one days without a day off, it takes something out of you." Any of the pitchers there could have added that if you are among the leaders in starts, innings pitched, and complete games, you have to be extremely lucky to last more than a few years in the major leagues.

The Koufax-Drysdale holdout during spring training had been an important rallying point for the players. I congratulated Sandy for standing up to Walter O'Malley and Buzzie Bavasi and wished him luck the rest of the season. I should have said the rest of his career. Koufax won a remarkable twenty-seven and lost nine in 1966. He pitched in the World Series that year, and that was it. Arthritis forced him to retire at age thirty-one. Had Koufax pitched in the era of five-man rotations and relief specialists, it's entirely possible he could have played several more seasons. And just imagine the kind of money he could have commanded today. He had charisma, control, and a ninety-five-plus mph fastball. Of course, I was partial to Koufax; like me, he was from Brooklyn.

In the airport the day after the game, I bumped into American League president Joe Cronin. I was flying to New York, and he to his office in Boston. (In those days, the league office was wherever the league president lived.) Both flights were delayed on a nonstruck airline—the strike was still on—so we decided to get a drink. Cronin had the wit and savvy of an old-time Irish politician. He was from a working-class family and, although he wasn't a supporter of the Players Association, he didn't treat us like radioactive agitators either.

When my flight was finally announced, he said: "Young man, I've got some advice for you that I want you to remember." Young man? I was forty-nine years old. The advice? "The players come and go, but the owners stay on forever." I would remember his remark, but not for the reasons he wanted. As much as any single statement I'd hear, it reflected the prevailing attitude of baseball's brass. A league presidency was and is a nothing job. Other than staying on the right side of the right owners, Cronin's biggest challenge was choosing between a pitching wedge and a nine iron. But Cronin—a Hall of Fame player, field manager, general manager, and now league president—had been a member of the patriarchal system for too long. He had completely misunderstood me, my motivations, and my means of operating. Basically he was saying, "Watch me and you'll understand what it takes to stick in baseball. If you don't play ball with the owners, you'll be gone." A year or so later, we met again to negotiate pension benefits, including retirement benefits for former players, long inactive. At one point in the negotiation I said something about the lack of understanding among members of the owners' committee. Cronin could not suppress a sly smile. He winked at me across the table and said, "I understand. You know, I'm one of the men you're negotiating a pension increase for."

A moment before the plane taxied out on the runway, a slender black man sat down in the seat next to mine. It was Dodger shortstop Maury Wills, on his way to New York too. Wills had made waves before the game by telling the press that he should have been the starting shortstop instead of Cincinnati's Leo Cardenas. In the bottom of the tenth inning, Wills singled home Tim McCarver to win the game. Though he felt somewhat vindicated, this most recent slight reminded him of past injustices. Wills grew up tough and street-smart in Washington, D.C. He played in the Tigers' minor league organization until he was twenty-seven. For an almost unbelievable seven seasons he endured the endless bus rides and fleabag motels, though he knew he was being bypassed by white players with less talent. When he complained loudly enough, Detroit released him. A Dodger scout signed him in 1959, and three seasons later he stole a major league record 104 bases, eight more than a surly racist from Georgia named Ty Cobb.

During the first part of the flight Wills seemed rather cautious in setting forth his views. He may have been testing me before opening up. But then he began talking about the special problems of blacks on teams training in Florida. He spoke about the time and money it took to hunt down decent, unsegregated housing and laundries, restaurants, and barber shops that would serve blacks. In many parts of Florida, black players and their wives were turned away from service establishments and forced to find Laundromats, beauty parlors, and so on, in black communities. Wills's intensity and sincerity made an impression on me, as had his enthusiastic encouragement and support of my candidacy during spring training. "The black and Latin ballplayers are especially eager to support this union," he said as the plane began its descent. "Discrimination is not dead." In 1980, Wills would become baseball's second black manager.

Two weeks later, an angry Johnny Edwards called me at Frank Scott's office. A sportswriter from Chicago named Jim Enright, reportedly in line for a public relations position if Judge Cannon had been elected commissioner, had misquoted Edwards in the *Sporting News*. Edwards vehemently denied making the antiunion remarks attributed to him and asked that I set the record straight. Widely read among the players, the *Sporting News* was supposedly baseball's bible. If it was, it was time for a new testament. Personally, I considered it management's mouthpiece, but it was undeniably a good way to communicate with the players. I wrote to the editor on Edwards's behalf.

A few days after my reply was published, Enright called. Now *he* was angry. "You should have written me," he complained, "instead of the paper. These matters are best settled privately." In effect, he was telling me to ignore the damage his distortions had on the players and public. I wasn't impressed by his argument, and told him so.

Several days later, I received an even odder request, this one from Robin Roberts, calling from Houston. "Have you picked your general counsel yet?" he asked hesitantly.

"No," I said, though I planned to offer the job to Dick Moss as soon as our funding was in place.

"Well, try this suggestion on for size. Richard Nixon is still interested in the job. I know you're not a big fan of his," Roberts said, "but he's in New York. Will you at least go talk to him as a favor to me?"

True, I had never rooted for Dick Nixon, but I was a big Robin Roberts fan. I agreed to call Nixon and arrange an appointment after Robin assured me that this was not an attempt to limit my authority to name my general counsel.

Nixon's apartment was located in the sixties on Fifth Avenue overlooking Central Park. I was greeted at the door by the butler, who escorted me into the living room. Nixon entered in the company of an associate at his law firm (Nixon, Mudge, Rose, Mitchell, etc.). "How are you, Mr. Miller? It's been a long time." At least forty-nine years, as far as I could recall. Then it hit me. We had met briefly (for possibly half a minute) during negotiations to end the 116-day steel strike in 1959. President Eisenhower was ill, and Vice President Nixon had attempted mediation in his place. I congratulated him on his sharp memory.

Drinks in hand, Nixon, his associate, and I amiably rambled on about the 1966 season. Thirty minutes passed. I didn't want to discuss politics, and I certainly was not going to bring up the matter of the next general counsel of the Players Association. Just before I was set to leave, Nixon's expression turned serious, or rather more serious. Here it comes, I thought. "Mr. Miller," he said, "you have a very difficult job in front of you. Let me know if I can do anything to help you. I am on very good terms with the owners." I thought to myself, "Yes, I bet you are." I expressed my thanks and headed home. He did not mention the appointment of a general counsel. And except for the gaffe about his closeness to the owners, I found him to be a lot brighter than I had guessed.

Three years later Nixon and I met again at a White House reception honoring baseball's All-Star teams and commemorating baseball's hundredth anniversary. When the crowd thinned, I approached President Richard M. Nixon. I was glad to see he had managed to find work after losing out on the Players Association job. Much had happened since we last met. He said nothing about my battles in the world of baseball, and I said nothing about his infinitely more important war in Southeast Asia. His memory was still very sharp. Bowie Kuhn, standing next to him, was introducing baseball personnel to the President. Before Bowie could begin the introduction, the President said he had been following Players Association developments with interest.

The question of funding the office of the Players Association continued to weigh on my mind. At the All-Star Game meeting of the player reps there was a fruitful discussion about raising money for operating funds until players' dues began coming in the next year. The idea of a group licensing program was hatched: selling to interested companies the right to use the names and pictures of the players—as a group—to promote the companies' products or services. After drawing up an appropriate authorization form and obtaining the signatures of the players in September meetings with all the players, Frank Scott and I got to work on a promotional deal that would pull us through the lean winter months. This was the modest beginning of the licensing program of the Players Association as it exists today. It led to drastic changes and mammoth expansion of the baseball trading card industry. But that's a story I'll tell later.

6...

Bowie Kuhn Was Not in the Best Interests of Baseball

ISASTROUS," "CATACLYSMIC," "end of baseball," "the game will never recover," "certain bankruptcy"—these were just a few of the adjectives and phrases that were used when I came into baseball (and for some time after). Predicting what the game would be like as the union pressed on to limit the century-old exploitation of players by owners became commonplace, but the prognosticators, it seems, had clouded crystal balls.

No one's was murkier than Bowie Kuhn's. In fact, Kuhn's predictions were so off that he couldn't even predict the past *after* it happened. As late as 1985, in his error-riddled autobiography, *Hardball,* he was still predicting that free agency (the right to work for another employer) would bring gloom and doom—this in the midst of a booming popularity such as baseball had never seen before. Kuhn's vision of the future was recorded in 1975 as he tried to influence the result in the most important arbitration case

• 85 •

in baseball history by asserting that free agency for players would mean the loss to bankruptcy of the entire American League as well as several teams in the National League. (Ironically, baseball prospered as never before, and the forecast fit only Kuhn's later personal experience with the law firm of Myerson and Kuhn.)

I met Bowie Kuhn for the first time in the summer of 1966 in Chicago. I had been invited there by then Commissioner Eckert after having been elected by the players as the Association's first executive director in the spring of that year. New network television and radio agreements for the next two years had been reached, and since the players' pension (and health insurance) plan traditionally was financed by a portion of the national radio and TV revenue, Eckert said he and baseball's Executive Council would like to talk to me about it. The Major League Baseball Players Benefit Plan was to expire at the end of March 1967, and a new arrangement would have to be made. I went to Chicago alone; I had to, since I did not yet have a staff. Because the baseball season was in full swing, no players were available for the meeting. I knew that the owners' group would include Commissioner Eckert, possibly some aides, lawyers, league presidents, and some of the owners on the Executive Council. Newspaper writers, apprised of the meeting by Eckert's office, lined the hall outside the meeting room in a downtown Chicago hotel. Seeing me walk down the hall to the meeting room reminded one of them of "Daniel walking into the lion's den."

I didn't exactly feel like Daniel, but I wasn't comfortable about meeting management without players as participants and as witnesses. Whether the owners' group felt like lions about to eat a meal I can't say; some of them qualified, though certainly not Spike Eckert. He was polite and pleasant, and struck me as rather innocuous. National League president Warren Giles didn't qualify as a lion either; he was small and round and jolly. In the years to come, I would discover also that he was a charming and truthful man in negotiations (truthful enough so that Kuhn and others would strive later to silence him in negotiating meetings or keep him away entirely). Gabe Paul's soft-spoken good manners removed him from contention as a big, predatory cat. About some of the others, though, I couldn't be so sure. They included Walter O'Malley, the rumored powerhouse among the owners (with his large jowls he had the look of a Cheshire cat, if not a lion); Joe Cronin, the American League president, former manager and general manager, and a Hall of Fame player; Bob Carpenter, owner of the Phillies and a member of the Du Pont family; and Bowie Kuhn. Except for Kuhn, I had met all the others at a prior meeting in May in New York on another matter.

Kuhn was at this meeting as assistant National League counsel. When I first saw him, I thought he was an imposing figure. He appeared to be about six-feet-five, but I soon discovered that one didn't have to deal with Kuhn for very long in order to be unimpressed by his height.

Even before I started as executive director, I knew that the owners had been financing the Players Association's so-called legal advisors over a period of years. This meant, of course, that the union was really a "company union." This use of owners' money was a violation of the Taft-Hartley Act, which banned employer financing of employees' unions. It is an offense punishable by fine, jail sentence, or both. (Somehow this basic point of labor law had gone unnoticed by the commissioner's counsel, Paul Porter, by the league's attorneys, and by all the other lawyers involved, including those who served as the Players Association's legal advisors and who had been the recipients of employer payments.)

All this being the case, it didn't surprise me that baseball's power structure had not invited me to negotiate *how* the pension plan would be financed over the next two years: their purpose was to inform me what *they* had decided to do. They had simply made certain decisions, and, being decent chaps, they wanted, as a courtesy to the newly elected executive director of the Players Association, to inform me of their decisions just prior to making a public statement. This was baseball's version of "good faith collective bargaining," the state of awareness of the labor laws which baseball had reached by 1966.

It needs to be stated that the decisions they were announcing were no small matter. They included the amount of money that would be paid to the pension fund in each of the next two years (slightly under $4 million) and a "decision" to terminate the method of calculating the owners' annual pension liability, which had been agreed to with the players in 1954 and had been in effect for the last ten years. Kuhn was present at the meeting, mostly listening. O'Malley did most of the talking; Bowie took notes and sometimes whispered to O'Malley and other management people. After a brief discussion, Bowie said they were scheduled to hold a press conference shortly in a larger room across the hall. Eckert had a prepared statement to read to the media. Glancing at his statement he paraphrased for me what he intended to say. It was, indeed, an announcement of the owners' decisions as to what the pension plan was to be for the next two years.

With my background of collective bargaining, I found the proceedings incredible. The pension and insurance plan, considered a major benefit by the players, was not due to expire for more than nine months. The players had not yet discussed changes or improvements they wanted to propose, so, of course, no proposals had been submitted to the owners. The owners, similarly, had made no proposals for change. In plain English, there had been no collective bargaining. No matter—they were about to make a public announcement that the players' pension plan for the next two years was a *settled matter!* I was to be present as a formality.

I looked across the room, hoping to find a sign that someone understood how blatantly illegal and offensive all this was. My eyes fell on Bowie, the only practicing lawyer in the room. I looked for a flicker of comprehension in his eyes, an awareness that his clients were about to display publicly their violations of law, demonstrating for all to see that they had engaged in a willful refusal to bargain. Didn't anyone see that such a display of ignoring their employees—the players, the players' union, and the players' elected representative—at the outset of the relationship was a crystal-clear example of attempted union busting of the most blatant type? Kuhn showed not the slightest sign of comprehension. As I think back on it now, I realize how naive I was to have expected to find any. Subsequent developments made it obvious that the owners and Kuhn tried to destroy the union even before it got started, before it presented to the owners its first proposal for negotiation. That early, mean-spirited, antiunion behavior of the handful of management people in Chicago on that day in July 1966 foretold later events and identified the provocateurs of problems to follow.

After Eckert finished summarizing his prepared statement, everyone rose to attend the press conference across the hall. I asked Commissioner Eckert if he could stay for a minute. He nodded. When the others filed out, I said, "Mr. Eckert, I wouldn't like to see this relationship get off on the wrong foot. The Major League Baseball Players Association is the collective bargaining representative of the players. There has been no collective bargaining at all on the renewal of the players' benefit plan, which will not expire for another nine months. No one can decide anything about the next pension plan without negotiation and an agreement. Any attempt to bypass us in collective bargaining is an outright violation of the law."

Eckert frowned and looked puzzled. No one, he told me, had informed him that there was anything wrong in what they were doing. I suggested that he consult his attorneys before making his intended announcement to the press. I don't know if he did or not, but I was told that at the press conference Eckert talked mostly about baseball's negotiations with the television networks and only spoke vaguely about the players' pension plan.

Eventually, "negotiations" did begin on it; that is, there was a meeting during the 1966 All-Star break in St. Louis. It produced talk but no movement from the owners' prenegotiation position. The stalemate continued until November, when I was informed by the New York State Department of Insurance (which was responsible for monitoring and auditing pension plans in New York State) that their examiner had found a violation of law by the owners in connection with the pension plan. Some years before, after appropriating the required amount of money for funding the pension plan, the owners had decided to return to themselves $167,440 which had been paid to baseball's Central Fund (maintained in the commissioner's office) for transmittal to the pension fund.* The state agency's examiner found that this "resulted in a depletion of the fund's assets."

The owners' decision to deprive the pension fund of the money, despite a contractual and legal commitment to pay it, was approved by John Galbreath, the pension committee chairman, by

---

*The Central Fund is made up of deposits by individual clubs for common purposes (such as financing the baseball benefit plan and the commissioner's office) and of income of major league baseball that is to be distributed to the individual clubs (such as television revenues).

the owners' attorneys, and by the players' legal advisor, Judge Robert Cannon, and the NL player rep on the pension committee, Bob Friend. The only dissent was by the other player on the pension committee, Eddie Yost.

At the next pension negotiating meeting I suggested that if the owners added $200,000 to the pension fund—$167,440 plus interest—the owners' legal problems with the New York State Department of Insurance might be resolved. Kuhn served literally as a messenger in these meetings, carrying messages from the Players Association's negotiating committee to Walter O'Malley, who was in his room at the same hotel, and returning with messages from O'Malley, who I began to see was the owners' chief power broker.

A settlement was reached eventually, but the aftermath was a prolonged exchange with Kuhn, lasting over several months, in which he concocted a variety of statements he wanted me to sign. These would deny any prior wrongdoing by the owners and their lawyers. This essentially meaningless exercise was amusing and pitiful. By this time the only people who cared—the players, coaches, managers, and trainers—all knew about the violation anyway. After the settlement it developed into a nonissue, but what I couldn't forget was the astonishing pettiness of the conduct of the owners and lawyers. For $10,465 each, the sixteen baseball clubs (in 1960) had willfully violated their written commitment to the players, and even after they had been caught by a government agency almost six years later, they were attempting to get away with it.

It was this pettiness that gave me my first hint that the owners were not really as formidable as they seemed. It was true that they had great power, a vast amount of money, publicists galore, lawyers by the dozen, and a press which seemed to swallow whole everything the baseball front offices handed them. But they were also arrogant, by which I mean that they made unwarrantable claims of superior importance and right. In that arrogance they believed that laws, federal and state, did not apply to them and that the ballplayers lacked the sense and determination to form a real union in the face of owner disapproval. To the owners the union in 1966 was an aberration, a temporary irritation. Surely, they thought, once they applied pressure, the players would give up and I would be gone, and in a very short time. And who could blame them for such beliefs? They had ridden over every single challenge to their absolute authority and control for almost a century. But aside from the illusions that arrogance brought, they had other serious weaknesses that I soon began to perceive. For one thing, most of them weren't very bright, and the people they selected to carry on baseball's operations were, with a rare exception or two, not all that bright either. Never having had to negotiate, they seemed totally unable, when faced with any real challenge, to develop realistic strategy or tactics to accomplish their aims. And they lacked even a speaking acquaintance with the notion of long-range planning.

From the outset of the reorganization of the Players Association in 1966 to the day when he was sent packing by the owners, Bowie Kuhn figured prominently (except for a brief period in 1969) in their never-ending effort to rid themselves of the union, or, failing that, to weaken and control it. While the total failure of that effort stemmed from the owners' blunders, Kuhn must be singled out as the most important contributor to the successes of the Players Association. His moves consistently backfired; his attempts at leadership created divisions. His inability to distinguish between reality and his prejudices, his lack of concern for the rights of players, sections of the press, and even of the stray, unpopular owner—all combined to make Kuhn a vital ingredient in the growth and strength of the union. To paraphrase Voltaire on God, if Bowie Kuhn had never existed, we would have had to invent him.

After the first collective bargaining contract was completed in December 1966, I turned my attention to the Players Association's financial structure. The problem was that there was no financial structure. Total assets were less than $6,000, and when I started as executive director there was no plan for a system of dues sufficient to support the organization. In September I had asked the players to authorize deduction of union dues from their salaries. To the astonishment of the owners (and, I must admit, to my own mild surprise) only two ballplayers declined. But there still was no agreement that the owners would comply with the players' requests to collect the dues. Bowie was assigned to work out this "checkoff" agreement with me. He used delaying tactics until that became too obvious, and then he substituted impossible concepts. For example, he insisted that this agreement would be terminable by the owners upon thirty days' notice at any time for any reason or for no reason. Since virtually all labor organizations are dependent upon members' dues to function, the purpose of such a demand was obvious. I had no reason to think that Walter O'Malley was prounion, but I thought he might listen to reason, so I called him. He heard me out, got back to me later, and said, "I think you will find that this checkoff agreement can be worked out rapidly and satisfactorily." The matter was completed within a week, not because of Kuhn, but in spite of him.

The checkoff agreement would provide income sufficient to operate the Players Association, but that income would not begin to flow until near the end of May 1967, about five months away. A number of player representatives suggested that money might be raised by selling rights to player endorsements of products. Such endorsements were a source of income to a very few superstars in major league baseball at that time. Through discussion we developed the idea of a group licensing project—that is, attempting to interest companies in utilizing the names and pictures of the players as a group to sell their products or services. The beginning of this program in December 1966 through a contract with Coca-Cola (which yielded the necessary operating funds for the Players Association over the next five months) and the tremendous growth of the licensing program is described in the chapter "Card Wars."

Observing the success of the Association's licensing venture, the owners decided to compete with us by creating their own licensing arm, Major League Baseball Promotions Corporation. Mike Burke, president of the New York Yankees, was named chairman. He approached me about the possibility of developing a joint licensing effort, and I agreed to explore the possibility with him. I found Mike to be an intelligent and a reasonable man. Bowie Kuhn, who was supposed to work with me, was less reasonable.

One problem faced us immediately: Each organization had an outside firm retained as licensing agent to find companies interested in using a baseball connection to promote their products. Our agent, Weston Merchandising Corporation, mistrusted the owners' licensing agent. Stanley Weston asked me to be extra cautious about revealing names or any specifics of licensing contracts which he had produced for the Players Association, or prospective licensing contracts that he was trying to finalize. Weston understood, however, that the talks with Kuhn had reached the point where both sides had to be frank about their licensing income and potential, since the end point of the talks, we hoped, would be an agreement to share such revenue. Because Weston was uneasy about letting the rival agent know about his clients for fear that he would try to steal them, I promised him I would not reveal such information unless Kuhn agreed not to let his licensing agent know.

After I explained all this to Kuhn, he agreed, with no qualifications, that the information I was supplying would be closely held within Major League Baseball Promotions and would not be made available to the corporation's licensing agent. Less than a month later, Stanley Weston provided me with indisputable evidence that the owners' licensing agent knew the names and specific terms of contracts Weston had secured for the Players Association, and in at least one instance had the same information about a prospective licensing deal. Moreover, Weston had received an inquiry from one licensee who said that he had been told that it would make more sense to deal with the owners and the owners' agent in the future. I was, to put it mildly, incensed; this went beyond shady business practices and into the realm of the low-down and dirty.

I called Kuhn and told him what I had learned. He expressed no surprise, as well he shouldn't. I asked how this information about the Players Association's licensees had gotten to his licensing agent; his reply was "These things happen." I answered, "I can't accept that as an explanation. You knew the importance of keeping this information confidential, and you gave me your word that it would be treated in that manner." Bowie's reply was as vague as his first statement. He accepted no responsibility for the leak; he offered no explanation of how it had occurred; he offered no apology.

Mike Burke, when I talked to him about it, was mortified. Ever the gentleman, he apologized for something we both knew he had not done. Perhaps his apology was for inflicting Bowie on me. "Mike," I said, "I don't blame you, but I don't deal with people who break their commitments unless I have to. And I don't have to in this situation." In collective bargaining, I explained, I had a statutory duty to bargain with whomever the other side named as its representative. Licensing didn't fit into that category. "A lack of integrity in these dealings is a serious matter," I told him. "So I'm afraid we'll have to pursue our licensing programs separately." Burke replied, sadly, that he understood fully and regretted what had happened. To this day the owners and the Players Association maintain separate licensing programs.

Mike and I developed a friendship after that, and on a number of occasions when problems arose he made himself available to assist in any way he could. He did not stand on ceremony, and when the occasion warranted it, he came to the offices of the Players Association, which had moved into the Seagram Building on Park Avenue. CBS owned the Yankees in those days, and Mike was technically not an owner, but as president of the Yankees he acted on behalf of the owner. To the best of my memory Mike Burke was the only owner to set foot in the union's office in all the years from 1966 to 1983 (when I retired).*

Mike regularly invited Dick Moss, my wife, Terry, and me to Opening Day at Yankee Stadium and to brunches at the CBS building and at the stadium before the game. These occasions were festive. The guests were interesting and sparkling and very different from the usual people around baseball owners. At different times at these lunches I met either Paul Simon or Art Garfunkel (I forget which, but since it was Simon who wrote the immortal words "Where have you gone, Joe DiMaggio?" it was probably him), the poet Marianne Moore, Walter Cronkite, and a former commissioner of baseball, Ford Frick, who, several years after leaving office, had a delightfully crisp and tart manner of speaking about then current baseball officialdom.

In one of those early years of my tenure—I think it was the year Marianne Moore threw out the first ball at the Yankees' opening game—Mike astonished me. There on the scoreboard, written in giant letters, was THE NEW YORK YANKEES WELCOME MARVIN MILLER, EXECUTIVE DIRECTOR OF THE MAJOR LEAGUE BASEBALL PLAYERS ASSOCIATION. Classy ges-

*With perhaps one exception: On one occasion Bud Selig and a National League owner may have come to the union office to discuss interleague play.

tures are made by people of class. Mike Burke was unique among the owners of baseball.

The first agreement in all of sports arrived at through bona fide collective bargaining was the benefit plan agreement of December 1966. It was a landmark, but it covered only pensions and insurance. The next big goal was to negotiate a basic agreement that would cover all other terms and conditions of a major league player's employment. This effort got under way in early 1967, and as you might guess, the first subject we tackled was the minimum salary. Twenty years earlier, in 1947, the owners set the player's minimum salary at $5,000 a year. The owners simply passed a rule to that effect. Between 1947 and 1967, a period of steep inflation, the owners generously increased the minimum salary once, by $1,000, to $6,000 a year. Fiat. Let it be done. And that was the way things *were* done.

Now it was time to introduce the owners to the myriad subtleties of collective bargaining. After discussion with the players, we decided to propose that the minimum be raised to $12,000 a year. We requested a negotiating meeting with the owners in January 1967. I prepared for it carefully and made a detailed economic presentation, setting forth our case for the proposed increase.

The owners assigned Kuhn, the National League's assistant general counsel, Joe Cronin, the president of the American League, Warren Giles, the National League president, and several aides as their negotiating committee. They listened to me in silence. They were entirely unprepared to discuss the matter on its merits. Shortly after the meeting, the owners decided they would need professional assistance, and Bowie began scrambling for advice. One person he approached was Jim Healy, a professor at Harvard who sometimes served as an arbitrator in labor-management matters. (Jim, whom I had known for years, told me about this much later on.) Kuhn had come to see him in something of a state. Baseball, he told Jim, was being confronted by this trade unionist who also was an economist, and he asked whether Jim thought it necessary for baseball to obtain technical and professional assistance.

Healy, who hadn't been following developments in baseball, asked who was leading the players' union. "Marvin Miller," Kuhn said. As Jim laughingly relayed the matter to me later, he replied, "Bowie, you need *lots* of help."

In truth, seeking help was one of Kuhn's more sensible ideas. It led, however indirectly, to the creation of the Player Relations Committee and a staff and to the appointment, in mid-1967, of the very professional John Gaherin as director.

But in early 1967 no one on the owners' side had so much as a clue as to how to proceed in labor relations. Kuhn, who allegedly had experience in the field, acted as spokesman for the owners' committee, although Joe Cronin nominally was chairman of the negotiating committee. For more than two months, Bowie stalled. Then another meeting was scheduled in Florida during spring training. This was attended by Kuhn, the two league presidents, and several assistants representing the owners, and by Dick Moss, Steve Hamilton, and Jim Pagliaroni—player reps of the Yankees and Pirates respectively—and me.

After the initial pleasantries, Bowie cleared his throat and, in a tone more pompous than usual, made an opening statement that was unbelievable. This was supposed to be a "negotiating" meeting on the minimum salary. As our part in the negotiations we had given a proposal to the owners months before, along with a detailed economic analysis as a basis for the proposed change. Now Kuhn was saying, in effect, We are here to listen to what you have to say, but we aren't here to talk. No one on the owners' side of the table will have any comments, observations, or questions. We will make no proposals or counterproposals of any kind. Kuhn, the self-proclaimed experienced negotiator, a man allegedly a veteran of collective bargaining in the can manufacturing industry, had simply refused to bargain.

After Kuhn finished, it was our turn to be silent. Steve Hamilton spoke first. This was not his idea of a "negotiating meeting," he said. It was "insulting and inconsiderate to waste everyone's time this way." He and Pagliaroni had taken time out of their training, and the four of us who were representing the players had better things to do than to talk to ourselves. In his soft and reasoned manner Steve said pointedly, "Since you had no intention of negotiating, or even of saying anything, you could have saved everybody's time by asking that we make a tape and send it to you." To this Pag, as his colleagues called him, added the very practical point that it was a disgrace to waste the players' money on transportation to a meeting that was a farce.

After the players had had their say, it was my go. The owners had made a mistake and would likely continue in it until they got appropriate assistance and cleaned up their act. I told them that. Dick and I both talked about their statutory duty to bargain in good faith; they had failed even to come close to fulfilling that duty. In the nicest way possible I explained to them that we had the option of filing an unfair-labor-practice charge with the National Labor Relations Board. We would certainly consider it.

Still, after all this, not a word issued from the mouths of the owners' representatives. In years to come, Kuhn would "disremember" this early history and his involvement in it. He and the owners had tried so hard to get things started on the proper foot, he proclaimed; they had really tried to establish a close relationship with the players and the players' union and with me. The truth is that their strategy was designed, right at the outset, to accomplish the opposite. And it was successful.

A complete collective bargaining agreement was reached in 1968. This basic agreement, the first ever negotiated in any sport, covered a two-year period, the 1968 and 1969 seasons. It was another landmark in many ways, and not just because of the economic improvements for the players. We had put real restrictions on the power of the owners either to change rules unilaterally or to ignore established ones when it suited their whims. The basic agreement incorporated the Uniform Player's Contract, which meant that the form of the player's individual contract could no longer be changed unilaterally by the owners and their lawyers. All changes now required agreement as a result of collective bargaining. The new agreement also contained the first formal grievance procedure. In other words, clubs could no longer play sheriff, judge, and jury with ballplayers.

It didn't seem earth-shattering at the time, but in many ways the 1968 agreement was the building block for major gains to come. A formal grievance procedure became the keystone of the next significant step, securing binding impartial arbitration, which we achieved in the next basic agreement (1970). The 1968 agreement even contained a basis for coming to grips with the most important issue in baseball—reforming the reserve rules under which players were held as property by the "owners," the major league franchise holders.

The reserve system was an issue in those first negotiations because I made it one; needless to say, no progress was made. I suggested that because it was a difficult and complex issue, it would make sense to create a study committee of representatives of owners and the Players Association to consider alternatives to the overly restrictive reserve rules system. To the owners, of course, the question was neither difficult nor complex; they had no intention of budging on it; so there was no issue at all. The idea of the study committee was accepted because it cost them nothing, and it led to nothing but two years of stonewalling by the lawyers—Lou Carroll, Kuhn, and Sandy Hadden—by the league presidents, and by John Gaherin, the director of the Player Relations Committee. It was apparent then, and confirmed later, that the owners had dictated that nothing was to come out of that committee—not even a recommendation for a change in punctuation in the reserve rules. If I wasn't sure before I started with the Association, I was sure now that negotiation could never be the avenue for change in the reserve rules without a lever of some major proportions to effect that change.

In the late summer of 1968 the basic agreement still had more than a year to go, but the benefit plan agreement was due to be renegotiated by the end of March 1969. After the talks began, it didn't take long to see that the owners were on the offensive. Although a new national TV and radio contract, effective in 1969, provided for record revenue, the owners' demands were all of the "turn back the clock" variety. Former players, coaches, trainers, and managers were to receive no increase in benefits—unlike the pattern of the past. The pension fund actually was to receive a much *lower* share of the television revenue than before. The language of the new plan, they insisted, would have to make clear that players were acceding to the owners' 1966 position that all television revenue belonged to them—another break with the past. And finally, even though four new clubs were added through expansion of the major leagues starting in 1969, no additional contribution for benefit plan coverage of these new employees was to be offered. War, not peace, was in the minds of the owners.

It was time to touch base, as it were, with the membership. I decided to alert the players in person, arranging meetings with all the players on the twenty clubs in September. I reviewed with them the lack of progress in the negotiations and the regressive nature of the owners' demands and indicated that united action by all the players might be needed to thwart this early example of "give-back" demands by employers. I was definitely lucky on one point: It was unnecessary to explain to them the importance of their pension and insurance plan. They knew that before I got there; it was virtually the only thing that many of them saw any use in a union fighting for. I did point out, however, that these benefits were an important part of total compensation. Therefore, it wouldn't be sensible to sign their salary contracts for the next year unless and until they had a benefit plan agreement—a player would be signing only part of a contract, without knowing what, if anything, would be included in the other part. For a veteran with perhaps a year or two of his playing career left, the pension and insurance plan would provide him with far more money than he'd receive as salary. No firm policy on the signing of contracts for 1969 was adopted. I alerted the players to the bleak outlook, stressing only that I'd continue to try to reach a negotiated settlement on the benefit plan.

The winter meetings were held in early December. Both the owners and the players' executive board had selected San Francisco as the locale. It was hoped that with the policymakers for both sides present in the same city, there would be an opportunity to resolve some problems. But no progress was made—none at all. As had happened the year before when both sides held their winter meetings in Mexico City, the owners gave the players the back of their hands—"too busy to meet with the players," they said, "too many important matters to attend to."

By the time we got to San Francisco, we were fed up with the runaround the owners had been giving us. We resolved never to invite rejection again by holding our meetings in the same place as the owners, who had never looked on the occasions as anything more than an opportunity to show the contempt in which they held the nascent Players Association. But the players also had more important things on their minds. After a discouraging discussion of the total lack of progress in the pension negotiations, they decided to go ahead with the previously discussed policy of recommending that no player sign his 1969 contract until a benefit plan agreement had been reached. This was a strong move. We recessed our board meeting so that the player reps could phone the players on their clubs, advise them of the board's unanimous recommendation, obtain the players' approval, and give the board permission to use their names publicly as supporters of the position of the Players Association. About five hours later we reconvened: The player reps had reached almost 450 players, including all of the top stars, and had received unanimous approval of the policy. I wasn't surprised that it passed, but I was quite surprised and pleased by the overwhelming show of solidarity in the ranks.

The reports of the player reps of their conversations with other players were most encouraging. They understood the need for this action and offered solid support. Yankees player rep Steve Hamilton reported, with a twinkle in his eye, that the most interesting conversation he had was with Mickey Mantle, who, although never hostile to the Players Association, had always seemed somewhat aloof. Steve thought of this when he called. Mickey's response was that it didn't really affect him because he had finally made his decision not to play in 1969. Steve, whose placid, laid-back manner conceals how sharp he really is, quickly asked Mantle if he had told the club or the press of his retirement decision. Mickey said he hadn't. Steve then made a request: Would Mickey delay announcing his retirement and give us permission to include his name with all the players who agreed not to sign contracts? Mantle had only one question: Would it help the players and the Association? "Yes," Steve replied, "it would." The implication was that even at the end of his career, the Mantle name had magic. "Then hell yes," Mick replied. "Use my name."

Armed with a list of the players who would not sign contracts, we held a press conference the next day at—why not? we thought—the owners' headquarters hotel. I briefed the media and then individual reporters began shouting questions concerning specific players on the clubs the writers covered. I decided that the best way to handle it was to read aloud the complete list of players supporting the nonsigning of contracts; I didn't realize until I heard myself reading it just how impressive a list it was. All the players of that day who took a stand in the first Players Association joint action deserve, like names in an ancient epic, to be given even though space permits only a partial listing: Brooks Robinson, Frank Robinson, Jim Palmer, Mickey Mantle, Willie Mays, Tom Seaver, Ron Swoboda, Carl Yastrzemski, Jim Lonborg, George Scott, Roger Maris, Dean Chance, Reggie Smith, Tommie Agee, Tommy John, Sam McDowell, Denny McClain, Mickey Lolich, Al Kaline, Mel Stottlemyre, Catfish Hunter, Felipe Alou, Bert Campaneris, Reggie Jackson, Tommie Davis, Jim Kaat, Rod Carew, Harmon Killebrew, Frank Howard, Willie Horton, Davey Johnson, Clete Boyer, Ed Kranepool, Phil Niekro, Joe Torre, Jim Fregosi, Tony Oliva, Gaylord Perry, Jim Bunning, Eddie Mathews, Jim Grant, Jeff Torborg, Hank Aaron, Ernie Banks, Ken Holtzman, Ron Santo, Bill Freehan, Pete Rose, Joe Morgan, Rusty Staub, Gary Peters, Don Sutton, Maury Wills, Tug McGraw, Rico Carty, Bob Gibson, Tim McCarver, Bill Singer, Dick Allen, Joel Horlen, Willie Davis, Roberto Clemente, Willie Stargell, Donn Clendenon, Bobby Bonds, Steve Carlton, Lou Brock, Curt Flood, Bobby Murcer, Roy White, Milt Pappas, Vada Pinson, Juan Marichal, Willie McCovey, Don Drysdale—this was the way I began. I would have read them all, just to make a point, but just then we received about a dozen copies of the total list, which were distributed quickly. Nothing further needed to be said. It really was quite simple. Baseball players and the sportswriters who covered games were familiar with individual player holdouts. For nearly a century it was the only weapon available to a player who felt that his club's contract offer was unfair. Everyone knew that holding out to gain bargaining leverage, even when the holdout was Joe DiMaggio, was notoriously ineffective. But in December 1968 we embarked on an uncharted course: The first mass holdout in baseball history. We would soon learn its effectiveness.

The owners' initial reaction to the policy was one of confidence that the unity of the players would not hold. Besides, they had other immediate problems of their own creation. In a somewhat surprising move, the owners announced the firing of Commissioner William "Spike" Eckert at this December 1968 winter meeting. He had been in office for only about three years of his seven-year term. I am always amused when subsequent commissioners of baseball get carried away with their own importance and assert the fiction of their all-powerful role, or when writers accept this same malarkey. (Commissioner Fay Vincent was the latest to proclaim his imaginary immunity to discharge by the owners.) All commissioners are controlled by the owners. They can persecute a stray or two who may be unpopular with the more powerful owners—a Finley, a Steinbrenner—and here and there a Turner, a Kroc, separated from the pack, can become victims of arbitrary actions by a commissioner. But make no mistake: The owners retain the real power within the management and owner hierarchy. And every baseball commissioner must eventually learn that reality or find himself unceremoniously booted out of his job. I believe that every commissioner who was fired—or who was asked to "retire"—or advised that his contract "would not be renewed"—(Chandler, Frick, Eckert, Kuhn, Ueberroth) absorbed this truth at long last. All of them, that is, except Kuhn, whose perception of reality was never his strong suit. Now Vincent shows the same failing.

When the owners fired Eckert, they apparently thought they'd be able to find a quick replacement. They scheduled a meeting in Chicago a month later, only to find that no candidate could muster sufficient votes in each league for election. They recessed, reconvened again in Florida a month later, and found themselves in the same ridiculous position. After long meetings, Papa Bear (Walter O'Malley) suggested that Bowie Kuhn, not heretofore considered, be given an interim appointment—for one year—as "commissioner pro tem," instead of electing him for the standard term of seven years. Kuhn was bland and inoffensive; he was a reasonably attractive alternative to a pitched battle over who should be commissioner.

Meanwhile the pension negotiations were going nowhere. In January, I convened a meeting in New York at the Biltmore Hotel to review our position with the players. From five to seven of the most prominent players on each of the teams, including the player reps, were invited. Something unexpected happened: 130 players came to New York for the meeting in the middle of the winter! Not only was it a great turnout, it was a stirring meeting. The issues were reported in great detail, and the players expressed themselves clearly and forcefully. The Players Association was instructed to continue negotiations, take no backward steps, press forward with all our aims for the Major League Baseball Players Benefit Plan, and take all the necessary steps to implement the policy of nonsigning of players' contracts for 1969 until a settlement was reached. The most prominent players in the game were solidly united. The press had a field day after the meeting as these stars all stayed for interviews. Their solidarity and knowledge of the issues were eye-openers to at least the younger writers—who seemed to sense that this was something new and different to write about. That was more than twenty years ago, but I still remember the whole experience with great pleasure.

I recall the positive contributions of many players at that meeting, but for some reason I recall most vividly Dick Allen. Always an impressive figure, he came to the meeting dressed in a dashiki. He did not speak in the early part of the meeting but later spoke with quiet dignity in a fashion that indicated he had been listening carefully. He was eloquent and forceful, and the other players listened intently. He didn't speak as a superstar, but as a player who understood both the issues and the importance of the players' moving forward as a group. I wish some of the writers who were so quick to jump on him in later years had seen him in this light.

The owners pretended not to be impressed with the obvious unity of the players, or perhaps they truly were ignorant of what they were seeing. The fact they couldn't ignore was that the players were not signing their contracts. There were exceptions here and there, such as players who were on major league rosters but who had not yet played in the major leagues. And there were a few journeymen players who signed contracts despite their commitment not to do so. I remember the fury of some of the Mets when their catcher, Jerry Grote, signed a contract despite a pledge not to. Grote had attended the large meeting in New York in January and had voted in favor of the no-signing policy (the vote had been unanimous). After he signed, several players telephoned to demand that he be billed for transportation to and from New York to attend the meeting; all he wanted, they alleged, was a free trip to New York. Ed Kranepool, the Mets' player rep, was particularly upset. Of course, no bill was sent, but I always thought it would have been a nice gesture for Jerry to have voluntarily sent the Association a check for his plane tickets.

In any event, the no-signing policy was a huge success, particularly considering there were no penalties for backsliders; it was totally voluntary. As February began, spring training was just a few weeks away, and it now became apparent to even the dimmest of executives that major leaguers were going to be conspicuous by their absence from the training camps. Pitchers and catchers report early. I still have a picture I clipped from the *New York Times* showing an empty playing field at the Yankees' Fort Lauderdale training site with a young man on the outside, his face pressed against the locked gate. The caption identified the man as a rookie catcher, Thurman Munson by name, and the large print read "Thurman who?" No one had informed him of the dispute. Thurman later became a member and staunch supporter of the Players Association and, of course, one of the great catchers of modern times. In August 1979—nearing the end of his eleventh season—he was tragically killed in a plane crash.

In that first week of February 1969 the owners had selected Bowie Kuhn as temporary commissioner for a year. Whether or not the owners recognized it—and Kuhn, who had been serving on the owners' negotiating committee, knew it well—the rapidly approaching showdown with the union was the new commissioner's first priority. As assistant National League counsel Kuhn had not risen above the role of glorified messenger boy in the negotiations, and he certainly was not a positive force for fashioning a reasonable settlement. Now, on his first day as commissioner, he had to face the unpleasant possibility that his first Opening Day would be remembered for not opening. It had to have been a sobering thought.

On his first day in office, Bowie flew to New York from Florida and telephoned me from the airport. We made an appointment for later in the day, and he appeared at the Association's office at the appointed time. He had been there many times during negotiations because such meetings generally were held alternately in the office of the Player Relations Committee and in the Players Association's office. But this visit during his first day in office would prove to be Bowie's last—after all, Bowie was now a "czar," and czars do not visit peasants. The meeting on this day was pleasant enough. We touched lightly on his new responsibilities, and Dick Moss and I wished him luck. We sent him a formal telegram congratulating him on his appointment as baseball's chief management official.

The events of the next few weeks turned out to be Bowie Kuhn's finest hours as commissioner. Whatever the reasons, and granted that his own self-interest surely was involved, his efforts to persuade the owners to drastically revise the regressive position they had taken in the pension negotiations were in the best interest of the game, and they were successful: The owners' position on the issues changed 180 degrees. John Gaherin's prior marching orders were rescinded.

Gaherin wasn't pleased with his new orders, but negotiations became constructive. The "give-back" demands of the owners were removed from the bargaining table. Their proposed contribution to the pension fund was increased to a realistic figure, from $4.1 million to $6.5 million a year. They fully recognized the cost of expanding the benefit plan coverage to the four new expansion teams (something I thought would have been obvious from the beginning). The final financing figure again equaled one-third of the total of the recently increased national television and radio revenue. The amount negotiated was significantly in excess of the figure which the old 60–40 formula would have yielded. (In his book *Hardball,* Kuhn wrote that it was a mistake to replace the 60–40 formula. His abacus must have been out of order.) Benefits of former players and others were increased along with the benefits of active members. And the union was even successful in reducing the requirement for pension eligibility to four years from five—and applying it retroactively (to 1947!). Numerous former players, coaches, managers, and trainers suddenly became eligible. A final settlement was reached in the early morning hours of February 25. The union's executive board, which had been standing by, ratified it. The ban on player signing of contracts was lifted, and we kept the traditional date for opening spring training, March 1. A lot of factors went into making the settlement so amicable, but much of the credit belonged to Kuhn, and I was happy to tell him so.

Early in his tenure, Kuhn decided to emulate my practice of meeting with all the players in spring training. There was nothing wrong with the idea, but he suffered from role confusion, a problem which would dog him in years to come. He couldn't seem to accept the idea that he was *not* the players' representative, no matter how badly he wanted to think of himself as such and no matter how many times he said so publicly. Further, he had no inkling of how to relate to players, and had nothing to offer them except the clichés and bromides of the bosses. (My personal favorite was "My door is always open for the little people with problems." I always pictured Frank Howard, all six-feet-eight-inches and 260 pounds of him, walking into Kuhn's office and announcing, "Bowie, I'm one of those little people with a problem.") Kuhn's talent for self-deception was amazing. He told everyone, including me, about his great reception by the players, but all I got from the players were comments such as "What a stuffed shirt," and questions such as "Is he for real?" and "Does he take us for dumb kids?" and "Do we have to go to those meetings and listen to that crap?" I don't know if it ever got across to him that the players were laughing at him, but after a while he mercifully discontinued the meetings.

His confusion about his role appeared in other ways. He announced, for instance, that he wanted to attend the Association's executive board meetings and address the board. After requiring him to clarify that this was a request and not a demand, I told him I'd take it up with the board. Initially, the members were opposed, but remembering his good will during the negotiations I said, "What the hell, let's give him a brief period for whatever he wants to say, to be followed by a question period." He came to two meetings. His remarks were inconsequential, and the board members were irritated when his answers to their questions were uninformed and evasive. There were no further appearances by Commissioner Kuhn before the players' executive board. This probably led Kuhn to have some bad feeling toward the Association, but he had only himself to blame for believing the fiction that the commissioner of baseball is "impartial," that he is a "representative of the public," and that he "represents the players as well as the owners." To the contrary, Kuhn was an employee of the owners, and every time he forgot that, he brought misery to himself and to baseball.

Kuhn was a victim of illusions about his job, but he didn't summon them from nowhere. The owners started it all with the appointment of the first commissioner, federal judge Kenesaw Mountain Landis, after the Black Sox scandal in 1919. (In truth, Landis had been the owners' boy in a black robe before his appointment.) For nearly half a century the press scarcely questioned the impartiality of a man chosen by baseball executives to make decisions about players. Even today it wouldn't surprise me to learn that a survey of baseball writers, of Congress, of the antitrust division of the Justice Department, and of the courts disclosed a prevailing view that the commissioner of baseball is neutral. It would probably still shock some of the most avid baseball fans to learn that commissioners are hired by the owners, that no one else has a voice in the process, that owners determine his duties and responsibilities, and that they decide his compensation and pay every penny of it. The owners decide whether the commissioner is representing their interests, and their interests alone, in a satisfactory manner. If they decide, at any time, for sufficient (or insufficient) reason that he is not representing their interests, they fire him. All of that is hardly rare or unusual. What is startling is that, despite the facts, the mythology—the hoax— the lie that the commissioner is above the fray and is anything more than the owners' designated spokesperson in limited areas continues in some quarters. Fortunately, the players no longer believe it. I can only take a small amount of credit for their enlightenment. Kuhn deserves most of the rest.

To understand how backward baseball was in the area of labor relations, recall that as late as 1965, when I was approached by the players' search committee about becoming the Players Association's first executive director, I was told that they had discussed their plans with (then) Commissioner Eckert. Robin Roberts, a leading member of the committee, was later quoted as having said that he had told Eckert the names of the people being considered for the job and had assured Eckert that no one who did not have the approval of the commissioner would be selected as a candidate for executive director! That would be like the fledgling Steelworkers Organizing Committee thirty years earlier going to the chairman of the board of U.S. Steel Corporation and asking him if it would be all right for John L. Lewis to appoint Phil Murray as chairman of the union's organizing committee. Of course, steelworkers had a union mentality, while there was virtually no one in major league baseball who had ever associated with a union of any kind. But within a few years, things changed. Kuhn could not get away with the things his predecessors did, and I don't think he ever forgave me for it.

Following his assist toward an equitable settlement of the 1969 benefit plan negotiations, Kuhn reverted to form. Attempts to discuss revisions in the reserve system again got nowhere in the negotiation of the 1970 basic agreement, and although he would later declare that he had felt the reserve system was overly restrictive, the silence from his office at the time was deafening. In 1970, Curt Flood, irked at being traded to the Phillies, decided to test the legality of the reserve rule system under which a player was considered the property of the owner. His lawsuit was filed in January 1970 and was backed by the Players Association. With the baseball monopoly being challenged under the antitrust laws, Kuhn meekly followed the industry line, condemned Flood, and testified against him.

The following year, Alex Johnson, of the California Angels, the reigning American League batting champion, found himself placed on the restricted list as a disciplinary action. (A player on that list is disqualified from playing, receives no salary and no credited service, and can be kept there indefinitely.) Use of the restricted list for disciplinary purposes is not permitted; it's baseball's form of jailing political dissidents. The action was taken by Kuhn, at the request of the Angels, *without a hearing*. No attempt was made by management to ascertain the cause of what seemed to be really bizarre behavior by Johnson, conduct totally different from anything he had exhibited over his many years as a major leaguer.

The union filed a grievance on Johnson's behalf, and long and painful hearings were required before an arbitrator rendered his decision. The arbitrator, Lewis Gill, found that the actions of the club, the league president, and the commissioner in disciplining Johnson were improper. Evidence of emotional illness required, Gill established, that the player be placed on the disabled list—with full pay and credited service—rather than under disciplinary suspension. Kuhn's inability or unwillingness to acknowledge that a major league player can become emotionally disabled indicated to me that baseball management was even farther behind conventional business establishments than I had thought.

The 1972 pension negotiations, strike, and settlement proceeded from beginning to end with little to indicate that there was a Bowie Kuhn. One writer—I forget who—amended the popular refrain of "This would never have happened if Judge Landis were alive" to "This would not have happened if *Bowie Kuhn* were alive." I have since heard and read Kuhn's theories of that strike, particularly the notion that "Miller and the union wanted a strike in 1972 to send a signal to the owners about the following year's negotiations on a basic agreement," and I'm almost prepared to believe what I didn't believe then: that he may have been one of the prime instigators of the strike. Is it possible that Kuhn could have been unaware that the owners' behavior in the last three weeks of negotiation in 1972 represented a classic example of employers spoiling for a fight? The very last thing I wanted at that time was a strike; the truth is that I wasn't sure we were strong enough. I've never been entirely sure what Kuhn's role was, but I'm sure it was one of two: Either his errors in judgment or his impotence in the face of the owners' determination to humble the players provoked the strike, thereby allowing the players to demonstrate their solidarity under fire. The players and the union were never the same again. Neither was major league baseball.

With the basic agreement and the pension agreement negotiated in 1973 we won many important gains for the players, including the right of players to have salary disputes with their clubs decided by impartial arbitrators whose decisions were binding. The difference between a ballplayer's being required to accept whatever a club offered him, as had been the case almost from the beginning of professional baseball, and the new system of salary arbitration was like the difference between dictatorship and democracy. Salary arbitration has been a major factor in eliminating gross inequities in the salary structures from club to club (and sometimes on the same club) and, along with the right of free agency, negotiated three years later, produced the most rapid growth of salaries *ever experienced in any industry.* What's not often noted, however, is that an integral part of the players' electrifying salary growth has been the spectacular increase in the revenue taken in by owners in the same period. A fact never noted by the owners (or their commissioners) and seldom noted by media observers is that baseball owners keep, after taxes, far, far more money than they ever did in what they call "the good old days" when players' salaries were a small fraction of today's payroll.

The groundwork for much of this new prosperity was laid in 1973, but Bowie Kuhn and his sidekick, Sandy Hadden, didn't surface often in those negotiations. For reasons of their own, they felt it important to present the commissioner as being above the fray; apparently he wanted to create the perception that the commissioner operated from Mount Olympus, from where he could descend when it pleased him to untangle the sordid affairs of men and money. Bowie was in the clouds all right, but it was cloud nine. Dick Moss and I had many occasions to meet with John Gaherin and Barry Rona, some meetings in our office and some in John's office on Forty-second Street, where the Player Relations Committee was located. I remember once when Dick and I arrived at John's office for a meeting about fifteen minutes early. Shortly after we were seated, we heard what seemed to be a lot of scurrying around in an adjoining office and in the hall. I looked questioningly at John. He said nothing and seemed embarrassed. Dick got up, opened the door, and looked out into the hall. He came back, smiled, and said to John, "Who are you hiding back there, John? I think I saw some familiar faces." Gaherin looked uncomfortable and disgusted. Dick thrives on this kind of situation. He said to John, "Why don't you ask Bowie and Sandy to join us?" John just shook his head, and I motioned to Dick to leave it alone. Gaherin then confirmed what we had already concluded: Kuhn insisted on being briefed on all developments in the negotiations. Nothing wrong with that. But his involvement was to be kept secret from the Players Association and the media. Because Dick and I had arrived earlier than expected, the Bobbsey twins had to scoot around from room to room in an effort to avoid being seen.

The whole thing was ridiculous, but in truth it was no more absurd or childish than much of the behavior we got from Kuhn. It had been during these negotiations that Bowie had telephoned me from time to time to ask about what was happening, what did I think about the progress or lack or progress, what were the stumbling blocks, and so on. The impropriety of this never seemed to dawn on him. Regardless of his pretense of neutrality, I knew that he was an employee and representative of the owners. I treated his inquiries cordially, but I told him nothing that I would not have told John Gaherin if he had asked, or an owner if he had called. It was pretty funny, though, to listen to Bowie talk as if he had not already been briefed on the negotiations, when I knew— and he knew that I knew—that he had been. It was also amusing when, a day or so after a telephone conversation with Kuhn, John Gaherin would say to me, with a knowing smile, "I understand you've been talking to the commissioner." Undoubtedly, for what it was worth, *Bowie* would report to *John* what *I* had said to *him*. It wasn't worth much.

Kuhn has written that despite all his friendly approaches to me, I did not reciprocate. There's a bit of truth in this. Bowie's approaches through the years were invariably for one of two purposes. He literally wanted to spy, albeit clumsily, to see if he could obtain "advance information" of what was about to happen. In those instances I did not "reciprocate" because I had no need to indulge in such foolishness. Bowie's other intention was usually to pick my brains. There was scant possibility of reciprocity in that department.

In 1974, after winning twenty or more games for the fourth straight year, Jim "Catfish" Hunter, one of the premier pitchers in baseball, signed a two-year contract with owner Charlie Finley of the Oakland A's. Finley, who often acted as his own attorney despite his lack of qualifications or knowledge, negotiated and signed the contract and even suggested some of the language incorporated into the contract. One provision required that one-half of his salary was to be paid to an insurance company, named by Hunter, for the purchase of an annuity; the money was to be paid as earned *during the season.* In other words, it was to be paid in installments each payday during the season. The contract provision was brief and to the point. It was written in plain English; it was written in order not to be misunderstood, and in fact it could not be misunderstood.

You wouldn't know that from the Kuhn version of this simple contract provision in his book *Hardball* and the equally false and distorted Lee MacPhail version in his book *My Nine Innings.*

After the season began, Hunter gave Finley the name of the insurance company to which the money should be sent. The entire

1974 season passed without Finley's having paid one cent to the insurance company named by Hunter. With Finley and the Oakland club now in default, we sent a written notice to the club after conferring with Hunter, calling for it to remedy the default within ten days. It is important to point out that the notice was sent in conformity with the contract. This default and termination clause had been in all Uniform Player's Contracts for upward of forty years, having been placed there by the owners and their attorneys long before there was a union. Its language is explicit. It provides that if a club fails to remedy a default within the specified ten days "the Player may terminate this contract upon written notice to the Club." Before the Players Association came into being, there had been no means of enforcing this provision; no matter how obvious the violation of a player's contract, league presidents and commissioners conspired with club owners to obliterate the player's rights. The same pattern was followed with Hunter, but not successfully.

Finley ignored the written notice of his default in the payments due under the contract, and he ignored Hunter's subsequent contract termination notice of October 4. League president Lee MacPhail pretended not to see the club's violation. He met with Finley, and the two of them, together with the Player Relations Committee, set up a scheme to deprive Jim Hunter of his rights. Finley, accompanied by MacPhail as a "witness," met with Hunter in early October. Finley offered to pay Hunter *now* the money that should have been paid to the insurance company throughout the season for the purchase of an annuity. Hunter's attorney instructed him not to accept it. Finley's and MacPhail's solution was to ignore Hunter's contract, pretend that it called only for salary payments to Hunter, and arbitrarily remove from the contract a benefit to Hunter which he considered important: namely, the deferral of $50,000 each year (which meant that no current tax would be due on that sum by Hunter) for the purchase of an annuity which would be payable to him after his career as a player was over. The Finley offer obviously did not cure the Finley default. MacPhail would later testify at the Hunter arbitration hearing about his shameful role, but without a trace of shame.

Under the terms of the contract Hunter was now a free agent, and in mid-October we sent a letter to Kuhn requesting that his free-agency status be recognized after the World Series and all the clubs be so informed. Of course, that was just a formality; we knew Kuhn would refuse. And he did. But the reasons he gave were pitiful. He pontificated that free agency was too severe a "penalty"; after all, Finley had offered to pay the money to Hunter on October 4! It was not even arguable that Finley's offer cured his default, which began early in the season. Kuhn's statement was pure gibberish, and especially unforgivable for having been written by a lawyer. Furthermore, the so-called penalty of free agency was Hunter's absolute right under the contract. And no one could set aside that right for any reason.

Kuhn's antiplayer bias was not new; it was simply a continuation of what had gone on for decades before the union. What was new was the arrogance and the failure to even try to adjust to the reality of new circumstances. By 1974 baseball's management had had more than eight years in which to learn that arbitrary, antiplayer actions could be challenged and reversed, but the behavior of Finley, the AL counsel Jim Garner, Lee MacPhail, the Player Relations Committee and its counsel, Barry Rona, and above all, Bowie Kuhn, revealed that they still had not a clue that times had changed.

The Hunter case finally got the union's message across: The baseball establishment did not have the ability to set aside the terms of a contract. Neither did an arbitrator or the courts. We promptly appealed Kuhn's refusal to recognize Hunter's free-agency status to arbitration. At the hearing in November Finley squirmed, invented things, contradicted himself, and made it altogether apparent that he had no credible defense. MacPhail did no better.

Some weeks later, in December, the arbitrator upheld Hunter's grievance. In noting that Hunter was now a free agent, Peter Seitz, the arbitrator, wrote that the remedy of the player being able to terminate his contract when it had been violated was not *his* remedy: *It was the remedy specified in the contract itself.* Finley appealed the decision in the California courts, and the American League counsel assisted in the appeal. But the California courts agreed that Seitz's decision reversing Bowie Kuhn was "final and binding."

One year later, the most important arbitration in baseball

history was pending. It involved two fine pitchers—Andy Messersmith of the Dodgers and Dave McNally of the Montreal Expos. Each had been dissatisfied with the terms offered by his club for the 1975 season and therefore had not signed a new 1975 contract. The clubs responded by renewing their 1974 contracts, without the players' signatures, for the 1975 season. The clubs had a right to do this because of the renewal clause. This clause provided that a club could renew a player's contract for "one additional year."

It was my contention that when the 1975 season expired, there was no contractual connection between these players and their former clubs; the players were free agents. One did not have to be Dr. Samuel Johnson to understand the meaning of such explicit language; the clubs, the leagues, and the commissioners had simply ignored the plain meaning of the contract from the time far back in history when that language first appeared. Baseball's owners and officials had long determined that, since players had no effective recourse to the tightly drawn monopoly known as baseball, the language of contracts and of rules meant whatever the owners and their stooges said it meant. The courts stood by and nodded their assent, as did state and federal legislatures and elected and appointed officials and virtually all of the sports press.

The Players Association filed grievances on behalf of Messersmith and McNally in October and sent the ritually meaningless formal request to baseball's "czar" to recognize the free-agent status of the two players. Like a good servant, Kuhn promptly and dutifully denied the request on behalf of his masters O'Malley and Charles Bronfman (Expos) and all other owners intent on maintaining their lifetime hold on what they regarded as their property. After extensive hearings, the arbitration panel once more reversed Kuhn and ordered that free-agent status be accorded to the players.

Baseball officialdom went its usual route of refusing to accept the arbitrator's decision as final and binding, although they had agreed to do so, and appealed to federal district court (rejected); they appealed to the federal circuit court of appeals (rejected). And still they were not through. They continued the fight, including locking out the players in February and March—a lockout designed to reverse the arbitrator's decision *even after the federal courts refused to reverse it.* A significant number of baseball writers and commentators took the occasion to reveal that they didn't know the difference between a strike and a lockout—a distressing number of them still don't—by roundly condemning the players and their Association for striking!

The lockout was called off by the owners about halfway through March when it had become clear that neither I nor the players would buckle on the issue of our hard-won free agency. Bowie's 1987 book spells out the details of his and the owners' panic at the thought that players might win the unimaginable if not un-American right to change employers when their contracts expired. Astonishingly, Kuhn contends that he had the option of removing the case from the jurisdiction of the arbitrator and deciding the case himself. The legal basis for this action, he says, was the provision in the basic agreement which gave him that right in cases involving gambling and corruption, that is, the throwing of games, as in the Black Sox scandal. He abandoned this ploy only after being advised that the Players Association would strike if he invoked his "authority" and interfered on a phoney basis. Here are his words: "In hindsight, my greatest regret about my sixteen years as commissioner is that I did not take that grievance and head off [Peter] Seitz." The truly amazing fact is that Kuhn makes perfectly clear in print *that he had already made up his mind about the case!* He already knew how he would decide it if the case were before him. He expressed his contempt for the idea that there was anything in the contract or the rules that provided for free agency.

Kuhn did not try to hide his bias against free agency. He ridiculed the entire concept as "nothing more than one of those myths Miller spent so much time inventing." (Some myth, as it turned out.) He said that the case had no merit whatsoever, that there was no basis for awarding free agency to players, and that such an award would result in chaos for baseball. He predicted the loss of an entire league (through bankruptcy) and the end of all controls over the minor league system, and stopped just short of a plague of locusts (or maybe I didn't read far enough—that may be in there). He concluded in advance that the Messersmith-McNally grievance had no merit and had to be denied—and all of this before any hearing, before any presentation of briefs, before any testimony by witnesses. Before any of that, *Kuhn wanted to take jurisdiction of the case and rule on it—when he already had decided it!* To understand the monstrosity of this position, picture a judge in a civil or criminal court, local, state, county, or federal, demanding that a particular case be given to him for decision when he has already decided the verdict before the trial begins. In such a case the grounds for impeachment or worse are present, the lack of integrity apparent, the rape of justice obvious. Perhaps I'm being naive; perhaps this happens in real courts with real judges. But I know of none where the judge involved provided *written evidence* that the fix was in, that the case was rigged to produce a result known in advance, before the trial or hearing even began. In this respect, Bowie's written confession may be a first.

Just in passing, it should be noted that Kuhn, of course, had no "option" to decide the case himself, nor did he have the option, as he later contended, to fire the arbitrator, Peter Seitz, when the Messersmith case was pending. The question of whether the owners could fire an arbitrator with a case pending before him was itself arbitrated, and the result was a decision that, of course, that could not be done or else a decision could be delayed forever. That is a settled matter. Kuhn's so-called option to fire Peter Seitz in 1975 was no option at all. Any such action would have been reversed immediately. It's possible that Kuhn didn't know that in 1975, but is it really possible no one explained it to him by the time he wrote his memoirs?

The Kuhn administration was, I believe, a downward toboggan ride from the beginning, but it accelerated as we approached the 1980 negotiations and climaxed its downhill run in the 1981 negotiations and strike. Once the strike began, I knew his days as commissioner were numbered, as was the case for his lieutenant, Ray Grebey. I don't know if Grebey saw the end coming; I'm pretty sure that Bowie didn't. After all, when you view yourself as a Gilbert and Sullivan character such as the Lord Chancellor in *Iolanthe*—"And I, my Lords [of baseball] embody the Law"—it must be difficult to imagine being kicked out on your rump by the very lords over whom you allegedly rule.

A reporter once asked me, "If you were Bowie Kuhn and you were up against Marvin Miller, what would you have done?" I replied that I'd have pointed to the state of baseball in the early 1980s and noted that we had expanded into new markets, that attendance had skyrocketed, that TV revenue had set new records, that there had never before been so much money for owners and players, that we'd never had better pennant races or more competitive balance, and that there have never been as many people avidly following baseball as there were since I became commissioner. I would have added: "Miller had his job to do representing the players, and I have represented the interests of the owners. The results speak for themselves. I have done all I can do, and it is time to retire." But that would have been out of character for Kuhn. His approach could best be described as a will to fail.

In late 1979, negotiation of a new basic agreement and a pension agreement for 1980 was about to begin. Bowie invited me for a drink at "21," one of his favorite hangouts. When David McDonald was president of the Steelworkers Union, he got in trouble with some of his constituent union members when his political opponents called attention to this watering hole as one of his favorite haunts. This was different. Bowie represented wealthy owners, not union members, although he had a fantasy that he did.

That day, after some small talk over a drink, Bowie told me what was on his mind. He started, uncharacteristically, by pouring out compliments about all that I had accomplished for the players since 1966. His thesis seemed to be that with the union having made so many gains, it now was the owners' turn.

I took a sip of my drink and replied that the owners *had* participated in baseball's new prosperity: their total revenue had risen remarkably; the value of their franchises, as shown by the price of those sold recently, was many times what their purchase prices had been.

Bowie waved that off. He was not interested in the economic facts. With some agitation, he said, "It's important for you to understand. You've had so many victories. Now *the owners need a victory.*"

At this point I was ready for a second drink. Kuhn had actually asked for a meeting to tell me that the wounded psyches of men like Gussie Busch and Walter O'Malley needed tending. Unspoken, but unmistakably there, was Bowie's plea that *he* needed a win.

I thought about how best to deal with this. Negotiations had not yet begun. The Players Association had made no demands; we hadn't even formulated them yet. The owners' Player Relations Committee had not given us their proposals for change. Given this situation, what exactly was I being asked to do? I decided to find out in a direct manner. I said, "Bowie, are you, in effect, asking me to *throw* the game?" Bowie began to deny it vehemently. "Okay, then," I said. "Exactly what are you asking for?"

He hemmed and hawed and began to chatter about the need to "water down" free agency, the gist of it being that he believed it was necessary for a club losing a free agent to be compensated by getting a major league player in return from the club that signed the free agent. He said that compensation was needed to insure "competitive balance." I disagreed, stating that by every measurement there was now better competitive balance than had existed *before* free agency, when just a few teams won all the pennants and World Series.

Bowie did not respond to this. Instead, he launched into a lecture about how something had to be done to stop the growth of the players' salaries. The owners, I pointed out, were making more money in this era of higher player salaries than when salaries were much lower. Kuhn seemed increasingly upset. He shifted gears a bit, telling me that in the upcoming negotiations the players would find the owners "united as never before." "They want compensation for the loss of free agents, and I am going to support them."

In his memoirs Kuhn gives his version of my reply to this. It is inaccurate. He claims I said that he and the owners would get compensation for free agents only over my dead body, or words to that effect. What I really said was more characteristic of my trade union background. I said, as I got up to leave, that no evidence had yet been presented which would require or justify compensation; that it should be clear by now that the Players Association would not be taking any backward steps; that there would be no give-backs without compelling reasons; that all matters were negotiable, but that it would be a serious error on his and the owners' part to create a confrontational situation with a solid, united Players Association.

The 1980 negotiation went to the wire—to the strike deadline—but a settlement was reached on all issues in the pension agreement and in the basic agreement. No agreement was reached on compensation for the loss of free agents. I had proposed that the matter be postponed for a year and a study committee be formed to review the whole problem. This became part of the settlement. The study committee effort failed and, as the basic agreement provided, two things happened in 1981. The owners announced that they would put into effect their compensation plan, and the Players Association announced its opposition and a strike date.

Bowie Kuhn and the hardliners among the owners were in control. Negotiations throughout the spring, led by Kuhn's hand-picked man, Ray Grebey, were a farce. The owners' plan would have destroyed the value of free-agent rights, as well it should, since this was the principal reason it had been developed. A player was either a free agent or he wasn't; anything that restricted a team from wanting to deal with him restricted his bargaining power. There was no such thing as a semi-free agent.

From the start I had made it clear that the owners' compensation plan was unacceptable, but for some reason I'll never fully understand, Kuhn (and Grebey) virtually ensured the 1981 strike by telling the owners in 1980 that their compensation scheme had been won.* This lie—I don't know of a kinder word for it—was intended to get the owners to ratify the 1980 settlement, which contained substantial gains for the players, and avoid a strike. Kuhn also told the lie in print, in the form of a press release issued by Kuhn-Grebey before the settlement was six hours old.

I knew this deception would mean trouble in the future and did my best to blow it away immediately by calling a press conference at which I assured everyone in no uncertain terms that we did *not* accept the owners' compensation plan. Kuhn later wrote that the owners were resolved "to *retain* the compensation *agreement* they had obtained in 1980 bargaining," but of course there was no agreement on compensation in 1980, so there was nothing for the owners to "retain." In 1980 the only agreement on the subject was that we were in disagreement; that the issue was to be postponed for one year; that a study group would be formed to study the subject in that year. Under the 1980 agreement the owners were

---

*A club, before signing a free agent, would know that the signing would result in the loss of a major league player from its roster, selected (as compensation) by the club that formerly employed the free agent.

given the right, absent an agreement, to announce before the 1981 season started that they would implement their plan (effective after the season was over), but in that case the union would have the right to strike to prevent the implementation of the owners' compensation plan. That was the extent of the agreement.

But Kuhn and Grebey had fed their bosses pap: that they "had" their compensation scheme. That deliberate mischief by the not-so-dynamic duo to save their political behinds in 1980 was a significant factor in bringing on the 1981 strike and the owners' subsequent ignominious defeat. Kuhn's role in bringing on the strike of 1981—supporting the owners' demand for a compensation plan that was not attainable—was mandated by what he had done in 1980. Having told the owners then that they already had their compensation plan, how could he tell them in 1981 that they did not have it and could not get it even after a long strike? Kuhn and Grebey were in a corner of their own making, and there was no way out; that is, there was no way out unless someone, or some circumstances, would at last persuade these "leaders" that truth and rational behavior might serve them better.

It wasn't to be. There were a few owners who were sufficiently enlightened to see the debacle into which they were being led, but not enough of them. Even the U.S. Secretary of Labor, Raymond Donovan, tried to head off the conflict through mediation and failed. The union's filing of an unfair-labor-practice charge with the National Labor Relations Board could have saved the situation. The NLRB sought to enjoin the owners from implementing their free-agent compensation plan. This would have meant there would be no strike since the compensation plan was the only issue. But Kuhn and the owners and their attorneys fought against the NLRB in federal court. Federal judge Henry Werker misunderstood the situation. He tortured the facts in order to defeat the government's proposed injunction, apparently convinced that he was aiding the owners.

Some aid! Within forty-eight hours, as we had advised the judge, baseball was shut down. The strike lasted fifty days until the owners collapsed, waving a white flag and asking for peace. From the standpoint of labor it was the most principled strike I've ever been associated with. Many of the players struck not for a better deal for themselves but for a better deal for their colleagues, and for the players who would be coming into baseball in the future. From the standpoint of management, forcing that strike absolutely was the most senseless policy decision I've ever seen.

In June Bowie testified in federal district court in Rochester, New York, before Judge Werker that he took no responsibility for labor-management relations. The contradictions between those allegations and his activities as described in his book are remarkable. The owners' lawyers told the judge that "compensation to be paid to a club losing a free agent was not an economic issue." Not an economic issue! Then what, perhaps a spiritual one? Whatever, Werker bought their argument.

While the case was pending in federal court, negotiations continued. In a final effort to avert a strike, the Players Association offered our own free-agent compensation plan; since it didn't meet the owner's insistence on a scheme which would convert free-agent rights to a trade of players, they sniped at it. They were demanding a give-back of major proportions.

In taking such an uncompromising position, I do not know how much Grebey and the owners were influenced by the industrial and political climate of the time, but as the 1980s got underway, the labor-management climate definitely changed. With the election of Ronald Reagan and his subsequent ruthless destruction of the Professional Air Traffic Controllers Organization, reactionary management became emboldened. We were suddenly in the era of give-backs, whether justified by economic circumstances or not. Unions throughout the country—even the major ones such as the Auto Workers and the Steelworkers—were pressured by threats of plant closings and mass layoffs into foregoing even modest wage and benefit adjustments. Wages and salaries were cut, benefits were reduced, and work practices it had taken years of struggle to obtain were drastically changed for the worse. In the 1980s the labor movement seemed cowed; it would be difficult to find any significant strikes won by unions.

It is not improbable that these events influenced baseball's owners to bring on a confrontation with the union in 1981. They weren't the first management people to make a major error because of an inability to perceive distinctions in totally different situations.

My own strongly held views that give-backs undercut everyone's wage and salary standards and do not result in saving jobs differ from the views of many traditional labor leaders. Kuhn, probably on the assumption that he was rapping me, wrote approvingly of Douglas Fraser, who, as president of the United Auto Workers, agreed to substantial give-backs. "It is inconceivable to me," Kuhn wrote, "that Miller would do the same."

Well, Bowie finally got something right. There is no greater compliment to the head of a union than to find it inconceivable that he could be conned into an agreement that went backward instead of forward. The give-backs in the automobile industry didn't save jobs; they were instead followed by layoffs, plant closings, and record high bonuses, salaries, stock options, and pensions for the top and middle executives of the auto companies. I was never a give-backer; management doesn't volunteer to share its prosperity with labor when profits roll in.

Baseball's economic condition in 1981 required no subsidies. There was no scarcity of poor-mouth speeches, but there was an unwillingness to furnish economic data to document this mysterious poverty. Besides violating the law, this refusal to provide evidence of their so-called losses made it impossible for the union to deal with these claims in any logical way. What evidence there was (record attendance and gate receipts, record radio, television, and cable revenue, record franchise prices) indicated a very profitable, solvent industry.

Unlike the auto and steel industries, and others, baseball wasn't threatened by foreign competition. We certainly didn't have a falling market for the product. In fact, baseball was still an expanding industry; *we had no unemployment.* The number of jobs for major league players, coaches, trainers, managers, and umpires (and executives of clubs) had increased by 30 percent since the union had come into baseball.

It bordered on insanity for anyone on the ownership level to interpret these facts as calling for a confrontation to produce give-backs. Nevertheless we now know that they fell into, or were led into, or were persuaded into, believing that that was their best course. Ray Grebey, their chief spokesman at the time, his counsel, Barry Rona, the two league presidents, Lee MacPhail and Chub Feeney, their counsel, Lou Hoynes and Jim Garner, seemed more like passengers on a speeding train to nowhere than motormen or conductors. No owners, general managers, or other officials ever appeared at a single negotiating meeting. Kuhn, of course, was simply above the sordid details of baseball business. So he never came either.

It was apparent to me, to our counsel Don Fehr, and to the players on the executive board and negotiating committee that the owners were committed to forcing a strike, and in fact had been even before the negotiations began many months before. It was no secret that the owners had invested a large sum of money for "strike insurance" through Lloyd's of London to provide each club with several million dollars to see them through a strike. In addition, a large strike fund had been built from a percentage of gate receipts starting the year before the negotiations began. This was kept in the Central Fund in the commissioner's office, and it had a special purpose: to provide support to those clubs which might waver first and start pressuring the others to make a reasonable settlement.

The key to understanding the owners' strategy was to comprehend that they were convinced that the players would fold rapidly. Each time baseball's management had been forced to retreat because of their inability to remain united or to stomach the loss of revenue and profits, there were a few militants who believed that they had cut and run too soon. Their theory was always the same, from 1969 to 1980: If only the hardliners were given their way, the players could be defeated, and I'd be sent packing. Pile up the number of missed paydays and those spoiled brats who don't know what it's like to do real work will revert to where they were before I came along and brainwashed them. I was told, though I was never able to confirm it, that the owners' negotiators had a pooled bet on how long the strike would last before the players accepted the owners' terms. The guess as to the longest period was five days. What, I ask myself as I think back on all this, could they have been thinking? Where had their heads been for the previous fifteen years?

I think they may have been influenced by their own propaganda. With average salaries in six figures, and some in seven figures, the rationale was that players were "making too much money" to risk a strike. Some sportswriters and TV and radio personalities picked this up, and soon the owners were reading and hearing this speculation, and that, in turn, reinforced their views. They should have known better than to believe everything they planted in the newspapers.

When the strike was over and the owners had surrendered unconditionally, I did not gloat. I saw no point in pouring oil onto the fire, and I did not even claim "victory." At a TV and press conference in the early hours of the morning of the 1981 settlement, I described it as a victory for "the spirit of the players." And it was. I am willing to concede, however, that it may be a mistake not to describe an event like that, and its results, in very specific, factual terms. Not to do so leaves the way open for self-serving revisionists like Kuhn.

They told me when I started, "Players come and players go, but the owners will be here forever," but the truth, as I found out, is that club owners come and go, too, and the new ones aren't told anything about the history of labor-management relations. There's no one to tell them. It is only ten years since the owners' resounding defeat in 1981, but the commissioner who led them to failure, or who let them fail so dismally, is out of office—and he never knew what was happening even when he was there—and there have been three new commissioners since. The AL president has been replaced, and the NL presidency has changed hands twice. The NL counsel is gone from baseball. The director of the Player Relations Committee was fired after the 1981 strike, and his successor was fired on the eve of the 1990 negotiations.

It is all too apparent why the owners repeatedly make the same mistakes: They have no sense of the history of their own industry. The 1981 strike was a watershed event. As such, it deserves to be described accurately. And it is not difficult to do, because the most salient facts of how it came about, and its results, are, for the most part, a matter of public record. The details are in the chapter entitled "Strike Two"; the fantasy version is in Kuhn's book. As Satchel Paige used to say, you pays your money, and you takes your chance.

When I read something about the selfishness of ballplayers—or when I actually see an example of it—I think back to something that happened in the latter days of the 1981 strike. Several of the players who were earning higher salaries took me aside at different times to inquire if I needed any help financially. This was a reference to the fact that I had taken myself off the payroll on day one of the strike. I was quite touched. Although I wasn't wealthy, I had enough to fall back on for a long period to come, and I told them so. In union life, you learn to plan ahead, I pointed out. I had weathered a 116-day steel strike sans salary in 1959 without much trouble.

I had similar conversations with other players. One said to me that he understood why I refused to accept my salary during a strike; it demonstrated that we were all in this together. But, he said, it didn't seem fair; at least the players were not working, but "you're working like a dog and not getting paid. You can bet your ass that Grebey, Rona, Kuhn, MacPhail, and the others on that side are not going without getting paid." I told him I agreed with the last point, but assured him that I considered the principle to be important for unions.

Other players were concerned with more than financial problems. As the negotiations dragged on, there was a period when briefing the press and television people became a daily routine. Sometimes there were several briefings a day. I began to feel the cumulative stress of all the strike activities. At some point I must have appeared especially haggard before the television cameras. I began to get calls from players around the country, and some from former players, asking if I was all right. These expressions of concern, and entreaties to get some rest, and so on, acted like a tonic. The feelings of the players for my welfare really gave me renewed energy. I was never so happy to have so many people tell me I was looking terrible.

There were fifty days of no work and no pay for the ballplayers in 1981; a strike settlement was reached after the owners' strike insurance ran out, and the splits in their ranks became cavernous, with terms less favorable for the owners than they could have had without a strike. Several were heard to comment about the settlement terms: What the hell did *we* get out of this? I could lose a major league player even if I don't enter the free-agent market. (This in fact happened to the Mets when they failed to protect Tom Seaver and lost him to the White Sox, a team that had lost a free agent to a third club.) I won the right to lose a player?

This is what we had a fifty-day strike for? Before, even if I signed a free agent myself, I wouldn't lose one of my players, now they can take one of mine out of the compensation pool when another club signs a free agent? Bowie Kuhn thinks that's a victory. What would he call a defeat?

And so, one of the inevitable consequences of the strike was the owners' decision to fire Ray Grebey and Bowie Kuhn. Grebey left when asked to leave; Kuhn lingered until it became impossible for him to ignore the fact that he was not wanted. He returned to his old law firm, Wilkie, Farr, but that didn't last very long. He moved on to a partnership with Harvey Myerson, which ended in disaster. (It is interesting to note that this humiliation has not interfered with his membership on the Hall of Fame committee, the one that has recently set itself up as upholder of the nation's morality by voting to exclude from the Hall of Fame players deemed ineligible by a commissioner—i.e., Pete Rose.)

It is not at all unreasonable that Bowie Kuhn should dislike me. I was a thorn in his side at every step along the way. He so wanted to believe himself to be the Lord High Commissioner. He was able to issue edicts and interdicts of many types against players, coaches, trainers, managers, umpires, club officials, league officials, owners, former players, even minor leaguers, but he had no jurisdiction whatsoever over me. He was impotent as far as I was concerned, and I thwarted his autocratic procedures when it came to disciplining players. The record is replete with examples of Kuhn's less than evenhanded treatment of players like Curt Flood, Andy Messersmith, Jim Hunter, Alex Johnson, Willie Mays, Mickey Mantle, and others. What all had in common was the knee-jerk judgments of Kuhn, which he pronounced *without affording them any opportunity to be heard.* Except for Flood, each one of these players found justice when Kuhn's ex cathedra pronouncements were overruled by arbitrators and the courts and, finally, even by the commissioner who succeeded him.

Many more people were bushwhacked by Kuhn's favorite method of operating—a variation on the Queen of Hearts method—sentence first, verdict later, and no trial or hearing at all. It was not just players whose basic rights were totally ignored by Kuhn in his efforts to give the impression that he was in control. Under the pretext of protecting "the best interests of baseball," he managed to trample, at various times, the rights of selected owners: Charlie Finley, Ted Turner, Ray Kroc, George Steinbrenner. Players, by virtue of their union, the collective bargaining agreement, and the labor laws, are entitled to due process. But management people—Pete Rose (as manager),Ted Turner, George Steinbrenner, and others, are on their own and subject to the harshest of penalties—permanent banishment from the game—with no right to due process, to a fair hearing, or even to an appeal. The Players Association, of course, has no jurisdiction over management and owner personnel and therefore could not protect their rights. Baseball is a strange world, indeed.

To my mind, the most offensive and distasteful actions of Kuhn's baseball career were directed against players accused of misdeeds away from the baseball field. In 1980 Ferguson Jenkins, an outstanding man with a fine reputation on and off the field, held in high esteem by his community near Toronto, Canada, a great pitcher with a fair chance of reaching three hundred victories as his career moved toward its conclusion, was pitching for the Texas Rangers. On a road trip to Toronto, all the other members of the club retrieved their baggage when the plane landed, but Jenkins's did not seem to be there. After some delay he was told to go with the other players to their hotel. When the bag was located, it would be sent there. But no luggage was sent to the hotel that night or the following morning. Fergie accompanied the team to the ballpark, where, after a short interval, he was arrested by Canadian authorities. They claimed they had found a small quantity of a controlled substance in his suitcase. Jenkins obtained a lawyer and was arraigned in court, a trial date was set some weeks hence after Jenkins pleaded not guilty, and he was released on his own recognizance.

Enter Kuhn. Not on his white charger, but more like a bull, the one in the china shop. He ordered Jenkins to come to the commissioner's office in New York City and provide him with a sworn statement of the facts. Jenkins's attorney quite properly pointed out to Kuhn that shortly there would be a trial. There was as yet no finding of guilt by a court, and the lawyer had quite sensibly instructed his client, Jenkins, not to make any statement to Kuhn or to anyone else until after the court matter was resolved. In Canada, the attorney pointed out to Kuhn, no one can be required to testify against himself, and perhaps that right existed also under the United States Constitution.

Obviously, as an attorney, even a nonpracticing one, Kuhn should have known how off base he was to demand that Jenkins give him a sworn statement when a criminal case was pending in court—even a Canadian court. Kuhn argued that Jenkins's statement could be given confidentially. The attorney gently pointed out that Kuhn would be unable to provide any assurance that such a statement by Jenkins could not be subpoenaed by the court and subsequently used against Jenkins. That didn't deter Carrie Nation Kuhn. It didn't even slow him down long enough for him to think about it. He announced that Ferguson Jenkins was suspended.

We were in the last month of the season. With no chance of the court case's being resolved for several weeks, the suspension terminated Fergie's season unless he ignored his attorney's instructions and testified against himself in Kuhn's office. Unconscionable, undemocratic, and ignorant were the appropriate adjectives for Kuhn's actions. My action was swift in response. We asked the permanent arbitrator for an immediate, expedited hearing because of the circumstances.

Within a few days a hearing was held by arbitrator Ray Goetz. At the hearing Kuhn testified, as did Jenkins's attorney. Kuhn sounded like a complete fool. Arbitrator Goetz, a professor of law, clearly found it incredible that another attorney, Kuhn, would even attempt to justify an indefinite suspension because of an alleged offense which had not yet been heard, and to do so without any hearing whatsoever, using the excuse that the player would not disobey his attorney's instruction and give a sworn statement that might later be used against him by a prosecutor in court. The arbitrator's award a few days later on September 22, 1980, was restrained, but his contempt for Kuhn's position was discernible. He reversed Kuhn's suspension of Jenkins and reinstated him to the active roster of his club.

Arbitrators routinely reversed Kuhn's actions or severely modified the penalties he attempted to impose, usually on the quite understandable ground that a person charged with an offense is not guilty until proven so. These American concepts of justice seemed foreign to Kuhn.

In Jenkins's case, apparently his luggage had been left unattended and unlocked at the airport for many hours before it was opened and a controlled substance allegedly found. Without evidence that Jenkins alone had access to the luggage, any prosecutor would have obvious problems of proof. In any event, although Jenkins was technically convicted at a later date, the case was discharged and the conviction erased from the record. This is the incident that may well have delayed Ferguson Jenkins, one of the three or four best pitchers of his time, in gaining his rightful place in the Hall of Fame until 1991. It was one of Bowie Kuhn's more unfortunate legacies to baseball.

I know nothing of Kuhn's life after he was fired by the owners in 1984 except what I've read in newspaper and magazine stories. I gather that he had an unsatisfactory return to his old law firm, and after that connection was terminated, he joined forces with another attorney and established a new law firm, Myerson and Kuhn. The new firm, after a relatively short time, ran into difficulties, including public accusations of overcharging made by a major client, and later Myerson and Kuhn filed for bankruptcy. Subsequent allegations circulated that creditors of the firm were seeking to obtain assets of the former partners, Myerson and Kuhn, to satisfy debt claims. There were allegations also that Kuhn had sold his house in New Jersey and bought one in Florida where apparently the laws insulate one from creditors somewhat better than in New Jersey or New York. Bowie issued a denial that he was unavailable to creditors' attorneys or that he had moved his domicile to avoid creditors. Litigation to establish Kuhn's liability or the lack of it to the firm's creditors may still be pending.

Bowie Kuhn's dislike of me (an understated term, I think it is safe to say) is understandable. He saw me as his competitor, the one who beat him at every turn for the seventeen years I was the executive director of the Players Association. That seldom leads to kindly feelings even by good losers. But deep down, Bowie was a bad loser, and that led him to ever greater errors of judgment, almost all of them justified by that all-purpose phrase: "in the best interests of baseball..."

I never wished Bowie harm. Although I felt certain that he would be fired, along with Grebey, as a result of the owners' failure in the 1981 strike, of course I had no say in the matter, nor did I get any satisfaction when it came to pass. Similarly, reading about the sorry events that have been a part of his life after baseball only makes me wonder how such things could happen. I confess, however, that I did have one strong feeling when I read that he would be testifying before a grand jury in New York City and that one possible outcome of litigation is that his entire net worth could be imperiled. That would be a terrible outcome for anyone, but especially for someone like Bowie Kuhn at age sixty-three.

My wish is that before anything like that should happen, even before any court judgment whatsoever is issued concerning him, he be given his full rights: that he have an attorney of his own choosing; that he not be required to testify against himself; that he have full opportunity to present evidence and confront and cross-examine adverse witnesses; and that he have a judge (or a judge and a jury) who is *impartial, and who has no connection whatsoever with those allegedly seeking to establish fraudulent behavior.* In short, I sincerely hope that he will be given due process in a court proceeding unlike any he ever conducted as commissioner.

7 . . .

Alex Johnson: The Maligned Angel

THE FIRST ARBITRATION of significance involving a black player arose from the disciplining of Alex Johnson by the California Angels, American League president Joe Cronin, and Commissioner Bowie Kuhn. A gifted hitter and outfielder for most of his thirteen-year career, Johnson played with the Phillies, Cardinals, Reds, Angels, Indians, Rangers, Yankees, and Tigers. Traded to the Angels after the 1969 season, Johnson capped his third consecutive season of hitting .312 or better by winning the American League batting title in 1970 with a .329 average.

Despite his success, Johnson's world began to crumble the following spring. I read in the newspapers that Alex had been fined repeatedly during spring training for "loafing" on the base paths and in the outfield, but when I visited the Angels in Palm Springs (on what had now become the last stop of my annual spring training tour), these fines were not discussed by Alex, or anyone else, including player rep Jim Fregosi. Alex's silence on the subject didn't surprise me. He had attended all spring training meetings since 1966 as well as other in-season meetings and rarely had much to say. Had I known at the time, however, that he was well on his way to a record twenty-five fines (totaling $3,750)—a telltale sign that he was deeply troubled—I would have surely sought him out.

Johnson somehow made it through spring training without being suspended. He even started the regular season with a bang, hitting so well in April that he was named the Angels' Player of the Month. But by May his erratic behavior had resurfaced. Manager Lefty Phillips fined Johnson several times for not taking outfield practice, then pulled him from games for not running out ground balls and for making lackadaisical throws from the outfield. Then, on one of California's first road trips of the season, Johnson made headlines nationwide. Odd as it may seem, Dick Miller, a sportswriter for the *Los Angeles Herald Examiner*, decided to play a practical joke on Johnson by hiding his bat before batting practice. Alex almost never lost sight of his precious hardwood. When he couldn't find his "stick" and heard several of his teammates (as well as Lefty Phillips) chuckling, he realized that he'd been the victim of a prank. Clued in on the joke by the bat boy, Alex confronted Miller, who admitted with a shrug that he had in fact hidden his bat. Johnson was already miffed at Miller. Earlier in the season, Miller, as official scorer, had given him an error on a line drive that Alex had lost in the lights. Alex felt the batter should have been credited with a hit. Now he located his bat and proceeded to pour coffee grounds into Miller's typewriter— saying, in effect, "Mess with the tools of *my* trade and I'll mess with *yours.*"

Needless to say, Johnson's already shaky relationship with the press hit rock bottom. Several of the beat writers who covered the Angels already considered Johnson surly and uncooperative; in fact, in 1970 Bill Shirley, the sports editor of the *Los Angeles Times*, wrote a formal protest to Angels' GM Dick Walsh, regarding Alex's (alleged) use of obscene language to one of his young reporters. After the coffee incident, many writers around the country, indignant over this "unprovoked attack" on "one of their own," raked Alex over the coals.

Not long after that, Alex was embroiled in another highly publicized incident when he accused utility infielder Chico Ruiz of pulling a pistol on him in the Angels' clubhouse. No one would corroborate Alex's story, and he was portrayed in the papers as hostile and deluded. But these initial reports left out several telling facts: Not only had Ruiz brandished a pistol at Alex, but the Angels had more guns in their clubhouse than the Jesse James gang. Tony Conigliaro had a shotgun in his locker, and Eddie Fisher, the owner of dozens of weapons, kept several guns in his.

Then again, what would you expect from a team owned by that old singing cowboy Gene Autry, a man known to tote a six-shooter into the clubhouse and routinely give guns to his players as gifts. California's PR people tried to downplay Autry's firearm fetish, so when Alex's gun charge surfaced, they emphatically denied it to the press. A staff employee of the Angels later admitted seeing Ruiz point a gun at Johnson, but the fact was never made public.

Johnson's version of the story was substantiated at the arbitration hearing months later when Dick Walsh was cross-examined. "Ruiz did point a gun," he admitted finally, "but the weapon wasn't loaded." (Walsh did say that Ruiz had shells for it in his locker.) Never mind that Walsh had issued a report to the press stating there was no gun or that he later admitted that "since there were no witnesses it was obvious that nothing could be served by going public with it." The way the story appeared one could only come to one of two conclusions: Either Alex Johnson had delusions or Alex Johnson was a liar. Walsh and the Angels knew for a fact that neither was true. Of course, allowing others to think ill of Alex Johnson beat having to admit that the club had lied.

Johnson's teammates and coaches refused to come to his aid. Manager Lefty Phillips denied that Angels players carried guns. "Johnson," he said, "doesn't give you his best effort, and he won't accept criticism from the other players, the coaches, or the manager." Even veteran reliever Eddie Fisher, a staunch union supporter, felt that Johnson was "jaking it"; in other words, he thought Alex just didn't want to play ball.

Not all players who are accused of dogging it encounter the degree of hostility Alex Johnson received from his teammates and others. My experience is that those in positions of authority in baseball have a tendency to assume that a black player is more likely to "jake it" than a white player. For example, a superstar on the Red Sox was widely rumored to be a player who didn't play with minor injuries or run out every ground ball, but he *never* faced anything like the amount of criticism and hostility that Johnson endured. And lest one think this a thing of the past, in 1989–90, when Mets right fielder Darryl Strawberry was in a slump, he was reviled by the press and fans alike, while his teammate, left fielder Kevin McReynolds, who temporarily experienced a marked performance drop-off at the same time, wasn't subjected to nearly the same critical onslaught.

Among Johnson's teammates, however, there were three players who seemed to understand what Alex was going through. They were Dave LaRoche, the relief pitcher and assistant player rep, Andy Messersmith, then a young pitcher on his way to his first twenty-win season, and Tony Conigliaro. "Tony C" was even quoted in *Sports Illustrated* as saying that he could tell that Alex was sick just by the way he walked. "He's so hurt inside," he said, "that it's terrifying."*

By June 15, the trading deadline, Johnson's relationship with club GM Dick Walsh had gone from lousy to worse. Walsh had tried, unsuccessfully, to trade Johnson, and attempted two weeks earlier to intimidate him, saying, in effect, that he would "blacklist" him if he didn't shape up. Walsh even called Alex's wife and asked her to use her influence to get him to behave better. An intensely private man, Johnson was incensed.

On June 16, 1971, Johnson was placed on the thirty-day "suspended list" for "failure to give his best efforts toward the winning of the club's baseball games." He was sent home to Detroit and suspended without pay.

The Players Association filed a grievance demanding that Johnson be placed on the disabled list at full pay. A player on the DL, whether he breaks his leg rounding third or in the bathtub or, as I contended, is emotionally disabled, like Alex, should get his full salary and full credit for his major league service. To me, this was legally, logically, and ethically sound, but it was a novel claim—at least novel to baseball. In baseball, it was claimed, a disability was only a physical condition.

---

*Conigliaro was trying to make a comeback from severe injuries caused by an errant fastball some years before. He died, sadly, of a heart attack in 1990.

Two weeks before the grievance meeting on July 21, Johnson flew to New York to tell me his side of the story. Once he started speaking, the words poured out of him like steam from a boiling teakettle. He showed up at nine A.M. and, except for a forty-five-minute lunch break, didn't stop talking until seven P.M. With him he had dozens of pieces of paper of all sizes—envelopes, ticket stubs, airline folders, matchbooks, you name it—filled with his grievances against management, the press, and even some of his teammates. Two things became quite clear: Many of Johnson's grievances were legitimate, and he had serious emotional problems.

I listened intently, taking notes about the events relevant to the fines and suspension. One incident, early in spring training, typified the misunderstanding between Alex and and Angels management. Struck by a foul ball that injured a nerve in his left hand, Johnson was told by the team doctor to take off a few days and, when he resumed playing, not to get his bandaged hand wet. Johnson tried to resume working out the next day, but when he started to sweat, left the field without telling anyone. The next day, the coaches bawled him out, but Alex didn't explain. Instead, he went to the outfield to shag flies. Soon he was sweating all over his bandage, found some shade, and again, without saying anything to anybody, sat down. Outfield coach Pete Reiser, the old Brooklyn Dodger who shortened his own career by recklessly running into walls chasing fly balls, confronted him. To which Alex replied, "I'm here not to sweat."

"Why," I asked, "didn't you try to explain *why* you did what you did?"

His response, which he would repeat over and over was, "It just wouldn't have done any good." I think he was talking about people's inability to understand him, but also about his inability to explain himself.

After talking to Alex, I called Joe Cronin in Boston. Cronin, who had been on hand when outfielder Jimmy Piersall was hospitalized after suffering a breakdown in 1951, was strangely unsympathetic.

"I don't see how the suspension can stand," I said. "Alex may be ill. We should determine that question first and then help him, not suspend him without pay."

"This is a terrible situation," he said gravely. "His behavior is hurting baseball."

"You can't think he's faking it, Joe. You were on hand when Jimmy Piersall initially had his emotional problems. Did you think Piersall was just fooling around when he ran around the bases backward?" (When Piersall, then with the Mets, smacked his hundredth career home run, he rounded the bases backward.)

"No, no," he said. "It's clear *he* wasn't. But that was, well, different." He never explained why.

To Cronin, our grievance on Johnson's behalf was setting a dangerous precedent for baseball. As nutty as it sounds, he felt that if we won the grievance, any player who was fined similarly would claim that he had had a mental breakdown.

I didn't know how to respond. Why would a player of Johnson's obvious talent play so far beneath himself? Sure, an injured or disgusted (or even hungover) player will occasionally half-ass it down the line on a routine ground ball, but did a former major leaguer like Cronin really think Johnson, or any highly skilled athlete, would alibi by saying he didn't hustle because he had had a nervous breakdown?

According to Joe Cronin, apparently so. He said that I was making a bad mistake by seeming to excuse players from playing as hard as they could, and that this was especially so in the case of players like Johnson. His comment astonished me. "What," I asked, "do you mean by 'players *like* Johnson'?" He didn't respond and terminated the conversation. I suppose I will never be sure what he meant.

Even though erratic behavior and its connection with emotional breakdown was something within Cronin's experience, and despite the fact that baseball's history was riddled with alcoholics, petty thieves, and other aberrant individuals, baseball officials acted as if they had never seen anything like this. Yet only the year before, Tony Horton, Cleveland's talented first baseman, had popped out to Thurman Munson on one of Steve Hamilton's high-arching "folly-floaters," dropped his bat, and *crawled* back to the dugout. Everyone laughed, thinking Horton was clowning around, until a short time later, when he left baseball and was hospitalized for a while. In his book *When in Doubt, Fire the Manager*, Alvin Dark called it "the most sorrowful incident I was ever involved in in my baseball career." The simple fact is, the macho world of professional baseball refused to recognize emotional weakness. Not only were baseball executives prejudiced against players with emotional problems, they pretended they didn't exist.

This became clear at the grievance meeting held in our office on July 21. Dick Moss and I told John Gaherin, Joe Cronin, and Dick Walsh that we planned to contest the fines and the suspension, informing them that we had retained a psychiatrist from Wayne State University, Dr. Lawrence E. Jackson, to examine and work with Johnson. No matter. The Player Relations Committee held to the position that we hadn't proved that Walsh's charge of "malingering" was untrue. Regardless of the PRC's official position, I knew that John Gaherin had tried to get the club to withdraw its disciplinary action and settle the case. The club refused, and neither Kuhn nor Cronin had the guts to buck general manager Dick Walsh or Angels owner Gene Autry and end the persecution of a player who was ill.

The hearings before the arbitration panel were scheduled in Anaheim on August 28 and in Detroit three days later. Roughly two weeks before the hearings, the Angels came to New York to play the Yankees. Jim Fregosi told me that John Gaherin had held a meeting in Bowie Kuhn's office with ten of the Angels players and all the coaches, including manager Lefty Phillips, to "discuss" Johnson's upcoming arbitration. I was incensed. I called Gaherin immediately and said, "If I discover that you're trying to coerce potential witnesses, I'll file an unfair labor practice charge against you faster than you can blink!"

Gaherin denied the accusation, but I made plans to counteract his move by meeting with the Angels in the visitors' clubhouse before the game with the Yanks. I made several simple points as clearly as I could. "There's no problem with any of you testifying," I said. "The case doesn't hinge on *what* happened, but rather on *why.*" I told them what I had learned about Johnson's case, including the likelihood of his emotional illness. I think it's fair to say that most of the Angels didn't grasp the depth of Johnson's psychological problems, although after the meeting Dave LaRoche and Andy Messersmith thanked me for coming and made it clear that they thought Alex had gotten a "bum deal."

Then, speaking of bum deals, Commissioner Bowie Kuhn changed Alex's status—without a hearing—from the suspended to the restricted list. Of all the moves taken against Johnson to that point, this was the most arbitrary and improper. The restricted list had been created for a player under contract who failed to report to his club. Kuhn's move, no doubt, was intended to drive Alex out of baseball. A player on the suspended list can be kept out of uniform for only thirty days; a player on the restricted list can be kept there indefinitely.

The arbitration hearing began on August 28 at the Grand Hotel in Anaheim. Management's first witness was Lefty Phillips. The Angels' skipper laid it on thick, citing all of Alex's offenses dating back to 1970, the year he won the batting title. Phillips was especially embarrassed, he said, because Johnson didn't run out a ground ball when President Nixon was at an Angels game in Anaheim, an act of civil disobedience that cost Johnson $200. Phillips criticized Johnson's regimen of rigorous calisthenics, his habit of carrying his bat around with him, and his lack of zeal for exhibition games.

Walsh testified next. An imperious, arrogant man, Walsh was also, according to Johnson, extremely hypocritical. And after his testimony, I had to agree. Walsh began by saying that Johnson was lazy and his actions willful. Yet, as Barry Rona questioned him, he seemed to forget what he had said and why he was there and stated that Johnson always arrived at the ballpark early and got out to the batting cage to hit against "Iron Mike" (the automatic pitching machine, not Mike Tyson). He continued, like an adoring fan, to describe Johnson's pregame routine. "He'd put 'Iron Mike' at the regulation distance [60'6"], hit thirty, forty, fifty line drives, stop, load the machine, move it in five feet, repeat the routine until it was forty-five feet away—and still he'd hit these vicious line drives." And this continued, he volunteered, during Alex's troubles in 1971. If Walsh felt that was an indication of a lazy ballplayer, I'd be curious to know what he considered a motivated one.

The hearing, which continued in Detroit three days later, was gut-wrenching. Johnson and his psychiatrist, Dr. Lawrence Jackson, were the chief witnesses. Alex handled himself rather well, although after one of Dick Moss's questions, he rambled on for minutes at a time. Sadly, later on, he broke down, pouring out every bad experience he ever had in baseball and even before he entered the game. He'd been subjected to racism in and out of baseball (not-yet integrated hotels, swimming pools, restaurants), and he had been treated unfairly, he felt, by coaches, managers, and owners. Walsh's maltreatment was just the last straw. By the end of his testimony, it was obvious Alex needed psychiatric help. It wasn't so much that what he said about racism wasn't valid; it was that he seemed completely lacking in ability to cope with it.

Dr. Jackson, who had met with Johnson over a period of five weeks, testified that much of Alex's detailed (and often irrelevant) explanation of his troubles was a way to hide feelings of persecution and self-doubt. Johnson suffered from severe reactive depression,* said Jackson. Playing baseball was out of the question for the remainder of the 1971 season, but with continued psychotherapy he felt that Johnson could be fully recovered by next season. He said: "Johnson has a great deal of pride in himself and for the profession of baseball." And he concluded, "I see nothing that is willful [or that] falls in the category of malingering."

After all the witnesses had been called, it was up to arbitrator Lew Gill to reach a decision. He did, almost a month later, on September 28, 1971. Gill, Gaherin, and I met in Philadelphia to discuss his written opinion before it became final. Gill ruled in our favor, reversing Kuhn and stating that Johnson should be placed on the disabled list with full pay and full credit for major league service retroactive to the date of the suspension. But Gill decided to throw management a bone, and upheld the $3,750 in fines levied against Alex. "It should be said with emphasis," he wrote, "that this ruling is not intended to suggest that players may now avoid disciplinary action simply by asserting that their conduct is due to emotional stress or mental illness." (Gill had bought management's absurd notion. The record shows that not one player in the twenty years since the Johnson case has claimed disability due to emotional illness.)

For several long minutes I sat silent. Then I exploded. Gill, like many "neutral" arbitrators, had a tendency to "split the baby,"

---

*A diagnosis seconded by management's psychiatric expert, Dr. Jonathan Himmelhoch, an assistant professor of psychiatry and pharmacology at Yale Medical School.

trying, if he could, to placate both sides. (Either side could fire the arbitrator after a case.) I carefully cited chapter and verse on past baby-splitting decisions of his and stated that this time he had gone too far. "We've just heard countless hours of testimony detailing Alex's illness; he was fined more times during spring training than any player has been during an entire career! How can you justify these fines when *two medical experts agree that Alex was ill?*"

Gill said very little in reply. He felt I had attacked his integrity. I had not. If I had thought he lacked integrity, I would have fired him. Instead, I voted yes to his decision to place Johnson on the disabled list and registered a dissenting opinion on his upholding the fines. Almost a year later, Gill resigned.

Once the facts of Johnson's illness became public, the decision was hailed by the sporting press as an important precedent. And it was, I suppose, given the insensitive way baseball dealt with the problem. I, on the other hand, thought it was crystal clear that Johnson had serious emotional problems and initially should have been placed on the disabled list. Instead, as I've written, Lefty Phillips, Dick Walsh, Gene Autry, Joe Cronin, and Bowie Kuhn disregarded his obvious illness, encouraged the press to ridicule Johnson, suspended him without pay, and sought to bar him permanently by placing him on the restricted list.

At the end of the 1971 season, the Angels fired Phillips and all of his coaches. Right behind was Dick Walsh, even though he had four years remaining on his seven-year contract. Walsh, just for the record, called Gill's reversing the suspension "completely without justification."

Johnson followed the recommended treatment during the winter and resumed his career in 1972 with Cleveland, where he struggled at the plate. He spent almost two years with Texas. He played for the Yankees starting near the end of the 1974 season and in 1975, and finished up his career in his hometown with the Tigers. He never regained his great batting touch, although he hit .291 and stole twenty bases in 1974. More important, he was able to resume his career and better handle the pressures inside and outside of baseball.

One final word on the Johnson case. Even though Jackie Robinson broke baseball's color barrier in 1947, his presence hid the fact that major league baseball made little progress toward true integration for decades afterward. The increased number of black and Latin players was, in effect, a foundation for progress rather than progress itself. Their presence allowed baseball (and perhaps the country) to feel good about itself. Too good. Twenty years after Jackie Robinson endured torment and ridicule, baseball owners refused to advance blacks to management positions—not a single field manager, general manager, or high club official was hired for two decades. Sadly, what was true of management was, generally speaking, true of the players as well. When Robinson made his major league debut, there was talk among the players of organizing a *strike:* Apparently, players who didn't have enough sense of purpose to unite and organize for their own improved conditions were ready to strike to keep blacks off the field. And to go one step further, prior to 1966, the same was true of the Players Association organization. It was a company-dominated outfit with no real structure and had never had a black player representative. While I don't know how the players' "legal advisors" (J. Norman Lewis and Judge Robert Cannon) felt about civil rights, I do know that they never lifted a finger to talk to players about a more representative player group, and they never got involved in a grievance of a black player. It should come as no surprise that by the mid-1960s blacks and Latin players didn't have confidence that the Players Association was any different than before or, for that matter, different from other organizations and institutions in America.

Remember that Johnson's case came before Curt Flood's suit against Bowie Kuhn. And after we went to bat for Johnson, there was a whole new attitude among blacks about what the Association was all about. The Players Association hadn't suddenly become a savior—and I had not become a white knight—but the Johnson case was a bridge to a new era, a passage to a new feeling of solidarity.

8...

Card Wars

ORGANIZING A NEW UNION is a formidable task. Not only do the organizers have to counter the prejudices and fears of the employees they are trying to unite, but they inevitably have to contend with the employer's opposition and hostility. The organizer's job in baseball had to deal with that and much more. When I was hired as executive director, this new, theoretically independent organization had the financial stability of a third world nation. Bowie Kuhn later wrote wistfully about the "advantages" I had in the union's struggle with the owners. Here's what we had: no money, no office, no staff, and no union consciousness. Even the players who were the activists had no real idea of how to finance the organization or what its functions should be.

Early in 1966, the Association had a makeshift dues structure of $50 a year. If all the players, coaches, managers, and trainers supported the organization (and a considerable number did not), dues would provide about one-fifth of the budget of $150,000 a year that they had decided the Association needed to become a

• 142 •

self-sufficient union. To understand how *dependent* the union was, consider that the leading player representatives had already approached the commissioner and several owners with a plan to support the organization by each year drawing $150,000 from the All-Star Game. When I heard that the owners had approved this plan, my jaw dropped. Financing a union with employers' money is illegal. Both the provider of the funds and the recipients can be punished with a jail sentence—but it was common to ignore such trifles in the world of baseball. After all, only a misguided few regarded the game as a business.

When the players finally elected an experienced union man several months later, management shot this "charitable" arrangement out of the park like a hanging curve. Stated simply, the owners figured, if they could starve the union financially, I would disappear, and the players would revert to their pattern of accepting whatever happened.

Not until December 1966—after I had successfully established a new dues structure ($344 a year), obtained individual deduction authorizations from the players, negotiated a change in the pension plan, making it noncontributory, and negotiated a check-off agreement for the payment of dues totaling about $200,000 a year—was the issue resolved.

This still left us with *one* financial problem. The dues would begin to be transmitted during the 1967 season, and that was about five months away. Until then the union would have *no* source of income at all. When I started on the job on July 1, 1966, the Association had $5,400 in a checking account with Chemical Bank of New York and a battered filing cabinet in Frank Scott's office in the Biltmore Hotel on Forty-fourth Street and Madison Avenue. Scott was a commercial agent for some players (making arrangements with companies to pay players for product endorsements) and performed some administrative functions for the Players Association.

Luckily, we had anticipated this problem. At the 1966 meeting of the player reps during the All-Star break, we tried to come up with some plan to stay afloat during this interim period. Frank vaguely recalled an old baseball promotion which involved players' pictures on cards inside boxes of Wheaties and suggested we try a similar idea to produce the necessary funds. I was concerned about anything which might interfere with an individual player's endorsements, but I thought perhaps we could develop a promotional program that involved the pictures or signatures of major league players as a group and which would be structured so as not to reduce individual players' endorsement opportunities.

While sifting through the Association's one file cabinet, I kept coming across references to Topps, the bubble-gum trading-card company. There were form contracts and records of payment to players and records of a dispute with another card company, Fleer, in Philadelphia. Topps had signed contracts with almost every major league player and many minor league hopefuls as well. A player received $5 to sign and $125 a year for each year he played in the majors for exclusive use by Topps of his photo for trading cards, either sold alone or sold in conjunction with a confectionary product. Players didn't get a percentage of sales. Nothing, not even free bubble gum. Additionally, the structure of the contract was unconscionable.

Back in 1962, Fleer had filed a complaint with the Federal Trade Commission, claiming Topps had a straight monopoly, a violation of the Clayton Antitrust Act. Although the trial examiner said Topps was guilty, the decision was reversed on appeal. Sometime during my first year with the Association, Donald Peck, the president of Fleer, contacted me to express his frustration with Topps. "Competing with them," he said, "is like running in quicksand." Fleer had managed to sign a handful of players to nonexclusive contracts, but these agreements could not take effect until the player's contract with Topps expired, and good luck trying to find out the date of expiration. Topps *claimed* that they gave players copies of their contracts, but we never found a player who had one. Peck had some players write to Topps and ask for copies. Topps refused them. A player could come to the Topps plant in Brooklyn, they said, if he wanted to *look* at his own contract, but he couldn't take a copy from the premises. Somehow I couldn't picture Carl Yastrzemski driving to Brooklyn after a Red Sox–Yankee game to check the fine print of his contract.

Since no company other than Topps could sell the players' pictures alone or with a confectionary product, Fleer tried selling cards with a cookie that had so little sugar in it that it was not technically a confectionary product. A good idea—except that the cookies tasted like dog biscuits. They tried selling the cards with a balloon—and that went over like a lead cookie. I could see no reason why there shouldn't be two or more competitors—all their talk about the market not being big enough to support competition sounded like the usual rationalization in defense of a monopoly. From the FTC hearings I learned that Topps annual sales totaled millions of dollars, making the sums they paid the players seem even more paltry.

After gathering the facts, I called Joel Shorin, Topps president, to arrange a meeting. We spoke frankly, culminating in my proposal that we redraft the form contracts and make appropriate revisions in the payments to players—including a percentage of sales as well as amendments in the "rights" provisions so that Topps no longer owned exclusive rights to the use of players' pictures.

Shorin listened calmly and spoke coolly. "There will be no changes," he said, "because, honestly, I don't see any muscle in your position. Topps has the players signed to [bubble gum] contracts, and I don't see what you can do about it."

His response didn't surprise me. Shorin was a bright and dedicated businessman. For many years he had operated only one way: signing up an inexperienced player with no knowledge of the potential value of his name and picture, and who was flattered just to have his photo on a trading card. And men like Joel Shorin don't change their practice simply because men like me make arguments that have merit. They change, as Shorin said, when they can see your "muscle." I understood his position very well. I thanked Shorin for his time and told him I would be in touch.

Topps was by no means the first company to sell baseball cards with bubble gum—trading cards date back to the 1870s, back to the days when tobacco companies used players' pictures to sell their products. Like millions of other kids, I collected picture cards of major leaguers and memorized the stats on the back of the cards when I was a child, but once I stopped feeling nostalgic, I started getting angry. Topps had, in effect, a perpetual reserve clause. After a player had been in the majors for two years, Topps would give him a contract renewal—a check for $75—insuring that the player was always three to five years away from being free of the contract. Even worse, Topps maintained that the contract provided that while he was under contract with them, he couldn't sign with another company even if the second company's contract was not to be effective until after the Topps contract had expired! It was a microcosm of the position the owners had the players in with the reserve clause.

Topps was aggressive, signing up most players while they were still in the minors. The company had its own scouting system and handed out gifts to managers, coaches, trainers, and establishment scouts, then signed the most promising young talent to five-year deals that didn't take effect until the player made it to the majors. If the player was sent down, the time spent in the minors didn't count against the five years.

Topps engineered all kinds of subterranean deals. Players had the option of getting paid in cash or applying the payment to a "gift" selected from a color catalog with everything from radios and television sets to luggage, refrigerators, and lawn furniture: a kind of S&H Green Stamps setup, if you will. This enabled Topps to make discount deals with manufacturers as well as pay off resistant name players who were dissatisfied with the paltry $125 figure.

Topps also gave card contracts to major league coaches and trainers, never intending to use them (though a card with a third-base coach, say, Yogi Berra, tugging on his ear, or a trainer taping Mantle's brittle knees would be worth a mint today), but those contracts provided loyal Topps employees like Sy Berger access to the clubhouses. Berger wandered around the clubhouse like he owned the place. He was in there more often than I was, and I had a right to be there under the collective bargaining agreement. The only way he could have done that was with management's permission.

As controlling and venal as the Topps contracts were, we at the Players Association had more pressing problems. How were we to raise money until the union dues structure became effective? Our prospects didn't look promising. Only a surprisingly small handful of players had endorsement contracts; almost all the players were tied to Topps; and except for a dimly remembered deal with

Wheaties, baseball had no history of a group promotion. Nevertheless, a group promotion was our best bet.

To get one going, we needed to get written authorizations from the players that would enable the Players Association to act as the contracting party. Dick and I designed the authorization, making sure any player under contract to a group licensee who received an individual endorsement offer from a rival company had the right to accept that offer unless the group licensee agreed to match it. In other words, if we had a group promotion with Kellogg's and a competitor offered Mickey Mantle a contract, Kellogg's had to match the competitor's offer or forfeit the right to use Mantle's name or picture. This concept of individual authorization, just like the checkoff agreement, required that we get each player's signature. Just as I had done during spring training, I visited each club in September of 1966. The players backed the group licensing concept wholeheartedly, and also signed dues deduction authorizations.

Armed with the authorizations, Frank Scott, a longtime commercial agent for players with respect to endorsements, went to work. When Coca-Cola expressed interest, Frank and I met with several of their executives and negotiated a deal that paid $60,000 a year for two years for the company's right to use the pictures of five hundred major league players on the underside of their bottle caps. (Today those caps sell at card shows for as much as $30 each.) The contract also provided an additional $20,000 annually for individual players who agreed to make appearances for the company, as well as $10,000 a year for Frank's commission.

Before the ink was dry on the contract, the first problem occurred. Coca-Cola wanted to use pictures of the players in uniform; however, to do that, major league team owners had to grant permission for them to use the team logo, and for that they wanted a fee. Coke balked. They felt the owners' request was exorbitant. This, of course, didn't bode well for our dwindling funds. When Coke finally accepted our proposal to airbrush the logos from the player's caps, the owners were removed from consideration, the deal went through, our financial troubles were solved, *and* the licensing program of the Players Association was born.

The Coca-Cola money carried us through the winter of 1966 and the spring of 1967. In fact, the entire fee from Coca-Cola became surplus. According to what I had written in the licensing authorization, all money not needed to meet the operating budget of the Players Association would be distributed to the players pro rata. During spring training in 1968, every player, manager, coach, and trainer who was in the majors for the entire 1967 season received a check for one hundred dollars; those on the big clubs for only part of the season received a proportionate amount. It was not a lot of money, but salaries in those days were miserable. And since players received only expense money during spring training, they were happy to have the extra dollars.

That licensing arrangement accomplished something even more important. It demonstrated that there was a potential for making the union financially secure; if it were developed properly, we could eliminate the possibility that the owners might bust the union by hitting it financially. In 1990 the licensing program generated more than $57 million, and licensing revenue paid to the union's members through the years exceeds, many times over, all the dues paid by all the members of the Players Association from the beginning of the union until now.

Throughout our dealings with Coca-Cola, I never forgot about Topps. I told the player reps how they were being shortchanged and described how Joel Shorin reacted when I reasoned with him. I said, "The only leverage you have is not to sign renewals. Eventually Topps will have contracts with no one." Painting as accurate a picture as I could, I also reported that this could cost some players five to six hundred dollars in lost payments from Topps; others would reap nothing for their sacrifice because they might no longer be in baseball by the time we reached an equitable arrangement. But, I predicted, if the players demonstrated solidarity by not signing contract renewals with Topps, the company would come around and want to negotiate a settlement that was more fair.

Sy Berger got wind of what was going on at these meetings and changed his schedule in order to speak to a few clubs before I did. Nevertheless, once the 1968 season was underway, players were declining across the board to sign a contract or a contract renewal.

Sometime after the All-Star break, I received a phone call from

Joel Shorin. "I see your muscle," he said. "Let's sit down and talk." I think it's fair to say he now understood my position perfectly.

We started our meetings in September. After a long, hard fight (Shorin's attorney had a heart attack and died right in the middle of the talks: I'm a tough negotiator, but not that tough), Topps agreed to double the payment from $125 to $250 per member and, more important, pay 8 percent on sales up to $4 million a year and 10 percent on sales above that figure. This was a real bonanza. Sales kept climbing. The royalties in the first year came to about $320,000 (on sales of approximately $4 million) and almost twenty-five years later, with five trading-card companies under contract, stand around $50 million a year. That baseball card collectors are making so much money today is an outgrowth of the companies' making so much. (Though it's not just baseball. Collecting has grown phenomenally over the last twenty years and has included everything from Super Bowl ticket stubs to Frank Merriwell novels to Elvis Presley memorabilia. But it started with baseball.) The March 1991 sale of one Honus Wagner trading card at a Sotheby auction for a reported $451,000 indicates that the collecting phenomenon is still flourishing.

We didn't get everything we wanted, and we didn't end the Topps monopoly. (That came later.) But where Topps literally had had all the rights on *any* pictures sold alone, it didn't anymore. We got specific language that allowed the players to grant the use of their pictures (of a certain size) to other companies.

This, however, didn't snuff another raging controversy. The Players Association began signing licensing agreements with companies giving them the right to use the players' picture on trading cards with "nonconfectionary" products. Joel Shorin, who was as protective of Topps as a mother hen, went nuts. He fought us over an agreement with Kellogg's to use trading-card-size 3–D pictures of the players inside the cereal box and threatened a lawsuit over pictures on boxes of Milk Duds. (Shorin argued that since the boxes had dotted lines around the players' pictures, the producer of Milk Duds was selling players' pictures.)

It didn't take us long to see that Shorin was trying to knock out all competition even when Topps' contract rights were not violated. And it was just one fight after another; some we worked out, some we didn't. Sometimes we dared Shorin to sue us because his objections were not valid. Though I was learning a lot about licensing—something I had previously known nothing about—I really didn't welcome it. It wasn't part of the job I was hired to do, I had no expertise in licensing or marketing, and, besides, the office was understaffed. It became almost a full-time job just administering the agreement, handling players' grievances with licensing companies, and dealing with pirate manufacturers— businesses that used the players' pictures illegally on T-shirts, glasses, gasoline promotions, you name it. Which was why, not long after, we decided to branch out by hiring an experienced firm to get new business—an exclusive licensing agent of the Major League Baseball Players Association.

Around 1968 or so there was another significant development— the owners set up the Major League Baseball Promotions Corporation to compete with us. The National Football League had a licensing arm—not the players', but management's—and a very successful one at that. Baseball did some licensing on an individual club basis, especially the Yankees, but baseball had nothing that pulled together the licensing rights of the leagues and the clubs into one entity—that came after the players began marketing themselves. Because we had the rights to the players and Major League Baseball Promotions had the rights to the clubs' logos, things became complicated. The two groups could have cooperated with one another, but major league baseball didn't think the town was big enough for both of us. They would get wind of a manufacturer who was interested in using players' pictures and instead try to talk him into using the owners' logos. What manufacturers wanted, of course, was both.

So the Players Association and MLBP went their separate ways. Through the years there were some disputes, but we were able to work out many of them.

In the middle of all this, Fleer offered the Players Association a $25,000 advance and 5 percent of receipts on sales of 5″ × 7″ glossy pictures. Topps no longer held the exclusive rights on pictures of this size or larger, but they did have the right of first refusal. I presented Fleer's offer to Shorin, but he wasn't interested. It wasn't the paltry $25,000, Shorin said. "The pictures won't sell. There will be large returns of merchandise, and worse, it would impede trading card sales." Although I was used to

Shorin's exaggerated reactions, I had to agree with him this time. So did the players.

I told this to Don Peck, who kept mumbling about how terrible this all was. Before you could say "five-by-seven glossy," we were served with papers: Fleer was suing both Topps and the Players Association on the grounds that we had banded together to keep Fleer out of the market. I had to laugh. Shorin had threatened us with lawsuits many times, claiming that our licensing program was a restraint of trade, and now we were codefendants in an antitrust suit! The card wars had intensified.

What happened next still baffles me. The industry of baseball, surely in violation of the antitrust laws, was declared exempt by the federal courts, while the Players Association—the representative of the longstanding victims of the Supreme Court's whitewashing of the owners' antitrust violations—became a defendant in an antitrust action...*and we lost.* The federal court ruled in *Fleer v. Topps and M.L.B.P.A.* that we were in restraint of trade, ordered the Players Association to offer to sign contracts with other interested bubble-gum card companies, and said Topps must grant us this right despite the fact that they had had exclusive rights.

Ironically, we lost the case *and accomplished our main objective.* But imagine the stupidity of such a decision. The record, and plain common sense, showed that the Players Association could only benefit from breaking the Topps monopoly, and, in fact, it had struggled to do just that. Regardless, a federal court decided that the Association had joined with Topps to *prevent* competition. Go figure.

Anyway, after the court's decision, Fleer rushed in with an offer, as did a third company, Donruss. So instead of one contract, we had three.

Shorin had always claimed Armageddon if something like this were to happen. His marketing studies had consistently shown that the market for trading cards wouldn't grow and, in fact, if viable competitors were able to enter the market, the total sales of cards would decline. For all I know, he may really have believed this nonsense. He seemingly had convinced himself that the Topps monopoly—by virtue of its contracts with the major league players—had succeeded in building and maintaining the largest possible market for trading cards. It followed, therefore, that it was in the interests of the players, the company, and the consumers that the status quo remain.

Nothing I said could convince him otherwise. I maintained it was far more likely that strong competition would result in an improved product, better merchandising, more realistic pricing, and a larger market for the product than had ever existed before—and that this would clearly be in the best interests of everybody. (Soon after the 1980 federal district court decision, sales went wild; today there are five major card companies, and card sales are still climbing to new records.)

Our trading card wars—competition against monopoly—paralleled the union's struggle against the owners in baseball. Both Topps and the owners gave lip service to free enterprise, but both have shown a decided preference for a lack of competition. I have little doubt that if organized baseball were opened to competitors, as was the case with Topps, the results would be similar: The brand of baseball shown to the fans would be superior, it would be promoted more effectively (probably on a worldwide basis), the competition would be more intense, there would be more leagues, franchises, and players, and fans would benefit by paying less at the box office.

In any event, the Players Association filed an appeal in the circuit court to clear our name as violators of antitrust. We won. The United States Court of Appeals for the Third Circuit reversed the lower court's decision, finding, among other things, that there was no basis for deciding that the Players Association had conspired to keep Fleer out of the card market in violation of the antitrust laws. The ruling, incidentally, didn't affect the long-term deals we had signed.

These court decisions are the bases of the giant card shops. And this was the beginning of the card boom. The card wars were over, and with peace came prosperity.

9 . . .

The Six-Thousand-Dollar Man

RICHARD MOSS became the general counsel of the Players Association in January 1967. A graduate of Harvard Law School, he had been a first-rate associate counsel at the Steelworkers Union for six years and a passionate Pittsburgh Pirates fan since childhood. One month after he eagerly took the job in baseball, we embarked on our first spring training trip together. It was, to paraphrase Humphrey Bogart in *Casablanca,* the start of a beautiful working relationship—one that lasted ten and a half years.

The tour in 1967 was a marked contrast to the one I had made by myself the previous spring. That trip was filled with one obstacle after another; even some of the player reps—the people who had nominated me as executive director—made derogatory statements to the press about unions and union men. It was hard not to think: "What am I doing here?"

The second time around, I was able to report not what the union *could* do, but what it had *done.* We had a new pension agreement and a dues structure in place, supported by more than

99 percent of the players. We had doubled benefits in one fell swoop, including the largest increase in retirement and health-care benefits that had ever been achieved. The Association now had a staff (albeit a tiny one) and an office all its own in the Seagram Building in New York. We had also set our sights on negotiating the first basic agreement in all of sports—a contract that would cover all the players' benefits, rights, and working conditions not covered by the pension plan.

It was, as I recall, a memorable spring.

One of the first stops was the Yankees' camp in Fort Lauderdale. After meeting with the players, I was leaving the clubhouse when the most elegant ballplayer of his era—perhaps of *any* era— approached me in the doorway. "Hello, Mr. Miller," he said, extending his hand. "I'm Joe DiMaggio."

Rarely has an introduction been more unnecessary. Joe was working with the Yankees as a batting instructor for a few weeks, and though I had hated the Yankees as a kid (you had to if you loved the Dodgers), I was thrilled to meet him. I had always enjoyed watching DiMaggio play. As I grew older, I was also impressed by his attempts to break the mold of the obedient player who would accept whatever salary was offered him. In the late 1930s, DiMaggio was coming off, back to back, two of the most phenomenal seasons any player has ever had. After those two years, DiMaggio walked into the Yankee front office and asked for $40,000 a year for his next contract. Management said, "Sorry, Joe," citing the fact that the great Lou Gehrig only made $40,000. DiMaggio paused, and was said to have replied, "Well, that means Lou is underpaid too." (The outcome was predictable in those days: Joe held out for weeks until Opening Day and was compelled to accept a grossly inadequate salary or be forced out of the game.)

In all, Joe DiMaggio had twelve glorious seasons—he missed three seasons during the war—and went on to become one of the first players to be paid $100,000 a year. In 1951, his thirteenth season, he suffered from a recurring bone spur in his heel, hit .263, and retired, because, in his own words, "he couldn't be Joe DiMaggio anymore." He was wrong; he would always be Joe DiMaggio.

Considering his stature in baseball and as a public figure,

DiMaggio was unusually soft-spoken and unassuming, almost retiring, but at the age of fifty-two, the tall, trim, gray-haired Hall-of-Famer was still speaking about players' rights. He described the shortcomings of his (and other former players') medical and dental coverage because they were no longer covered by the Major League Baseball Players Benefit Plan. (Health-care benefits were not extended to former players at that time.) He was also concerned about the inadequacy of his pension entitlement and asked if the increased retirement benefits I had negotiated a few months earlier would apply to him if he returned to baseball as a full-time coach.

After I had answered his question, he stepped back, pointed to a ragged patch in his baggy pinstripes, and said: "Take a look at this uniform."

It was poorly stitched, ill fitting, and nearly worn through. In fact, most company softball teams were better outfitted.

"I think I might have deserved something better," he said with a slight edge to his voice.

As we talked, we walked back into the clubhouse, now deserted except for one player who sat by himself taping his left knee. His right leg was already heavily wrapped from calf to thigh. The player was DiMaggio's heir to center field, Mickey Mantle. From the thighs down, Mantle looked like a mummy. Where, I wondered, was the trainer? Why was no one helping him get ready for the workout? Staring at Mantle's bandaged legs, I thought not so much of the tremendous power he once possessed from both sides of the plate, but of his fantastic speed on the bases and in chasing down fly balls in New York's expansive outfield. By 1967, however, Mantle was a gimpy thirty-six-year-old first baseman with sixty-six-year-old legs.

I was surprised by how much the scene affected me. It seemed wrong. Watching these two all-time greats walk slowly out to the field, I couldn't help but agree with DiMaggio: He deserved better. So did Mantle. So did all the players.

It was satisfying to see that the players had a new attitude toward the Association; "union" was no longer considered a dirty word, and many of the players now referred to the Association as "the players' union." We still, however, had a long way to go. Like most unorganized employees, the players were very reluctant to talk about their salaries with each other. Which was the way management wanted it. The less the players knew, the easier it was for the owners to manipulate them. Employee ignorance about salaries eliminates employee pressure to correct inequities.

My first problem with the salary issue was rather serious: I had no idea what the players were making. The minimum salary in 1967 was ridiculously low—$6,000 a year. In order to assess the impact of raising the minimum I needed to know how many players were at that level and how many were at various levels above it. As the sole collective bargaining representative of the players, the Players Association had a legal right to this information for bargaining purposes. But in baseball, rights are often conveniently ignored. The owners had no intention of supplying the information. When I pressed Joe Cronin, Warren Giles, and Bowie Kuhn about it, they looked at me as if I were speaking a foreign tongue: Why on earth would the head of the players' union need to know what the people he represented were making?

Not only was there confusion and secrecy about the minimum salary (Tom Seaver, the Rookie of the Year in 1967, assumed it was $7,500 because that's what the Mets were paying him), few players had any idea what salaries were around the two leagues. Many didn't even know what their teammates were paid! Years later, I heard Mickey Mantle say that when he found out that Yogi Berra and Whitey Ford were making $50,000, he felt guilty because he was being paid $100,000!

Even more outrageous than a $6,000 minimum was the fact that it had risen just $1,000 in twenty years. One thousand dollars since 1947! I could have pursued the matter of obtaining salary information with the National Labor Relations Board, but I didn't want to take the time. I also wanted to let the players see for themselves that the more they knew, the better off they would be, come contract time.

If the owners wouldn't tell me the salaries, I'd have to ask the players. I wasn't interested in *who* made *what* (that would come later and prove to be significant), I just needed to know *how much*. So at the end of each team meeting I asked the player rep to ask each player on his team to write his current salary on a blank piece of paper, without signing his name. The results were to be sent to our New York office by the player reps.

Not long after I returned to New York, the Dodgers came to town to play the Mets, and L.A.'s player rep, Ron Fairly, called to ask if he could deliver the results in person. Fairly showed up the next day, closed my office door behind him, and handed me an envelope full of salary slips. He was upset. "Buzzie Bavasi [the Dodger's GM] told me that after Koufax, Drysdale, and Wills, I was the highest paid Dodger. He said if I got paid more, I would throw the team's salary scale out of whack. Do you know where I rank?"

I shook my head.

"Eighth!" he exclaimed. (The year before, Fairly had played in 158 games, led the club in RBIs, and was second behind Wills in batting average.)

All I could do was shrug. Fairly's salary education had begun.

When all of the returns were in, we tallied the figures: The *average* salary of the five hundred major league players in 1967 was $19,000 a year. The *median* was $17,000 (that is, half of all the players earned less and half more). Seven percent of the players were at the minimum salary; thirty-five started the season at $6,000 (traditionally the salary paid only to rookies). A larger number of players were paid only slightly higher figures—$7,200, $7,500, $8,000; *one-third* of all players were at $10,000 or less; and more than *40* percent were paid $12,000 or less. Obviously, a raise in the minimum salary to, say, $10,000 or $12,000 a year would affect a great many players and *all* of the owners.

Given the compressed nature of baseball's salary structure, pushing the minimum up in succeeding negotiations would affect not just players at the low end of the scale but those at every level. From 1967 to 1976—when free-agency rights began—raising the minimum required a struggle each time. Prior to 1976 individual players had no real bargaining power at contract time; hence the importance of the Players Association in the struggle to raise the minimum salary.

Getting the players to understand this connection was one of my chief aims that spring. To make my point, I often used the following (hypothetical) example. Imagine, I told the players, the impact on your salary if the minimum was raised from $6,000 to *$100,000* a year. It usually took a minute or two for the players to stop laughing. In those days, the top salary any club would pay was $100,000 a year. This was, mind you, an "unofficial" ceiling paid only to superstars like Ted Williams and Joe DiMaggio, and, later, Mantle and Mays.

The idea of a rookie making $100,000 a year was simply fantastic. In 1966, Bobby Bonds was a twenty-year-old rookie making $6,000 a year. Had I told him that his son, if he made it to the major leagues, would make as a rookie what Bobby's teammate Willie Mays was paid—he would have rightly told me to take a hike. And had I added that his son, if he became an outstanding player, would be guaranteed millions of dollars a year—more in one season than the great Willie Mays would make during his *entire* career—Bobby Bonds would have concluded that I needed psychiatric help.

Twenty-four years later—in 1990—the minimum salary negotiated in the basic agreement was $100,000 a year. And Bobby's son, Barry, the 1990 NL MVP, is an All-Star making millions a year. The descendants of the $6,000 man have become $100,000 men and more. And the union produced that salary structure.

In 1967, of course, that was pure fantasy. The players, responding to my explanations, approved a demand for a minimum of $12,000 a year. But throughout that season, the owners, league presidents, and attorneys did their best to delay coming to grips with the issue. They even refused outright to bargain for an extended period. With nowhere else to turn, I began to present our case publicly, explaining to the press that the minimum salary in baseball had failed to keep pace with trends in industry and in other sports or with the rise in the cost of living over the last decade. Even *New York Daily News* columnist Dick Young (before he started bashing the union as a matter of course) called on the owners to raise the minimum. He wrote: "How many Lords of Baseball have priced groceries lately?" (When Young wrote a line like that, you remembered it.)

Baseball, however, was not the only sport in flux. The National Basketball Association had the high-scoring American Basketball Association to worry about. The National Hockey League added six new teams in 1967. The upstart American Football League threatened NFL sovereignty, luring away a cocky college quarterback from Alabama named Joe Namath and later dangling big bucks before established stars like John Brodie and Roman Gabriel. I was pleased by these developments, but that didn't last long. In June 1966 the two football leagues agreed to end their bidding war by merger. Unfortunately, Congress had passed legislation making the merger exempt from antitrust laws. As a result, the NFL swallowed the new league whole, yet the AFL had to pay reparations to NFL owners. If *that* wasn't a violation of antitrust rules, then Andrew Carnegie wasn't a Scot and a capitalist. The action of the Congress made more sense after I learned that Louisiana senator Russell Long, an influential member of the Senate Finance Committee *and* a vocal supporter of the merger, was rewarded with an expansion franchise in New Orleans. The name of the team, the Saints, was clearly a misnomer.

I was touched by football's tug-of-war when Bernie Parrish, a defensive back with the Cleveland Browns, asked if I would take a look at their pension plan. "You don't even have an agreement," I told him bluntly after studying it. "The owners can abandon the plan with a majority vote." Bernie called back a few weeks later with another proposition. Tired of the NFL's paternalistic control, Parrish had spoken to a liberal Teamster leader from St. Louis named Harold Gibbons who was interested in forming a union of *all* professional sports. Despite the Teamsters' "iffy" reputation, Gibbons was considered an honest and progressive union official. Parrish asked if I was interested in discussing the idea. I had too much to do as it was, but I found the concept intriguing. I agreed.

We had two meetings. Representatives from baseball, hockey, football, and basketball gathered in our office in April 1967. Among those present were Parrish, Buck Rodgers (California Angels), Mike Pyle (Chicago Bears), Jack Kemp (Buffalo Bills), Bobby Orr (Boston Bruins), and Oscar Robertson (Cincinnati Royals), along with my counterparts: Larry Fleisher (NBA), Alan Eagelson (NHL), and Creighton Miller (NFL). The reps from these other sports had very little conception of the way management operated. As you might have guessed, the most misinformed of all was Jack Kemp, the head of the AFL Players Association. The Buffalo quarterback sounded as if he had been brainwashed (although given his natural political bent, his brain didn't require a lot of "washing") by the commissioner's office. Not only was he antiunion, he seemed to have no idea that the organization he headed *was* a union. He spent considerable time showing that he was more concerned about the owners' profits than the players' welfare. Several months later, Kemp damaged the players by accepting a substandard contract on behalf of the American Football League Players Association; it contained terms rejected by the NFL Players Association. After his playing days, Kemp became a U.S. congressman from Buffalo, and in 1988 he sought the Republican presidential nomination. He was a better quarterback than he was a presidential candidate, but he never made the Super Bowl in either league.

The meeting accomplished very little. The philosophical differences, especially in football, were so great that when the elected player reps tried to hold meetings, various factions formed and met separately in different rooms.

The idea of a superior organization was dropped. A measure of cooperation among the players' associations became possible in later years, but for the time being we tried to forge ahead without them.

Though my public relations campaign eventually dragged baseball to the table, it didn't get the owners to bargain. Dick Moss, Tim McCarver (player rep of the Cardinals), and I met with the Player Relations Committee just before the 1967 All-Star Game at the "Big A," the Angels' new stadium in Anaheim. Before the meeting, McCarver asked Dick, "What do I say when they make us an offer?" Dick looked at McCarver earnestly and said, "If the offer is below twelve grand, it would be very helpful if you could throw up on the table."

McCarver came close to obliging. When PRC Chairman Joe Cronin made the first formal offer of $8,500, Tim grimaced as if he'd been nailed with a foul tip. Regardless, the owners' committee refused to budge.

McCarver and the other players were frustrated. They understood the importance of raising the minimum salary, but they weren't sufficiently moved to get the owners to do anything about it. Instead of negotiating a new minimum, as originally planned, and then addressing all the other terms and conditions of employment to be included in the first collectively bargained basic agreement, I served notice on behalf of the players that we intended to negotiate an overall contract. In addition to the minimum salary, this included scheduling rules, the length of the season, a formal grievance procedure, official recognition of the Players Association as the sole collective bargaining representative, limiting of salary cuts, increases in spring training and regular season allowances, moving expenses when traded, first-class hotel accommodations and air travel, restrictions on rules changes and amendments of the standard player's contract, modifications of the reserve rules—and much more.

Now we had the owners' attention. More important, we got the players' attention as well.

Several days later, Commissioner Eckert called. He didn't mention our contract demands, but he did tell me that the owners had made a change by hiring an experienced labor negotiator. Warren Giles and Joe Cronin and their lawyers would continue to attend negotiating meetings, but this new man would be the owners' spokesman for the Player Relations Committee. His name, I would soon learn from a press release, was John Gaherin. Soon afterward, Leonard Koppett, a reporter for the *New York Times*, telephoned for a comment and told me that Gaherin was an ex-FBI administrative employee with years of experience in labor relations in the railroad and airline industries and, more recently, had been the head of the New York Newspaper Publishers' Association. (Four years earlier, a disastrous newspaper strike had resulted in the collapse of the *Herald Tribune*.)

"This is a good move," I told Koppett. Baseball's owners had never had anyone with experience in this role. I said I was hopeful that this would improve the collective bargaining relationship.

My statement proved to be a good forecast. Hiring Gaherin in the fall of 1967 moved Bowie Kuhn into a subordinate role and helped professionalize the negotiations. Gaherin acted in good faith, though his hands were tied by the hardline, antiunion owners, and try as he might, he was unable to put the owners in touch with the realities of dealing with unionized employees.

While our negotiations were no longer farcical, progress was painfully slow. This was, in part, because no owners or club officials ever would meet with the players' negotiators. The so-called Player Relations Committee, which included at various times Bing Devine (Mets), Dick Meyer (Cards), Jerrold Hoffberger (Orioles), Tom Yawkey (Red Sox), Peter O'Malley (Dodgers), Clark Griffith (Twins), Robert Reynolds (Angels), Bob Howsam (Reds), Ed Fitzgerald (Expos), Francis Dale (Reds), Dan Galbreath (Pirates), John McHale (Expos), John McMullen (Astros), and others—not one attended a negotiating meeting from 1967 to 1985.

I dubbed them the "backroom negotiators," which is what they were, except they "negotiated" only with themselves. This head-in-the-sand approach denied them any first-hand experience, any ability to gauge the reactions of the players and their representatives, and certainly diminished the possibility of being influenced by the facts. Nonetheless, these "backroom boys" called the shots for management. It was an idiotic strategy. More often than not, it insured a breakdown in negotiations and led to one crisis after another.

After a series of meetings between Thanksgiving and Christmas produced more stalling than substance, our next hope for legitimate progress was the December winter meetings in Mexico City, where the owners planned to meet among themselves for four days. It had been agreed that after they discussed the players' proposal, a meeting would be arranged with the players' negotiating committee. But after our executive board arrived in Mexico City, we received word that the owners were too busy to meet with us. And to avoid criticism, the owners apparently lied to the press, denying that a meeting with the union had ever been planned. (This didn't go over too big with the players who had been present when the meeting was scheduled.)

Highball in hand, Atlanta's general manager, Paul Richards, even sounded off with a drunken tirade directed at me for telling the press that the owners had canceled a negotiating meeting. "Somebody's lying, and I don't think it's the owners," he said. I wonder who that left. The press was kind enough not to reveal that Richards had to be propped up to prevent his falling down.

Other officials were more apologetic. Mike Burke of the Yankees called the situation a "misunderstanding," and Bob Reynolds of the Angels expressed "chagrin." But the bottom line was that the owners had been sidestepping our advances for almost a year. As 1968 drew near, the minimum salary for a major league player was still $6,000.

The executive board's meetings south of the border brought a couple of surprises. In a meeting without me, the board made a decision that was announced to the press by NL player rep Tom Haller. He reported that the executive board had replaced my first contract, which had another year to run, with a new three-year contract extension through 1970 and a $5,000 raise, bringing my salary to $55,000 a year. Jim Bunning, who had become one of the stalwarts of the Players Association, told the press about the board's action by saying, "I know that baseball people resent our new leader. . . I have news for them. Marvin Miller will be around for a long time!"

Bunning wasn't—at least, not with Philadelphia. He had had a frustrating season in 1967. He had an outstanding ERA of 2.29, walked just seventy-three, and led the National League in games started, innings pitched, strikeouts, and shutouts, but he had the painful distinction of losing five games by the score of 1–0, and he finished with a modest won-lost record of 17–15. Despite his stellar stats, the outspoken NL pension rep and player rep of the Phillies was traded to the Pirates a few weeks after he returned from Mexico City in exchange for southpaw Woody Fryman (3–8 in 1967) and two minor leaguers, Don Money and Larry Hisle. I don't know how many times pitchers with a 2.29 ERA have been traded, but I'd bet it happens much more often among pitchers who are player reps.

Shortly after the New Year, John Gaherin responded to charges of stalling by telling a newspaperman, "Baseball is not Neanderthal . . . Yesterday died with the sunset." I took this to mean that he was ready to talk.

By February 19, we had hammered out a two-year agreement. The minimum salary for players on the roster on Opening Day was increased from $6,000 to $10,000. The maximum salary cut allowed was reduced from 25 percent to 20 percent. Spring training allowance ("Murphy money") increased from $25 to $40 a week, and we raised the allowance for meal money during the season from $12 to $15 a day.

The first basic agreement also provided the players with other important advances. Progress had been made on all our basic demands, except changes in the reserve rules and shortening the season to its original 154-game schedule. And on these last two subjects we proposed, and received, an agreement to create study committees so that we could seek to resolve our differences in the ensuing two years.

What's more, we had won the right to a formal grievance procedure, the importance of which Dick and I stressed to the players. At last they had a mechanism which they could use to fight violations of their contractual rights. If you exercise this right, I said to each and every club we visited that spring, Dick and I will provide all the necessary help to process your grievances.

Right after the start of the 1968 season, Baltimore's Curt Blefary contacted us. The Orioles had fined the outfielder for playing in an off-season charity basketball game along with members of the Washington Senators. Despite the fact that the game had been sponsored by another team, the Senators, and though the Senators' officials had recruited Blefary to play, we lost the grievance (the rule prohibiting off-season play still stood).

We did, however, win the next two.

The basic agreement required that the players fly first-class. This had been no small issue. Players spend a lot of time in the air, and coach seats are too cramped for large athletes who often have to play soon after a flight. Cincinnati GM Bob Howsam insisted that the writers, broadcasters, and coaches also be allowed to sit in first class. This was fine with me as long as a player wasn't bumped from his seat to accommodate a nonplayer. When pitcher Milt Pappas, the player rep, told me that his general manager was violating the agreement, I decided to fly to Cincinnati to speak to Howsam. I asked to meet privately with him. The last thing I wanted was to read about "selfish" ballplayers who had privileges the press did not.

When I arrived at his office, a hostile press corps was there in strength. Howsam had invited them to a grievance meeting! I went on with my business. It was not my job to negotiate for either coaches or newspapermen. We had bargained hard to secure this provision, and we were not going to see it ignored. "I know first-class seats are sometimes hard to come by," I said. "But not as hard to find as chartered planes, which is what will be needed if you ignore the contract." Howsam relented. But a month later—surprise!—he traded player rep Milt Pappas to Atlanta.

The third grievance, filed by a group of American League players, was directed against the clubs that used the Lord Baltimore Hotel when they were in town to play the Orioles. John Gaherin and Dick Moss checked it out, finding tiny rooms with peeling paint, atrocious beds, faulty air conditioning, and dining facilities that closed before the players returned from night games. Commissioner Eckert ordered the road secretaries around the league to find "first-class" accommodations. But Eddie Stanky, the manager of the White Sox, whose club was one of those that stayed at the Lord Baltimore, attempted to ignore the ruling. He said that the Players Association couldn't tell him what to do. Gaherin had to step in to shut him up and get him to comply.

Stanky was always trouble. Nicknamed "the Brat," Stanky had played in Brooklyn with Leo Durocher and later joined the Lip in the Polo Grounds with the Giants. (In 1968 Durocher was managing the Cubs.) Despite his antiunion stance, Stanky did pay union dues. Durocher never did. Like most people, I thought that Durocher and Stanky were clones. Each would kick and spit and scratch and scramble until he won or passed out. But Jerry Holtzman, a sportswriter who covered Chicago's skippers for the *Sun-Times*, told me otherwise. "There's a difference," he said. "If they both happened upon a drunk in the street, Stanky would say, 'Look at the no-good bum!' but Durocher would strut over and kick the poor guy."

Commissioner Eckert soon had other worries. At the end of spring training, Martin Luther King Jr. was assassinated. Many players, including Maury Wills, Roberto Clemente, Bob Aspromonte, and Rusty Staub refused to play on the day of his funeral. To his credit, Eckert supported the players and urged the respective owners not to fine them for staying away from the ballpark—and was criticized by many baseball officials. In June, after presidential candidate Senator Robert Kennedy was killed, Eckert yielded to the owners and did not postpone the games scheduled on the day of his funeral. (Sadly reminiscent of Pete Rozelle's nonaction after JFK was shot.) But the damage was done. Eckert seemingly had defied the owners, and they never forgave him. His days as commissioner were numbered.

During these turbulent times, I learned that management was going to take a hard line as far as renegotiating our pension agreement, which was going to expire March 31, 1969. Preliminary indications from Gaherin and Kuhn were that they were going to insist that the new agreement specify that all television revenue belonged to the owners and that any increases in retirement benefits which might be negotiated would definitely *not* apply to former players, managers, coaches, and trainers. It seemed to me that the owners were intent on harvesting 100 percent of the anticipated television revenue down the road, a move which would endanger the pension plan.

I informed the players about this impending crisis by meeting with them in September 1968. I suggested the possibility of a group holdout, which meant none of them would sign their 1969 contracts until the new pension agreement was satisfactorily settled. Although later that policy was adopted unanimously, the real test would come on February 13, the early reporting date for pitchers and catchers.

The only veteran to report was catcher Russ Nixon. (That somehow seemed appropriate to me for a guy named Nixon.) Call it karma, but he failed to make the team; they didn't have Nixon to kick around any more. As spring training grew near, several more broke ranks, including (I'm sad to say) pitchers Jim Palmer and Pete Richert from Baltimore and Clay Carroll of the Reds. Mets ace Tom Seaver signed a contract, but publicly announced that he would stay away until March 1. Jerry Grote, the Mets catcher, also signed. Obviously, with so few defections the season was in jeopardy.

The most articulate of all was Leon "Daddy Wags" Wagner, an outfielder entering his last season with the Giants. Daddy Wags said, "We let it hang out in front of seventy thousand fans. We deserve something. If that many people turned out to watch a guy lay linoleum, then he should get a likewise pension." As to my role in the boycott, he said, "Miller's a union dude all the way. He's the most unionizing man I've ever seen. He'll help us get the moon. But he's only following our orders."

Ironically, Kuhn's election as commissioner helped resolve the situation. He let it be known to the owners that the last thing he wanted to happen during his first days in office was a stoppage. On February 20, talks resumed. Four days later, we reached an agreement that extended the pension plan through the 1971 season.

On the morning of the February 25, the players' executive board approved the settlement in a meeting in New York, and the players flocked to the spring training camps, eager to begin the 1969 season.

When I returned from spring training, the study committee resumed meeting about alternatives to the reserve rules. After useless meetings in 1968 and 1969, we no longer had any doubt that the owners never intended to modify the rules at all. We were exactly where we were when the "study" first started, and Gaherin had written a memo which said, "The reserve clause as it now operates is in all respects satisfactory to the clubs." No kidding! This was, by the way, what was known in the owners' circles as keeping an open mind.

When it no longer made sense to meet on this matter, I drafted (more for self-amusement than anything else) a mock advertisement in the form of a leaflet:

OUTSTANDING INVESTMENT OPPORTUNITY FOR INDIVIDUALS, PARTNERSHIPS, CORPORATIONS OR ANY COMBINATIONS:

Invest in a business with the following advantages not found in any other industry in the United States:

1. A record of more than 100 years of great consumer appeal. Revenue has grown year after year and is at an all-time high.

2. Material costs are negligible; machinery and equipment costs almost nonexistent; physical plant leased on extremely favorable terms; municipalities eager to serve your needs through use of municipal funds, bond issues with tax-free interest and in other ways.

3. Only assets needed are skilled personnel. The displayed performance of such personnel constitutes the commodity to be sold. An ample supply exists.

4. Labor costs for skilled personnel total less than 15 percent of revenue, have been stable proportionate to

revenue for a decade, and are spectacularly below the 35 percent of revenue which labor costs represented forty years ago!

5. Secondary revenue—from radio and television contracts—is sufficient to meet all skilled labor costs twice over!

6. Capital gain is virtually assured. 500 percent increase in market value of franchises in last ten years is not unusual.

HOW CAN YOU RESIST?

OWN YOUR LABOR SUPPLY. As long as your employees retain their skills, their services are yours to command. You may sell them for cash or trade them for other skilled personnel to associated firms in your industry when it suits your purpose. You determine the compensation of your employees. You determine when their skills begin to fade and when to remove them from your employ.

ENJOY THE FINEST TAX SHELTER IN THE NATION. This is an industry in which you can depreciate, for income tax purposes, your skilled personnel. Since your assets are almost totally in such personnel, you can depreciate almost all assets over a short number of years. If your enterprise is organized on an individual owner basis, or a partnership, or a Subchapter S corporation, you may utilize excess depreciation to reduce or eliminate income taxes on your personal income.

FINALLY—Your methods of operation, your business practices—such as the use of blacklists, group boycotts, and conspiracies in restraint of trade, including combinations with foreign associates—are free of legal restraint.

The United States Supreme Court has determined that the industry is not subject to the antitrust law of the United States or of any state, *unlike your closest competitors, who are subject to such restraints.*

You are therefore free to utilize what would otherwise be illegal sanctions to enforce your will in controlling the entire skilled labor complement of the industry, to deprive cities and entire areas of your product when you choose to do so, to maintain with your associates a complete monopoly by barring would-be competitors, to fix prices and to allocate divisions of the market.

Perhaps I should have released the mock ad just to see what, if any, reaction it produced. In any event, two weeks after the "Miracle" Mets defeated the heavily favored Orioles in the 1969 World Series, a phone call from St. Louis brought this problem into sharp focus. It was Cardinal center fielder Curt Flood. A twelve-year veteran, Flood had been traded to the Phillies and did not intend to go. He said: "I would like to talk to you about the reserve rules, and the possibility of a lawsuit against baseball under the antitrust laws, or any other options I might have." We spoke briefly, and decided it best to meet in New York. When I hung up the phone, I knew Flood wasn't fooling around. That much was evident from the grave tone in his voice. No, clearly, he was a man on a mission.

10 . . .

Flood Gate

I WISH I could start this chapter by saying, "The first time I saw Curt Flood I knew I was looking at someone who was going to change baseball forever." I wish I could, but I can't. For one thing, Curt Flood didn't actually change the game, though he was a positive force and an example for others who did. For another, when I met all the other major league players, that is, in the spring of 1966, just before I was elected executive director, Curt Flood was one player in a group of standouts.

The Cardinals were a team of interesting characters, maybe the single most interesting group of ballplayers at the time. Other teams have had more *great* players, and many teams (including an earlier version of the Cardinals, the "Gas House Gang") had more *colorful* characters, but how many teams have had so many interesting players who *stayed* interesting after their playing days were over? From their championship teams of 1964 and 1967 that beat the Yankees and Red Sox, respectively, to the 1968 squad that lost a great, seven-game World Series to the Al Kaline–Denny

• 170 •

McClain–Mickey Lolich Detroit Tigers, the Cardinals roster included:

- Bob Gibson, one of the great right-handed pitchers and fiercest competitors of all time, also a very outspoken player on the subject of civil rights.

- Tim McCarver, then the Cardinals' player rep, a fine catcher who helped win pennants for the Phillies as well as the Cardinals. An author, a contract bridge player of note, and, perhaps, the most articulate of baseball TV broadcasters.

- Lou Brock, later an outspoken player rep, a Hall of Fame outfielder and one of the true gentlemen of the game. In his own quiet way, a man of firm conviction when it came to matters of principle.

- Dal Maxvill, also a future player rep, a scrappy, light-hitting infielder who carved out a major league career largely on the basis of smarts and determination.

- Orlando Cepeda, a terrific hitter deserving of induction into the Hall of Fame and a colorful character who carried several teams to the top on his broad shoulders.

- Steve Carlton, one of the game's best left-handers, an intellectual, and a man who got nearly as much ink for *not* talking to the press as most players who do.

I'm only mentioning a few. I could also include standouts like Mike Shannon, Roger Maris, Vada Pinson, Julian Javier. For whatever reason, the Cardinals of the sixties had a habit of producing ballplayers with minds and personalities of their own. On such a team even someone like Curt Flood doesn't jump right out at you.

Curt Flood was a good player, and at his best a *very* good one. He played in fifteen seasons in the major leagues and hit over .300 six times; by the time the Cardinals won pennants in 1967 and 1968, he had probably surpassed Willie Mays as the game's best defensive outfielder. In 1969 the Cardinals traded him to Philadelphia. (Trivia question: Who were the other prominent players included in the trade? Curt Flood got so much publicity in the deal that to this day most people don't remember that it was a four for four deal. Tim McCarver was also sent to the Phillies and Dick

Allen to the Cardinals.) At that point, Flood decided that he had had enough of being handled as a commodity.

Flood was a quiet, sensitive man, a portrait painter who has since made a name for himself outside of baseball. In 1968 *Sports Illustrated* featured Curt on the cover with his self-portrait and the caption, "Baseball's Best Centerfielder." Now he was thirty-one years old. He had been a Cardinal since 1958—actually, he had been a Cardinal for all but eight games of his entire career. In the fifties he had played baseball in minor league cities with major league prejudices in North Carolina and Georgia, in towns that were, for all intents and purposes, unaware that Jackie Robinson had broken the color line.

After all this, Curt Flood had somehow gotten a strange idea into his head: He believed that he wasn't a commodity and that he had earned the right to decide where he would finish out his baseball career. Flood got this strange notion that the Constitution and laws of the United States also applied to him. In his autobiography, *The Way It Is*, he described the trade like this: "If I had been a foot-shuffling porter, they might at least have given me a pocket watch."

At the time of the trade, Flood was making about $90,000 a year, which doesn't seem like a great deal today, but was really in the very top brackets of what ballplayers were getting back then. Some people thought he was the best at his position in the game. He was still relatively young. He had played all this time with an organization reputed to be one of the best in the game in the way it handled its players, and he had helped them win three pennants and two World Series in five years. Then came the morning in the fall of 1969 when he was awakened by a phone call from a newspaperman who wanted to know how he was reacting to his trade to the Phillies. *That* is how Curt Flood first found out he was no longer a St. Louis Cardinal.

As he told me later, the indignity of it all was harder to take than the fact that the Cardinals were letting him go. After spending virtually all his professional life with one organization, Curt Flood found that his personal life—his business connections, his friends, his family, the roots he'd put down in the community—were of no importance to his employers, who for years had made such a public display of demanding devotion and loyalty from him and his teammates. That Curt Flood was being forced to leave one of baseball's best organizations for one of the worst, that he was being sent without discussion to a city which he considered racist—all these things were of no account to Curt Flood's employers.

The first thing Flood did was to consult a local lawyer in suburban St. Louis. The lawyer advised him to attack the trade under the antitrust laws. At that time the Players Association basic agreement had no provision for impartial arbitration of grievances. There was a grievance procedure, but when an issue could not be resolved between the owners and players, it went to the commissioner—the owners' handpicked man, whose job it was to defend the reserve rule system. One of the bitter ironies of the Flood case is that by the spring of 1970 the Players Association was able to knock out the commissioner as the arbitrator and install a real arbitrator. But in the winter of 1969–1970 we were still without any hope of fairly resolving any dispute over the meaning of a clause in a player's contract.

So Flood's attorney correctly told him that the only way to void the trade was through a federal case attacking the reserve rules as being a violation of the antitrust laws. The position would be that Flood's contract with the Cardinals had expired, and therefore he was free to pursue his profession by finding another employer. In other words, to win some measure of respect and dignity—some degree of choice in determining his own future—Curt Flood had to first take on a hundred years of baseball injustice.

Flood called me early in November and said, briefly and in a businesslike way, that he had thought long and hard about the matter and that he simply was not, under any circumstances, going to report to the Philadelphia Phillies for the 1970 season. There would be no going back on that. He told me about his conversation with his attorney, Allan Zerman, and what he had told him about the antitrust laws.

After confirming pretty much what Flood's attorney had said, I gave Curt a brief history of the laws as they applied—or rather, as they *didn't* apply—to baseball. I told him that back in 1922 the *Federal Baseball* case had gone all the way to the Supreme Court, which had ruled that baseball wasn't covered by the antitrust laws. In 1953, in a case brought by a minor league player named George Toolson, the Court upheld the 1922 decision (*stare decisis*); that is, they let the old decision stand and didn't get into the merits of the new case. In other words, there had been, up to 1970, two Supreme Court rulings that baseball was *not* covered by antitrust laws. While there were indications that those decisions might not stand a third time, he'd be foolhardy to bet on it.

But Curt Flood had made up his mind. He wasn't betting on his chances to win; he had just made up his mind he was going to take a stand.

I decided the matter was too important to handle over the phone, and I asked Curt if he could come to New York. A week later Curt and his lawyer met Dick Moss and me at the Summit Hotel on Lexington Avenue. Their first question was, "What did I mean that there was 'some indication' the Court might go a different way this time?" I proceeded to give them the background of the 1953 decision in the Toolson case.

The name of George Toolson isn't well known today, but he very nearly became as famous as Curt Flood and Andy Messersmith. Toolson was in the Yankee chain at a time when the Yankees were well stocked at all positions. He probably could've caught on with another team, but he was tied to the Yankees through the reserve rules. They wanted to keep him in the minor leagues indefinitely as insurance against injury to a starting player at the big league level.

Toolson sued baseball for violation of the antitrust laws. After reviewing the case, although the Court earlier had declared that horse racing, boxing, and football were subject to antitrust laws, it now decided, somehow, that baseball was not. The reasoning behind the ruling was fuzzy, at best, and when you broke it down to basics the Court, including several of its most "liberal" justices, was really saying, "Right or wrong, we exempt baseball from the antitrust laws. That's the precedent. If the Congress thinks that is an error, it can change the decision by legislation." And so, in a routine that has become familiar, the Court passed the buck to Congress, which dropped it. Neither institution had the slightest concern for the rights of employees—the players. Both always have had great concern for the "property" rights of owners.

Still, it's an improvement when football players have *some* rights, but I felt the odds were stacked against the Supreme Court's upholding the law if it would discomfit the owners of the "national

Marvin Miller today. (Andy Freeberg)

With Yankee third baseman Clete Boyer and Mets shortstop Roy McMillan, player reps of their teams when I was elected in 1966. (UPI/Bettmann)

Club owners Charles Finley and George Steinbrenner. Yankees President, Gabe Paul, is at the right. (New York Times Pictures)

Robin Roberts, who was instrumental in my election. (Noel Clark, Life Magazine)

With Curt Flood, returning to the Federal Court Building in New York on May 21, 1970, after midday recess. Flood challenged organized baseball's reserve clause. (UPI/Bettmann)

Awaiting the start of the first salary arbitration session, February 12, 1974, with Rollie Fingers and (in background) Darold Knowles of the Oakland A's. (AP/Wide World)

Peter Seitz, arbitrator of the Catfish Hunter and Messersmith–McNally disputes, at December 23, 1975, news conference. (UPI/Bettmann)

Bill Campbell of the Twins, first player signed after the 1976 free-agent draft. (New York Times Pictures)

Preparing for a closed door meeting on March 2, 1976, with players (from left) Dave Duncan, Dick Drago and Mark Belanger, who is currently an officer of the players' union. (AP/Wide World)

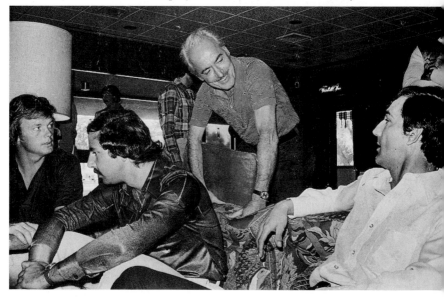

With Baseball Commissioner Bowie Kuhn on November 4, 1976, when both were smiling. (UPI/Bettmann)

Talking to the Phillies and Red Sox during spring training in March 1977, after the free-agent victory. (New York Times Pictures)

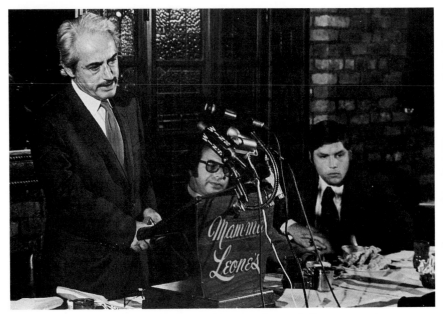

With Dick Moss and Tom Seaver at Mamma Leone's Restaurant just before reaching agreement on the arbitration of salary disputes. (New York Times Pictures)

Miller the Matador, 1981. (Courtesy Bill Gallo. New York Daily News)

With Reggie Jackson on July 1, 1981, after leaving the bargaining table on the twentieth day of the baseball strike. This photo ran in newspapers nationwide with the quote, "The gap between us is so wide that it defies my vocabulary to describe it." (UPI/Bettmann)

Visiting Athens on holiday, 1989.

Wife Terry with grandson Neil, 1991.

Son Peter and daughter Susan, 1991.

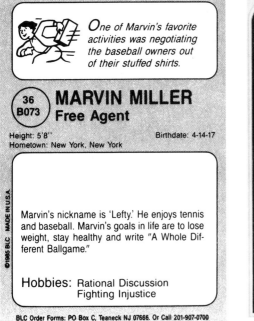

One of Marvin's favorite activities was negotiating the baseball owners out of their stuffed shirts.

36 B073 **MARVIN MILLER** Free Agent

Height: 5'8''   Birthdate: 4-14-17
Hometown: New York, New York

Marvin's nickname is 'Lefty.' He enjoys tennis and baseball. Marvin's goals in life are to lose weight, stay healthy and write "A Whole Different Ballgame."

Hobbies: Rational Discussion Fighting Injustice

©1985 BLC   MADE IN U.S.A.

BLC Order Forms: PO Box C, Teaneck NJ 07666. Or Call 201-907-0700

MARVIN MILLER
FREE AGENT   2-6-91

Baseball card of Marvin Miller created by Jim Bouton, February 6, 1991.

pastime." I felt also that no matter the outcome, Curt Flood would not have much of a major league career left. I could promise him nothing more than that I believed in his cause and would fight for it as best I could. Curt Flood looked me in the eye and said he understood the difficulties, that my promise to fight on his behalf was good enough for him, and that he wanted to challenge the reserve clause. And that was it; there was no going back from Flood's decision.

I knew how much the case would mean to Curt personally, but I also knew how explosive a Flood victory could be and how it could change things for all the players. I couldn't just sit there and say, "Okay, here's my evaluation of the situation. Now you do what you think best." Curt's attorney seemed competent but clearly did not have the experience or the stature to handle a case of this magnitude. He had never argued a case before the Supreme Court and was not experienced in antitrust cases. This case would be of great importance not only to Curt Flood but to all the players, including thousands who might still be in Little League. I told Curt's lawyer that I wasn't denigrating him in any way but that Flood's case required experience and expertise in antitrust cases, and I added that it wouldn't be a bad idea to have a lawyer with a national reputation who could bring the case the kind of publicity it really deserved. Both of them understood this; Curt's lawyer said he had no illusions of being able to handle such a case himself and would be there to assist in any way he could.

I began to realize that Flood really knew what he was getting into when he said, "You know, I made a good salary, but I'm told by my lawyer that a case like this will cost a fortune before we're through." And I said, "Indeed it can." The only plausible way to deal with this was to discuss it with the union's executive board so that the players themselves could determine whether to support Flood's struggle against the baseball monopoly.

While I was explaining all this, I was also thinking as fast as I could. I realized that once we started down this road, we couldn't abandon the case or turn away from it. We'd have to follow it through to the end, no matter how long, expensive, or bitter the struggle. And so, our lunch turned into a four-hour meeting. As our waitress glared at us and refilled our coffee cups, we discussed what would be involved in the first sustained assault on the handful of words that had held baseball players in bondage for a century.

It's best, I've always believed, to explain all of the downside risks to any union member about to enlist in a struggle against industry. The best way to give Curt and his attorney an idea of what they were up against was by telling them about previous players who had challenged the monopoly of the American and National leagues. The most famous challenge occurred after World War II when two wealthy Mexican brothers named Pasqual succeeded in luring a number of U.S. big leaguers to the Mexican League. They hoped, eventually, to upgrade the league to a major league level. Three St. Louis Cardinal stars, Max Lanier, Lou Klein, and Fred Martin (who was to become a pioneer of the splitfinger fastball) were among the earliest to go south after the war. The Dodgers' catcher, Mickey Owen, and the St. Louis Browns' shortstop, Vern Stephens, were among their other big-name recruits. Starting pitcher Sal Maglie also accepted a Mexican contract. Their contracts provided considerably higher salaries than the players' previous salaries in the major leagues.

For a while there was panic among the owners of U.S. clubs that the Mexican League would turn into a legitimate third big league that would touch off a salary war for top players. They needn't have worried; by the end of 1946 it was obvious that the Mexican league was poorly organized and did not have the financial resources to sustain a challenge to the American and National leagues.

In June of 1946 Happy Chandler, who had been named commissioner of baseball in 1945, announced that Americans who "jumped" to the Mexican League would be barred from American baseball for five years. (No players had "jumped" their contracts, of course. They had gone to Mexico *after* their American contracts expired.) Vern Stephens made it back just before the edict was passed. Mickey Owen wasn't banned for the full five years, but he did miss three years, and they probably would have been the most productive of his career. From 1938 to 1944 Owen had never caught fewer than 117 games in a season; after his ban was lifted in 1949, he played four seasons and never again caught more than 86. This was his punishment for trying to make the best living he could playing baseball. After Owen returned to the United States, Jim Gallagher, the Cubs' GM, wrote to Happy Chandler that "the spectacle of Mickey Owen languishing on a Missouri farm will do more to keep players from jumping this winter than anything Mr. [Branch] Rickey or the rest of us could do." This expressed the contempt that the men who made their fortunes from ballplayers' skills felt for the men who brought in that money.

One player, a young man from the Bronx, N.Y., had an even tougher time of it. Danny Gardella had turned down an offer of $5,000 to play for the Giants in 1946, opting to play for Vera Cruz of the Mexican League. In 1947 he came back to the States with Max Lanier and other players on a barnstorming trip that soon disbanded. He returned to New York, and soon his wife was expecting their first child. Danny continued to play ball, this time for the Gulf Oilers, a semipro team. Irony of sad ironies, a game between the Oilers and a Negro team, the Cleveland Buckeyes, was canceled when the black players found out Gardella was playing on the opposing team. Though the blacks had been *unofficially* banned their whole careers, they didn't want to risk what little chance they had of making it to the big leagues by playing with or against someone who had been *officially* banned.

Danny Gardella probably wouldn't merit attention today if it hadn't been for a lawyer named Frederic Johnson. Johnson knew the law, and he knew baseball. He had written extensively about baseball contracts, but his conclusions certainly didn't suggest that one day he'd champion the case of Danny Gardella. Commissioner Landis, he wrote, was to be praised for helping to bring about the longest "uninterrupted peace" in baseball history.

But that was in 1939, and by 1947 Johnson's opinion of baseball's power structure had begun to sour. The owners' attempts to use the courts to fight competition from the Mexican League particularly angered him, and when he heard about Gardella's Mexican League odyssey and the troubles he encountered on his return to the States, he could see a clear case of injustice. There was a basic legal difference between Gardella and players like Lanier, Stephens, Maglie, and Owen. They had had contracts before going to Mexico; Gardella had never signed a contract with an American team that contained a reserve clause. All he had done was to turn down the New York Giants' offer of

$5,000 as a signing bonus. The way Johnson saw it, there was no legally valid reason why Gardella should not have been allowed to play professional ball in America on his return. Johnson decided that Gardella had a legitimate case against major league baseball, and he advised him to sue.

In his affidavit filed with the lawsuit Johnson attacked the reserve clause as being "contrary to settled principles of equity...a conspiracy in restraint of trade and commerce." Baseball's owners, predictably, argued that the 1922 Supreme Court exemption was still valid, and that the reserve clause was not in restraint of trade but merely a tool for "conservation of personnel." The case opened early in October of 1947, and in 1948 the federal district court dismissed Gardella's suit.

Johnson appealed to the Court of Appeals for the Second Circuit. The three-man appellate court (which included a former FDR New Deal official, Jerome N. Frank) heard Johnson's argument that radio and television revenues had incontestably turned baseball into a national business and, on February 10, 1949, announced that it had voted two-to-one that Danny Gardella's case was strong enough to merit a trial.

Frank, in particular, had become convinced that baseball's employer-employee structure was fundamentally wrong, even if a few players were relatively well paid. "Excusing virtual slavery," he wrote, "because of high pay is only an excuse for the totalitarian-minded." The argument Frank was responding to would be revived many times in the coming decades, but Frank's reply to it would almost never be quoted.

Judge Frank wasn't the only one who felt passionately about the issue: An Arkansas congressman named Wilbur Mills helped introduce a bill to legalize the reserve clause and grant baseball legislative exemption from the antitrust laws. This was, apparently, to make sure that the baseball monopoly could continue no matter what the Court did. Nothing came of Mills's effort, but over the next twenty years grandstanding politicians introduced some sixty bills on the subject of baseball's antitrust status. None came really close to becoming law.

It would be nice to report that his fellow players flocked to Danny Gardella's side, but at this time there was no union to defend or even help define the interests of major league players, and all of them feared the vindictiveness of baseball executives. Max Lanier visited Gardella and asked him to drop his suit, apparently hoping that the action would cause Happy Chandler to reinstate him. Mickey Owen even recanted, apologizing publicly and implying the players deserved punishment since they went to Mexico out of "weakness." Gardella admitted no weakness.

With *Gardella* v. *Chandler* heating up in the press, Branch Rickey was quoted as saying that those opposed to the reserve clause had "Communistic tendencies"—which was certainly the right button to push in 1948 in the climate of the cold war, even if Rickey was indulging in the "logic" of the "big lie." No one bothered to point out that what opponents of the reserve clause were trying to do was bring the free enterprise system *into* baseball. There were a few independent voices in the press who at least had the courage to point out that the reserve clause furthered monopoly and inhibited competition, but hardly anyone had the courage to attack it openly.

Still, Chandler must have felt some pressure: On June 5 he offered a surprising amnesty—baseball's first amnesty international, as it were—to all players who had defected to the Mexican League. Two months earlier, a New York judge had denied a petition from Gardella, Lanier, and Fred Martin asking that they be reinstated to baseball; now Chandler relented. "The threat of compulsion by a court having ended," he said, he felt "justified in tempering justice with mercy."

Maybe. It's much more likely that Chandler was simply trying to undercut the effects of an upcoming decision in *Gardella* v. *Chandler*. Lanier, Martin, Owen, and Sal Maglie all returned to baseball under the amnesty, but Danny Gardella was left out. Frederic Johnson vowed to continue Gardella's fight, but privately he knew that Danny couldn't stand up to what surely would be a protracted court battle. He urged him to accept a settlement. The owners were only too happy to offer one: Their new chief lawyer, John O'Brien (a former antitrust lawyer, of all things!), had warned them of the money they'd have to spend if the courts ruled for Gardella and held that the reserve clause was illegal. On October 8, 1949, the owners settled for what Gardella acknowledged years later to be around sixty thousand dollars (from which, presumably, he had to pay Johnson).

And so baseball defused Gardella's case with an amnesty and an out-of-court settlement. "I'm so relieved," Chandler told the press, "if I were a drinking man, I'd get drunk." Danny Gardella, by the way, finally returned to the majors; in 1950, he flied out in his last major league at-bat. He was playing for, yes, the St. Louis Cardinals, who, in the interim, had purchased his contract from the Giants.

Soon after news of Flood's lawsuit was out, Frederic Johnson contacted the Players Association. Of course, he had been long retired from legal practice, but he volunteered to be of whatever help he could. As it turned out, we had all the relevant documents from *Gardella* v. *Chandler* and we didn't need Johnson's aid, but I was glad to hear from him. We were going to need all the moral support we could get.

Technically, of course, Danny Gardella hadn't lost his protracted court battle with the major leagues and Happy Chandler. But by finally settling with Gardella out of court, baseball's power structure had helped to avoid what could have been, from their point of view, a very damaging court decision. I knew that the owners would try the same tactic with Flood if it appeared in any way that he might be successful in his suit. "It's going to be a very difficult fight," I told him, "and I fully expect that if your lawsuit appears to be going well they'll attempt to buy you off. What will your reaction be if they throw a huge settlement figure at you?" Flood didn't blink. "I wouldn't accept that," he said. "If I accepted help from the Players Association on a commitment that we carry this to a conclusion, that's what I'll do. I'd be in it till the end." He offered to put that promise in writing. I told him that wouldn't be necessary; his word was sufficient.

Still, I wanted to be absolutely sure that he understood the implications of what he was about to do. I said: "Curt, you're past thirty now. The odds are that if we file this suit, you will not be able to play for at least one season, and God knows how long it might take to fight this case all the way through. *Even if you win, it could mean the end of your career.* I'm not saying that you can't do it, but I am saying that if you were out even for just a year it might be impossible to come back at your age. I don't think anything like that has ever been done before." Again, he didn't hesitate: "I'm prepared to make this the final fight of my career. I really don't want to play for those people."

I didn't doubt the sincerity of what he was saying. But if this was going to involve the Players Association, I had to consider the long-term possibilities. I had a lot of respect for Curt as a ballplayer, but I didn't know how well *he* knew the owners. "In some ways," I told him, "you know some of those guys better than I do, but on the other hand I've learned a lot in dealing with them over the last three years, and if you don't know it, I can tell you I've learned that they are a mean, vindictive bunch. If they think you're endangering their monopoly, they'll do anything they can to destroy you in baseball. I'm not calling them racists—not all of them, anyway—but being black isn't going to help you with them. If you win, you might be too old to come back, and if you lose, you'll certainly be blacklisted. Let me put it to you the simplest way possible: The way I see it, the moment you file that suit, you're probably through in baseball. And there could be more to it than that. These people are influential in other industries besides baseball. Your own boss, Gussie Busch, is a giant in the brewing industry and a big influence in St. Louis, if that's where you want to live."

This gave him pause, but just for a moment. "I hadn't thought about it," he said, "but if that's the way it is, okay, I'll live with that and deal with it somehow." At the time, Curt was just starting to establish his reputation as a portrait painter. He thought that he could support himself through his painting, having just moved his business into a studio. I couldn't help but think that few artists ever had to paint with such pressure on them.

One of my last considerations was a delicate one. "Is there anything in your private life that could be used to denigrate you? If there is, it's likely to be used against you." He said that didn't worry him. Finally, I said that we could win the lawsuit for future players, but there was a good chance that he wouldn't benefit. Again, he said that it would still be worthwhile.

At this point there was nothing to do but ask him to go home and think over our entire discussion. I appreciated Curt's honesty, but I wanted to be sure that he understood how bad all of this could get. The baseball owners were men with resources and had influence with the media. I asked him to talk it over with his family and then get back to me. Meanwhile, I planned to talk to some of the player reps to see whether the players themselves would back the case enthusiastically.

After saying good-bye to Curt and his lawyer, Dick Moss and I wasted no time in diving into the legal aspects of the case. In 1957 the Supreme Court had decided a pro football case that was strikingly similar to Flood's. The ruling had been favorable to the player, William Radovich, who had refused to play for the NFL team that had drafted him and later sued when he was blacklisted by another pro team affiliated with the NFL. Not only had Radovich won, the Court had commented that baseball's continued exemption from antitrust was "unreasonable, illogical, and inconsistent." Why, then, had a football player been granted a right a baseball player had been denied? The answer was that football had no *history* to go by; the judges simply looked at the evidence and reached a logical conclusion. Baseball had history, and judges were faced with the reality that their decision could change, perhaps radically, the nature of the game that had been America's national pastime for a century. Unlike William Radovich, Curt Flood was squarely up against this history, the history of an earlier, *negative* decision.

Dick and I began meeting with the player reps, and it proved to be a much more exacting task than we had anticipated. Today's players and fans have grown up with the benefits of free agency, but the climate was much different twenty years ago. Only a few players really understood what the reserve rules were and what they meant to baseball; none of them really understood how abolishing the rules would change the game and their lives. Many of the players we talked to about the reserve clause simply echoed the owners' line, as thorough a job of brainwashing as I had seen in all my years. And I don't just mean a brainwashing by the *owners;* it wasn't that easy to find sportswriters in the late sixties who didn't take the owners' line on most issues in contention. It would really have been easier if none of the players had ever *heard* of the reserve clause, because then they might have approached the subject with open minds. One of the truly amazing things about the players of this time is how many of them *absolutely believed that the elimination of the reserve clause would destroy baseball.* On the other hand, who could blame the players for feeling this way? The Supreme Court and the Congress had been passing the buck on the issue for nearly five decades.

The funny thing is that after you've heard for years about baseball's antitrust exemption, when you study antitrust legislation—particularly the Clayton Antitrust Act and the Sherman Antitrust Act—you expect to see some specific piece of writing in them exempting baseball. Of course, there isn't. There is no language that would even remotely suggest baseball is not included with other industries operating in interstate commerce. The exemption which influential baseball men succeeded in carving out for themselves was a strictly *judicial* one, totally inconsistent with the federal statutes the Court was supposed to interpret. In my lifetime, literally scores of bills have been introduced in both the House and the Senate to correct the Supreme Court's error by amending the antitrust laws to make it clear that baseball is not exempt from coverage (and never was!). Every one has ended up buried in committee in one house or the other. Congress has never accepted the challenge of stating simply that baseball was *not* exempt from antitrust laws.

Of course, neither Congress nor the courts have been, nor should they be expected to be, sympathetic to players' problems. The Supreme Court's bias toward property interests has been observable in every baseball case (as well as in numerous nonbaseball cases). Politicians aren't stupid when it comes to matters of what it takes to get reelected, and it's doubtful that any politician is going to be responsible for sponsoring legislation that alienates big-time sports owners. States and cities are always in fierce competition for big league baseball, football, and basketball franchises, and many team owners are big contributors to campaign funds. The point is that politicians aren't neutral observers in baseball labor problems. In Phillip Roth's political satire *Our Gang,* Curt Flood is named on Nixon's enemies list. Roth was joking, but the point survives the exaggeration: What Flood was trying to do was perceived as a revolution. Curt Flood had to go into his lawsuit knowing that neither the Congress nor the courts would be numbered among his allies.

Flood went back to St. Louis. He called about two weeks later, saying he had thought over everything that Moss and I had told him. He had taken our words to heart, and still he wanted to proceed. My feelings were mixed at that moment. Realistically, we had little chance of overthrowing a reserve clause that had a half a century of court precedents on its side, but at least in Curt Flood we had the right man and the right situation with which to mount the challenge. Since this could turn out to be a landmark case, it was absolutely essential that the man at the center of it be someone with great personal integrity. As to Flood's personal qualities there could be no doubt, but I would still have to convince the players that Flood would not back out on us once the Association committed its resources to his case. If Flood turned out to have feet of clay, the players' chances of ever modifying the reserve rules through legal action would be damaged. But I was persuaded that Flood meant what he said and that he was in the case to the end. While Curt Flood's place in baseball history was not as important as Jackie Robinson's, his decision to challenge the reserve clause took at least as much courage as Jackie Robinson needed in his rookie season. Certainly, before the case was over Flood learned things about pressure that he hadn't learned in three World Series.

One of the first matters to resolve was the problem of financial backing. I had already been considering the point when Curt brought it up. I told him that I didn't feel comfortable asking the Association to support him in terms of his living expenses, but it would be appropriate to seek their approval to pay all the legal costs as well as expenses incidental to transportation to and from St. Louis for the trial in New York. Can you, I asked, live with that arrangement, assuming the executive board goes along with it?

As with many important questions I put to him, Curt answered almost without hesitation, and in a tone that indicated he had already given the matter serious thought. "That's absolutely fair," he said. In turn, he had a question for me: "Who did you have in mind for a lawyer?" I had someone in mind, but I begged off giving his name to Curt just yet as I hadn't had a chance to talk to him. By now it was the third week in November; the way to proceed, I said, was to wait till the first week in December when the board had its winter meeting. Under the constitution the board was the decision-making body, and if they gave their approval, things would begin to move quickly.

A short time later Curt came to New York again, and we had dinner—Curt, Terry, myself, and a friend of Curt's. I told Curt that I wanted him to meet with the board in Puerto Rico. I had talked briefly with the two league player reps about what had transpired and indicated that the matter would be on the board's agenda. I would report to the board in detail, I told him, but I was sure the board members would want to hear from him directly. Almost all the veterans in both leagues knew and respected Flood, so it seemed logical that he should be present at the meeting before the player reps made their decision. Curt agreed.

The board met in the first week of December, and I gave them as complete a background as I could. I told them that Curt was in the hotel and ready to answer their questions. Here was a case that might have a major impact on their futures, and they could begin confronting it *now*. We first discussed the case in great detail among ourselves; then Curt was sent for, and the questions began. Many of them were questions I had already asked Curt, such as, "Have you thought of the fact that you may never play again?" "Are you aware that, win or lose, you might be doing a lot for the players of the present and the future but that your career may come to an end without your having gotten anything tangible from the suit?" Flood fielded that as cleanly as he fielded sinking line drives. He stared solemnly at the board and said, "I've thought that through, and I've made my decision. I'm willing to do it anyway." Then Jim Bunning asked, "Suppose the owners do what they did with Gardella and offer you a lot of money to drop the case?" To which Flood answered: "If the Players Association commits to help me in this lawsuit, I will make the commitment that I will not withdraw the suit."

Then Tom Haller put the question that was on the mind of a lot of players but which many were uneasy about bringing up. He mentioned first the turbulence of the 1960s, the struggle over civil rights and black power, a new consciousness about race relations and past injustices and the righting of wrongs. Haller's question then was: "Are you doing this simply because you're black and you feel that baseball has been discriminatory?"

Haller's question caught me by surprise. It hadn't occurred to me that race might be a factor in Flood's actions, but it evidently had occurred to several of the players. All watched Curt carefully for his answer. He remained impassive.

"All the things you say are true," he replied, looking directly at Haller, "and I'd be lying if I told you that as a black man in baseball I hadn't gone through worse times than my white teammates. I'll also say that, yes, I think the change in black consciousness in recent years has made me more sensitive to injustice in every area of my life. But I want you to know that what I'm doing here I'm doing as a ballplayer, a major league ballplayer, and I think it's absolutely terrible that we have stood by and watched this situation go on for so many years and never pulled together to do anything about it. It's improper, it shouldn't be allowed to go any further, and the circumstances are such that, well, I guess this is the time to do something about it."

Before the meeting Curt and I had discussed what he would say to the board and what questions they were likely to ask him. At one point he interrupted to ask, almost offhandedly, "Why is it nobody's ever done this before?" And I said, "Well, it isn't that nobody has. George Toolson and Danny Gardella did it, as you know. But it almost takes a situation where a player has no alternative, where he has nothing to lose by challenging the powers that run the game. That's why there have been so few challenges." He nodded. Curt Flood understood that he was all but finished as a major league ballplayer if he pressed this suit. I don't know how many of the players on the board understood all this in precisely those terms, but on some level Curt convinced them that he was serious about sticking it out. This was not a strike. In that situation Flood would have the organized backing of his teammates and colleagues. In this situation he stood alone, and he would, to some, be a pariah. Flood understood this much more clearly than the players at the board meeting.

The board then excused him. They had some questions for me. What was I proposing? If we were to go forward, I told them, we would have to be empowered by Curt to select and retain highly qualified attorneys. The case was too important to all the players to do anything less. We had to commit ourselves to paying all the legal costs (excluding Curt's personal attorney) and all Curt's expenses incidental to his travels to New York to prepare for the trial and to participate in it.

This loosed questions they hadn't asked Flood, including one very good one: If Flood wins the case and wins damages, would we not ask (in the form of a pretrial written agreement) that the expenses be repaid? In other words, if our legal expenses amounted to, say, a quarter of a million dollars—and they very easily could—and Curt was awarded, say, $600,000 or perhaps even half that, would it be fair to ask him to reimburse the union?

I thought it was fair, and I said so. Curt had stated clearly that he wasn't bringing suit for the money. The alternative, I added, was also fair: Curt was taking the risk for what could benefit *all* the players, so if he lost, then we would just have to bear the loss. (And I have to add that $200,000 or even $600,000 may not seem like a lot of money to fans accustomed to reading about today's multi-million dollar salaries and endorsement fees, but it was a substantial sum of money for the Association at a time when the organization's total annual dues from all the members was less than $200,000.)

The board moved unanimously to support Curt Flood's lawsuit. I then talked to Curt about drawing up a written agreement to repay expenses from a possible damage award, and he agreed without hesitation. The day after I returned from Puerto Rico, I telephoned my choice of attorney in the case, Arthur Goldberg.

When I went to the Steelworkers Union in 1950, Arthur Goldberg was general counsel for both the Steelworkers and the overall federation, the CIO. He was remarkably young to have reached such a position—he was only thirty-seven in 1950—and in fact he had been in those positions for only about a year when I was hired. Even then he had acquired a reputation as a brilliant policymaker and negotiator, and justifiably so. Goldberg was a kind of majordomo of the Steelworkers Union and with his very capable staff was assuming a more and more important place in the union. Many thought he came to be more important than the *president* of the union.

I worked closely with Arthur through those years in all the major negotiations in steel, aluminum, metal fabricating, the can manufacturing industry—the whole jurisdiction of the Steelworkers Union. I didn't always agree with him on policy matters, but I respected his ability; his oral arguments in federal district court and then the circuit court of appeals in opposition to the government's imposition of an eighty-day Taft-Hartley injunction against the 1959 steel strike were models of clarity and logic. He could be brilliant on his feet: I had seen him present a case in the circuit court for well over two hours with just a couple of notes to fall back on.

Goldberg left the Steelworkers Union in 1961 when President Kennedy appointed him secretary of labor, and later he was Kennedy's choice for the Supreme Court. There he had written the majority opinion in a number of antitrust cases. In 1964, Lyndon Johnson persuaded him to resign and replace Adlai Stevenson as United States ambassador to the United Nations. By 1969, Arthur was back in private practice as a partner in a prestigious New York law firm.

Today, I think, most New Yorkers remember Arthur best for campaigning against Nelson Rockefeller in the 1970 race for governor. But there was another side to him. Like most kids who grew up in Chicago he was a lifelong baseball fan (when he was campaigning for governor I reluctantly allowed him a "photo opportunity" by taking him into the Mets locker room). It would have been impossible to imagine anyone better suited to lead the fight against the reserve clause.

Goldberg seemed fascinated by the idea of representing Curt Flood and agreed to have breakfast with Dick Moss and me to discuss it. He had some familiarity with the reserve rule and shared our feelings of outrage that in this day and age such a thing could be allowed to exist. He had an appreciation for Flood's courage in wanting to fight the reserve clause. I couldn't have been more pleased at his response, but one thing had me worried: On the way into the hotel where we were to meet I had seen a headline in the *New York Times* which indicated that New York Democrats wanted Goldberg to run for governor against Rockefeller.

After we had made our pitch and Goldberg seemed receptive, I produced the paper and asked him what his intentions were. "Arthur," I said, "I'm not trying to get any inside information, but our situation is that Flood's case is not going to be decided in just a few months, as you know. In fact, it's probably going to go all the way to the United States Supreme Court, and if you have to drop out to become a candidate, it could really cripple things for us. And if you *win,* I *know* you're not going to have time." We *all* laughed about that; I probably should have said "when you win." Goldberg replied that he had absolutely no intention of running for governor. "I haven't informed them yet," he told me, "but I'm going to withdraw. I'm flattered that they want to nominate me, but I really don't want to be governor." At this point I had no option but to accept his word or find a new lawyer, and since it didn't seem possible that we could get a better lawyer than Arthur Goldberg, I decided to trust him.

There was still the matter of his fee. As I said before, the Players Association had limited resources compared to today, and I had no illusions that we could pay an Arthur Goldberg his usual fee. "Look," he told us, "the case is of tremendous interest to me and I would regard it as *pro bono* work, a public service to upset a series of unconscionable rulings that should have been overturned by courts a long time ago. I won't bill you for any hours myself, though you'll have to pay my associates at the firm who assist me in the case. You can have me for expenses, travel, and what-not." This was much better than anything I'd hoped for. Arthur Goldberg for expenses! That was like Sandy Koufax pitching for pass-the-hat. We made plans to meet with Flood as soon as possible.

Like all good lawyers, Goldberg wanted to be fully briefed on all aspects of the case. I told him that the first basic agreement the union had negotiated with the owners covered the 1968 and 1969 seasons. That contract included an agreement of the parties to conduct a study of alternatives to the reserve clause. During the negotiation of the 1968 agreement we had demanded an end to the absolute control of a player by one team for his entire career. Needless to say, we got absolutely nowhere with this demand, but the provision to study alternatives held out hope for change.

As anyone who had studied the owners' conduct over the previous century could have guessed, the study group proved to be a farce. At every meeting, all of the ideas for study were presented by the Players Association *alone;* all alternatives to the reserve rules, all study suggestions, all possible revisions, came from the players' side. Not only did the owners have nothing to say on these matters, the union never got any real discussion of the ideas it put on the table, and never, never was there a hint that the owners were looking for an alternative to the reserve clause. What they were really saying, of course, was "It's nice that you took the time to do all this, but we really think everything is working fine just the way it is. The system's not broken, so let's not try to fix it."

It's not just that we couldn't make any progress: It's that the owners were purposely stalling so that we *couldn't* make any progress. In the strict sense, we weren't dealing with the owners at all; their study group was made up of league presidents and their lawyers, people who had no authority to make any decisions and move ahead. This was deliberate. It was very much in the minds of the people who ran baseball at that time to break the union when the opportunity might arise, and they weren't going to put themselves in a position to yield anything that might lead to the erosion of their power. Their final response to every proposal was a thinly disguised version of "Thank you, but the bottom line is that we own the players. We like it that way. When does the study group meet again?"

Dick Moss and I went through all of this with Goldberg and related the facts of the *Federal Baseball, Toolson*, and *Gardella* suits. Arthur told us he would try to bring in some associates to assist: a very bright partner, Jay Topkis, a Yale Law School graduate, who in 1948 had written an article for the *Yale Law Review* on baseball's reserve system, and an intelligent young associate, Max Gitter. We all met, I believe, on December 15, and Flood took an instant liking to his new attorneys. Almost immediately we began to plan the letter that was to fire the first shot.

In the interest of historical accuracy I have to admit that Dick Moss and I thought of suggesting to Curt that he start out, "I'm free, black, and thirty-one"—it does have a nice ring to it—but finally decided it was too corny. We worked on the letter with Curt and reviewed it with Arthur, and Curt signed it. On December 24, 1969, Flood sent the letter to Bowie Kuhn.

Dear Mr. Kuhn,
    After 12 years in the major leagues, I do not feel that I am a piece of property to be bought and sold irrespective

of my wishes. I believe that any system that produces that result violates my basic rights as a citizen and is inconsistent with the laws of the United States and the several states.

It is my desire to play baseball in 1970 and I am capable of playing. I have received a contract from the Philadelphia club, but I believe I have the right to consider offers from other clubs before making any decisions. I, therefore, request that you make known to all the major league clubs my feelings in this matter, and advise them of my availability for the 1970 season.

Curt Flood

After Kuhn received Flood's letter, there was an inconclusive meeting between Kuhn and Goldberg. More of this later—for now, let's contrast the letter you just read from Flood with the one Bowie Kuhn sent Curt in reply on December 30, 1969:

Dear Curt,

This will acknowledge your letter of December 24, which I found on returning to my office yesterday.

I certainly agree with you that you, as a human being, are not a piece of property to be bought and sold. This is fundamental in our society and I think obvious. However, I cannot see its applicability to the situation at hand.

You have entered into a current playing contract with the St. Louis club, which has the same assignment provision as those in your annual major league contracts since 1956. Your present contract has been assigned in accordance with its provisions by the St. Louis club to the Philadelphia club. The provisions of the playing contract have been negotiated over the years between the clubs and the players, most recently when the present basic agreement was negotiated two years ago between the clubs and the Players Association.

If you have any specific objection to the propriety of the assignment, I would appreciate your specifying the objection. Under the circumstances, and pending any further information from you, I do not see what action I can take and cannot comply with the request contained in the second paragraph of your letter.

I am pleased to see your statement that you desire to play baseball in 1970. I take it this puts to rest any thought, as reported earlier in the press, that you were considering retirement.

Sincerely yours,
Bowie Kuhn

"I would appreciate your specifying your objection." Close your eyes and poke your finger at Flood's letter; you will scarcely find a sentence that doesn't "specify" Curt Flood's "objection."

While we thought Flood's case was not complex, we certainly had no illusions that the trial was going to be easy or that it would move through the judicial system rapidly. The disposition of a case in federal court *always* involves a lot of time. The court dockets are always crowded, and lengthy postponements are easy to get. It's no surprise that some cases remain unresolved for many years. Which is to say, we fully expected serious delays in Flood's case.

Instead, *Flood* v. *Kuhn* moved through the courts like Willie Mays going from first to third. The case was filed in January 1970, and the Supreme Court ruled in June 1972. By the spring of 1970 all the preliminaries were over. In May, we were in Judge Irving Ben Cooper's court in Foley Square to begin the trial. On August 12 Judge Cooper ruled against Flood. To this day I'm not sure why it all went so quickly. And not only did the case go quickly in district court, our subsequent appeal to the circuit court, their hearing and decision, and our appeal of that decision to the Supreme Court asking for certiorari (asking the Supreme Court to take jurisdiction) all happened with remarkable, uncharacteristic swiftness. The one thing we had no right to complain about was the speed with which the trial and the appeals were handled.

In a sense I had no reason to complain about the lower court decision, either; it's very rare that a federal district court will directly reverse a decision of the Supreme Court. We all knew that, but Goldberg emphasized from the beginning that the only way we could win was to fight it out all the way through the Supreme Court, hoping that it would accept jurisdiction so it could finally decide whether it would reverse the 1922 *Federal Baseball* decision and the 1953 *Toolson* decision.

So we assumed from the start that we weren't going to win in district or circuit court, and we saw them as obstacles we'd have to pass through. Let me stress that we were not without *some* optimism for the long haul: Judge Harold Burton's dissent in the Toolson case had become law in the case of the football player, William Radovich, as well as in the antitrust suit against the International Boxing Club in the mid fifties. All of us involved in the case were keeping our fingers crossed that eventually the Supreme Court would have to face up to the logic of its own decision in other cases and begin applying that logic to baseball. We were simply hoping that Curt Flood and his contemporaries would be first to benefit from that sudden burst of sunlight. It was not to be.

As in the past, I believe that the judges in this case simply let their awe of baseball—that is, their awe of being in a situation where their verdict could have a lasting impression on the national pastime—affect their judgment. A prime example was Judge Irving Ben Cooper. In early March, when the arguments were completed, Cooper told us: "Now you have thrown the ball to me, and I hope I don't muff it." What he meant, of course, was that the ball was too hot to handle, so he was going to toss it onto the next court. This was particularly interesting because, while Cooper's decision was pretty much pro forma, he threw in some dicta—having nothing to do with the actual decision—which concluded that the reserve rules were overly strict and that it would be in the interest of "everybody" to sit down and negotiate "appropriate modifications."

Cooper's commentary made me wish that Cooper could have been at the meeting in early 1970 when Jim Bouton jokingly asked if the owners would consider terminating the reserve clause obligation when a player reached age sixty-five. No, replied NL attorney Lou Carroll with a straight face, "because next time you'll want it reduced to age fifty-five."

Judge Cooper, who had baited Flood when he was on the witness stand ("This isn't as easy as playing center field, is it?"), ruled against Flood, but did not deal with the reserve rule itself. What he decided was that baseball was exempt from the requirements of all federal and state antitrust laws—in other words, the exemption created by the Supreme Court especially for baseball was still intact.

In 1971 the court of appeals upheld Judge Cooper's decision. That might have been the end of the case, but the Supreme Court then surprised most of the legal profession by agreeing to hear an appeal. (In most situations the votes of at least four Supreme Court justices are required for certiorari.) But on June 6, 1972, the Supreme Court, by a vote of five to three (with one abstention), upheld the lower court as well. We were defeated.

The majority opinion was written by Justice Harry A. Blackmun. Here's some of what he wrote: "We continue to be loath, fifty years after *Federal Baseball* and almost two decades after *Toolson,* to overturn those cases judicially when Congress, by its positive inaction, has allowed their decision to stand for so long and, far beyond mere influence and implication, has clearly evinced a desire not to disapprove them legislatively."

If this sounds confusing, let's note that six of the eight justices held that baseball *was* "interstate commerce," which was contrary to the 1922 decision, but that three of those six *still voted to abide by the precedents!* Baseball, despite all logic, was to continue as an exception to other entertainments and professional sports which the courts had already ruled *were* subject to antitrust laws. In other words, or in Latin words, it was a case of *stare decisis;* let the previous decision stand.

Chief Justice Warren Burger recognized the error of baseball's exemption, but wrote that the lives of too many people would be affected by a reversal of the error. I don't think I've ever read such criticism of a majority decision of the court by the very justices who formed the *majority*. The majority described their decision as an "aberration" and an "anomaly." Their criticism was correct, but their decision was, unfortunately, wrong. All in all, the *Washington Post* described the decision aptly when it noted that "tradition had once more won out over logic."

I think it is worth taking a look at the dissenters on that Supreme Court. Two of the justices, William O. Douglas and William Brennan, felt that baseball's judicial exemption from antitrust laws was wrong. In perhaps the most strongly worded statement connected with the case, they wrote, "Were we considering the question of baseball for the first time on a 'clean slate,' we would hold it to be subject to federal antitrust regulations...." They added that "the unbroken silence of Congress should not prevent us from correcting our own mistakes."

I must also point out that Justice Thurgood Marshall, in a separate dissenting opinion, correctly pointed out that if the Supreme Court *had* decided to overrule the 1922 and *Toolson* decisions (and thus subject baseball to antitrust regulation), that wouldn't automatically mean that Flood would win his case. Flood was suing on the basis that his treatment by baseball was a violation of antitrust law, so first he had to establish that baseball was covered by antitrust laws, and only then would it become necessary to establish *how* baseball violated those laws. To show that what baseball *did* to Flood was *in violation* of the law would have been the easy part.

The efforts of Curt Flood and the Players Association were not wholly lost. First of all, we presented a good case in the trial court. The arguments against the reserve clause had never before been made so lucidly or so forcefully. Much more important—what *Flood* v. *Kuhn* really accomplished—was, in the much-used phrase of the 1960s, raising the consciousness of everyone involved with baseball: the writers, the fans, the players—and perhaps even some of the owners.

There is no evidence, however, that Commissioner Bowie Kuhn learned anything. "I concluded," he wrote in his autobiography, "that it would be impossible to maintain the integrity of the game and maintain honesty among clubs and players without a reserve system." (Apparently Bowie would have it both ways: "The last thing I wanted," he wrote two pages later, "was for the clubs to view the Flood decision as an excuse for doing nothing. Change was in the wind." Precisely how Bowie proposed to change the reserve rule when he had concluded there could be no integrity or honesty without it can only be guessed at.

Change, indeed, was blowin' in the wind, but throughout his reign as commissioner Bowie was always spitting into it. But many outside of the immediate power structure of baseball *did* begin to understand that the reserve system was wrong and that baseball as we knew it might not vanish if it were abolished or drastically reformed.

Of course, when I say "raised consciousness," I mean "raised" in a relative sense: The norm before *Flood* v. *Kuhn* wasn't very enlightened. I think the trial caused a lot of judges and lawyers to recognize that major league baseball was, after all, a monopoly and that it had been granted a license against being penalized for operating as a monopoly, and they began to ponder why that should be. The trial caused some sportswriters to say, "Hey, I didn't realize baseball alone *isn't* covered by antitrust laws. Is that what the Supreme Court decided in 1922?" The Flood case caused everyone connected with baseball—and that includes millions of fans, of course—to realize that the 1922 decision was absurd. It was absurd to contend that baseball was not an industry engaged in interstate commerce, and it was just plain nonsense to rule that football players and boxers had certain basic rights that baseball players did not have.

It's an old adage that hindsight is easy, but if that's the case, why do we repeat our mistakes so often? It is painful for me to think back over the history of *Flood* v. *Kuhn,* but that's necessary if we're to learn from our mistakes. And we made mistakes in this case.

What did we do wrong? For one thing, the players themselves could have taken a more visible and active part in the trial. This may seem like a small point, but it was foolish to overlook the media appeal of big-name athletes. They could have been seen attending the trial, going in and out of the courthouse. That, I think, would have given the Players Association more of a human look to the public and shown that ballplayers were capable of demonstrating courage and solidarity off the field as well as on.

Why didn't I encourage it? Well, for one thing the trial was held during the season, and I was reluctant to urge players to do anything that would distract them from their jobs. For another, it was in the back of my mind that a great many marginal players might be the targets of owner revenge if Flood lost: A utility infielder who was active in the union and made a public show of support for Flood might find himself losing a job to a utility infielder who *wasn't* active in the union. Union reps had a tough time as it was; they tended to be traded more often than players who were less active in the union.

But there was little element of risk to the major stars, and they were the ones we needed most. To my knowledge, not one of them attended a single session of the trial. This was as much my fault as the players'; if I had it to do over again I would say, "For God's sake, this man is a colleague of yours! What happens to him could have a dramatic impact on *your* life, so when your team comes to New York, if you've got a night game, come on down to Foley Square for a couple of hours during the day and show him some support."

To be honest, I wasn't as certain of the unity and solidarity of the Association then as I became a few years later. By the time *Flood* v. *Kuhn* came to trial in 1970 I had been executive director only four years, and we had not been tested by our first strike. We had been unified to an extent by the players' refusal to sign contracts in the winter of 1968–69, and the players had remained firm through successful negotiations on both the pension plan and the first collective bargaining agreement. But we were still feeling our way as an organization; for instance, I think it would have been different in 1973, after the players had stuck together during the 1972 strike. Still, if I had to do it again, I'd do more to get players to show up in support of Flood.

That was undoubtedly a failure of leadership—my leadership. And it was yet another example demonstrating that players, like other people without leadership, *always* seem to fail to act in their own best interests. Fear aside, it must be remembered that players are profoundly affected by the press, and one can't minimize the impact of the media working in conjunction with the owners, hammering away on the theme that without the reserve clause, baseball will fall. Flood's suit was painted as an attempt to undermine the entire sport.

It was also true that many players simply didn't care. They may have wanted Flood to win, but they felt that they had their careers to be concerned with, and that was that. Even though I had explained the importance of modifying the reserve clause, many of the players remained in the dark about what the case might mean. In 1970 I had no idea of the magnitude of the salary increases down the road, but I did know that once real competition came to the baseball labor market, there would be terrific salary increases. Any student who had taken Economics 101 could have told you that. Nevertheless, the fact that not one player showed up at the trial to demonstrate his support highlighted the "me-first" attitude that, regrettably, has always been a part of the game and perhaps a major element in our society as well. Because in the final analysis, the Flood case was the players' case, and *some* of them should have been there.

There's something else I should mention under the category of mistakes, and it, too, is traceable to me. Before retaining him, I had asked Arthur Goldberg point-blank if he intended to run for governor against Rockefeller, and he answered no. If he had said yes or equivocated, I would have sought a different counsel. I accepted what he said about not running and made no back-up plan in case he changed his mind. When he did change his mind, I should have retained someone else as lead counsel. For as the trial went on, he spent more and more time campaigning and less on *Flood* v. *Kuhn*. I can't say this crippled us; Jay Topkis became, for all intents and purposes, the lead attorney of the case, and he is a brilliant lawyer. But I can't say the distraction of our chief counsel helped all that much, either.

Later, after he lost the election, Goldberg went back to Washington and established his own firm, eventually deciding to argue *Flood* v. *Kuhn* for us before the Supreme Court. Though I never told Arthur so, I felt he had betrayed us by deciding to run for governor—or more to the point, by not telling us he might change his mind and run—but I didn't feel we were in any position to turn down a lawyer of his stature when the case went before the Supreme Court. I guess I underestimated the allure of political office even to a man like Goldberg.

More important, whether because of the distraction of a political campaign, or the reaction to a stunning defeat by Governor Rockefeller, or some other reason, Goldberg, according to all qualified observers, performed way below his ability in arguing the Flood case before the Supreme Court. In retrospect, I realize it would have been better if Topkis had argued the case all the way through.

Sometimes the sins of men live long after them. In the case of

Presidents, occasionally the decisions of their Supreme Court appointees continue to do damage long after the President has left office. With respect to the Flood case, I have never seen any commentary on the fact that of Richard Nixon's four Supreme Court appointees (William Rehnquist, 1971, Lewis Powell, 1971, Harry Blackmun, 1970, and Warren Burger, 1969), three were made while the Flood case was pending and one at about the time the case was filed—and these four justices cast the crucial votes: three against Flood with one abstaining. The three negative votes were of course vital to the five-to-three decision against Flood. When Nixon told me in 1966 that he was a friend of the baseball owners I believed him; I certainly didn't need the point driven home by his court appointees six years later. Regardless, when I am in the mood to play "What if," I think: "What if Justice Hugo Black, a liberal, and Justice John Harlan, an intelligent conservative, had not resigned from the bench in 1971 but had served just one more year? Would they have joined Burger, White, and Stewart and voted against Flood, or would they have joined Justices Douglas, Marshall, and Brennan to produce a five-vote majority for Flood?" Tantalizing, but unanswerable.

In time, some other things about *Flood* v. *Kuhn* came out that I hadn't realized—for instance, how close we actually came to winning at the Supreme Court level. Or at least, how close we *might* have been. Bob Woodward's book *The Brethren* deals with much of the private discussion among the judges when they were considering and preparing their opinions. There are, of course, no written records of this, so the sources are questionable, but if Woodward is correct, the conference votes of the justices kept shifting. The first one, on March 24, allegedly was five to three against Flood, with one abstention—Justice Lewis F. Powell, who, of all things, owned stock in Busch Breweries, and that's the same Busch that Curt Flood had been playing for in St. Louis. Justice Marshall, again according to Woodward, then shifted to Flood's side, giving a four-four split. White showed signs of doing the same, and Powell's clerk urged him not to abstain and to cast his vote for Flood. But neither White nor Powell shifted his position. However, Chief Justice Burger changed his mind and voted against Flood, bringing the final tally to five to three against, with one abstention.

It was a curious coincidence that *Roe* v. *Wade,* the case dealing with a woman's right to make decisions about her body should come before the court at the same time as *Flood* v. *Kuhn,* about a man's right to make decisions about his body. Blackmun wrote the opinions in both cases. How this came about is the stuff of history.

Woodward's book makes it clear that Blackmun yearned to write a majority opinion in an "important" case; apparently, in his view, he had never had one.* After Marshall shifted his vote in favor of Flood, the resulting four-four split meant there would be *no* published opinion. When Chief Justice Burger then changed his vote to a negative one, making the final tally five to three against Flood, Blackmun, allegedly an ardent baseball fan, finally had his opportunity to write his first "important" majority opinion, one which, according to Woodward's account, was considered something of a joke by other justices.

If Woodward's version of events were true in any significant part, it certainly would not enhance the perception of the integrity of the court. Vote trading is not considered beneath congressmen, but in the U.S. Supreme Court?

After the case was tried in district court, Flood went to Denmark. We had some correspondence and a few telephone conversations when the appeal was pending. Curt was stoical about the decision; I don't think he really expected to win, any more than we did. He didn't appear to be bitter about the lack of support from his fellow ballplayers—at least Hall of Famers Jackie Robinson and Hank Greenberg had taken the stand in his corner, and he was justifiably proud of the linking of his name with theirs in baseball history. He also appreciated former major leaguer Jim Brosnan and Bill Veeck serving as witnesses on his behalf.

No one anticipated it, but Bob Short, owner of the Washington Senators, showed an interest in having Curt play for his team in 1971. I must admit that, given the circumstances, the salary he offered—$110,000, about $20,000 more than Curt made during

---

*Blackmun had been assigned to write the majority opinion in *Roe* v. *Wade* by the chief justice. However, Burger was in the minority in the vote taken at that point and, according to Court precedent, was therefore not entitled to assign the writing of the opinion. Senior members of the Court protested. In any event, the decision in *Roe* v. *Wade* was postponed until the following term.

his last season with the Cardinals—was quite fair. *Flood* v. *Kuhn* had not reached the Supreme Court yet, so we were all skeptical about the deal. If Flood accepted, would the case become moot?

That was the big obstacle, but after some discussion among Goldberg and Kuhn's lawyers and the counsel for both leagues, a written agreement was reached providing that Flood's appearance in a Senators uniform would not be made the basis for an argument that the case was moot and should be dismissed by the Court. It worried me a bit because an agreement between parties cannot bind a court—that is, a judge was free to interpret Flood's actions in his own manner. Still, Curt wanted to play—he certainly needed the money by now. He didn't talk about it, but I think some of his personal obligations, such as child support payments, were weighing heavily on him.

Our first meeting with Short was in a New York City hotel room shortly after Flood was "traded" to the Senators by the Phillies in November 1970. Goldberg and an associate, Flood and his attorney, Dick Moss, myself, and Short with his attorney were the participants. Short was a decent man, certainly progressive in his views (for an owner), was, in fact, a liberal Democrat, and had been the national treasurer of the Democratic Party. Goldberg was making his pitch about how the contract would have to take into account the difficulties of his client's having missed a year, etc., and Short chimed in, "Well, I understand, and these are all good points and we're going to do everything possible to make sure that the boy is comfortable."

Curt Flood was thirty-two years old. I looked over at him, wondering how he was going to react to Short's remark. Was he thinking, *"This,* after all I've gone through!" Curt saw me looking at him; he gave me a straight look back and winked. The gesture told me: "Stay cool. It's par for the course. The insensitivity of an owner is nothing to get excited about."

He decided, of course, to play again. I wish I could report that things worked out better. But after thirteen games and with a .200 batting average, he knew, or felt, he had lost it. His wire to Bob Short said: "I tried, a year and a half is too much. Very serious problems mounting every day. Thank you for your confidence and understanding."

Eight years later, at a Yankees-Athletics pregame ceremony,

Flood, who was working for Oakland as a broadcaster, met Bowie Kuhn for the first time. They shook hands. What did they say? Kuhn tells us in his book, published in 1987. "Finally the old schoolteacher inside me said, 'But you were wrong to walk out on Bob Short in 1971 after taking his money.'" As if Flood had been paid for anything more than the few games he played! After all Curt had gone through, I couldn't imagine a more insensitive remark, nor one that was more quintessentially Bowie Kuhnish— totally preoccupied with saving the owners' money. If I had been there, Curt surely would have winked at me again.

11 . . .

Strike One, 1972

I'M ALWAYS SURPRISED when I read a baseball historian who writes about the 1972 strike as if it were inevitable. The last thing I expected in 1972 was a strike; it really caught me unawares. It was not only the first in baseball history—it was the first in the history of professional sports. The issue described as the cause of the stoppage was only a mask for the real issue. The owners had decided to bring the Players Association's progress to a halt either by provoking a strike, which they felt confident of winning, or by forcing the players to back down and accept their unreasonable position in the negotiations.

Only the benefit plan (pensions and health insurance) was open for negotiation. The cost of the players' health care had risen by about $500,000 a year since the prior settlement in 1969. The union wanted the owners to meet that rise in costs and wanted payments to the pension plan increased so that retirement benefits could be adjusted to match the 17 percent jump in the cost of living over the prior three years. It was a modest request, especially in light of the four-year television contract major league baseball had signed recently with the National Broadcasting Company for the World Series, All-Star Game, and Game of the Week. That contract was worth $70 million.

Negotiations had gone slowly, but with no sign of a crisis. John Gaherin had made an offer—$500,000 a year—on the health-care contribution, but management was reluctant to increase retirement benefits. There was, however, surplus income from the pension fund that could be used to fund an increase in the retirement benefits. This meant that it could be financed without additional cost to the owners. It seemed to me that a settlement was within reach. In fact, on my annual spring training trip in early March I discussed the pension negotiations with seven teams without mentioning the possibility of a strike. And I'm not an optimist.

Things changed fast. The night before Dick Moss and I were set to meet the Chicago White Sox at their spring training facility in Sarasota, Gaherin surprised us. "The owners aren't going to increase pension benefits at all," he said, "and we're going to *reduce* our offer on health care." Reducing a bargaining proposal which Gaherin knew was inadequate in the first place was an unmistakable signal: Management was baiting us into a strike. Their position was, "Take it or leave it! There's nothing you or the players can do about it."

Before I could even consider a long-term plan, I was faced with an immediate logistical problem. Having already visited seven clubs, I had to backtrack to tell them about the threat without disrupting my scheduled meetings with the seventeen remaining teams—eleven more in Florida, five in Arizona, and one in California. I also had to find a way to continue pension negotiations, conduct the rest of the Association's business, and keep the press up to date on what was happening. All within a span of twenty-three days. That night Dick and I mapped out a strategy, making the necessary calls to rearrange our schedule.

The next morning we went to the White Sox meeting with an entirely different mind-set. "Negotiations will continue," I said, "and there's always the possibility we'll reach a settlement, but it's beginning to seem unlikely." Over the next ninety minutes I explained how important it was to keep retirement benefits on the same level as rising living costs; if not, inflation over the next twenty-five to thirty years (when the players would begin drawing benefits) would reduce the value of their pensions to a tiny fraction of the current worth. I explained what the options were (stand or fold), what each option would lead to, what would be involved if the players decided to walk out, and the procedures we'd follow until the benefit plan expired on March 31. Before leaving the meeting, I asked Jay Johnstone, the White Sox player rep, to conduct a strike authorization vote—the first in baseball since Robert Murphy's attempt to get the Pirates to walk out in 1946 was derailed by Commissioner Chandler's labor spies on the Pittsburgh ball club. The White Sox voted to support a strike, 25–0. (In the next eight days I met again with the seven clubs where no strike vote had been taken; the players unanimously endorsed a strike.)

As the March 31 deadline approached and the negotiating sessions produced no change, my hopes of reaching a settlement faded. If I still hadn't known which way the wind was blowing, all I needed to do was feel the hot air billowing from St. Petersburg, where, after an owners' meeting, Gussie Busch announced to the press, "We voted unanimously to take a stand. We're not going to give them another *goddamn* cent! If they want to strike, let them strike." Busch's war cry was heard throughout the spring training camps. Of all his confrontational statements, this may have been the dumbest. It became a rallying point for the players, a factor in their rapidly spreading solidarity against the owners' arbitrary, antiplayer position. As for Bowie Kuhn, his contribution to the governor's dinner at St. Petersburg was to deliver pious platitudes. "The club owners...are a group of sportsmen whose hearts are in the game we all love."

Busch, the "malty proprietor," as Red Smith labeled him, had become a caricature of the factory owner resisting unionization, but he was by no means acting alone. The Player Relations Committee in 1972 contained scarcely a "moderate." There was Reds owner Francis Dale, a publisher and later treasurer of CREEP—the Committee to Re-Elect the President (Nixon)—the organization whose activities were exposed at the Watergate hearings; brewery owner Jerry Hoffberger of the Orioles; Royals owner Ewing Kauffman, who made his money in pharmaceuticals;

Dick Meyer representing the petulant beer baron Busch; Wall-Streeter Donald Grant of the Mets; Twins owner-by-inheritance Calvin Griffith; and Dan Galbreath of the Pirates representing his father, John, who had amassed a fortune in construction and real estate. These hardliners didn't hide the fact that they were out to destroy the union. From 1971 to the spring of 1972, the rate of "disposal" of elected player reps had jumped dramatically. Of twenty-four reps, sixteen had been cut or traded.

The press generally followed the owners' lead. The public heard that the players had the most generous pension plan in America and they were greedily grasping for more, even though what we were seeking was stable pension benefits. We endured editorials like "The fan goes from steak to hamburger while the ballplayer rides a golden gravy train"—as if *we* were taking steaks out of the fans' mouths! And they echoed management's line that the athletes were well paid for "playing a game." (In case anyone thinks allegations of players being overpaid began when salaries reached seven figures, major leaguers were averaging roughly $22,000 a year at the time.) I wondered how the same writers would have responded had newspaper owners asked why grown men demanded payment to *watch* games and *write* about them—and still expected decent salaries and benefits.

The more I read the more I was persuaded that the owners were not only out to break the union, but also intent on achieving a "victory" over me. After all, I had cost them a fair sum of money. Since 1966, the minimum salary had more than doubled, from $6,000 to $13,500, the players' various allowances had been substantially increased, the pension and medical benefits had grown by many millions, and the Association had demonstrated an ability to defend players' rights. I was portrayed in the newspaper as the villain, the union man who had introduced the evil serpent of money into baseball's Garden of Eden. Atlanta executive Paul Richards said that a stand must be taken or "there isn't going to be any baseball for a long, long time. The owners...simply aren't going to let Marvin Miller run over them any more."

The columnist who seemed most obsessed with me was Dick Young, who wrote, "Clearly, to the owners, the enemy is not the players, whom the owners regard merely as ingrates, misled ingrates. The enemy is Marvin Miller, general of the Union. The showdown is with him. It is not over a few more thousand dollars, not the few thousand demanded for some obscure pension inflation, it is over the principle of who will run their baseball business, they, the Lords, or this man Miller." Young was overstating the case, as usual, but he wasn't entirely wrong. I had every intention of making the Players Association into an effective, independent organization. I had no desire to "run" baseball, but I was determined that the players' importance to the game be fully recognized and the concept that they were property be eliminated.

On the sixteen teams I visited in Florida, only eight players voted not to strike. When I got to Winter Haven, in the middle of the trip, Carl Yastrzemski and Reggie Smith asked several questions, the tone of which indicated that they were opposed to a walkout. A Red Sox player since 1961, Yaz had already spoken out against Curt Flood's struggle to end baseball's monopolistic practices. Management had treated Yaz well, and he was close to Sox owner Tom Yawkey. Yaz and Smith influenced another two players, making a total of four negatives, but they were outvoted by their teammates, 26–4.

In his book, *The Wrong Stuff,* Sox pitcher Bill Lee wrote: "Reggie Smith stood up the day we took the vote, announcing that he was voting no because every week out was going to cost him four thousand dollars, while it would cost most of the other players less than eight hundred. I looked at him and said, 'Reggie, you didn't say that, did you? That didn't come out of your mouth?' But it had.... The rest of the club voted strike and the brief discussion between Smith and me was forgotten. By everybody but Reggie. From that day on I was *numero uno* on his shit list."*

In the Dodgers camp there were other minor cracks. On March 17, St. Patrick's Day, Dick, my wife, Terry, and I arrived at Vero Beach, the site of Los Angeles's newly renovated sprawling spring training complex known as "Dodgertown." The meeting went well. It was a lively, interesting group, with veterans Frank

---

*It's worth noting that all four Boston players came around to supporting the Association. Before a strike vote in 1980, Reggie Smith, then with the Dodgers, made an emotional speech about the value of a strong union. He told his teammates that he regretted his vote in 1972 and urged a unanimous vote to strike. He got it.

Robinson and Maury Wills (later, baseball's first black managers); pitchers Don Sutton and Tommy John; and Davey Lopes, Ron Cey, and Steve Garvey, the nucleus of the club that would advance to four World Series in eight seasons.

Afterward, player rep Wes Parker reported the results of the vote: 21–4 in favor of a strike. While I was talking to a few sportswriters, a messenger interrupted in order to invite us to Walter O'Malley's annual St. Patrick's Day party that evening. Ordinarily I would have declined—nothing against St. Patrick, but Dick and I still had nine clubs to meet. But a thought came to me that this might be the best time to talk to Walter O'Malley. He carried a lot of clout and possessed a quality many other owners did not: He was a realist. Perhaps he could talk some sense into the rest of the owners and possibly avoid a strike. "We'd be delighted," I said to the messenger, "but could you ask Mr. O'Malley to set aside some time for a private meeting?"

The party was a big league bash. Everything was green: water, scotch, beer, potatoes, tablecloths, you name it. O'Malley had chartered a plane from Los Angeles with scores of season-ticket holders, and everybody was whooping it up. I hadn't been there very long before I began to feel uncomfortable—and not because I was wearing a green party hat. Ex-Dodgers Sandy Koufax and Roy Campanella were there, but none of the current players had been invited. Their absence dampened my spirits.

I was talking to team executive Al Campanis when Dick and I were summoned to meet with Walter and his son Peter O'Malley. O'Malley Sr., his party hat still perched on his huge head, was puffing on a fat cigar, laying a cloud of smoke throughout the room.

We got down to business quickly. "Walter, I don't really understand what's going on. This isn't a new issue. And we're not asking for anything out of the ordinary. The amount of money separating us isn't even that large, certainly not large enough to require a strike. Unless you confirm what I think—that the owners are deliberately challenging the players, the Association, and me—I don't get it."

Instead of discussing the issue seriously, O'Malley said, "Oh, well, don't worry. There's not going to be a strike. We'll resolve this."

I told him I hoped he was right, but that it was getting close to the deadline.

"A lot can happen in two weeks," he said, sipping a glass of green Scotch.

Either O'Malley was ignoring the facts, or he didn't understand them. I never really understood which. In any event, O'Malley's remark caused me to despair; if the most rational businessman among the owners didn't understand that their stance was about to force a strike, none of the owners did.

As I stood up to leave, O'Malley said, "I heard the strike vote was twenty-one to four. Who were the four?"

I thought he was kidding. He wasn't. "I have no idea," I said, "but I wouldn't tell you if I did. Why do you want to know?"

"A baseball team is only as good as its unity," he said. "I don't want players that cast themselves as management tools on my team." He explained, "Don't get me wrong. I'd prefer the players to vote unanimously not to strike, but if the majority decides to walk out, I don't want dissenters on my club opposing their teammates. A winning ball club is unified, not split."

I didn't know whether to believe him. But much later, after I learned their identities—Wes Parker, who told me about his vote; two veteran stars who were managerial candidates, and a utility catcher—I realized O'Malley had been telling the truth. Two were traded, and two retired.

I left the meeting with him and his son convinced for the first time that there would be a showdown by March 31.

Supported overwhelmingly by the clubs in Florida, Dick, Terry, and I flew to Arizona where Dick and I would meet with the players on the six clubs in the "cactus league." By the time we completed our tour out west, only two players had voted against a strike—a Milwaukee Brewer and a Seattle Pilot—pushing the final player vote to 663–10.*

Unfortunately, this impressive show of solidarity didn't persuade the owners to bargain in good faith. On March 29—two days before the pension agreement expired—I proposed that the dispute be decided by an impartial arbitrator in order to avoid a

---

*Two players abstained.

strike. Among other things, this proposal was an excellent way to determine whether the owners wanted the matter resolved or whether they were hell-bent on *not* finding a solution. I even suggested that the arbitrator be selected by ex-President Johnson, President Nixon, or former Chief Justice Earl Warren. My only stipulation was that he be a "professional" arbitrator. John Gaherin said no, issuing the stock alibi that baseball was a unique business and hence an outside arbitrator couldn't understand the issues. (When it suited the owners to admit it, baseball was magically transformed from a "game" into a "business.") Actually, Gaherin was partially right. Baseball's exemption from federal antitrust laws was *unique* in American industry; it was even unique among the other professional sports.

We scheduled a meeting for March 31 in Dallas to inform the player reps and their alternates of the latest developments. The night before, in a hotel in Scottsdale, Arizona, Dick Moss and I reviewed our options. The amount of money we wanted for health care and retirement benefits was chicken feed compared to the $70 million the owners were getting in television revenue, the traditional source of funds for the pension plan. Money was not the issue. That had been obvious for several weeks.

The real issue was power. Set on having their way, the owners believed the players would back down or, if they did strike, fold before you could say "pension plan payments." I suppose it was inevitable, given the Association's gains over the past six years, that management would eventually test us. We were armed with a vote of 663–10 in favor of striking, but the owners were checking to see if we'd be firing bullets or blanks. Management was certain it would be the latter.

To strike or not to strike, that, as one playwright almost said, was the question. It was a rough decision. The players were inexperienced (none had ever been out on any kind of strike), and the Association lacked the financial and public relations resources the owners had at their command. Postponing the conflict wouldn't damage the players in the long run, but if they struck and couldn't sustain it, the blow to the still young Association could prove disastrous.

After a long discussion with Dick and several phone conversations with player reps, I decided to recommend the strike be postponed. Before we shut down baseball, I wanted the Association to have a stronger base and better funding. I wanted the players to be better informed and prepared and the issues to be more meaningful to the players' long-term interests. As it was, I didn't like the odds.

So Dick and I worked on an alternate plan. We would negotiate during the season, a scenario that would also give us more time to educate the players. If we couldn't come to an agreement during the season, we'd be able to try again when the basic agreement (and the pension plan) were renegotiated in 1973. By then we would be in a stronger position to strike, if need be. Under no circumstances, however, would we accept an inadequate settlement. The old benefit plan agreement would remain in effect, and retirement benefits could be increased retroactively after we had come to terms. Dick set down our recommendation and the reasons for it in longhand.

The three of us flew to Dallas on the morning of the thirty-first. Sitting behind Terry and me on the plane were Chuck Dobson, Oakland A's player rep, and Reggie Jackson, the team's alternate rep. They had been following the negotiations in the Phoenix newspapers, and their view was that the owners thought the players were afraid to strike. Reggie and Chuck certainly didn't seem afraid. We arrived at the airport motel near Love Field around two P.M. and were greeted by a swarm of reporters and photographers. I had been involved in five nationwide Steelworkers' strikes, but I'd never seen anything approaching this. Such was life in baseball.

The meeting got underway. After reviewing all that had happened during the negotiations, I recommended that we delay striking. Hands shot up all over the room. The players were more committed to accepting the owners' challenge to strike than I had realized; in fact, they were positively militant. Soon I found myself playing the role of devil's advocate, trying to be as realistic (even pessimistic) as possible. I explained the hardships involved. I pointed out that we had no strike fund, no field offices, and no public relations staff; the press would likely be hostile; and on and on. To no avail. Player after player stood up to convince *me* that they were united, that *they* were hell-bent on taking the fight to the owners—even though it was impossible to know how long the strike would last.

Roughly four hours into the meeting, one of the player reps, impatient with the continuing discussion, started to chant: "Strike! Strike! Strike!" It was picked up by the others and repeated over and over. It reminded me of a scene from Clifford Odets's play, *Waiting for Lefty,* in which a group of cab drivers, preyed on by racketeers and exploited by corrupt taxi owners, have gathered for a meeting. They wait, but the union leader, Lefty, doesn't show, and they finally learn he has been murdered. The cabbies refuse to be intimidated and begin shouting in unison, "Strike! Strike! Strike!" The play presented an overly sentimental view of the labor movement in the 1930s, but that scene packed an emotional punch. I was similarly moved by the dramatic turn of events at the Dallas meeting, more so since this wasn't staged. For the first time in baseball history, the players wanted to fight management head on. Our new draft resolution would be a lot simpler—a declaration to strike immediately. The remaining exhibition games on or after April 1 would be canceled, as would the regular season games until a satisfactory settlement was reached.

The final tally was 47–0 in favor of a strike. Wes Parker, the Dodgers' player rep, abstained. Parker had been quoted several times as being opposed to players receiving "ridiculously high" salaries (such as $150,000 a year); not long after the meeting he was removed from office by his teammates, who described their action as "impeachment."

After the vote, we worked out a strategy to communicate with the rest of the players, who would soon be scattered around the country (and throughout Latin America). I announced that Dick and I would remove ourselves from the Association's payroll as we had when the Steelworkers Union went out on strike.

When I called John Gaherin with the final tally, he was flabbergasted. Then again, so was I. Both of us knew the odds were stacked against the players, but Gaherin and the owners had no idea how determined the players were. I could only hope the players' resolve would last—though the tenor of the meeting had made me a believer.

Meanwhile, the meeting had lasted much longer than anyone

anticipated, forcing us all to scramble for new flight reservations. Unable to get a nonstop flight to New York, Terry and I were forced to stop in Baltimore. Around midnight, I stirred from a nap to find a dozen of the biggest men I'd ever seen boarding the plane. I sat up, looked closely, and focused on the familiar faces of the New York Knicks who, hours earlier, had been battling the Baltimore Bullets. The Knicks greeted us with cries of "Right on!" Bill Bradley, Dave DeBusschere, Earl Monroe, Walt Frazier, Willis Reed, and most of the others came over to talk about the strike, which was how we spent the rest of the flight. It was a satisfying end to an emotional day.*

We returned home in the early hours on April 1. The morning newspapers would soon announce the unexpected. It might be April Fool's Day, but no one would be laughing. I slept for a few hours and called John Gaherin early in the morning to discuss resuming our negotiations. Over my second cup of coffee, I thought back on the events of the past six years, trying to understand the owners' fury against us. Soon I found myself thinking about their folly in bringing on baseball's first strike.

The owners' efforts to bust the union made a bit more sense when you considered the strides the Association had made during the previous six years. Before 1966, the owners had a unilateral right to do, literally, anything they pleased; they could change the rules in the middle of a player's contract and say, "Here are the rules that *now* apply to you." The owners routinely tied players to documents—the Major League Rules, the Professional Baseball Rules, the league constitutions and bylaws—without even giving them copies of what they were agreeing to be bound by.

The first basic agreement, in 1968, required that players at least be given copies of every document that became a part of their contract. Then we insisted that the owners had to advise us of proposed changes. Later, we insisted and obtained agreement that no rule would apply if it conflicted with a provision of the basic agreement.

*A few days later, Bill Bradley (now U.S. Senator Bradley, D–N.J.) wrote a letter to the *Daily News* in response to one of Dick Young's hateful columns. He called me and asked if I'd check his facts on the baseball dispute. It was an intelligent letter, and the paper ran it right away.

We had them put that language in a *big box* in the major league rule book to make clear to anyone who opens it that any rule which is inconsistent with the conditions of the basic agreement is null and void. But we still weren't home free; we would negotiate something in the basic agreement, and the owners wouldn't change the blue book—the book that encompassed the Major League Rules and the so-called major league agreement. And since the rules weren't brought up to date, you had owners and general managers saying, "How was I to know I couldn't follow this rule? I followed it for thirty years, and it's still here."

Over time, the language protecting the players' contracts and the collective bargaining agreement became stronger and stronger until the leagues finally understood that any time they wanted to change a rule affecting the players' rights, they had to negotiate the approval of the Players Association. The same became true of any playing rules that could affect a player's career.

These were important changes, but they were a mere prelude to the Association's most important victory: impartial grievance arbitration, won during the basic agreement negotiations in 1970. The pressure of the recently filed Curt Flood case had a large impact. In order to maintain in court the fiction that baseball was governed impartially and not by the commissioner, a paid employee of the owners, the owners (or at least their lawyers) had to concede that any disagreement about the meaning of the provisions of the collective bargaining agreement would be resolved by impartial, binding arbitration.

The owners ultimately agreed to grievance arbitration on two conditions. The first involved television rights. There was a clause in the players' contract which granted the owners the right to all pictures of a player for *publicity* purposes. While I had no problem with that, I fought hard to retain a player's right to his picture for *commercial* purposes. Management eventually conceded this point, but they were worried that I would take a grievance to arbitration on a player's right to his television image. We finally agreed that such a dispute would be resolved in court.

The second exception involved the issue of "the integrity of the game." Lou Hoynes, counsel for the National League, argued on management's behalf that in the event of another scandal such as the 1919 Black Sox scandal, baseball didn't want the commissioner overruled in court. (Remember, Commissioner Kenesaw Landis had banned Shoeless Joe & Co. for life *after* the players had been *absolved* in court.)

It was finally agreed that any grievance arising out of alleged corruption could be ruled on by the commissioner as long as the player's right to a fair hearing was protected. Hoynes didn't want the contract to contain any language which even *suggested* the throwing of games and came back with a draft that substituted "public confidence in the game of baseball" for "alleged corruption." I grudgingly agreed on two conditions: We would have the right to renegotiate the provision if Kuhn were replaced as commissioner; and if any commissioner improperly removed a case from arbitration, we had the right to reopen the agreement, demand the end of his authority to deal with any grievance, and, if necessary, strike to support our position.

At the time Hoynes (on Kuhn's behalf) agreed to grievance arbitration, management didn't see the eventual cost to them of this "noneconomic" issue. But this victory was as important as any we would win. Any collective bargaining agreement which can't be enforced by binding, impartial arbitration (or by a strike) isn't worth the paper it's written on. Grievance arbitration put us on the track that led to the Messersmith decision. There were a lot of turns, but we were on track.

As soon as the 1972 strike was announced, the owners and the press sounded off immediately. Red Smith and Leonard Koppett of the *New York Times* provided, I thought, accurate and balanced reporting, but over all, the players were blasted. Some of the criticism bordered on hysteria. C. C. Johnson Spink, the editor of the *Sporting News,* called the walkout the "darkest day in sports history," adding, with breathtaking stupidity, that "the whole idea of pensions for major league players may have been a mistake growing out of a misconception of what constitutes a career." Paul Richards of the Braves said, "Tojo and Hirohito couldn't stop baseball but Marvin Miller could." When California owner Gene Autry learned that the Angels-Dodgers exhibition game had been canceled, he said: "We ought to close baseball down forever!" And he called *me* an extremist!

The press in Cincinnati was particularly virulent—no surprise considering that Reds owner Francis Dale also owned the *Cincinnati Enquirer*. Reds player rep Jim Merritt was concerned and asked me to talk to the players on April 5, the traditional Opening Day of major league baseball. I flew to Cincinnati.

Roberto Clemente called to ask if I would visit Pittsburgh as well after speaking to the Reds. The Pirates were a loose, fun bunch of guys. Dave Giusti was the player rep in 1972, but Roberto Clemente was the real leader of the clubhouse. He himself was known to stand up to the owners. Dave Giusti told me a Clemente story that I'll always treasure. Pirates owner Dan Galbreath was in the locker room talking to the players. The club would draw better, he said, if the players signed more autographs and made more public appearances. Galbreath piled it on, claiming that the players weren't appreciative enough of the fans. According to Giusti, the team had had enough, but nobody had the audacity to speak up.

Finally, Clemente said, "Mr. Galbreath, I had a dream last night about this. I had terrible neckache, and suddenly I had become so old and tired and injured that I could no longer play. But those *wonderful* fans out in right field banded together and said, 'Even if the Great One can't play, we can't let him go. He belongs in right field.' So the fans presented me with a rocking chair and said that I should sit comfortably between the stands and the right-field foul line and relax all through my retirement."

The rest of the Bucs didn't know what to think. Was he buttering management up? Had he gone loco?

But Clemente continued in his heavily accented English. "You know, Mr. Galbreath, what that dream is?"

Galbreath hesitated. "No, what?"

Clemente replied firmly, "It is *bool-sheet!*"

Everybody busted up. Except Galbreath.

Thinking about it now, I can just see Clemente moving toward the plate, flexing his neck muscles and turning his head from side to side while everyone waited expectantly for him to step into the batter's box. And as I write this, I greatly regret that I never took him up on his numerous invitations to Terry and me to visit him in Puerto Rico. The only time I ever visited his home was the day of his funeral. On December 31, 1972, Roberto Clemente was killed flying on a relief mission to earthquake victims in Managua, Nicaragua. He was thirty-eight years old.

Not only Clemente but the Latin American players in general often expressed tremendous gratitude for the gains we made on their behalf. In the winter of 1971, soon after Pittsburgh had come back from a two-game deficit to upset the Orioles in the World Series, I was invited to throw out the first ball of the annual Puerto Rican Winter League All-Star Game. I had expected the traditional ten-foot flip from the stands. Much to my surprise, I was led onto the field, past a horde of photographers eager to record the "event" and onto the pitcher's mound. Elrod Hendricks, the Orioles catcher, pulled down his mask and crouched, spotting his glove for a low target. Without warming up, and wearing a suit and tie, I reached back and let her rip; I needed just one bounce to reach the plate. Elrod short-hopped the ball and fired it back to the mound, insisting I throw a strike—something I hadn't done since 1937. My next pitch—it would have been a fastball except for its lack of speed—did the trick. I trotted off the field as relieved as any pitcher who has worked his way out of a bases-loaded jam.

Shortly after that, I returned to New York. Mets ace Tom Seaver stopped by my office and noticed some photos lying on my desk.

"What's this?" he asked.

I told him about the all-star game. "Care to comment on my delivery?" I asked.

Seaver played it straight. He studied the pictures carefully, looked up with a serious expression, and said, "Do you always pitch with a wristwatch on?"

After meeting with the Reds and Pirates in the strike's first week, I stopped in Baltimore at the urging of club and American League player rep Brooks Robinson. Robinson had reason to be concerned. After the walkout, Orioles owner Jerry Hoffberger had called a team meeting and blasted the players for hours. Hoffberger had two prominent allies on the team: manager Earl Weaver and pitcher Jim Palmer. Weaver told the players that the strike would ruin the club's chances of returning to the World Series. Palmer said I had "brainwashed" the players. (He must have been anticipating a column Dick Young later wrote, which read: "[Miller] runs the players through a high-pressure spray the way an auto goes through a car wash, and that's how they come out, brainwashed." Maybe Young brainwashed Palmer.) After the meeting, Weaver announced to the press that a poll he had conducted showed that twenty-one of the twenty-six Orioles were against the strike and sixteen of the twenty-one were willing to play a scheduled exhibition game against Atlanta.

I spoke with the team at Brooks and Connie Robinson's home in suburban Maryland. Brooks was one of the real heroes of the 1972 strike—not the only one, but one of the most important. Perhaps the best defensive third baseman of all time, he *had* been a hero in Baltimore until the virulent press (among the worst in terms of union bashing) turned on him like a traitor; after the strike was settled, the fair-weather fans showered him with choruses of boos. A kind and modest man who did a lot for the community, Robinson remained the same calm, level-headed person he had always been; undeterred, he carried out his duties as player rep superbly. He regretted the fans' reaction, no doubt, but he didn't show it. I never heard him criticize them. I did criticize them— publicly. Recalling their jeers still galls me.

The meeting at Brooks's house was a good one with a full airing of the relevant issues. I'm not sure why, but that Orioles team produced several of the Association's most vociferous supporters. Robinson's successor at third base, Doug DeCinces, went on to become the American League's player rep. Shortstop Mark Belanger, the O's alternate rep in 1972, became the club's player rep and a special assistant for the Association after he retired as a player in 1983. And some time after the 1972 strike, Earl Weaver, of all people, became a vocal and eloquent union stalwart.

The players surprised everybody during the walkout, even themselves. Players around the country kept in constant contact with their team reps; others worked out together at high schools; and many veterans invited the younger players to stay at their homes to lessen the financial strain. Twins pitcher Jim Perry was a case in point. Perry had grown up in a farm community in North Carolina. He had no experience with unions, and yet overnight he became an efficient, dedicated leader. He was the first to organize the housing of younger players with veterans, and he rented a school bus to transport players back and forth to a local gym which he had arranged to use for workouts. He telephoned me each day for reports on the negotiations and even put together a public address system in the gym so that I could report directly to all of the Twins working out there.

When there were potential cracks, players stepped forward to prevent them. Maury Wills led a meeting of thirteen players in Los Angeles and announced that they had voted to play the Dodgers' home opener on April 7, but Wes Parker—the lone abstainer from the strike vote one week earlier in Dallas—contacted the press to say that Wills didn't speak for the rest of the players, who would remain solidly on strike.

While Wills's conduct turned out to be an aberration, it did feed my biggest concern—division in the ranks. I had to keep reminding myself that the players had never struck. But then, in New York, Willie Mays addressed the players' executive board and my doubts disappeared like one of his towering home runs. Mays had always supported the union, but he hadn't been particularly outspoken—not strange, really, since Willie's career was winding down just about the time the union was solidifying. In 1971—Willie's twentieth big league season—owner Horace Stoneham had traded Giants player rep Hal Lanier and alternate Gaylord Perry. Mays, the forty-one-year-old superstar (he, too, would be traded in a few weeks to the Mets), became the acting player rep.

At the meeting in New York, Mays quieted any doubters with his speech: "I know it's hard being away from the game and our paychecks and our normal life," he said. "I love this game. It's been my whole life. But we made a decision in Dallas to stick together, and until we're satisfied, we *have* to stay together. This could be my last year in baseball, and if the strike lasts the entire season and I've played my last game, well, it will be painful. But if we don't hang together, everything we've worked for will be lost."

The silence in the room spoke volumes. Mays's on-the-field brilliance had dimmed, but his influence off it remained strong. Sometimes I wish I had come to the Players Association ten or twelve years earlier, if only to see what Willie Mays (or Mickey Mantle or Sandy Koufax, among others) would have pulled in as a free agent near his prime.

As the standoff moved into its second week, negotiations progressed at a snail's pace. But on April 8, forty-eight hours after telling me the owners wouldn't contribute a dime more, Gaherin announced that the owners planned to add another $400,000—the "revised" estimate of the increased cost of insurance benefits.

He was only doing his job. Divisions had begun to appear among the owners. The White Sox, Pirates, and Phillies opened their stadiums to the players for workouts. When the league offices ordered them to stop, Sox owner Arthur Allyn barked, "Nobody is going to tell me what to do with my team!"

After a meeting of the owners in Chicago on April 10, Gussie Busch was reported to have said that the clubs should band together to raise a $1 million emergency fund to help the poorer teams during the strike. Supposedly, Walter O'Malley shot back, "You idiot, the Dodgers alone lose one million dollars each weekend the strike goes on!" That was the refreshing thing about O'Malley: You always knew his bottom line.

Charlie Finley, who had made his millions selling medical insurance to doctors, said after the owners' meeting, "Very few owners knew there was any surplus in the pension fund. That was the main problem....The owners didn't understand what this was all about." (Apparently, they hadn't read the memorandum I sent to them documenting the surplus in the pension fund.) It was a far cry from his stance ten days earlier, when he claimed the players had forgotten two things: "First, they don't contribute one red cent to their own pension plan, and, second, they already have the best pension plan in America." Dick Moss noted Finley's turn-about by saying, "Charlie's going to be my hero yet." In ten days, Finley's consciousness had been raised 100 percent. If we could make a fraction of that progress with a few of the other owners, we were home free.

Several hours after Finley's proclamation, the owners revised their offer by adding $500,000 for health-care benefits and agreeing to a cost-of-living increase in retirement benefits.

But no sooner had we settled that than another problem threatened to wreck the agreement. The owners wanted us to make up all the games lost during the strike *without* pay. The hardliners didn't give up easily. They suggested extra doubleheaders and games on scheduled off-days. The players scorned the plan.

At this point, Gaherin and I were in my office when I asked him, in total confidence, to think about an idea. I said, "What if we make up all the lost games due to the strike with neither the owners nor the players receiving compensation? Make admission to those games free as a way to make it up to the fans, and have the proceeds from concessions, parking, and radio-television go to mutually agreed upon charities."

Gaherin almost fell out of his chair. "Are you nuts?" he asked. "The owners would never go for it, and do you realize the lousy PR we'd receive if this leaked to the press?"

"Okay. Let's forget it," I said. "It was only an idea."

What followed was the one and only time Gaherin broke a commitment to me. After leaving my office, he told the owners and their lawyers the idea I had spoken of in confidence. Management exploded, just as he had predicted. Not only were they shocked, but they cleared out of New York *just in case* word leaked to the press. From then on, the remainder of the negotiations were conducted by phone to the owners' new headquarters in Chicago.

On April 10, I called Gaherin with our proposal: "No canceled games will be rescheduled, and the players won't be paid for the days we were out on strike." (I never expected that they would be paid for the struck games.)

The owners' answer was the same: "No dice."

On April 13, after three days of batting this back and forth, the owners okayed our proposal. Had they agreed to our proposal on April 10, only about half as many games would have been missed. The owners then refused to settle unless the players lost credited service for the nine days of the strike in the season. I rejected their demand out of hand. They folded, and the agreement specified that players would lose no credited service time because of the strike.

The strike lasted thirteen days (nine during the season) and forced the cancellation of 86 games. Some clubs played 153 games, others played 156. That twist of fate may have cost the Red Sox the pennant—they finished behind Detroit by one-half game. The owners lost an estimated $5.2 million. Major league players lost nine days' salary, or about $600,000. Starting in 1972, the increased pension benefits represented a gain of an even greater sum *each year* into the future. Pete Rose, who finished with 198 hits, sounded off by saying, "If there's another strike...the Players Association will not get my support....Last year's strike cost me seven thousand dollars and a chance for two hundred hits." I'm happy to say that Pete changed his tune in 1981, backing the Association all the way. He did the same in 1985, even though he was a manager. Thanks to the Association, Pete became a free agent in 1978, signed a four-year, $3.2-million contract with Philadelphia, and earned more money *each day of the season, every year,* than he "lost" in the entire 1972 strike.

Baseball was back, and the Association—now stronger than ever—had successfully stood up to the owners. Leonard Koppett of the *New York Times* summed up baseball's first strike like this:

Players: We want higher pensions.

Owners: We won't give you one damn cent for that.

Players: You don't have to—the money is already there. Just let us use it.

Owners: It would be imprudent.

Players: We did it before, and anyhow, we won't play unless we can have some of it.

Owners: Okay.

Between the last two statements, thirteen days elapsed and eighty-six games went unplayed. Koppett was making a very basic point; the terms accepted by the owners on April 13 would have averted a strike had they accepted them on March 31.

In later accounts, Koppett provided an analysis of greater depth, pointing out that the real significance of the strike was that the owners never again would be able to exercise the control over players that had been the hallmark of the owner-player relationship for so many decades.

When a settlement was reached, I told the press, "All fans should be proud of the players. They showed courage and hung together against terrible odds. They made the owners understand that they must be treated as equals." I felt very hopeful. Weathering such a crisis, of course, would enable the Players Association to stand up against further assaults: the 1976 lockout and the 1981 strike. Of course, those battles were years away.

The 1972 strike was settled on April 14—my fifty-fifth birthday. The season was free to begin. I don't remember any other gifts I received, but I do remember celebrating late into the night.

12...

Catfish...

JAMES "CATFISH" HUNTER, of Herford, North Carolina, lists "farmer" and "author" as occupations. He also accomplished a few noteworthy things in baseball in a fifteen-year Hall of Fame career. He won 224 games, including 21 or more for five consecutive seasons; he pitched more than 230 innings for ten straight years; he won 9 postseason games and helped the Oakland A's and New York Yankees to five World Championships; he won the 1974 Cy Young Award after winning 25 games; and on May 8, 1968, he pitched a perfect game against the Minnesota Twins. He was also a terrific hitter—in 1971 he batted .350, making him the first American League pitcher since Walter Johnson in 1925 to win 20 games and hit .300 or better in the same season. And to be fair, in his career he gave up 374 home runs, more than anyone else in league history. He accomplished all this without the little toe on his right foot, which he lost in a hunting accident in 1963. However, one thing that Jim didn't accomplish was something he often gets credit for: he *didn't* abolish the reserve clause and win free agency

• 224 •

for ballplayers. True, he was the first bona fide free agent, but his freedom arose from the club's violation of his contract.

One of the first significant cracks in the brick wall of the reserve clause began when Hunter's contract was breached by the A's owner, Charlie Finley. When it was explained to Jim that he had a right to terminate his contract and become a free agent unless Finley corrected the violation, he filed a grievance to do just that. Hunter's victory and subsequent contract offers were significant because they were tremendous eye-openers to the players as well as the press and public. Why would a team pay a player who had been making $100,000 $3.75 million for a five-year guaranteed contract, as the Yankees did, unless they thought him to be worth the money? Remember, this was a time when pitchers were paid, on the whole, less than everyday players. If Hunter was worth that kind of money, what were Johnny Bench, Joe Morgan, Reggie Jackson, and other superstars worth? And what effect would that have on player salaries all the way to the bottom? Once Hunter signed with the Yankees, those questions and issues were out in the open, and the owners would never again succeed in sweeping them under the rug.

It might surprise baseball fans who grew up after 1974 to realize this, but the size of the contract the Yankees offered Hunter came as a shock to his teammates and competitors alike. Not because they sold his abilities as a competitor short. With the possible exception of the Orioles' Jim Palmer, there may have been no more respected starter in the American League, and after he compiled a 4–0 record against the Reds, Mets, and Dodgers in the 1972, 1973, and 1974 World Series, the National League knew all about him as well. But this was still a time when, despite the Association's best efforts, many players still bought the owners' claims that free agency would damage and impoverish baseball and that they were well paid. And so Hunter's case was the forerunner of later victories in the sense that it awakened players to how much they had been exploited.

Catfish Hunter's free agency was not the result of a prolonged assault on the reserve clause by the Players Association but of the violation of a contract between Hunter and Charlie Finley. Technically, the breach of contract that freed Jim Hunter could have happened at any time in baseball history. But it's unlikely that before the formation of the Players Association Hunter's rights would have been recognized. If the incident had occurred in the old days, the sequence of events would have gone pretty much like this: Finley might have gone to the American League president and said, "Come with me, I owe Jim Hunter some money for a part of his contract I reneged on, but I'm going to go offer it to him now. You'll be a witness. If he takes it, the contract is fulfilled, and if he refuses, I can't be faulted—because I did offer it to him." (And if that sounds like an exaggeration, you'll see very shortly that something very much like that was attempted.) If, in the preunion period, Hunter hadn't been satisfied with this, where would he have gone? There was no grievance and arbitration procedure before the Players Association negotiated it in 1970. Without the union there would have been no place for Catfish to obtain redress for Finley's violation of his contract.

So, in this sense at least, the victory for Hunter was the direct result of the new arbitration rights in the 1970 collective bargaining agreement. Without that, American League president Lee MacPhail and Commissioner Bowie Kuhn would have excused the contract violation and, in essence, told Hunter, "Run along, my boy, and continue to play for a man who deliberately violated your contract and who pays you a salary that's roughly one sixth of your actual worth."*

The basic facts in the dispute were these: Hunter and Finley had clashed a couple of times over the years, though the same could pretty much be said of anyone who played for Finley long enough. Hunter was involved in what he later termed "a pretty fair pissin'" match,† when Finley fined pitcher Lew Krausse five hundred dollars for "raisin' hell"—for too much drinking, Finley said—on a plane flight. Hunter was one of several A's players who signed a letter protesting Charlie O's action, a letter prompted by player rep Jack Aker, who was then suspended for his part in the letter. Finley made headlines by firing manager Alvin Dark when

---

*If this seems like a guess as to what would have happened without a union, see Kuhn's *Hardball: The Education of a Baseball Commissioner* (New York: Times Books, 1987) and MacPhail's *My Nine Innings* (Westport, Conn.: Meckler Books, 1989), which spell out how they would have screwed Hunter!

†Jim Hunter and Armen Keteyian, *Catfish: My Life in Baseball* (New York: McGraw-Hill, 1988), p. 73.

he refused to back the suspension of Aker, then, after a change of heart, hiring him again just two hours later. Shortly after that, a beat writer for the *Kansas City Star* showed Finley a copy of the letter; Finley exploded and fired Dark again. (Somewhere, a Cleveland shipbuilder named George Steinbrenner must have been taking notes.)

Hunter had his moments of peace with Finley. He even reported years later that Finley had helped him make $50,000* on an investment deal. But he spoke out in no uncertain terms when Finley tried to humiliate Mike Andrews in the 1973 World Series, calling it "the most despicable act I've ever witnessed in baseball";† and in general, for a quiet, rather easygoing man, he was quick to let Finley know how far he could push him.

Finley had only himself to blame for what finally happened with Hunter. In 1969 he had loaned Hunter $120,000 to buy farmland in North Carolina, with an agreement that Hunter would repay it at the rate of $20,000 per year plus 6 percent interest. That was the agreement, but just a few months later Finley began demanding that the money be repaid—all at once. Hunter, of course, didn't have the money; he had purchased the farmland. But Finley, insisting that he needed the money for purchases of new hockey and basketball teams, was adamant. He began badgering Hunter on days when he was scheduled to pitch, which partly explains why he finished the year at 12–15. Eventually, Hunter had to sell thirty acres of land in North Carolina in order to repay Finley. Hunter later admitted that the bitterness from this incident set the stage for what happened in 1974.

Hunter's contract for the 1974 season specified that he was to be paid a total of $100,000, $50,000 to be current salary, and the other $50,000 to be paid during the season *as earned* (that is, each payday—which was twice a month) to purchase a deferred annuity from a life insurance company to be named by Hunter. In his autobiography, *My Nine Innings*, Lee MacPhail wrote, "The contract provided that Hunter would receive a total sum of $50,000 to compensate him for insurance covering his farm in

North Carolina."* Wrong! No such provision was in the contract, and at no time during the entire case did anyone ever say that there was.

At some point during the 1974 season—after Hunter had named the insurance company to which $50,000 should be paid in installments—Finley discovered what he should have known when he signed the contract. (He had made his fortune in insurance.) Much to his dismay, the $50,000 for the deferred annuity was not a tax deductible item like current salary. He couldn't deduct the payments to the insurance company until Hunter received his deferred annuity payments years later.

The bottom line was that Finley refused to purchase the annuity, an outright default under the contract, and Hunter proceeded to take action under the terms spelled out in Paragraph 7(a) of the Uniform Player's Contract signed, of course, by Finley and Hunter. This provision, which is very specific, predates the union, and was composed by the owners' lawyers. Let's take a look:

"The Player may terminate this contract, upon written notice to the Club, if the Club shall default in the payments to the Player provided for in paragraph 2 hereof [payment for the player's services] or shall fail to perform any other obligation agreed to be performed by the Club hereunder and if the Club shall fail to remedy such default within ten (10) days after the receipt by the Club of written notice of such default...."

Hunter wanted the annuity to reduce his taxable income while he was an active player in a relatively high tax bracket; he would draw on the annuity for income after retirement, when, presumably, he would be in a lower tax bracket.

Deferred payment arrangements are not uncommon, and the right of the club and the player to agree on such payments has been spelled out in the Uniform Player's Contract since 1968. It's not that Finley was against the idea of deferred payments. He had made many such contractual agreements with players over the years. But prior to the negotiation with Hunter and his lawyer, he had been dealing with money-ignorant players and some unknowledgeable lawyers. Finley was able to keep the player's money for, say, a five-year period in his own bank, so *he* could

*MacPhail, *My Nine Innings,* p. 134.

either pocket the interest or funnel the player's money into business ventures of his own without paying any interest for the use of the player's money. But if he paid the money to Hunter's insurance company, as required by the contract, then Finley could neither use the money nor declare it a deductible expense for tax purposes until years later. One commentator on this incident used Hunter's deferred payment plan as evidence that players had become too "money conscious." I don't suppose it occurred to him that Hunter's owner had been "money conscious" all along.

Our first indication that there might be an incident which would involve the Players Association came when I read that Hunter was accusing Finley of "reneging" on a part of his contract. I called him to verify the charge. He felt there was nothing ambiguous in the wording of the contract. Dick Moss and I read the contract and agreed. With Hunter's consent, we sent Finley written notice of the contract violation and asked him to remedy it, noting that he had ten days in which to comply, as the contract set forth. More than ten days passed without the default being remedied. In fact, we received no reply at all. So, on October 4, 1974, Moss sent a telegram to Finley's business office in Chicago. It read, in part, that the "contract is terminated due to Club's default in making payments in accordance with said contract and its failure to remedy said default within ten days after receiving written notice thereof."

We also asked Bowie Kuhn to notify all clubs that Hunter was a free agent. Bowie, of course, refused. I had asked Hunter if pressing the case just then would hurt his concentration during the most important time of the season. No problem, he said, and the record shows that he was right. The last postseason game was on October 17, when the A's beat the Dodgers 3–2 to win the Series in five games; Hunter racked up a win and a save. His regular season had been a gem: 25 wins, 318 innings pitched, an ERA of 2.49, and an amazing total of 23 complete games. He was at the height of his talent, and Finley was at the height of his arrogance. It proved to be a highly combustible combination.

Charles Finley was a shrewd judge of baseball talent—I don't think I ever met an owner who knew more about the game from the ground up. But he was burdened by a very bad advisor: himself. Worse, he was given erroneous information. Kuhn records that the Player Relations Committee told Finley that he was not legally obligated to purchase the annuity but that he should send Hunter the second $50,000 in cash. "Which he did," Kuhn wrote, "on October 4."*

As usual, Bowie had the facts wrong. Finley "sent" Hunter no money. What happened is that Finley collared Lee MacPhail at the League Championship Series and asked that he serve as witness while he went through the motion of presenting Hunter with a $50,000 check, thus "fulfilling" his obligation. Hunter, as cool off the field as on, wisely refused, saying that he had been advised by his attorney that the money should be sent directly to the Jefferson Insurance Company (of North Carolina) as provided by the contract. Finley asked that the room be cleared except for himself and Hunter. He then switched the subject from money to baseball, telling Hunter, "We're gonna win tomorrow, then it's on to the World Series!" And it was, with Hunter going seven innings and allowing just three hits in a 2–1 win over Mike Cuellar and the Orioles.

The Players Association filed a grievance against Kuhn and organized baseball on Hunter's behalf, demanding Hunter be recognized as a free agent. Finley's response was to offer to pay the money to the arbitrator. Once again, Charlie must have been listening to the wrong people. The arbitrator, Peter Seitz, saw no point in accepting it, since the question was never whether Finley *owed* the money, but whether he had violated the terms of the contract by not paying it to the named insurance company, and, thus, whether Hunter was a free agent.

The possibility of Catfish Hunter's becoming a free agent occupied as much space in the newspapers as Watergate. At first, no one could quite believe that it was possible. When Hunter told Jim Kaat that he had become a free agent, Kaat responded, "Oh, no, you're not." Dick Young was another skeptic. "I've got inside information on this," he told me one afternoon at the ballpark. "The decision will go against Hunter." "Oh, really," I replied. "I didn't know you could have inside information on an arbitration

*Kuhn, *Hardball*, p. 139.

case." But Young was certain that Finley was going to win. (Apparently his source wasn't so reliable after all.)

Amazingly, Hunter's own agent, Jerry Kapstein, didn't think his client would win. I regarded him as an example of the poor excuses for players' agents that existed in the early 1970s. During the NFL strike in 1974 he committed the inconceivable act of advising several of his clients, most of them rookies, to cross the picket line; he even bragged about it during a television interview. He had become friendly with media people—columnist Dave Anderson wrote and Howard Cosell spoke well of him. Like a lot of agents then and now—in fact, like a college football coach recruiting blue-chip high school players—Kapstein knew how to ingratiate himself with a player and his family. The difference is that after a coach gets his player, he becomes the boss, whereas an agent like Kapstein becomes a full-time babysitter. The player has problems with income tax, the player doesn't like the rooms he's getting on the road, the player doesn't have time to get a birthday present for his wife—the agent has to be prepared at virtually all times to perform these and even more demanding, but essentially menial tasks.

Kapstein blazed the hand-holding trail for future agents. But he was a much better suitor than he was negotiator. The year before free-agency rights, Kapstein had difficulty getting Joe Rudi, a terrific player, a salary in the neighborhood of $74,000 a year. When the union changed the owner-player relationship the following year, Rudi was able to get a million-dollar bonus for signing, a five-year guaranteed contract, and an annual salary many times his seventy-four grand. Kapstein received accolades for his bargaining skills, but it doesn't take a genius to see that the difference was due solely to the union's achieving free-agent rights for players.

Hunter and his lawyer, J. Carlton Cherry, were scheduled to appear on the day of the arbitration hearings in November. I hated that part of the process: You're supposed to put people on as witnesses with almost no briefing and virtually no reviewing of the facts except what you can go over on the way to the hearing. Dick Moss and I decided to do the best we could, meeting Jim and his lawyer at the airport. To our unpleasant surprise, Kapstein was with them. Jim announced that "Jerry will be my agent," to which my unspoken response was "Oh, brother." Kapstein had not represented Hunter up until then. He had had nothing to do with Hunter's contract or with the subsequent events or the processing of the grievance.

We had to wait for Jim's luggage, so, not wanting to waste any more time, I began briefing Jim. I was perhaps a minute into it when Kapstein interjected, "You can't be serious about free agency. That's never going to happen." Under normal circumstances I might have said something like "Oh, and why do you think so?" But these weren't normal circumstances. We had minutes to prepare Jim for perhaps the most important off-the-field moments of his career (not to mention the information we still needed to get from Hunter, since we had inklings that Finley's defense was to accuse Cherry of negligence), and Moss and I were stuck with a meddling agent who was taking management's side!

Instead, my reply was "Yeah, I'm serious. In fact, I think it's an open-and-shut case. If the arbitrator interprets the contract to the letter, yes, I'm certain we'll win. And since you've brought it up, I don't appreciate your putting yourself in the middle of this case, given that you know so little about it. You didn't negotiate this contract, and you have nothing to testify about in this case. And while I'm on the subject, precisely when the hell were you retained?"

Kapstein said nothing, but Hunter mumbled something about having hired him about a week into the case. I was a little taken aback. How, I wondered, could a pitcher who made his living primarily through his guile and wits make such a blunder when it came to his bank account? Apparently, Hunter gave more thought to what he would throw a .220 hitter on an 0–2 count than to his financial future, which is why I always have to smile when I hear an old-guard sportswriter say that modern ballplayers are too money conscious. A lot of them would be much better off if that were true.

Kapstein's comments got me heated, so I decided to vent everything that was on my mind. "When you get right down to it," I told him, "I don't see what you're doing here at all. You don't know anything about the case, and now it's obvious you don't even know anything about the contract. If Jim wants you to be here, it's okay, but I don't want you to open your mouth during the proceedings."

He didn't, but despite Peter Seitz's request that everyone at the meeting refrain from discussing it with outside sources, someone did. After the hearing, Frank Dolson, a sportswriter from Philadelphia, called and asked me how the meeting had gone. I told him simply that I thought it had gone quite well, that not being in the category of comment we were asked not to make to the press. Then he said, "I understand from an inside source that it's clear that Hunter will not be made a free agent."

That was the tipoff. No other "inside source" at the meeting would have hinted such a thing. I told him, "Look, I know better than to ask you who your 'inside source' is, but let me tell you something about that source. I'm willing to give you odds it was someone at the hearing, which means it was someone who broke his word to the arbitrator by talking to you, so whoever your source is, he's an unreliable person."

The following day I got a copy of a telegram sent by J. Carlton Cherry and Hunter to Kapstein dismissing him. Afterward I heard that Kapstein blamed me for the firing. I can't take the credit. If he hadn't been so intent on making uninformed predictions, he would have walked right into a bonanza: Only a short time later, his former client's contract was worth thirty-five times what it had been.

On December 13 Peter Seitz announced his decision: Finley would have to pay the second $50,000 in the manner specified by the contract *and* that the contract with Hunter was terminated *and* that Hunter was a free agent who could negotiate with any major league team.* The transcript of Seitz's decision is forty pages long, every one a model of lucidity and balanced judgment. But the

---

*Arbitrator Seitz's draft opinion required payment of the money owed to Hunter and terminated the Hunter-Oakland contract, but it did *not* state that Hunter was a free agent. In executive session with Seitz and John Gaherin, I pointed out the omission. Seitz had not understood that the omission would open the door to a claim by Finley et al. that Hunter was still the property of the Oakland club. Once he understood, Seitz added a few words to his award and opinion specifying that Hunter was a free agent able to contract with another club.

final three pages, I think, are as accurate a summation of the incident as anyone could present:

Mr. Finley has stated that at all times during the 1974 playing season he stood ready to pay the $50,000 to Mr. Hunter; and that he repeated the offer in the presence of Mr. MacPhail and others in October shortly after the receipt of Mr. Moss's telegram. Mr. Hunter's testimony is that on that occasion he told Mr. Finley, "I don't want the money paid to me. I want it paid just like the contract calls for, deferred payments to an insurance company or whoever I designate."

Obviously, payment in 1974 to Mr. Hunter would have completely thwarted the objective of the Special Covenant, which was to defer payment to the employee in order to avoid taxes on current income, as Mr. Hunter testified, and I find, that the deferral program was an important consideration in his agreeing to play with the Club at the salary stipulated in the Player's Contract. A payment of the $50,000 to Hunter in the tax year 1974 would mean that he would have to pay income taxes on that amount and the particular purpose of the Special Covenant will have been defeated.

Plainly, Mr. Finley's offer to pay the amount to be deferred *presently* to Mr. Hunter is not a satisfactory answer to the charge that the Club violated the contract.

If Mr. Finley was surprised by the character and the details of the deferral program as revealed to him in the papers first presented to him for approval and signature on August 1 and he felt that there were aspects of the program as devised by Mr. Cherry that were of dubious legality or went beyond the deferral program as he envisaged them there were alternative courses of action available to him. He could have made a counter-suggestion to Mr. Cherry as to procedures and action that would achieve the objectives of Mr. Cherry's deferral plan in ways not objectionable to Mr. Cherry. He could have negotiated further with Mr. Cherry and Mr. Hunter to canvass other possibilities of action less repugnant to him that would meet the goals of both parties and satisfy the objectives of the Special Covenant.

He did none of these things. Following the August 1 meeting he gave Mr. Cherry to believe that the only thing standing in the way of completion of the program was the difficulty of persuading his estranged wife to attest to the regularity of the corporate signature. Then, in their September 15 telephone call (a month and a half after the papers had been presented to him), he bluntly stated that he would not sign them; and in response to Mr. Cherry's request, refused to write a letter to that effect and said the papers had been thrown away.

The record, as a whole, compels the conclusion that Mr. Finley, some time after August 1, decided that the undertaking set forth in the Special Covenant, as executed by the papers presented to him, was an improvident one, principally because it denied him the use of the deferred compensation during the period of deferral as in Mr. Jackson's case. It is not known when he reached that conclusion; but he did not state his refusal to sign definitively until a month and a half after the papers were given to him for signature. In the meantime he had the use of Mr. Hunter's services, which was the consideration for the salary and deferred compensation the Club was under a duty to pay. This was a material breach of Mr. Hunter's Player's Contract.

Mr. Finley's refusal to accept the insurance company as the "person, firm or corporation" designated by Mr. Hunter to which the compensation should be paid, as deferred compensation, constituted a violation of the Special Covenant and justified its termination by Mr. Hunter.

Bowie Kuhn led the negative chorus for management's side: "To forfeit the contract over a few days delay* in paying the $50,000 was like giving a life sentence to a pickpocket." After all, Kuhn reasoned, "Hunter's contract was of enormous value to the Oakland club." And indeed it was, though no one had any idea how

---

*Payments were supposed to be made during the season. None were. And not one cent was paid during the League Championship playoffs or the World Series, or during the rest of October and November. On December 13, when the arbitrator's award was made, Finley had still not made any payments to the designated insurance company. Some few days!

much until other teams had a crack at it. It was understandable that Kuhn was miffed; Seitz's decision had reversed his own, a rebuff he took personally.

There was rejoicing at the Players Association. After decades in which the owners had things entirely their own way, one player had won his freedom. Naturally I was happy for Jim, but I knew that his newfound freedom was largely the result of Finley's arrogance and Seitz's fairness in interpreting the contract. Still, I was certain that Jim would now be offered a contract that would more closely reflect his true worth and would set a standard for top players that would be difficult for baseball's power brokers to pull back from. Not that they ever stopped trying.

A final thought about Catfish. I always liked and respected Jim Hunter. When Finley was going off the deep end in the 1960s—releasing slugger Hawk Harrelson, then in his prime, for disciplinary reasons, fining pitcher Lew Krausse and suspending player rep Jack Aker over a relatively minor incident, and firing manager Al Dark—Hunter showed courage and solidarity with his teammates. Later that season, Hunter, then a young, not-yet-established major leaguer, stepped up and became the acting player rep. When Hurricane Charlie continued to storm, I filed an unfair labor practice charge against Finley with the NLRB. Finley then tried to coerce some of the players, including Catfish, to pressure me into withdrawing the charge. It didn't work.*

Given Hunter's consistent union support during his fifteen-year career, I was stunned by some of his comments at his well-deserved induction into the Baseball Hall of Fame. After all of Hunter's battles with Finley, Kuhn, and MacPhail (and in fact the entire baseball establishment, which tried diligently to derail him time after time), Catfish stepped up to the microphone in Cooperstown, N.Y., and credited his economic security to the *owners*—specifically, George Steinbrenner.

Had Hunter forgotten all that the Players Association did for him? In 1974, he had no agent, and his legal advisor from

---

*The matter was resolved after an all-night meeting in Commissioner Eckert's office with Finley, his lawyer John Paul Stevens (now a justice of the U.S. Supreme Court), Dick Moss, and me.

Herford, N.C., J. Carlton Cherry, had no baseball experience. After Finley violated Hunter's contract, Dick Moss and I intervened and advised him every step of the way. We filed a grievance on his behalf; we dealt with the public relations hubbub that surrounded him; we prepared the case for arbitration (which Dick argued expertly); as a member of the arbitration panel, I stressed to the chairman that the contract itself mandated the penalty—free agency; and I dealt with John Gaherin's repeated attempts to confuse Peter Seitz. After Hunter became a free agent, I fought to keep Kuhn from advising clubs to limit the offers to Hunter. I had to convince Cherry, who hadn't a clue to Hunter's actual value on the open market, not to accept Finley's ridiculously low offer of $200,000 *before* Catfish had entertained offers from other clubs. And even after Hunter had signed his five-year, $3.75 million deal with the Yankees, Finley sued in the California courts to overturn Seitz's award—an action supported by the entire baseball establishment, including George Steinbrenner. (Finley lost. The Players Association retained counsel and defeated this attempt to negate Hunter's rights.)

Nevertheless, in the world according to Catfish, there was no Major League Baseball Players Association; Steinbrenner was responsible for the economic security of James Hunter and his family. I still have not figured that one out.

13...

Messersmith-McNally...

ANDY MESSERSMITH and Dave McNally didn't go Curt Flood's route of trying to establish that baseball was a monopoly in violation of the antitrust laws. They didn't band together to battle the baseball establishment with a dual holdout like Koufax and Drysdale, who took on the Dodgers in 1966 in a salary dispute. Nevertheless, their willingness to challenge the reserve clause—what many called "the backbone of the game"—led to the most important arbitration decision in the history of professional sports.

I had never made a secret of my contention from the beginning, that Paragraph 10(a) in the Uniform Player's Contract clearly stated that the owners had a right to renew an unsigned player *for one year, and one year only*. Management had always said that if a team and a player couldn't agree on salary, the club could renew the player's last contract for one additional year *without* his signature and that this right of renewal had no limit. Simply stated, the claim was that a club had the right to renew a player's contract *forever*. The only alternative a player had to complying with the rule was to quit playing baseball for a living.

The uproar over *Flood* v. *Kuhn* in early 1970 distracted attention from an important advance: We did get a basic agreement negotiated by May. And we made sure it was carefully worded in regard to the reserve clause and the pending litigation: "...this Agreement does not deal with the reserve system. The parties have differing views as to the legality and as to the merits of such a system as presently constituted." This was to forestall any future arbitrator or judge who might be tempted to say, "Well, you *agreed* to the reserve clause in the basic agreement." We wanted it as clear as mountain water that we had *not* come to an agreement on the clause—we had come to a contract settlement *in spite of it*. And, the agreement said, once the Flood case was adjudicated, "either party shall have the right to reopen the negotiations on the issue of the reserve system."

The point we were determined to make was that the Players Association, in not pressing for a *negotiated* settlement of the reserve clause issue in 1970 in the face of the owners' resistance, was by no means surrendering its right to do so. We had made a tactical decision: We would fight the reserve clause in court rather than at the bargaining table so as not to divide our energies and resources. But when the Supreme Court in *Flood* again upheld its fifty-year-old decision (which it called an "aberration" and an "anomaly") exempting baseball from antitrust laws, we were back to square one.

Square one, that is, on paper. For I could sense that the pressure we had put on the owners would cause them to yield somewhere down the line. The judges, after all, had not said that our desire to reform the reserve rules was wrong; they had just said that reform should be accomplished through collective bargaining. Many of the owners' advisors realized, in the back of their minds, that if there were no modifications to the reserve clause, judicial patience would eventually wear thin. Then the owners might lose all their advantages at once. Even Curt Flood, discouraged as he was after the Supreme Court decided his case, had realized this. "If I had six hundred players behind me, there would be no reserve clause."

With impartial arbitration in effect, we could argue the meaning and interpretation of a contract provision. It was only a matter of time, I felt, before we could test whether a club's right of renewal of a contract lasted forever or existed only for one additional year.

An incident in 1969 was illuminating. In that year Yankee pitcher Al Downing became the first to play in spring training without a newly signed contract. When he arrived in camp, GM Lee MacPhail told Downing he couldn't play unless he signed a new contract—even though Downing readily acknowledged that he was already under contract for one additional season because the Yankees had renewed his contract from the prior year. Al and I discussed his options when he telephoned me early in March. Downing then told MacPhail he was under contract and had reported to camp to perform under that contract; if he were turned away by the Yankees, they would violate the contract, and that could result in free agency. Not much later, MacPhail made Downing a slightly better offer, and Downing signed.

The incident told me that the owners were not quite so confident of their interpretation of the reserve clause as they made it seem. If nothing else, the owners were wary of testing Paragraph 10(a). It seemed that they didn't really believe that a player's contract could be renewed more than once without his signature; otherwise, they would not have coerced holdout players for decades into *signing* new contracts even though the renewed contracts were valid and binding.

Three years later, in 1972, Ted Simmons and St. Louis could not agree to terms. Unlike Downing, Simmons did not sign a new contract before the season began. He played half the season under a renewed contract and thereby became the first major leaguer to play in a regular season game without having signed a new contract for that year.

In 1973, Sparky Lyle had the same problem with the Yankees, but George Steinbrenner signed him to a lucrative multiyear deal two weeks before the end of the season.

In 1974, in San Diego, Bobby Tolan went right down to the wire before signing. Prior to the 1973 season, Tolan had been an integral part of Cincinnati's Big Red Machine. He hit for average and power, and he had great speed (his uncle, Eddie Tolan, had been an Olympic sprinter). But in 1973, the Reds' front office complained about his "attitude." Tolan, who is black, complained publicly about racism. When he refused to shave off his beard, he was suspended without pay. Tolan's charge was given credibility at the arbitration hearing of his grievance protesting his suspension. Reds president Bob Howsam, in an effort to denigrate Tolan, testified that during the outfielder's suspension, the club could not find him at home because "he was shacking up with a white woman." (I wondered if Howsam had considered placing Tolan under house arrest.) The arbitrator ordered Howsam's comment struck from the record and reversed the suspension. At the end of the 1973 season, Tolan was traded to San Diego.

There had been no agreement on terms for the next season, so Bobby was playing in 1974 under a contract renewed by the Padres without his signature. On the very last day of the season, San Diego made Tolan an offer he couldn't refuse. Padres GM Buzzie Bavasi offered a significant salary increase, and the team owner, Ray Kroc, offered a large loan for a house that Tolan wanted to buy. "Unless I sign," Tolan told me hesitantly, "none of this will be available." I made no effort to talk him out of signing the Padres contract. I had never interfered with a player's contract negotiations, and I wasn't about to start then.

The evidence was mounting: The clubs, in spite of what they said, didn't believe an unsigned contract could be renewed more than once. Before too long, a player would find it in his own best interest to finish a season under a renewed contract and then assert that he was a free agent on the grounds that he had no contractual connection with any club.

Enter Andy Messersmith, a thirty-year-old right-hander from Toms River, N.J., the best pitcher in the National League in 1974. Before going to the Dodgers, Andy had enjoyed five productive seasons with the Angels, and he had been shocked when he was dealt to the Dodgers. In 1974, he signed a one-year, $90,000 contract and led the league in wins (20) and winning percentage (.769). In 1975, the Dodgers and Messersmith were apart on salary, and he asked for a no-trade provision, or at least the right to approve any trade involving him. Walter O'Malley refused, and the club renewed Messersmith's 1974 contract with a modest salary increase. Andy did not sign. Although he did not talk to me at that time about his problem with the club, I knew he was playing under a renewed contract. And Andy, as he told me later, was aware, from numerous statements I had made at meetings with the players, that I did not believe a player's contract could be renewed more than once without the player's signature.

Messersmith was having another terrific season in 1975. When he pressed for the no-trade provision, O'Malley countered by saying, "Can't do it. The league wouldn't approve the contract."

"Bull," I said, when Messersmith told me of O'Malley's reply. "Absolute bull! There's no such regulation."

It reminded me of a story Buzzie Bavasi had told me several years before. Buzzie had been the Dodgers' general manager since before the team moved out west. Around 1968 he learned what kind of money some of the other general managers around the league were making and realized he was underpaid. "The Dodgers were making money hand over fist," he said, "and I hadn't received a raise in years." Bavasi's contract was about to expire, so he gathered his courage and went in to see "the old man," as he referred to O'Malley. The Czar of Los Angeles considered Bavasi's request and said, "You've done a fine job, but your timing stinks. We lost two million dollars last year." Not until later, when Bavasi moved to the expansion franchise in San Diego, did he discover that two years earlier the Dodgers had netted a profit of more than $4 million. When O'Malley said, "We 'lost' two million dollars," he meant, of course, there had been two million dollars *less* in profits than the year before.

In August, Messersmith called, and we discussed filing a grievance at the end of the season if Andy had not signed a 1975 contract by that time. O'Malley had come up with an acceptable salary offer (even though he had been speaking about the need to hold the line on "outlandish" salary demands), but he was still stonewalling on the no-trade clause. In fact, O'Malley had accused Andy of being a pawn in the Association's plan to file for free agency. Messersmith said he was no such thing, reminding O'Malley that he'd sign if he were given the no-trade clause.

On the phone to me, Andy apologized when he told me of the negotiations. He felt terrible, he said, but he intended to sign if O'Malley met his demand for a no-trade provision. This would mean that no grievance would be filed to test the renewal clause.

"It's okay," I said, repeating what I had once told Al Downing, Ted Simmons, Sparky Lyle, and Bobby Tolan. "Do what you feel is in your best interest."

Despite his policy of nixing no-trade contracts, my guess was that O'Malley would sign Messersmith. First off, he was the ace of the Dodgers' staff. He had won 19 games in 1975 with a 2.29 ERA. Secondly, though management professed they would win should the case go to arbitration, they certainly preferred to postpone a grievance as long as possible. After all, if the decision didn't go their way, they were in danger of losing it all.

Checking the records, I found that the only other unsigned player during the 1975 season was former Orioles pitcher Dave McNally. McNally had pitched thirteen seasons for the Orioles, including four straight twenty-win seasons. After the 1974 season, Baltimore traded him to the Expos. After starting the 1975 season there, McNally decided to leave baseball.

I spoke to Dave, who was working as a Ford dealer in his hometown of Billings, Montana.* He'd been unhappy with Montreal's offer and hadn't signed his contract. Then his wrist had been bothering him. After a 3–6 start, he decided he couldn't pitch with anywhere near the effectiveness he once had. On June 8, he walked away from the $85,000 remaining on his contract.

McNally was the perfect player to challenge the reserve rule. He was a good union man; he had once been player rep in Baltimore. And having no intention of pursuing a career in baseball, he was immune to retaliation. Messersmith could sign with the Dodgers and we would still have a test case.

I told McNally, "I'd like to add your name to the grievance as insurance if Andy decides to sign a new Dodger contract."

"If you need me," he said, "I'm willing to help."

That was a stroke of good fortune, having McNally to fall back on. Still, considering his former role as player rep, luck might be seen as the residue of design. McNally had been a starter for fourteen years, but the last act of his career was to serve in arbitration as a reliever.

---

*An inactive player was still owned for life by the last club he played for. This prevented "retired" players from coming back with another club. Without Montreal's permission, he couldn't have even become a manager for another team.

Once we had McNally as a reserve test case, O'Malley no longer had any reason to offer Messersmith a no-trade clause. In *Hardball*, Bowie Kuhn wrote, "Before the arbitration was slated to begin, the Dodgers actually could have signed Messersmith and avoided the grievance. It would have required their giving him a no-trade clause, which they were prepared to do....The PRC asked them not to do so and the Dodgers, being good organizational soldiers, complied."

Wrong. O'Malley, more than any other owner, set league policy; rarely (if ever) did he do what was requested of him unless he felt it to be in his own interest. My guess is that other prominent owners were opposed to the loss of control implicit in a player's being able to veto a trade and, having been erroneously informed by Kuhn and the lawyers that the arbitrator would rule against the Association, urged O'Malley to stand firm. Besides, the challenge to the reserve rule could no longer be sidetracked by signing Messersmith. Dave McNally was waiting in the wings—a fact Kuhn conveniently forgets.

We filed two grievances on the last day of the 1975 season. Predictably, management screamed that the sky was falling. National League president Chub Feeney said that if owners bid for players' services, it would be so disastrous that "we might not have a World Series." Dodger manager Walter Alston predicted graver consequences: "If Messersmith is declared a free agent, then baseball is dead." I half expected him to claim that Los Angeles would fall into the Pacific.

The PRC filed a lawsuit in Kansas City, asking the court to enjoin the arbitrator from hearing any grievance involving the reserve rules. The owners' stance was that contract renewal was part of the reserve system, which was not a part of the basic agreement.

Federal district judge John Oliver denied the injunction. He also ruled that if the clubs concluded that the arbitrator had exceeded his authority, they could ask the district court to set aside his award.

Early in November, a few weeks before the arbitration hearing, Dave McNally called. "Guess who was in town last night," he said.

"I have no idea."

"John McHale [Montreal's president] said he just happened to be at the airport in Billings," he said, chuckling, "and he wanted to know if he could buy me a drink."

The image of John McHale telling McNally that he just happened to be passing through Billings, Montana, in November tickled me silly. Perhaps the pilot had misheard Montana for Montreal. My guess is that only a few hours before his plane set down, McHale couldn't have told you what state Billings was in if you led him to a map.

McHale offered McNally $25,000 for signing a contract and $125,000 for playing in 1976—more than he had ever earned in a single season. Of course, if McNally signed, O'Malley would have offered Messersmith a no-trade contract, and we would have been right back where we started.

McNally replied that he wasn't sure that he could pitch at a major league level any more. McHale then told him, hey, no problem, even if McNally didn't play, *even if he didn't last through spring training*, the $25,000 was his just for signing. The fact that they were willing to pay a disabled pitcher more than $100,000 not to go to arbitration told me that somebody knew how much more was at stake.

"What are you going to do?" I asked him. This wasn't an easy decision. Dave was being offered $25,000 to leave a Montana winter and come down to Florida.

But he turned the Expos down: "McHale wasn't honest with me last year, and I'm not going to trust him again. It's tempting to show up in spring training for twenty-five grand, but I have no intention of playing, and it wouldn't be right to take the money."

Peter Seitz, the arbitrator who had ruled against Charles Finley in the Catfish Hunter case, set the hearing date for November 21. An experienced lawyer, Seitz had been a full-time arbitrator for twenty years. He had a reputation as a professional, intelligent arbitrator, but I didn't consider him to be prounion. I hadn't been particularly impressed by the decisions he'd made in basic steel when I was with the Steelworkers Union.

Some of his more recent opinions and awards had impressed me with their objectivity. While reviewing his record, however, I found something that seemed significant. As an arbitrator for the

National Basketball Association and the NBA Players Association, Seitz had noted in an opinion the 1969 California Court of Appeals ruling which gave NBA star Rick Barry the right to sign with the Oakland Oaks of the rival American Basketball Association after playing out his option year with the San Francisco Warriors. That court found that the standard basketball contract permitted a club to renew a player's contract for one year only. The wording of the renewal clause in the NBA's Uniform Player's Contract was almost identical to ours—in fact, it was copied from baseball's. Given the similarities, Seitz's opinion containing that reference to the California court ruling caught my eye. It seemed significant to me.

The owners and their attorneys in baseball were, of course, hypersensitive to any developments involving the reserve rule. When a vacancy opened for a permanent baseball arbitrator following the resignation of Gabriel Alexander in 1974, Peter Seitz was one of a number considered for the post. He was chosen by agreement with the owners. Considering his reference to the Rick Barry case (a decision he seemed to support), I can only guess that Kuhn, Hoynes, Gaherin, and Rona had not done their homework.

By the time the Messersmith-McNally grievance was filed, Seitz had already heard a number of baseball grievances. Determining the impartiality of an arbitrator by counting wins and losses is an unproductive exercise, but considering the criticism Seitz later received from Kuhn and others, it is worth noting that Seitz had ruled in the owners' favor more often than not. In the end, that's probably the reason the owners agreed (despite Bowie's objections) to keep him when the Messersmith case loomed.

Two weeks before the Messersmith hearing, the Player Relations Committee met to decide whether to fire Seitz. Kuhn and Hoynes felt he was "dangerous" and recommended taking their chances with someone else. Kuhn later said of him: "Kindly and well-intentioned, [Seitz] was a prisoner of his own philosophy and would rationalize his way to the destruction of the reserve system."* This is a classic bit of revisionist history. Considering Seitz's record in baseball the only possible cause for rejecting him was his ruling in the Catfish Hunter case, and all he had done there was

*Kuhn, *Hardball*, p. 157.

acknowledge a contract provision (which predated the union) that was too obvious to ignore.

The seven-member panel of the PRC voted six to one to retain him, the lone dissenter being John McHale, the Expos' general manager, who had just happened to be passing through Billings, Montana. Kuhn says he urged the panel to reconsider and vote again. The result was identical, six to one.

Once the hearing started, the first matter to be considered was management's argument that the grievance was outside an arbitrator's jurisdiction. After each side had presented its case, the hearing recessed for a week. Seitz reviewed the transcript and ruled that the grievance was arbitrable.

The arbitration panel consisted of John Gaherin, Peter Seitz, and me. Kuhn described the panel this way: "Seitz, benign and gracious with visions of the Emancipation Proclamation dancing in his eyes; Miller, full of mock judicial gravity and anticipation of a succulent chicken dinner [he had referred to me as a fox sitting in the hen house]; and Gaherin, looking worried."*

Kuhn's implication that Seitz had decided the case beforehand is inaccurate and insulting. The transcript of the hearings and the correspondence between Seitz and the principals shows that Seitz did all in his power to get the parties to take the case from him by negotiating a settlement. Kuhn's description of Gaherin, however, was accurate. John had good reason to be concerned. He had failed to convince Kuhn, Hoynes, Feeney, MacPhail, and the owners that their case was weak and that common sense dictated a negotiated settlement. A settlement would be much wiser than risking the whole ball game.

A quick note on National League counsel Lou Hoynes. Hoynes was a good lawyer. He was quick on his feet and argued well in court, but he had a couple of weaknesses: a lack of experience in labor relations and the belief that the courts would always do what the owners asked of them. Admittedly, given the courts' record of docile acquiescence to baseball's demands over the preceding fifty years, it's hard to fault such a belief, but Hoynes had failed to judge this case on its own merits. He paid the price.

With the proceedings about to resume, Hoynes asked the panel

*Ibid., p. 158–59.

to permit Kuhn to make a statement at the opening of the hearing. Hoynes made it clear that Kuhn wanted to appear *not* as an owners' witness but as the lord high commissioner delivering an "impartial" judgment on the foolishness of the Association's case. I objected. If the owners wanted him as their witness, obviously he was free to "testify." I said the Players Association wouldn't call him as a witness. Bowie Kuhn, owners' man, could testify as a witness and, like any other witness, he would be subject to cross-examination. If, as Bowie says, I had been anticipating a chicken dinner, here was the feast.

In any event, Kuhn's testimony was largely irrelevant. He launched into a sermon which boiled down to this: "Without a reserve system, our vast array of minor leagues would hardly survive." And: "It is not hard to imagine that we could even lose a major league."

To this overwrought rhetoric Seitz calmly replied: "Mr. Commissioner, I don't doubt your sincerity, but you have to understand that the arbitrator's function is very limited. I'm not empowered to seek solutions to collective bargaining problems, merely to interpret the contract." Seitz wasn't trying to belittle Kuhn, who, as a lawyer allegedly with experience in labor relations, should have known the arbitrator's limited role, but Kuhn seemed oblivious. Seitz told him over and over that it was far better in a matter of such importance for the two sides to shape the settlement. And since the basic agreement was expiring on December 31, he reminded Kuhn that each side could take advantage of this "fortuitous circumstance" and work out an agreement. Seitz couldn't mediate the dispute, but he was pushing the parties to negotiate on their own. He had as much luck urging common sense as we did.

After three days of testimony, both parties were ready to rest their case. When post-hearing briefs were suggested, Seitz, ahead of his time, gently urged everyone to consider the impact on the environment: "Whole hillsides are being decimated for the exhibits in this case." The transcript alone ran 842 pages.

Just before the owners' winter meeting in Hollywood, Florida, Seitz sent John Gaherin and me an eight-page letter reiterating what he had already told Kuhn about finding a solution through collective bargaining. Short of chartering a plane to write it in the sky over the hotel where the owners were staying, he couldn't have stated the situation more clearly. For years the courts had told us: The reserve clause is subject to negotiation through collective bargaining. We had got the message. Now an arbitrator was telling the owners the same thing, and the owners still weren't getting the message.

Later, Kuhn wondered if Seitz was "just threatening an adverse decision so as to bring about a solution through supervised bargaining?"* Unbelievable! Seitz had told him to his face: "Take the case away by negotiating a settlement." How Kuhn could go from that direct statement to a theory that Seitz wanted to be involved in collective bargaining is inexplicable. But as Kuhn writes, "The lawyers felt they had presented an overwhelming case. After all, no one had ever seriously imagined that the reserve system had a large, heretofore undiscovered ocean of free agency floating in its midst. That was nothing more than one of those myths Miller spent so much time inventing. The PRC certainly wanted no part of Seitz's supervising their negotiations with the Players Association. There was no telling where that might lead. If Seitz went against the law and bought the myth, there was always judicial review. On balance, the PRC concluded, it was best to let Seitz go ahead and rule."†

If, as Bowie wrote, the lawyers felt they had presented an overwhelming case, they were alone in that view. What they had done was present a very complicated case in an effort to confuse. Perhaps it would have worked with a less intelligent, less experienced arbitrator than Peter Seitz. Dick Moss couldn't believe what a bad job the owners' lawyers did. Even Barry Rona, Gaherin's counsel, agreed. Gaherin refused to discuss it, but his attitude spoke volumes. Seitz expressed himself only with his decision. And though I usually tortured myself by imagining worst-case scenarios, I left the hearing room after the summation of the owners' attorneys reflecting on what the Players Association would do after the coming victory.

When Kuhn wrote that no one had ever seriously imagined that the reserve system had "a large undiscovered ocean of free agency

*Ibid., p. 159.

†Ibid.

in its midst," he was again wearing blinders. I had seriously imagined it the first time I read the Uniform Player's Contract and the Major League Rules in 1965. And there had been owners' attorneys who worried about it before Kuhn was out of diapers.

Finally, eleven years after the Messersmith ruling, Kuhn maintains that if Seitz "bought" my argument, it would be an "unlawful" decision that would be overturned after judicial review. (Judicial review had sustained the decision eleven years before Kuhn wrote this.) Then again, in his book Bowie repeatedly writes about my "luck" in rolling up tremendous gains for the players. In a sense, he is right. His inept performance as a thinker and as the owners' designated fall guy throughout that period was one lucky break for me, for the players, and for all of baseball. He was indispensable to our success.

The Seitz ruling was no bombshell. Gaherin had seen it coming during the arbitration hearings and had been given instructions to fire Seitz if he ruled against the owners.* On December 23, we met in John Gaherin's office. Gaherin, Barry Rona, Dick Moss, and I made small talk while we waited for Seitz to arrive. When he came in, he handed out copies of his decision, which ran sixty-one pages. Later, I would relax and savor every word, but at the time I flipped straight to the back. Seitz had ruled that Messersmith and McNally were free to negotiate and sign with other teams. There was nothing, he wrote, in Paragraph 10(a) that said the contract could be renewed for more than one year. The "myth" that I had supposedly invented was a reality.

And that was it. It was a key moment in baseball history, a moment I had anticipated since 1965, and I signed the award. Gaherin signed his name on the line that read "dissenting," looked up at Seitz, and said, "Peter, I'm sorry. I love you dearly, but you're out." Seitz had been fired, literally before the ink was dry. It might

---

*Labor-management arbitration most often involves a single impartial arbitrator selected by agreement of the parties. Sometimes, as in baseball, there is a three-person panel. In this case, each adversarial party selects its own representative on the panel, and the two in turn select, by agreement, the chairman, who is impartial and represents neither party. Regardless of the structure, the services of the neutral, impartial arbitrator typically may be terminated by either party—but not while a case is pending before him.

sound odd, but I believed that Gaherin was sorry. He was a good man forced to do a bad job. He had been telling the owners to negotiate a compromise for some time, but they had stripped him of his power.

Afterward, a frustrated Seitz said that if the owners had shown the slightest inclination to resolve their differences with the Players Association, he would have left ample time for the parties to negotiate and reach a settlement, thereby making it unnecessary for him to decide the case. "I begged them to negotiate," he said. But "the owners were too stubborn and stupid. They were like the French barons in the twelfth century. They had accumulated so much power they wouldn't share it with anybody."

Seitz has left his mark on baseball and sports history. His Messersmith opinion was thorough and balanced and, at times, eloquent. For example:

"It deserves emphasis that this decision strikes no blow emancipating players from claimed serfdom or involuntary servitude as was alleged in the *Flood* case. It does not condemn the Reserve System presently in force on constitutional or moral grounds. It does not counsel or require that the System be changed to suit the predilections or preferences of an arbitrator acting as a Philosopher-King intent on imposing his own personal brand of industrial justice on the parties. It does no more than seek to interpret and apply provisions that are in the agreements of the parties. To go beyond this would be an act of quasi-judicial arrogance!"

As soon as Gaherin fired Seitz, the PRC filed an appeal of the arbitrator's decision in federal district court in Kansas City. The owners argued that the arbitrator had exceeded his authority. After a hearing, Judge Oliver upheld Seitz's decision, even going out of his way to note that it was sound and balanced. The owners' appeal to the circuit court also was shot down.

It's interesting that the precedent for the actions of the district and appellate courts was a 1960 U.S. Supreme Court decision known as the "Steelworkers Trilogy," which said it was public policy to encourage arbitration of grievances in labor-management disputes and that arbitrators were better qualified than judges to interpret such action—and admitted only the narrowest of grounds for overturning an arbitrator's award. (The case was argued brilliantly before the Supreme Court and won by David

Feller, a friend and colleague at the Steelworkers Union at the time.)

The owners decided not to appeal to the U.S. Supreme Court—and Andy Messersmith was officially a free agent. He was the first real free agent (excepting Jim Hunter the year before) since the reserve rules were invented and instituted (around 1879) by the owners to save money and control players.

I called Andy with the news. He said, "Great! What do I do next?"

It was a good question. He should expect to receive offers, I said, but I wasn't sure exactly how or what kind. The only other procedure had involved Catfish Hunter, who had been declared a free agent for a completely different reason. Still, if the big money was available for Catfish Hunter, it was there for Andy Messersmith.

The first offers were few and far between. First off, the owners had locked the players out of spring training (something I'll discuss in detail in a later chapter), and second, the owners were hesitant to get involved in a bidding war like the one for Catfish Hunter. Red Smith said it best: "It is the *price* of human flesh that has scandalized the baseball establishment, not the *barter* of human flesh."

Cincinnati was interested, but decided to pass. Reds president Bob Howsam explained his reasoning: "Andy is a good athlete and would make a desirable addition to our pitching staff, but we have to operate our team on a sound basis. To sign him under these terms is poor business. No club in our industry can truly afford this and survive." Since Howsam had *no idea* what it would take to sign Messersmith, I wondered how he figured that signing him would threaten the survival of the major leagues.

Around this time, unnamed sources (alleged to be "two scouts") started a rumor that Messersmith had a sore arm. They reportedly said that the Dodgers had tried unsuccessfully to get Messersmith to have his arm checked the last two or three months of the 1975 season—a season in which he had led the league in starts (40), innings pitched (322), complete games (19), and shutouts (7).

I called Dodgers executive Al Campanis to see if the rumors were true. Campanis had always been a straight shooter with me. "It's a lot of baloney," he said. "We never asked Andy to take a physical, because there was nothing wrong with him. He never missed a turn." I asked him if he would have the team doctor issue a public statement. Much to his credit, he did so.

The New York Yankees pursued Messersmith, but their claim that Andy had agreed to terms was ruled invalid by Kuhn when it was revealed that Messersmith had not signed a contract or made any commitment to sign with the Yankees. Just after the start of the season, Messersmith signed a three year contract with Ted Turner and the Atlanta Braves, totalling $1 million. When he finally signed, Campanis said: "The Braves didn't get a sick horse. They got a healthy pitcher."

The ultimate irony of Messersmith's deal with Turner was that he signed a contract giving Atlanta, at the expiration of his contract, the right of first refusal. In other words, Andy (and his agent) had signed away his free-agent status—the very rights he had gained in the Messersmith decision! (Andy was a fine fellow, but he wasn't an astute businessman.) I never let the issue get to first base, or, in this case, the pitcher's mound. I called Chub Feeney and reminded him of the provision in the basic agreement which prevented a player (even if he does so knowingly) from signing away rights that the union has won in collective bargaining. Feeney quickly relented, and we weren't forced to go to arbitration. The offending clause was removed from the contract. This was a perfect example, I thought, of why players had never made progress in the past without a strong union. In fact, it was a warning that progress achieved by the Association could be reversed by individual players in the absence of a union.

To finish the saga: Messersmith pitched two years for Atlanta, the worst club in the National League, finishing with a combined record of 16-15. In 1978, Turner traded him to the Yankees, the club that had claimed to have signed him when he was first declared a free agent in 1976. Fittingly enough, Messersmith finished his career with the Dodgers, the team that very well could have prevented—or at least postponed—free agency by offering him a no-trade contract in the first place. Actually, that may have been the final irony in the Messersmith case. The Dodgers and the rest of the baseball establishment fought to keep him a Dodger; all that Andy had wanted was a no-trade provision so that he *could* remain a Dodger for the rest of his career. And O'Malley had refused.

14...

Not a Strike... *Not* a Strike... *Not* a...

ALTHOUGH THE arbitration in a landmark case, Messersmith-McNally, had been won, the biggest breakthrough in baseball—the actual modification of the reserve rules—had yet to come. Consider what happened:

After arbitrator Peter Seitz's award in the Messersmith case, the owners immediately challenged the decision by filing a suit in federal court in Kansas City. To this day, I can't say for sure why they chose Kansas City. (Then again, I didn't see the basis for the lawsuit in the first place.) But baseball's attorneys must have advised the owners that they could overturn Seitz's award in court.

Predictably, Judge John W. Oliver upheld Seitz's ruling and even praised him for the high quality of his reasoning and handling of the case. Obviously, I was pleased by Oliver's decision, but I did note sadly—as I had during the 1970 litigation involving Curt Flood—that not a single player showed up in Kansas City (this was during the off-season) to watch and listen to a courtroom

• 254 •

drama which would determine their future—not even the players who lived there.

Be that as it may, after Judge Oliver's decision the owners and their lawyers painted themselves into an even tighter corner. Instead of bargaining, they embarked on another useless stall tactic, appealing to the circuit court. As irrational as this may sound, baseball had always been rescued by the courts, and the owners, confronted by the fact that hundreds of players who hadn't signed contracts for 1976 had the same free-agency rights as Messersmith and McNally, were panicking.

While the appeal was pending, we went ahead anyway and scheduled meetings with John Gaherin, the director of the Player Relations Committee, and his associates in Scottsdale, Arizona. Right from the start, it was obvious that Gaherin's hands were tied. He played it as if there had never been a Messersmith-McNally decision, even saying at one point that he was perfectly willing to "consider" changes in the reserve rules—as if that hadn't *already* happened. It was not unlike, I thought, General Robert E. Lee showing up at Appomattox and telling General Ulysses S. Grant, "All right, we'll negotiate." I had little doubt that it wasn't really Gaherin talking. He had apparently been instructed that if he ignored the Messersmith decision, it would somehow disappear. For my part, there were some very good reasons to negotiate. First of all, the law required it. The basic agreement had expired, and a new agreement had to be negotiated. Second, I did not believe that free-agency rights after one year were in the best interests of the players—that large a supply of free agents every year would hold salaries down. And third, there was much to do to make the new system work, including the negotiation of a prohibition against collusion.

John lost his temper several times during our talks, which made it even more obvious that he was being forced by the owners to do something he didn't want to do. Gaherin was a professional, an experienced labor negotiator, but he was not the most patient man, and, apparently, he and the owners had had their own heated arguments. During the 1972 strike, he indicated to them that their acting like nineteenth-century robber barons was going to blow up in their faces. They let Gaherin know in no uncertain terms that he was to follow their orders. The general counsel of the PRC, Barry Rona, told me later that Gaherin had said, "I'll never survive this job. I'll have a heart attack, a nervous breakdown, or they'll fire me." Fortunately for Gaherin—the messenger who continually delivered bad news—the firing occurred first. Management sent him packing in 1977.

In Scottsdale, Gaherin did offer a proposal. It was preposterous. The proposal was that in order for a player to be eligible for free agency he would have to be in the majors for *nine* years. If no agreement could be reached after an additional year (his tenth season—the option year), that player would become a free agent, *unless* the club offered him a contract of $30,000 or more. The $30,000 would apply to all players, including superstars, and would remain unchanged over the next four years. In addition, the club that acquired the free agent would have to pay a large cash settlement to the departing player's team.

Considered in the climate of 1976, the owners were offering us ice in the winter. The arbitrator's decision provided free agency without a service requirement, without the club's right to retain him, and without cash compensation to the club losing the player. When I told Gaherin his offer was absurd and that he must recognize the Messersmith decision in the negotiations, he went bonkers. "There's no such thing as the Messersmith decision!" he bellowed. "You've got to get it out of your head! The owners don't recognize it!" This was gibberish, and Gaherin knew it, but his stonewalling did raise some interesting questions.

The basic agreement had expired on December 31, and technically the owners were free to propose anything they wanted. I didn't know if they had thought beyond their appeal to the circuit court or if they had come to grips with their shrinking options. But considering their tangible fear of having three hundred or so free agents set loose at the end of the season, I figured that management would (assuming they lost their appeal) take the offensive. In other words: a *lockout*. The lockout, of course, was management's way of testing their misguided theory that the players would be unable to remain united. By pressuring me, they hoped to force a "compromise" that would enable them to retain complete control of the players. While I didn't welcome that scenario, I certainly preferred a lockout to a strike.

A strike, at least in 1976, would have been a hard row to hoe. Many players still believed what the owners had been telling them for years: Free agency threatened the very fabric of the game. What's worse, some believed that free agency spelled the end of baseball. While none of these fears were logical, they were some of the obstacles that interfered with the drive, unity, and solidarity needed for a successful strike. Furthermore, the advantages of free agency to the players—multimillion-dollar salaries—had not yet been proven. And there were just enough doubts, hesitations, and what-ifs that I couldn't answer. The *biggest* was "What if we win and no club owner ever makes an offer to a free agent?" There was, at least, this advantage of a lockout over a strike: When the owners locked us out, they did my job for me—they united the players.

Remember, there was nothing in the expired collective bargaining agreement that made collusion a contract violation. Given baseball's antitrust exemption—a gift bestowed by the courts—it was not illegal to collude. If that sounds strange or even paranoid, don't forget that collusion had been an everyday part of baseball since 1876. The owners controlled everything from ticket prices to the color of a ballplayer's skin. Take salaries: There had been an unwritten rule for years (a collusive "understanding") that said no player—not Ted Williams, Joe DiMaggio, or Stan Musial—would be paid more than $100,000 a year. The reserve rules system was more of the same. Each club agreed not to talk to any player who *belonged* to another club; violators were to suffer stiff penalties.

It was unwise, I ultimately decided, to strike in order to win free agency. Would I strike to defend free agency once the benefits were in place? You bet! But until then, we ran too great a risk of winning the battle and losing the war.

One of the most surprising things to come out of those meetings in Scottsdale was how Dodgers reliever Mike Marshall misconstrued what was happening right before his eyes. Given the great victory of the Messersmith decision, I had assumed that most informed players (if not all of them) understood the upside to competitive bidding for their services. I was wrong. Marshall had a reputation as something of a maverick, an independent player rep who was less easy to satisfy than most. The Cy Young Award winner in 1974 (he appeared in a record 106 games), Marshall had been active in the negotiations. Many players had been indispensable because of their intelligence and levelheaded support under fire: Tom Seaver, for example, who had gained a much greater understanding of the issues since 1972; others included Bob Boone, Brooks Robinson, Bill Singer, Steve Rogers, Tommy John, Joe Torre, Jerry Reuss, Jon Matlack, Lou Brock, Rusty Staub, and more.

But Marshall, much to my surprise, was impressed by Gaherin's "free agency" proposal. "This represents a big advance," he told me, "and we have to consider it."

"A big advance from *what*?" I asked.

Marshall has always talked about his militancy, but at the time he was taking the most conservative position of any player on the committee. It should be said, however, that before the negotiations were finished, Mike regained his equilibrium; in fact, he fell over the other way. Perhaps he wanted to regain his vision of himself as an independent. I can't say. I do know that his was the only vote against the 1976 agreement on free agency—an agreement that has brought the salaries of *average* players to almost seven times the salary of a great relief pitcher and Cy Young Award winner of that time, a pitcher by the name of Marshall. Curiously, in articles he has since written about this period, Marshall has failed to explain the mixed-up expression of his views at the time.

We accomplished nothing in Scottsdale. John Gaherin had strongly advised the owners to negotiate a settlement, but the owners' legal counsel apparently told them what they wanted to hear, namely, that the court would overturn the Messersmith decision. It was a case of the emperor's new clothes. Shortly before the start of spring training, the appellate court in Kansas City upheld the district court's decision. Instead of turning on the people who gave them this terrible advice, management turned on Gaherin. The most militant of the Gaherin-bashers were Gussie Busch (Cards), M. Donald Grant (Mets), Calvin Griffith (Twins), and Walter O'Malley (Dodgers), though there were a handful of others. As soon as the court decision was handed down, the owners made two decisions: *not* to appeal to the Supreme Court and *not* to open spring training camps.

By flexing their muscles with a lockout, the owners hoped to negate the impact of the Messersmith decision, which meant that no players would become free agents, whether they had signed 1976 contracts or not. Throughout the winter, we had advised players wanting to become free agents not to sign. By the time spring training was scheduled to start, almost 350 players had followed Messersmith's lead. This led to two sets of nightmares: the owners' and mine. The owners', for obvious reasons—a potential "loss" of so many valuable players. To me, a large supply of free agents each year would defeat one of the purposes of free agency, namely, the bidding up of salaries. Luckily, Oakland's owner, Charlie Finley—who generally was ignored—seemed to be the only one smart enough to recognize that opening the floodgates by making all players free agents would work to the owners' advantage (by holding salaries down); the rest screamed bloody murder: "This SOB, Miller, said there'd only be a handful of free agents. Now I'm going to lose my entire infield, outfield, and pitching staff!" Instead of negotiating realistically, management insisted that a player be required to have ten years (nine years plus option year) of major league service (something few players achieved) in order to become a free agent and then hedged that with a provision that the player still could be held by his club if it offered him at least $30,000 a year.

Although league presidents had announced that spring training facilities would remain closed until there was a new basic agreement, many players had traveled to the camps in Florida and Arizona hoping that an agreement would be reached quickly. I understood why they went. Some had already laid out large deposits on housing for themselves and their families; others felt it important to be with teammates and organize informal workouts so as to begin getting into shape.

In 1969, I recalled, Ernie Banks and his wife flew to New York to explain to me that even though he supported the policy of not signing a contract until the pension agreement was reached, he and his family would be going to the Cubs' camp in Scottsdale because he had already made too many arrangements not to go. I understood Banks's motivation then and I understood what was happening now, but it was a bad move. It reminded me of the days when players held out individually for more money and then revealed their eagerness to play ball or anxiety about getting beaten out of a job by hanging around their clubs' spring training facilities. When an owner saw a holdout peering through the ballfield fence like a kid kicked out of a candy store, he chuckled, realizing it was only a matter of time before the holdout accepted *his* offer.

For the same reason I was also against the players staging their own practice sessions. Tom Seaver had organized workouts in the Tampa area. The closer the players were to playing condition, the longer the owners could afford to lock them out. What's more, if a player hurt himself during one of these workouts, or worse, suffered a career-ending injury, the owner most likely had no responsibility.

Nevertheless, there we were with several hundred players in Florida while the gates to the camps remained locked. I demanded that negotiations continue and suggested they be held in Florida (so as to have as many players on hand as possible). Gaherin agreed, and we arranged a series of meetings in St. Petersburg.

As the meetings began, Dick and I and some of the player reps called players and urged them to attend the negotiations. As might be expected, some of the sportswriters had been soliciting quotes from players to incite hostile comments about the lockout; instead of calling it a lockout, all but a few reporters called it a strike! In this manner the public became confused: Although it was the owners who locked the gates of the spring training facilities, the players' union was accused of starting a strike.

It's not hard to see why the locked gates would anger your average sportswriter. Many of them had rented houses in Florida and Arizona. Instead of hanging out at the ballpark for a few hours and golfing the rest of the day, they were forced to sit around in hotel lobbies, writing about labor issues which they knew nothing about. And without any baseball, some of them were going to be recalled to their ice-encrusted northern cities.

One of the biggest muckrakers—or maybe muckmakers is a better word—was a sportswriter from a Cincinnati paper, Earl Lawson. During the 1972 strike he did the owners' work by seeking out all sorts of inflammatory statements. Instead of asking Pete Rose how he felt about the issues at hand, he said, "Hey, Pete, what's going to happen to your streak of two-hundred-hit seasons?" Always concerned with his statistics, Rose made the mistake of rising to the bait and said all he wanted to do was "play ball." So, of course, did we all.

Four years later, Lawson was back to his old tricks. During the lockout, Rose, Bench, and a few others were quoted as saying they didn't want to *strike*. I did what I always did in that situation; I called the players who made the divisive comments and said: Obviously, you have the right to say anything you want to, but you're hurting the rest of the players because these "Let's play ball" statements are misinterpreted. If five players are quoted in that fashion, the most shortsighted of owners will draw two conclusions: There must be hundreds saying the same thing; and their desire to play means that the union can't stay united. Although both conclusions were false, the owners' belief resulted in a continuation of their refusal to bargain and an even longer dispute.

After I spoke to Rose and Bench, both sat from morning to night through one bargaining session after another. Once they came to understand the issues, they began participating and were a great help throughout the negotiations. (Just for the record: During the 1985 dispute, members of the press asked Cincinnati *manager* Pete Rose, "Hey, whose side are you on anyway?" Rose said: "After all the Players Association did for me, which side do *you* think I'm on?")

But Bench and Rose were only two of the many players who sat in on the negotiations. Attending day after day turned many of the players from interested spectators into hard-core union supporters. Several times during negotiations, Chub Feeney and Barry Rona were shouted down by players who couldn't believe what they were hearing. "How can you say a player must play ten years to be a free agent?" Bench said. "Only four percent of all major leaguers ever play that long!" Bench was one of that four percent; and it did my heart good to see him standing up for the other ninety-six percent.

During one recess, Willie Stargell said to me, "How do you keep your temper when they talk that trash? They're insulting us. Where I come from, we'd flip over tables if someone treated us like that. You're staying calm, so I keep biting my tongue."

"Look, Willie," I said, "*you* don't have to be restrained because *I* am. If you have something to say, let it fly." (Though I don't think I'd like to be around when Willie Stargell started launching tables into orbit.)

After each desultory day of negotiations I held a press conference, sometimes twice a day, and I'd get questions like: "Don't you realize that the merchants down here are being financially ruined by the players' demands!" This, of course, in an accusatory tone, the assumption being that *we* were the ones responsible for ruining the local merchants. Or "Don't you realize how much money you're losing by holding out?" (I always felt like slapping my forehead and saying, "*Damn*, I forgot all about that!") And once again I'd have to explain that we wanted to play ball, that players were down here on their own working out. "The *owners* are the ones who are locking *us* out. The players are ready to play, and continue to negotiate at the same time. All that stands in the way are the locked gates, locked, as you know, by the owners."

The inability (or unwillingness) of the press to distinguish between a lockout and a strike reminded me of the old story of the pedestrian who stumbles onto a group of Communists picketing city hall. He's watching innocently enough until a cop on horseback starts clubbing everyone in sight. As the cop heads for him, the horrified bystander screams out, "I'm an *anti*-Communist, I'm an *anti*-Communist!" And the cop, who continues to flail away, shouts back, "I don't care *what kind* of Communist you are!" Instead of billy clubs, the press wielded typewriters; the result was less brutal, but the effect was the same.

This public relations campaign was furthered by the various general managers around the league who were speaking to players, continually drumming into their heads that if *I* wasn't reasonable, there might not be a season at all. And there was also the pressure of general fatigue. During the 1972 strike, Leonard Koppett of the *New York Times* asked me if I thought that the owners deliberately tried to wear me out by continually carrying the negotiations into the early morning hours. I said I couldn't say for sure, but it certainly seemed like a good strategy, because I did get terribly tired.

The frustration that had been brewing during the lockout finally boiled over in a Tampa Airport hotel. The two sides convened in the auditorium. We sat in the audience—thirty to forty players joined us—and the members of the Player Relations Committee looked down on us from the stage. This wasn't a negotiating meeting (owners didn't attend those meetings), but a kind of "clear the air" session. Early on, Reds general manager and club president Bob Howsam launched into a monologue that had little to do with the way the negotiations had actually been going. It's one thing to mouth banalities about "doing our best to reach an agreement for the good of baseball," but it's quite another to falsify information to players who had attended the negotiations day after day, and even more galling considering Howsam hadn't attended a single meeting.

Howsam had no sooner paused to take a breath when Johnny Bench stepped into the aisle, picked up a floor microphone, and cut him off as swiftly as he would a base stealer trying to swipe second. "We're willing to make a reasonable agreement," he stated, "but we're *not* willing to give up free agency." Bench wasn't insulting or profane, but he was intimidating. He was telling his own general manager and club president, in no uncertain terms, that he was handing the players a load of hogwash.

It was the first time I'd seen Bench display off the field the kind of leadership he had been exhibiting on it for years. Bench seldom spoke up during spring training meetings; if he had a question or comment, he usually talked to me after the meeting broke up. Howsam had to be equally surprised by Bench's bold stance. He had always considered his conservative catcher one of the players he could count on to go along with management's position. But I was delighted to note that times had changed.

Stars like Joe Torre, Tom Seaver, and Mike Marshall (to name just a few) had been verbally sparring with baseball's brass for years. I encouraged players to speak out whenever possible, unless the complaint would damage their relationship with the club. In a business like baseball, before free agency, where you sat down with an owner or general manager to negotiate a contract, your career could be destroyed if you crossed the club's top officials. (This almost happened to Dave Winfield even after free agency, when he feuded publicly with the owner. After missing nearly the entire 1989 season with a back injury, he was platooned by Steinbrenner at the beginning of the following season, a severe penalty to an veteran player who was trying to ensure a place in the Hall of Fame, to say nothing of trying to extend a career another few years.)

The lockout lasted seventeen days, ending on March 17 when Bowie Kuhn reopened the camps. At least, that's the way it was reported. The truth is that Walter O'Malley, who saw that the owners were uniting the players instead of breaking them apart, had the lockout lifted and called both sides back to the bargaining table. (Though, to his credit, Kuhn was smart enough to follow through on it.) With the players back in camp, John Gaherin and I flew to New York to "begin" negotiations.

For the next month and a half, we went nowhere slowly. The owners continued their charade, insisting on nine plus one years of major league service for free-agent eligibility, plus an absurd amount of compensation. One high-level executive said: "These doggone players have a misguided view of themselves because they've never lived in the real world. They are going to have to accept some restraints on their movement. And they had better learn quick that if you like scrambled eggs for breakfast, it's not a good idea to eat the chicken."

With negotiations at a standstill and the season underway, I decided to travel around the country to talk things over with the players on all twenty-four clubs. Throughout that trip, the same question kept coming up: "Should we strike?" Some thought we should boycott the All-Star Game. This would have ticked off the owners (not to mention the fans), but I couldn't see the point. Management would not have granted us large concessions just to save the All-Star Game. (Technically, it wouldn't have been a strike because nothing in a player's contract said he was required to play in the All-Star Game.) Others suggested we strike the World Series. But that would have involved just two teams and demanded an unequal sacrifice from those players in terms of money and satisfaction.

The only alternative was to strike the remainder of the season. I've always believed that a union lacking the credibility to carry out a strike can't negotiate a decent contract—especially in an industry controlled by a group as reactionary as baseball owners. But the more I thought about it, the more I realized this was the wrong issue to strike over, however much I thought it a good idea to let the owners think we might. The players didn't seem to grasp the implications of the reserve rules or to foresee the tremendous progress they would enjoy after those rules were appropriately revised. No, the time for a strike on this issue had not yet arrived.

I decided to shift the emphasis somewhat by playing up the other issues in the dispute, familiar matters such as the pension plan and a dozen or more matters in the negotiations which were also important to the players. Had the owners joined together and said, "Look, I don't think the players fully understand the reserve rules. If we give them everything else they're asking for and isolate them on this issue, I think we can have our way," that might have been an approach worth trying. But this is where all those years of complete dominance worked against them. They had no experience in compromise, no inclination to do anything other than what they wanted when they wanted.

As the players rallied around these collective issues, it became increasingly apparent to everyone that—even without new agreements in place—the owners would need to change their tactics. Around this time, Gaherin was granted the authority to actually negotiate. My guess is that with the two league presidents (Lee MacPhail and Chub Feeney) on his side, Gaherin was able to convince the Player Relations Committee to consider the facts: As of the early spring, as many as 350 unsigned players were eligible for free agency at the end of the 1976 season, among them many of the game's biggest stars. Considering the fans' reaction, it was going to be hard *not* to sign All-Stars like Carl Yastrzemski, Reggie Jackson, or Rod Carew if they became free agents, to name just a few.

In mid-May, with no progress in sight, Gaherin suggested to me privately that we eliminate the attorneys from the proceedings until an agreement had been reached. He had become increasingly troubled by the attitudes of the league attorneys—Lou Hoynes and Jim Garner—and felt the possibility of reaching an agreement would be improved without their presence. John said he realized he would have to leave his counsel, Barry Rona, out of the meetings as well.

"Fine with me," I said, thinking that the owners' attorneys had yet to make positive contributions to a labor-management problem. "On one condition. I won't bar Dick Moss [who was an attorney] from the meetings."

John agreed.

For the next two months, the five of us—Gaherin, Lee MacPhail, Chub Feeney, Dick Moss, and I—met at the Biltmore Hotel nearly every day, and often into the night. No players were present during the meetings (the season was in progress), but Dick and I did consult with key members of the executive board as we went along. It was, thankfully, the first time any real progress was made.

Lee MacPhail, I have to say, played a major role in the negotiations. He had a rational view of free agency, saying, "We're trying to swim against the social current. We've got to change." He was also valuable because John Gaherin knew nothing of the mechanics of baseball. You could hardly blame him—the many books of Major League Rules, Professional Baseball Rules, the Major-Minor League Agreement, and much more are master-pieces of obfuscation, making even *Finnegans Wake* seem like a first-grade primer by comparison. MacPhail understood the nuts and bolts of the game as well as anyone, and he took great pains to draft proposal language between meetings. The downside, how-ever, was that he was very attached to his own writing. When we tried to reword the language, he reacted with the sensitivity of a poet who had just had a metaphor changed by an editor.

As the Fourth of July approached, a settlement seemed possible. The basic eligibility question—what conditions would a player have to meet in order to become a free agent—was a tough one, but it was only one of fifteen or twenty other complex problems that had to be resolved. I had taken a firm position that the union would do nothing to eliminate or limit free-agency rights of players *currently* eligible for free agency under the Messersmith decision. Our position was that any player who had not signed his 1976 contract could declare free agency at the end of the season regardless of how many or how few his years of major league service. This tug-of-war lasted longer than I care to remember, but Gaherin & Co. finally came around to our view. Only then were we able to move on to the eligibility question for all other players—present and future.

Initially, management had proposed, in essence, a ten-year service requirement and inched down in the next four or five months to seven years. But management's view of the problem made their position uncomplicated: The owners wanted as few players as possible to become free agents. I wasn't entirely opposed to this; I didn't want so many free-agent players as to flood the market. I had no doubt that my position was sound, but I agonized over the eligibility requirement. What would be likely to produce the optimal mix of supply and demand? With no history of free-agent movement to study, it was impossible to know which eligibility requirement would be best. I proposed four years. My feeling—and I stress "feeling"—was that five years would be better, and that if the choice lay between four and six years, I would choose the latter. The owners' committee proposed six years; I suggested five. However, as other essential parts of an agreement began taking shape, I agreed to the six-year requirement, *provided* we included the right of a player with five years of service to demand a trade, to designate up to six clubs to which he would not accept a trade, and to have the right to become a free agent if his club failed to trade him by March 15.

Management finally agreed.

The settlement was reached on July 12, the eve of the 1976 All-Star break. The memorandum of agreement covered all the changes in the reserve rules and all other issues in the new four-year basic agreement, as well as the improvements in the new four-year pension agreement. It also included agreements on so many matters large and small, simple and complex, on new issues not heretofore dealt with and revisions and improvements on more traditional matters than the reserve rules, that it still seems a small miracle that so much of a really constructive nature was resolved without a strike (or even a strike vote). By the same token, it seemed only fitting after completing such a revolutionary agreement to be headed to the City of Brotherly Love, where the All-Star Game would be played, nearly two hundred years to the day after the signing of the Declaration of Independence.

On the way down to Philadelphia, I considered all the work that still lay ahead. Dick and I would have to make a full report to the executive board so that a ratification vote could be held; there was the difficult and painstaking task of converting the memorandum of agreement into complete contracts (with arguments with the owners' lawyers almost line by line); and we had to police the revisions of the reserve rules in the new basic agreement as they would be put into effect at the end of the season.

Regardless, considering how momentous these changes were, and how many obstacles we had overcome to get there, I was as elated as a manager who has just won the pennant. My high, I think, was also buoyed by our return to Philadelphia, the city Terry and I had lived in during World War II and my days with the National War Labor Board, the city in which our son Peter had been born, and where we still had many good friends.

The day before the All-Star Game Dick and I met with the executive board at the Bellevue-Stratford Hotel, where the players ratified the proposed agreements by a vote of twenty-three to one! John Gaherin met a more hostile audience. After he briefed the owners on the settlement on the morning of the All-Star Game, the cries of discontent began to sound. The chorus would rise in a deafening crescendo in the days to come, and it would ultimately (and unnecessarily) worsen labor-management relationship in the years ahead. But for now, anyway, this was Gaherin's headache—and Chub Feeney's and Lee MacPhail's. They had to deal with the owners' sour faces and obtain ratification of the new agreement. They did.

One postscript to the proceedings in Philadelphia: A few weeks after the All-Star Game we received some unsettling news. While we were in New York grinding out a contract, a large delegation from the American Legion had their convention at the same Bellevue-Stratford Hotel we had stayed in during our three days in Philly. The word was that many of the legionnaires were stricken with a respiratory infection of unknown origin. It became known as "Legionnaires' disease." Many were hospitalized, and in the days and weeks to come, some died. All of us in baseball felt extremely fortunate not to have become ill. Had this mysterious affliction occurred two weeks earlier, it might now be known as the "Baseball All-Stars' Disease."

Actually, baseball was suffering from another disease: hardening of the arteries. While I was convinced that the lockout had been an ineffective ploy from beginning to end, Walter O'Malley andBill Veeck seemed to be the only owners who recognized this. Veeck called it "unfair and unreasonable"; but, then, he had been against the existing reserve clause for years. In fact, in 1941 he wrote Commissioner Landis and said that the system was "morally and legally indefensible." Landis wrote back: "Somebody once said a little knowledge is a dangerous thing and your letter proves him to be a wizard." To me Landis's letter confirmed that the commissioner as well as the reserve system was morally indefensible.

During the 1976 lockout Veeck announced that he was going to open the White Sox camp to his minor leaguers, prompting Clark Griffith of the Twins to say, "If we thought this was the act of a rational person, we'd worry about it." Griffith's attitude didn't surprise me, but I was amazed to learn, several months after the 1976 settlement, that John Gaherin still believed the lockout would have succeeded if it had lasted longer. Gaherin, Barry Rona, and I were discussing other matters over lunch when John brought up his favorite subject: my luck. He used to accuse me of being Irish because "when your back's to the wall, you always come up with a hole card." His favorite example was the time Gussie Busch unwittingly rallied the players during the 1972 strike by blurting out, "We're not going to give the players another goddamn cent." The press got hold of the quote, and, bingo, the players were infuriated and we won points with the public.

Pointing his sandwich at me, Gaherin said, "You pulled another lucky card when Bowie Kuhn showed he was gutless and opened the camp gates."

I reminded him that it was O'Malley, not Kuhn, who had really ended the lockout. "Where's the luck?" I asked.

Gaherin said, "We had you by the balls and let you go."

He wasn't referring to baseballs. "You've got to be kidding," I said. "How do you figure that?"

"The players were getting restless," he said. "It was obvious."

Gaherin was referring to a phone call I received during the lockout from a well-liked Houston player. After a few preliminaries, the player said, "We just can't have this lockout. It's going to ruin the entire season."

I said, "Do you want to give back free agency and go back to the way it used to be?"

"Well, you gotta do something," he said.

I was baffled. "Short of renting a tank and driving through the gates, I don't know what you want me to do. This is a lockout, not a strike. They won't *let* us go back unless we fold. Just what is it you want me to do?"

The player had no idea.

Two hours later, Houston pitcher Ken Forsch called. He said, "Marvin, I suppose I shouldn't be telling you this, but I just had to let you know that I was in the room when that call was made."

I said, "That's funny. He didn't say anything."

"It's not so funny," Forsch replied. "There were four other players with us. We were calling from Tal Smith's office." I wasn't surprised. Smith was the Houston general manager and club president and had used his position to try to intimidate players many times. "He's spoken to each of us almost every day and has been harassing us about this," Forsch said. "Smith intimidated [the nameless player] into making the call. The rest of us, I'm ashamed to say, stood by."

I wondered what buttons Smith had pushed to pressure his player into making such a call. I certainly wouldn't have put it past him to take advantage of any personal or financial problems the player might have had.

I was furious. I called John Gaherin and explained what had happened. "This is an unfair labor practice, as you know. I want assurances that this will never occur again!"

Gaherin called back quickly. He said, "I told Tal Smith that was a fool trick to pull, that it was illegal, that it could disrupt negotiations, and that he is not to try anything like that again."

I believed Gaherin. Apparently, the warning worked. There was never a hint of such a thing happening again.

Now it became clear. Somehow Gaherin had construed this episode to mean the players were "restless." Sure, one or perhaps two players in Tal Smith's office were restless: They had a loose-cannon general manager breathing down their necks. But the owners hardly had us by the balls. However, if John Gaherin thought it was my "Irish" luck that the Players Association had been developed into a solid labor organization able to surmount crisis after crisis, including the latest lockout, I wasn't going to argue. After all, as the saying goes: "It's better to be lucky than good."

But I remained curious and decided to follow up on this matter. "*Assuming* the owners' lockout had worked," I said to Gaherin, "how long would it have taken before the players pressured me into accepting management's proposal?"

"Another few weeks," he answered. "With Opening Day looming, the pressure would have been enormous for you to accept almost anything."

This, I thought, is what made negotiations so difficult. Not only had Gaherin confused a lockout and a strike, he had failed to understand the very people he was dealing with.

But no matter what I said, Gaherin remained unpersuaded. "You aren't dealing with what eventually would have occurred," he said. "If the lockout continued, the players would have crumbled and forced you to accept anything so that they could begin to draw paychecks."

One would have thought we were arguing about the existence of God. "You're dreaming," I said. "But let's suppose that several months into the season a significant number of players panicked and demanded the union surrender by accepting the owners' terms. What would you see happening next in that absurd scenario?"

"You'd be forced," he said confidently, "to do what the players demanded."

"Wrong!" I said. "I'd refuse."

He looked flabbergasted. "You'd be forced to!" he argued.

"There is," I explained, "no mechanism, no procedures, no laws, no provision in the union constitution, that could force me to negotiate, sign, and obtain ratification of what would be the equivalent of a scab contract. I'd never do it," I said again.

Gaherin countered with a quick, triumphant reply. "In that case the players would go back to work without an agreement."

He had completely forgotten that that was our position the entire time, that we had urged that the lockout be ended. This had not been a strike, I repeated for the thousandth time: *It had been a lockout.* And a lockout is *not* a strike.

EARLIER I SAID the players didn't understand the reserve rules. I don't think there was any better example than an incident during the 1976 season. Jerry Kapstein, an agent whose ability I had reason not to respect, had used the potential free-agent rights of his clients (which had been won by the union) to negotiate five-year contracts for three of his clients from the Boston Red Sox: Rick Burleson, Carlton Fisk, and Fred Lynn. The catch was that they also *gave up* their free-agency rights when the contracts expired. Kapstein had given Boston "the right of first refusal." I tried to tell him: "Don't you realize that means all Boston has to do is match the offer made by another club? If no other club makes an offer—a likely scenario considering that they could not get the player if Boston were interested—the player is right back where he started before free agency and able to negotiate only with his club."

Kapstein didn't understand that I was acting on *his* behalf as well as his clients'. Neither did Carlton Fisk or Rick Burleson. (Fred Lynn and I never discussed it.) Fisk argued: "We don't care if Boston has the right of first refusal. We like playing in Boston."

"That's no argument," I insisted. "You can stay with Boston *if you choose*, but you can't give away the *right* to be a free agent and leave. It violates the basic agreement." Had eliminating the "first refusal" clause spoiled an otherwise satisfactory contract, I could have understood their objections, but I made it clear that only the provisions that took away their rights would be eliminated, and the rest of the contract would remain unchanged. For them it was a total "no-lose" situation.

It was like talking to Fenway Park's left-field wall. Even Mrs. Burleson got into the act, telling the press that Kapstein was a wonderful agent and that I had "outlived" my usefulness. It was clear that Mrs. Burleson didn't have a clue as to what was going on. Her husband's rights had been given away, and I was returning them.

Finally, I said to Fisk: "Look, you and Kapstein can stand on your heads for all I care. I'm representing all six hundred players, and you, Burleson, and Lynn are *not* going to have something in your contract that jeopardizes the other five hundred ninety-seven! Kapstein told you there's a no-trade provision in your contract. But perhaps he didn't tell you that it's a limited one, and after the third year Boston can trade you to any team without your consent. You could end up with Minnesota or Oakland, the stingiest teams in baseball, who would then have the right of first refusal when your contract terminated. You wouldn't have the right to be a free agent, and you would be 'owned' by whatever team Boston traded you to."

That stopped him. The clause was removed from their contracts.

But that wasn't the end of the story.

Several weeks after the owners' 1980 winter meetings, I read an item in the newspaper that Fisk's five-year contract had expired. Under the basic agreement the team had to offer to renew a player's contract on or before December 20 for the following year. If not, he automatically was a free agent. December 20 had come and gone and Boston hadn't made Fisk an offer.

I found it difficult to believe that the team wanted to dump Fisk. He was a native New Englander, a perennial All-Star, and his game-winning home run in Game Six of the 1975 World Series was the most dramatic in Red Sox history. But when I called Fisk in January, he told me he and Red Sox executive Haywood Sullivan had been feuding all season over a new contract, and Boston *still* hadn't sent him a proposed contract.

"This makes you a free agent," I said.

He was amazed. Jerry Kapstein hadn't told him. Now it was my turn to be amazed. How could an agent not know that his client's bargaining power had suddenly been enhanced by his becoming a free agent?

"I don't know what their game is," I said, "but there's no way they can win. Call Kapstein, tell him what I've told you, think about what you want to do, and call me back when you've made a decision."

Several days later, Fisk said he wanted to be a free agent. He had also discovered that Fred Lynn hadn't received an offer.

The Players Association filed for free agency for both of them. The arbitration was set for January 23, 1981. The Boston club argued that our requiring a change in language in 1976 about the right of first refusal affected the date in 1980 by which they had to send out a contract. Not so. There was some peculiar language that Kapstein had agreed to, but nobody can amend the basic agreement without the consent of the Players Association.

By the time we convened in New York for the arbitration hearing, I had heard enough about the bad blood between Fisk and Sullivan that I wondered about the wisdom of leaving them alone in a room together. (The following season, I read that Fisk wore a T-shirt that said "Haywood and Buddy Suck" every time he faced the Red Sox. So much for Fisk's earlier claim that he wanted to spend the rest of his career with Boston.) Minutes before the hearing got underway, John Gaherin told me that the California Angels wanted to trade for Lynn and were offering a five-year guaranteed contract. A former star at the University of Southern California, Lynn was eager to return home. So everybody waited around, including the arbitrator, while Jerry Kapstein talked by phone with Angels officials. The Angels sent a telegram spelling out the contract's exact terms. We checked them with Lynn. He found them satisfactory, and the arbitrator had one less case to hear.

The Fisk arbitration proceeded. The Red Sox had no case to present. They had no defense against Fisk's claim for free agency, based on the basic agreement provision which stated: "The Player becomes a free agent [because of] failure by the Club to exercise its right to renew the contract within the time period specified [on or before December 20]." Haywood Sullivan and the club's attorneys had goofed; no renewal notice had been sent. (And Kapstein had goofed by not alerting his client.) As a member of the arbitration panel, I knew that the chairman, Raymond Goetz, understood the case, but he clearly was puzzled by one thing: Why had the Red Sox not conceded free agency instead of wasting everyone's time in an arbitration hearing?

Four days later, I learned the arbitrator's award over the phone: Carlton Fisk was a free agent. I dialed Fisk at home. His wife, Linda, answered and said Carlton would be home in a few minutes. She was ecstatic when I gave her the news. Fisk was a valuable property, one of the best catchers in baseball. He would command top dollar as a free agent, and they could leave Boston and the turmoil of the last season. I told her to have Carlton call Jerry and give me a call as well.

I was happy for Fisk, but saddened by what I knew would be one of the results. Both Lynn and Fisk had been poorly served by Kapstein, and the union had rescued them. They would now pay tremendous fees to the agent in conjunction with their new contracts with clubs of their choice despite the fact that the agent's role was mostly a negative one. And, worst of all, neither player was perceptive enough to understand what had happened, even though the facts stared them in the face.

Eventually I learned that the Chicago White Sox signed Fisk to a long-term multimillion-dollar contract. It has been ten years since then, and Carlton Fisk still hasn't returned my call. And I've yet to hear from Fred Lynn.

You're welcome, Carlton. You, too, Fred.

THE YEARS just after the 1976 agreement should have been a time of peace and consolidation. The climate after that drawn-out settlement, reached without a strike, should have produced four years of quiet on the labor-management front and led to a more constructive relationship. It should have, but it didn't. Nor, I suppose, did I have any illusion that it would. Still, I was surprised that the owners sounded the drums of war immediately when they couldn't wage one for another four years.

Sounding like a military man rallying the troops, Walter O'Malley proclaimed: "We've compromised and retreated so far, we have our backs to the wall. We may have to stand up and fight or be destroyed." (Fact: In 1976, major league attendance and television revenue had reached a then all-time high. A *Sports Illustrated* cover story proclaimed "The Baseball Boom.") Another of the old guard, Calvin Griffith, said: "I'm convinced that the only way baseball can survive, after the present four-year player agreement expires, is to return to the old reserve clause the way it was before Marvin Miller's entry into the Players Association." (It was said that swimming was invented when Griffith was confronted by a toll bridge.)

After the settlement, John Gaherin became a convenient and visible target for the owners, who felt he had been outmaneuvered at the bargaining table. But John had been forced into a no-win situation; first they tied his hands and then maligned him for "giving" too much away. By early 1977 they had handed him his walking papers. Speaking of the owners afterward, he said: "They naturally want to hold on to as much as they can for as long as they can. In my judgment it was time for compromise. I think baseball would be better off today if we'd taken this route. My advice was ignored and a hard-line strategy was adopted." (Gaherin had urged the owners to negotiate revisions in the reserve rules *before* the arbitrator decided the Messersmith case.)

I was sorry to see John go. And even sorrier to discover he had been replaced by Ray Grebey, a labor negotiator from General Electric, a corporation with a long history of attempted union-busting. Everyone I talked to who had encountered Grebey said the same thing: "He was a union buster." "He hates to be surprised, absolutely can't stand it." This last bit of information puzzled me, but sure enough, when John Gaherin introduced us, Grebey stated how much he disliked being surprised about anything. (I had no intention of surprising him, but if I had, that would have been valuable information.)

Grebey was pleasant enough at that first meeting, but he had the mannerisms of an old-fashioned industrialist. Odd from a man who wasn't even an owner.

"My door is always open," he told me, using a cliché from the last century. At the time, the expression meant something else: An employer was telling an employee, "You don't really need a union because if you have any problems you can always come in and see me"—even if it was the chairman of the board talking to the janitor on the night shift.

Later in the conversation, Grebey reminded me again of his open-door policy. Gaherin and I looked at each other, and I could tell John was stifling a laugh.

"That's good," I said earnestly, "because my door is always open, too. We'll talk to each other with our doors open."

Gaherin wasn't the only one to exit baseball's labor relations scene in 1977. That spring, Dick Moss informed me that after ten and a half years he had decided to resign as general counsel of the Players Association. Dick was an invaluable colleague; he would be hard to replace. Though his departure caught me by surprise, I did know how bothered he had become by the player-agent system of representation.

Over the past decade, Dick and I had watched, with a sense of satisfaction at first, then wonder, and ultimately horror, as the Association ushered agents into the picture in 1970 (by negotiating a player's right to have representation of his own choosing during individual salary negotiations). We had seen the union create a powerful bargaining position for players where none had existed before (by gaining salary arbitration, free-agent rights, and much more), providing the player and his agent with all the necessary comparative salary and service data. We had taught the agents the meaning and interpretation of the Major League Rules and provisions of the basic agreement and demonstrated the type of preparations needed for salary arbitration cases and how to present such cases. We had selected (jointly with management) the best-qualified arbitrators. We had furnished the agents with appropriate contract language, advised them on contract construction, administered the basic agreement and the players' contracts—filing grievances when necessary to ensure that contracts were not violated—and then watched players hand out to agents each year tremendous payments that dwarfed the *total* annual operating budget of the Players Association.

Aside from the costs to the players, there were problems of competence and, in some instances, honesty. In order to become an agent, all one had to do was say, "Hey, I'm an agent." We talked to the players about developing some type of agent-certification program, but for whatever reason, they didn't place too high a priority on a program aimed at giving them first-rate representation at a fraction of the cost.* Nothing I said on this point seemed to make a difference. I used to tell the players over and over that an agent representing two or three top-notch players could make a million dollars in a couple of days, say, in fifteen to twenty hours of work. "Think about it," I said. "The agents didn't create your multimillion-dollar contracts. The work they do basically involves answering the phone. You could hire a top senior partner in the most prestigious law firm in New York City, pay him five hundred dollars an hour to do this clerical work, and it would cost you eight thousand dollars for, say, two days' work instead of a million." A handful of players took this to heart, among them Bob Boone, who retained an attorney, but most players shelled out to agents sums that were (and are) completely disproportionate to the services rendered.

Some agents charged fees for negotiating the major league

---

*There is an agent certification program today, instituted after I retired.

minimum—when a lower salary was not possible! Some signed inexperienced minor leaguers to agency contracts that purported to tie them up for their entire careers. Some signed players to contracts that gave the agent a percentage of a player's *total* income, on and off the field. Some intermingled their own money with their clients' in investment schemes (many with disastrous results). Some received large sums up front (based on a percentage of a player's salary over a five-year period)—sometimes an entire signing bonus—for a few hours of work, which (after free agency) involved fielding offers over the phone from different clubs. In some cases these bonuses went *directly* from clubs to agents without even passing through the player's hands—a practice I outlawed at the first opportunity in 1977. Some agents charged players for filing income tax returns and failed to file them, costing the players fines and interest charges. Some played it too cozy with the club owners and commissioners. And many had other conflicts of interest.

It would have been hard to rationalize what had developed. The harder we worked, the more the players made, the more money agents made. Indirectly, however, the end result proved injurious to the Association, for we lost Dick Moss. In the wake of the first group of free-agent signings in 1976, Dick apparently decided that he didn't want to stand by and watch a repeat performance as these agents became instant millionaires for a modest amount of unskilled work. I didn't blame Dick. He was a dedicated and highly skilled lawyer, and he had spent thousands of hours each year on the players' behalf—for a fraction of an agent's income (or, for that matter, a fraction of that of a partner in a prestigious law firm). He did not, mind you, talk about becoming an agent; quite possibly he had no such intention at the time. (I thought he did.) Whatever the case, when he finally did become an agent, he became an important addition to the small complement of qualified, competent professionals.

Even if I didn't react the same way, I felt as disgusted as Dick with the players' practice of rewarding poor service with princely sums. In fact, an agent who represented ten or so big-name free agents made more money than even baseball's highest-paid player. Perhaps after sixteen years with the Steelworkers Union, I was better prepared for such inequities. By the time I had become chief economist and assistant to the president I was working with executives of major corporations whose salaries were ten to thirty times more than mine. This discrepancy, however, didn't concern me, and it was rarely, if ever, discussed at the union. It might sound self-serving, but *dedicated* union men didn't dwell on maximizing their income; their aim was to protect the workers' rights, perhaps even to correct some of society's ills. Working for a "not-for-profit" organization always has seemed to me to be in a different category than employment in a profit-making enterprise.

Ultimately, this was why I felt it improper to set up a salary structure at the Players Association that was comparable with the fees paid to players' agents, or competitive with salaries of management officials. Hefty salary increases for staff members at the Players Association would have enticed exactly the kind of union representatives no one should want. I felt then as I do now that to maintain the integrity of any service organization the top officers should place principles above a paycheck. Besides, it was impractical to even imagine an appropriate salary structure at the Players Association which would be in line with the fees of some of the prominent agents. They each were netting more than a million dollars from commissions for less than one month's work. What salary would be appropriate for, say, an experienced and competent general counsel who logged considerably more than two thousand hours a year? Would \$10 to \$12 million a year be enough?

The staff at the Players Association was well paid—not when compared to the players or their agents or baseball's brass, but in relation to the rest of the trade unions around the country (except for those whose legitimacy was suspect). I considered my salary more than adequate; in fact, sometimes I thought it embarrassingly high. I represented a union with fewer than a thousand active members, and I made more than many presidents of industrial unions with more than a million members. Sure, the players had become millionaires and could have easily afforded *whatever* salary might be proposed, but the comparison with players' salaries was unjustified. Professional baseball players are in the entertainment industry, a business with noticeably short careers, and it is my belief that neither union officials nor agents have a legitimate claim to pay based on players' peak earnings. However, not long after I retired in 1982, the executive director's salary was reexamined and, after consideration of a number of factors, including players' salaries, the executive director's salary (and the salary structure at the Players Association) was increased many times over. The implications of such a policy change on the operation of a union aren't easy to discern.

But back to Dick. Or more particularly, his replacement. After news of his departure became known, I began receiving letters and telephone calls from applicants and from friends and associates who recommended others for the job. Dick and I discussed the applicants at length and kept coming back to an impressive young attorney from Missouri who had worked with us during the Messersmith case in federal court in Kansas City. His name was Donald Fehr. A lawyer who specialized in labor law (as opposed to a trade unionist who happened to be a lawyer), Fehr had picked up on the nuances of the case quickly. I arranged an interview in New York, Fehr said he was interested, and I offered him the job. Considering the owners' efforts to have the Messersmith decision overturned in a Kansas City court, it was only just, I suppose, that their suit led, indirectly, to the hiring of Don Fehr as general counsel in 1977. All of the owners know what position he holds today. And all baseball fans should know that I found him to be a skillful, bright, hardworking lawyer who was totally compatible with the players.

In the spring of 1978, our clipping service sent us a strange headline from the *Chicago Sun-Times:* "Coming Next: Commissioner Marvin Miller?" Here's what followed: "There has been more talk than ever this spring about the possibility of Marvin Miller retiring as executive director of the Players Assn. 'If Marvin wants to be fair,' said Bob Scheffing, former general manager of the New York Mets, 'once he retires he then should go to work for the owners; it would help even things up.' It is Scheffing's opinion, and the view of many baseball men, that Miller would 'make a great commissioner.' Chances are he would, but Miller isn't likely to be interested in being hired by the owners. He'll probably retire after the next negotiations, which come in 1980, write a book, and serve the Players Assn. as a consultant."

Okay, the timing was off by several years, but the writer did call two out of three on the money. But obviously, these fabricated stories about my becoming commissioner were way off base. Neither the owners nor I would sanction such an outrageous idea. Such stories, which appeared from time to time, were planted, I think, by a writer or a club official who wanted to get a rise out of Bowie Kuhn. Usually they did.

Throughout the 1978 season, the owners and Kuhn continued to pop off about the need to put me and the players back "in our place." George Steinbrenner was a prominent part of the chorus, though I felt that George's comments were made largely to persuade the other owners that the man who was leading the way in signing free agents was still in their club. Gussie Busch was more militant. He said, "The owners are going to be better prepared than they ever were before, and they'll take a harder line than ever before. And if it means a lockout, baseball will shut down. We opened our doors two years ago without a new contract. I don't think that will happen in 1980."

At the Associated Press sports editors convention in Dallas, Steinbrenner threw down the gauntlet. "In our negotiations on the players' agreement two years ago, we were like David without a slingshot. Marvin took, took, took. I have a lot of respect for Miller. He is a brilliant man, but next year we will meet him head on. He will find himself in the toughest negotiations he's ever seen. This time he'll know he's been in a ball game." I felt like reminding him that I had been in one hell of a ball game since 1966.

As usual, Steinbrenner was wrong on all points. His characterization of the 1976 negotiations was incorrect and blatantly unfair. They were good-faith collective bargaining negotiations, and the result was an agreement that served the best interests of everybody. And since I had spent almost forty years in labor-management relations, including basic steel negotiations in 1950, 1952, 1953, 1954, 1956, 1959, 1962, 1963, and 1965—including a 116-day strike in 1959—he was off in saying that the next negotiations would be the toughest I had ever seen. I do, however, thank him for the "brilliant" comment, but I don't know whom he was comparing me to.

Of course, Steinbrenner was talking publicly about the need to limit the free-agency rights of players at the same time that he was busy signing Catfish Hunter, Don Gullett, Reggie Jackson, Luis Tiant, Goose Gossage, and Tommy John to lucrative contracts. When Richie Zisk signed with Texas for $2.7 million over ten years, Steinbrenner said: "Brad Corbett's crazy. He's ruining baseball." George neglected to mention that from 1975 to 1977, Yankee home attendance jumped from 1,288,048 to 2,468,092, bringing an increase in revenue of roughly $10 million a year. And that didn't include the additional millions of dollars from the playoffs and World Series, and from the vastly increased television and radio payments. Neither Corbett nor Steinbrenner was crazy, except as in the expression, "crazy like a fox."

While Steinbrenner & Co. talked tough, baseball's high priest, Bowie Kuhn, continued sermonizing. Free agency, he maintained, had affected competitive balance and brought baseball to the brink of financial ruin. At a news conference in Boston, Kuhn said, "The preferred way to deal with the issue is through collective bargaining, but I don't rule out the possibility of *trying to do something.*" (Was this the original seed of the collusion to come?) In the *New York Times*, Peter Maas delivered one of the best lines of the year: "Not since Nero scheduled the lions versus the Christians has the western world suffered the erratic pomposity [Kuhn] exhibits almost daily."

Neither of Kuhn's statements came near the truth. Most of the teams that signed free agents were second-rung clubs striving to become more competitive—Milwaukee, Texas, California, San Diego, Atlanta, Montreal, Toronto, and Cleveland. Maybe the commissioner was speaking of the "competitive balance" back when, *before* free agency, Cincinnati claimed *five* championships in *seven years*; or Pittsburgh finished first or second *six* times in *seven* seasons; Los Angeles *six* times in *seven*; and Oakland *five in a row*. As Red Smith said: "Year after balanced year, the rest were out of it."

At our winter meetings in Scottsdale, Arizona, I met the twenty-six player reps to discuss a special fund to be used in case of a strike or lockout. That was a strategy the owners didn't react kindly to. One unnamed owner told the *Baltimore Sun*: "I think what they're doing is an unfortunate move at this early stage. We're troubled by it and we don't know why the Association is doing it. It seems part of a program designed to create suspicion and crisis for the public far in advance. Miller doesn't have to engage in that kind of stuff."

My response then was the same as it is now: I wish the owners' comments after the 1976 basic agreement hadn't given me reason to do it.

Here we were, with two and a half years to go before the basic agreement expired, and the front offices were sabotaging negotiations for 1980. It was provocation without precedent in all my years of labor-management relations, and it was made even more outrageous by the boom in baseball's prosperity.

It must be said that the owners could not have waged this war of words without the complicity of the press. Their ability to manipulate the media was nothing new. During pension negotiations in 1969, the owners collected columns written by their pet writers and distributed them in packets to the "privileged, pampered" players. (This, when the minimum salary was $10,000.) This propaganda had an unholy purpose, but even at the time I recall getting a chuckle or two from some of the things I read.

For example: Angels owner Gene Autry told a reporter for the *Los Angeles Times* that, in the event of a strike, "I can still climb back up on my horse and earn enough to pay the rent without the players." The writer went on to say Autry "became an owner for a very simple, romantic and outdated reason. He loves the game of baseball. . . . Hurt and puzzled, Autry is ready to lock the doors to Anaheim Stadium." I almost felt compelled to mail a check to the poor cowboy so he didn't have to get back on his high horse.

No matter how hard I tried, keeping up with the media onslaught—correcting errors and writing letters and articles—was impossible. Probably the most consistently one-sided publication was the *Sporting News*. The columns were biased, the editorials error-strewn, the selected letters-to-the-editor vicious. I wrote the *Sporting News* so often they ran a cartoon depicting me hammering away at a typewriter with smoke rising from the keys. (Years later, when our relationship had mellowed, the publisher, Johnson Spink, sent me a framed copy of the cartoon.)

When I was in St. Louis, I used to visit their editorial offices. In fact, it wasn't long before I had developed a rapport with Spink and several of his writers. We had our share of arguments, including one in which I confronted Spink with the fact that the paper was subsidized by major league baseball in the form of subscriptions sent to American soldiers overseas. The deal apparently started during the Korean conflict and continued thereafter. Without those subscriptions, paid out of the commissioner's office's Central Fund, the paper would have had a rocky time financially. I don't know how much longer the subsidy lasted, but after I pointed this out the paper's coverage gradually became more balanced.

The opposite occurred with *New York Daily News* columnist Dick Young. Woody Allen once described his rabbi as "reform," so reformed in fact, that he was a Nazi. In the 1950s, Young was a maverick, perhaps the best in the business at bringing fans into the locker room. But by the midsixties, he was "reformed," as reactionary and virulently antiunion as *any* owner in baseball. With good reason. Young was *part* of management. He accompanied Mets executive Donald Grant to union grievance meetings! His son-in-law was employed in the Mets' front office. And he wasn't alone. There was a stable of sportswriters around the country spoon-fed inside information as long as they spouted the company line. Young used to brag to other sportswriters: "You'd kill for my access." But he never told them what he gave up in return.

By 1979, the stormy labor-management relationship had become worse. You wouldn't think an industry with the growth of baseball, with the unprecedented surge in popularity and television revenue, would want to get into a disruptive labor dispute. But that's what happened. The biggest issue was compensation (not payments to players, but payments to owners!). Instead of a draft choice, the owners wanted a major leaguer from the team that signed a free agent awarded to the club he used to work for; they wanted to scrap salary arbitration; they wanted to institute a pay scale. The list of give-backs went on and on. Their demands were in line with their real goal: the destruction of free agency.

Clearly, the battle over free agency involved more than just money. In 1978, baseball took in $277.7 million; salaries totaled $68.5 million, or less than 25 percent of total revenue. As for the remaining income of more than $200 million, nonplayer expenses did not come close to absorbing it. Owners' claims to the contrary, there were substantial profits. The real problem, as the owners saw it, involved power and control. Instead of the total domination of the game they had enjoyed for a hundred years, they were confronted with a contractual relationship between equal parties. It was a turnabout they weren't willing to accept.

As the 1980 negotiations drew near, my inclination was to look for some sane voice among management. But not even a whisper of sanity could be heard. There appeared to be nothing the union could do to avert a collision.

In the fall of 1979, Bowie Kuhn asked me to have a drink with him at the 21 Club. Our drinks had barely arrived when he said, "Marvin, the owners need a victory." What he was asking me to do, I replied, was akin to "throwing a game." From there the meeting went downhill fast.

When I returned to the Players Association office, I must still have been wearing my astonishment on my face. Don Fehr took one look and asked, "What's wrong?"

"We're in for a hell of a fight," I said.

15 . . .

Strike Two, 1980–1981 . . .

WE HAD JUST ENDED the longest strike in baseball history, and I was in no mood to smile and pose for pictures with Ray Grebey. (There had been a traditional handshake the prior year when a last-minute settlement averted a strike.) Before I had a chance to refuse, Doug DeCinces pulled me aside. "I don't think you should pose with him," he said, echoing the sentiment of several other players standing by. Such was the immediate aftermath of the 1981 strike, a long, drawn-out, bitter affair.

Although negotiations for the 1980 basic agreement began in 1979, related events leading up to a conflict began three years earlier, right after free agency came to baseball.

As soon as the 1976 basic agreement was signed (seven months after the Messersmith-McNally decision), the owners began moaning and groaning about the high salaries that *they* expected to offer the players. It was a chorus of woe and hostility that they kept up for the next three years. (By 1979, average salaries had risen from $51,500 in 1976 to $113,558.)

The owners insisted that free agency was ruining baseball. Their remedy was "compensation"—a scheme designed to penalize a club for signing a free agent. Charles Bronfman of the Expos warned that the owners had to be given their free-agent compensation demand because "baseball is not a healthy industry."* Calvin Griffith of the Twins said: "Some teams are going to go broke—it's bound to happen." Ray Grebey claimed that the Orioles, Cubs, and Braves had all lost money, ranging from $53,000 to $1 million. In addition, he said, "It is no longer pleasant or nicely profitable to run a ball club. Most owners don't take a damn cent out of their clubs, and they could [make more money] as a waiter at the ballpark."† And Bowie Kuhn, the leader of the doomsayers, proclaimed, "Unless we find oil under second base we will never survive."

The owners' line—that free agency and skyrocketing salaries were ruining competitive balance and thereby turning off the fans—was a smoke screen. In 1976 they had predicted that every eligible player would become a free agent that year (the actual number was twenty-three), that all the best free agents would wind up in New York or California, that there would be runaway pennant races, that one or two teams would dominate the World Series every year, that attendance and television interest would diminish, that the entire American League would go bankrupt and a handful of National League teams would vanish as well. (This was the testimony of Kuhn & Co. offered at the Messersmith arbitration hearing.)

None of that happened. Business in baseball was booming. Attendance and gate receipts, television and radio revenues, income from concessions, the value of franchises all set new records virtually every year. Looking at what had happened in the sport, one might be tempted to proclaim a "trickle-up" theory of economic development. The gains of the players had percolated, so that everybody—trainers, coaches, field managers, general managers, league presidents, club officials, umpires, owners,

---

*In 1990, a year of record-breaking profits, Bronfman was quoted again to the effect that "expenses may soon choke many of us," and that the existing salary structure "had to be eliminated."

†The waiter that made more than the average owner would have had to have been pushing something stronger than peanuts and Crackerjacks.

players' agents, and, yes, the commissioner—were making much more money. A *lot* more, in fact. For most of his tenure, Commissioner Kuhn's salary was reportedly $200,000 a year or slightly less; Commissioner "Spike" Eckert had earned roughly $65,000 a year. In 1990, Jack McKeon, the general manager of the Padres, had a contract for a reported $400,000 per season; several field managers are in the $500,000 a year (and over) bracket; and Commissioner Fay Vincent reportedly is paid in the $700,000 to $800,000 range. Yet many of the same front-office men who owed their newfound prosperity to the success of the Players Association continued to conspire against it and to complain about *players'* salaries.

Competitive balance was a phoney issue. If the real profit figures were revealed, I believed, the owners' true intentions— ending free agency, restoring the reserve rule, and reducing players' salaries—would come to light as well. In 1981, I decided to force the owners to "put up or shut up" by filing a charge of refusal to bargain with the National Labor Relations Board. Under existing law, an employer claiming poverty (that is, an inability to pay) in collective bargaining must document it. Failure to provide the relevant financial data is refusal to bargain in good faith—an unfair labor practice. The NLRB ruled in favor of the Players Association and moved for an injunction in federal court to prevent the owners from implementing their plan for compensating clubs that lost a free agent until the board finally adjudicated the refusal-to-bargain complaint. If the injunction were granted, there would be no strike. If not, as the owners had announced already, their 1979–1980 compensation proposal would become part of the basic agreement, and a strike was a certainty.

The injunction hearing proved to be an exercise in futility. Grebey & Co. asserted "Kuhn doesn't represent us" under oath. (I half-expected them to print the slogan on T-shirts.) If Kuhn wasn't speaking for management when he said the owners would have to discover "oil wells under second base" or be rescued "by some other miracle" to survive, who was he speaking for? And in case Judge Henry Werker wasn't listening, the owners sat in one group, the lawyers in another, and Kuhn sat off by himself. When a reporter asked Kuhn if his comments about baseball's alleged poverty represented the owners' view, he responded as he surely was told to respond: "I was really kind of a free agent when I said that. Those statements were mine." Kuhn's comments about the "fairness" of the owners' free-agent compensation made me wonder if he thought his old law firm, Willkie Farr & Gallagher, deserved compensation when he left to become commissioner of baseball. For that matter, I wondered if *they* thought they deserved compensation.

You'd almost expect a judge named Werker to have *some* empathy with labor. Werker was misnamed. The NLRB had filed three prior injunction requests on which he had ruled, and he had turned down all three. And the NLRB is quite selective—its request for section "10-J" injunctions under the law are few and far between and rarely rejected. The courts have established that there is a presumption in favor of granting the NLRB's motion unless there are compelling reasons to persuade a court otherwise. When NLRB counsel pointed this out to Werker, his response spoke volumes: "I don't recognize that."

Werker was a Republican hack appointed by Richard Nixon, and everything a judge shouldn't be: rude, sexist (his treatment of the female NLRB counsel was disgraceful), biased, incompetent, and, on top of everything else, a publicity hound. Werker held press conferences in his court between sessions, something I had never seen before. At one post-hearing news conference, Werker called the case "as extraordinary as throwing a manager out of a game."

"That's not extraordinary," one reporter suggested.

"I know it isn't now," he said, "but it used to be extraordinary. Billy Ball has changed that."

This was the man who had the power to decide whether there would be a player strike. What's worse, he misunderstood what was going on in his own court. If the injunction were issued, the clubs would be prevented from implementing their compensation scheme for at least a year, and, most significant, there would be no strike. So Werker assumed (because the owners told him so) that the Players Association had engineered this NLRB action because we were afraid to strike. The absurdity of this propaganda, which he had swallowed whole, soon became apparent.

Even more preposterous was his opinion that free-agent compensation—the only issue in the negotiations—was *not* an economic issue. Millions of the owners' dollars and players' salaries were at stake, but Werker found that *compensation* was not an economic issue. He found that the mandatory transfer of players worth millions on the open market was *not* an economic issue. Opposed to this view were simple facts: In 1976, Reggie Jackson left Baltimore and signed a five-year, $2.66 million contract with the Yankees; in 1978, Pete Rose left the Reds and signed a four-year, $3.2 million contract with Philadelphia; and in 1979, Nolan Ryan left the Angels and agreed to a three-year, $3.5 million deal with Houston; and starting in 1976, about two hundred players had become free agents—the majority of them changing clubs, a significant shift of assets. In order to rule against the NLRB, Werker somehow had to pretend to believe the fiction that economics and the owners' ability to pay were not involved.

He opened the hearings by saying, "In the words of Abbott and Costello, Who's on first?" I suppose he thought this was witty. On June 10, 1981, he delivered his decision, closing with "PLAY BALL!" (He *was* a comedian...but which one?)

He didn't realize how ironic these final words were. Forty-eight hours later, as we had assured him, we began what was to become the longest strike in the history of professional sports. For that, Judge Werker deserves a place in history—with a dunce cap on his head.

It had been a long time coming. On April 1, 1980, the players voted to cancel the final week of spring training (a total of ninety-two exhibition games), return to play the Opening Day of the season, and consider the possibility of a strike on May 23. Waiting until the twenty-third—the Memorial Day weekend—would inflict greater financial damage, as the early weeks of the season often draw poorly. The players voted 967–1 in favor of the strike. The lone dissenter was Minnesota infielder Jerry Terrell, who objected for religious reasons.

The owners were not quite that religious. They had seemed intent on provoking a strike. Their demands for an end to salary arbitration and individual player contract negotiations, the substitution of a fixed salary schedule, and compensation to a club losing a free agent were really extreme.

Six hours before the strike deadline, I said it would take a "small miracle" to reach a settlement. *Sports Illustrated* wrote: "On the negotiating table were large pitchers of water, but the two sides were separated by oceans." A week earlier, I had suggested settling all other matters—pension funding, minimum salary, eligibility for salary arbitration, and more than a dozen other issues—while submitting the subject of free-agency compensation to a one-year study group. The Player Relations Committee said no. If compensation couldn't be settled now, they wanted to play ball, negotiate during the season, and then put their compensation plan into effect.* I rejected the proposal for obvious reasons. Later that afternoon, Grebey came back to my study-group idea. Once that was worked out, the other issues fell into place as I had hoped. Negotiations into the early morning hours of the next day produced a four-year basic agreement and a pension agreement.

The basic agreement involved many improvements for the players, most notably, reducing eligibility for salary arbitration to two years of major league service. The new pension agreement increased all the basic benefits—retirement, disability, pensions of former players, health care, and so on—and we succeeded again in negotiating the owner contribution to the pension plan at the traditional level of one-third of the national television and radio package, which had grown dramatically. The owners' demands for ending salary arbitration and instituting a fixed salary structure were, of course, withdrawn.

The group to study the compensation issue consisted of two players, Sal Bando and Bob Boone, and two club officials, Harry Dalton and Frank Cashen. Dalton had been a rational voice at various times. In May 1980, thinking he was speaking off the record, he told a pool of reporters: "I hope that we are not about to witness another macho test of wills. From what I hear, the Players Association is genuinely looking for a compromise if we'll just give them something that they can accept without losing too much face." He went on to say that he feared the owners didn't want a settlement, they were looking for a "victory"!

Dalton's remarks cost him $50,000. Apparently he had violated Grebey's "media blackout" by making a public statement about the

---

*This scam was tried again by Commissioner Fay Vincent in 1990. The union gives up its only weapon, a strike, and the owners win by default! That's fair and equitable, isn't it?

negotiations. I was quoted as saying, "I had always realized that the truth had a price, but I never realized it was that expensive." Although Dalton was punished, one month earlier Gene Autry had said, "They [the players] keep wanting more with no consideration for the other side. There's only so far you can go, only so much water in the well, and for an owner who is trying to do the right things, it's all very frustrating." That didn't cost Autry a dime in fines. It all depends, of course, on what it is you don't want said.

The study group accomplished nothing. Dalton and Cashen brought to the table the PRC's proposal that a team signing a "quality" free agent (one chosen by eight or more teams in a reentry draft, which would henceforth be a draft conducted in private) would be allowed to protect fifteen players on its forty-man roster, leaving one of the remaining twenty-five available as compensation. In other words, a club signing a free agent could very well lose an established player more valuable than the free agent, or lose a prospect with All-Star potential. The scheme was designed to end free agency and would certainly have succeeded if it had gone into effect.

Though Dalton for a time seemed willing to work toward a mutually acceptable solution, apparently the PRC's instructions were to stonewall the meetings. Cashen clearly had a closed mind. The study group issued their report—two diametrically opposed opinions—on January 1, 1981. That gave us thirty days to try to hammer out an agreement. If no agreement was reached—and it wasn't—the owners could unilaterally adopt the last compensation proposal they had presented in the spring (or a less harsh proposal). They chose their harshest proposal, one consistently rejected by the players. Our only option was to strike not later than June 1, 1981 (the date set in the contract), or accept the owners' plan and watch free-agency rights become meaningless.

In his autobiography, *Hardball*, Bowie Kuhn refers to the 1981 strike as "Miller's strike" and says, "Miller was a prisoner of his own ego above all things. According to the press, he had never lost to the owners in collective bargaining and would not now."* (At least the press was accurate, even if Bowie wasn't.)

*Kuhn, *Hardball*, p. 346.

It's revealing that Kuhn phrases it that way. As the Players Association gained ground over the years, many writers painted Kuhn as the leading actor in a cast of defeated characters. According to the press, the Players Association was "unbeaten, untied, and unscored upon," but that was hardly an accomplishment, considering that Kuhn led the opposition. From time to time a writer would remark something to the effect that "this wouldn't have happened if Judge Landis were commissioner." A silly remark, but it must have stung Kuhn. But what must have really hurt was Dick Young's crack: "None of this would've happened if Bowie Kuhn were alive." I was dubbed the "real" commissioner of baseball. One columnist wrote: "Miller's playing with a stacked deck. He has arbitrators, judges, appellate courts and Congress on his side. Bugs Bunny could win with that going for him." I didn't mind being compared to Bugs, who would have made a skillful negotiator, but I would have loved to ask the writer, "What did Congress and the Supreme Court ever do for the players over the years except screw them?"

The press began to portray Kuhn as a dunderhead and called him a stuffed shirt. This must have hurt, but to his credit, he sometimes joked about it. Before a meeting he would occasionally tell a story, stop, and say, "Does that sound like something a stuffed shirt would say?" Sometimes he'd laugh about the barbs. But I know they bothered him.

Kuhn was a prisoner of his belief in the totality of the commissioner's power. He wrote: "The commissioner exists to tell the owners what to do and not the other way around." (Imagine anyone who had already been kicked out of office by the owners writing such words! But reality was never Bowie's long suit.) Kuhn was plagued by the ghost of Judge Kenesaw Mountain Landis. When Kuhn told me over drinks, just before the 1980 negotiations, that "the owners need a victory," he was saying, pointedly, "I need a win too."

This, I think, was the true source of the friction between Kuhn and me. All the Players Association's victories—achieving bona fide collective bargaining, a grievance and impartial arbitration provision to enforce collective bargaining contracts, salary arbitration, free agency, safeguards against collusion—involved the removal of the commissioner as the so-called impartial arbitrator.

No contract is worth its weight in salt without true impartial arbitration (or the right to strike to enforce the contract). Had the commissioner's office not been stripped of this power, overturning the reserve rules through arbitration could not have happened. And Kuhn took the loss of power and prestige as a personal insult.

Before 1970, baseball was like one of those tiny towns in which a stranger passing through gets arrested by the sheriff, who also turns out to be the judge and the mayor. If an owner violated a player's rights, the latter had no recourse but to appeal to the commissioner, and that was slim recourse indeed. The commissioner would remove his hat, which read "Hired and Paid by the Owners," and don another, which said "Impartial Judge." It was the removal of the second hat that Bowie never forgave me for.

I never saw my battles with Bowie Kuhn as clashes of personality. At times I enjoyed Kuhn's company. He had a decent sense of humor about most things, though not often enough about himself—and after just one martini he was able to improve in that area. He wasn't a big drinker, but once the alcohol loosened him up, he could be charming; the arrogance and inflated notions about the title of commissioner disappeared. He would refer to himself as "the Commish." And he stopped his usual knee-jerk defense of owners' actions and views. Sometimes he would even rip into the ones who had given him a hard time. One target was a general manager (still alive) whom he and his deputy, Sandy Hadden, referred to as "the Führer"—and not because he was of German origin.

But Kuhn's inability to face facts and his penchant for spouting nonsense long after events had proved his statements incorrect made me wonder about him. For example, he predicted free agency would ruin competitive balance and continued over the years to cry wolf in the face of facts to the contrary. By harping on competitive balance, Kuhn could maintain that he was looking after the best interests of the fans and the game when he was really serving as the owners' shill in an effort to end free agency. In reality, the game had never been *more balanced* than after free agency was instituted in 1976. Teams that had been perennial doormats became contenders and division winners. The Phillies (winners of two pennants in one hundred years) won pennants. Kansas City, a city that had never had a team in the World Series, defeated the Yankees, who just a few years earlier dominated the American League. Free agency had produced the best competitive baseball in forty years.

If ego was a factor in the 1981 strike, it was the ego of Kuhn and of those obstinate owners craving a "victory" and desperate for a means to make certain writers eat their words about their losing every "contest" they fought with the Players Association. Kuhn wrote: "No sensible person would have permitted the Players Association to strike over the compensation issue." What he doesn't say is that the demand for compensation was the owners' demand; it was a poorly concealed plan to reduce players' salaries and achieve greater control. The issue was so important that when the owners had unveiled their scheme the year before, virtually every neutral observer predicted a strike. (The players' strike vote had been 967–1.)

The owners *knew* that they were bringing on a strike. They had laid out large sums of money in advance for a $50-million strike insurance policy with Lloyd's of London. And they had created a $15-million fund to further bolster themselves against the losses of a strike. Kuhn is sickeningly disingenuous when he claims that the compensation issue was trivial, and that the owners were unprepared. What they weren't prepared for—almost inconceivable *after* the events of 1972 and 1976—was a union membership that would remain united until the owners sued for peace on terms we chose to give them. No, compensation was not about balance or fairness to the fans or financial instability.

Money, control of players, and management's great desire to stop their long losing streak were the issues. All the patent baloney was simply their attempt to conceal their objectives. There was also a group of "hard-core" owners, the Gussie Busches and Gene Autrys and Calvin Griffiths of the world, who quite possibly believed that a protracted strike would destroy the Players Association. George Steinbrenner said: "I've never seen the owners more unified and prepared for a strike. . . .Unless he handles this right, it could be Waterloo for Marvin Miller." I'm sure George didn't come up with that on his own; it was something being said in the circles in which George traveled.

But, as I said, management underestimated the players. They were banking on the fact that the players were making so much money they wouldn't stick together.* One general manager said, "We expect the players to take a hard look at where their interests lie. This [the owners'] approach isn't villainy. It's business." By 1980, players were too sophisticated to buy that. They knew that no matter how attractive their individual contracts, they would have no future bargaining power if they lost free-agency rights or if the Players Association were weakened in any way.

Restricting free agency would carry the owners a giant step toward regaining the control they had enjoyed *before* free agency. In 1979, the PRC proposed a salary scale for players with less than six years of big league service. Under this plan, no club, even if it wanted to, could pay the player above the pay scale. In this scenario the union would be policeman, holding salaries *down* (as in basketball) to the limits set forth in a contract. The proposal, aimed at ending salary arbitration, was inane and couldn't be taken seriously. There would be no more individual salary negotiation, a practice the owners had insisted on for a hundred years. A superstar would make only a fraction more than an average player. And the proposed salary figures were a joke. For example, Jim Rice's salary was about $700,000 a year. A future player of Rice's stature would be paid $153,600 with possible bonuses upping the figure to $187,900. They wanted to eliminate individual salary negotiation at precisely that time in history when it worked to the *players'* advantage.

In effect the PRC wanted the union to protect the owners from themselves. The Players Association was being told *it* had to restrain the owners from paying higher salaries. Bob Ryan of the *Boston Globe* may have overstated a bit when he wrote: "There is no sense in even dignifying the proposal by analyzing it as a legitimate expression of human thought. It is merely the depraved workings of some reactionary brains." But the idea was correctly perceived. When the PRC finally withdrew the salary scale proposal in 1980, even Ray Grebey hailed the move as a "major

---

*In 1972, when players' salaries were on the low side, owners and the media said players couldn't afford to strike. In 1981 they said players were making too much to strike. I have concluded, therefore, that management believes either that there is no salary level appropriate for a strike or that there may be some optimum level of salaries which supports a strike—but it has yet to be established.

breakthrough." I disagreed, and compared the PRC to a man who wants a medal because he no longer beats his wife.

As the 1981 strike deadline approached, various writers, general managers, owners, and agents began pressuring the players to make some concessions on compensation. I didn't think the owners deserved any compensation beyond an amateur draft choice, and they had had that since 1976. Should Ray Grebey's former employer, General Electric, have received a baseball executive when *he* jumped ship? When George Steinbrenner signed Padres free agent Dave Winfield in 1980, he said, "I don't think it's fair that I get a player of Winfield's talents and lose an amateur kid that may never play in the majors." The statement caught my attention. Steinbrenner didn't say it was unfair for him to *get* Winfield, just unfair for San Diego to *lose* him without compensation. I decided that it was time to create a fire on this compensation thing and see what we smoked out.

The next day I issued a statement. "Steinbrenner's heart is in the right place. I recommend that he decide now what he will give San Diego in return." I suggested he send Padres owner Ray Kroc a check for a million bucks. Don Baylor had an even better suggestion: "If the owners feel so strongly about compensation, why doesn't George Steinbrenner give the Padres his *sixteenth*-best player for Dave Winfield?" I thought that, at the very least, it would have been a nice gesture to send them one of George's racehorses, but Steinbrenner apparently didn't feel that strongly about compensation.

None of our suggestions went over too big with the front offices. I tried another idea: The owners could create a compensation fund. After all free agents have been signed, each club would receive a cash settlement from this new general fund to compensate them for the free agents they lost. Not surprisingly, the owners didn't bite. Such a proposal did everything they said they wanted except the thing they really wanted compensation to do: discourage clubs from signing free agents and thereby keep salaries down.

After Judge Werker's deluded decision—that compensation was not an economic issue—we had forty-eight hours to negotiate a settlement. But it was like negotiating with experts from the Flat Earth Society. Grebey maintained that the club that lost a free agent had to be able to receive *direct compensation from the club that signed the free agent.* And that compensation had to be *a professional player on that club's major league roster.* The Players Association proposed a variety of ways to compensate the club losing a free agent. But we focused on just that club, not on punishing the club which signed a free agent. If the punishment were severe, it would end free agency. Just before the strike I had made an offer that each club could "protect" the twenty-five players on its active roster. All others on the major league roster (up to a total of forty to a club) were subject to being drafted as compensation. When a club lost a free agent, it could pick a player from a pool made up of the unprotected players of all the clubs combined.

Grebey rejected it. Which I expected. The proposal had smoked them out. It provided professional player compensation, but it did not require that it be paid by the club that signed the free agent. I told Grebey, "This covers everything you said you wanted and needed. But you can't buy it because it would permit free agency to continue, and you're in here with instructions to restrict the movement of free agents and roll back salaries. I'm not going to allow that." He stared back at me and had nothing to say. The smoke had cleared. The cause of the breakdown in negotiations was clear.

So on with the strike.

I stayed awake all night before that first day of the strike. Money had to be wired to teams stranded on the road; plane tickets had to be purchased; player reps had to be contacted; press releases written; and on into the night.

Baseball was on hold.

Newspapers around the country ran photos of empty ballparks. Local TV stations that broadcast Mets and Yankees games filled the airwaves with reruns of shows like "Bonanza." NBC rebroadcast the 1975 Cincinnati-Boston World Series on its first Saturday afternoon show. Instead of "Monday Night Baseball," ABC featured a film called *Elvis.* In Cincinnati, they showed minor league games; in Montreal, *Dracula* replaced the Expos game.

America (and, for that matter, part of Canada) was angry. So was I.

Negotiations after the walkout were as unproductive as those leading up to it. Grebey called the strike unnecessary, saying all that mattered was the adjustment of "one small paragraph" in the 1980 basic agreement. "It doesn't even deal with free agency," he said, "just compensation."

As if one didn't have anything to do with the other! In essence, he was saying: "We're not trying to take away the players' free-agency rights, we just want to eliminate the value of such rights." The design was simple, but it escaped the perception of most observers. A free agent was to be held hostage; no other club could employ him unless the club he wanted to leave received ransom (compensation) from the club that wanted to sign him. The ransom, of course, would come from the free agent's pocket because his value to the new club would be diminished by the actual payment ("compensation") required from the new club. Instead of free agency, there would now be a trade, controlled by the clubs, of course. If Grebey, Kuhn, and Company had their way, the 1976 creation of free-agency rights, the most significant reform in sports history, would be eliminated.

"Why strike over such a trifling matter?" was Grebey's and the owners' and many writers' most frequent (and disingenuous) question. The question assumed that players would not see right through this repetitive nonsense. In this, they were proven dramatically wrong. I think it genuinely shocked them to find out just how wrong they were.

Given enough time, Grebey figured, the players would fold. The owners bombarded the players with mailgrams reminding them of how much money each of them stood to lose if the strike continued for the rest of the season. Dave Winfield was losing roughly $7,770 for each day of the strike; players earning minimum salaries of $32,500 were losing about $180 a day. An inside source informed me that some members of the PRC had each bet a few bucks on how long the Players Association strike would last: The long shot was five days.

If that prediction sounds arrogant, consider an incident that occurred one year earlier. Hours before the strike deadline in May

1980, National League president Chub Feeney stomped into the room minutes after a negotiating meeting had begun. The usually unflappable Feeney was visibly shaken.

"Do you know what's happening in California?" he gasped.

"No," I deadpanned, "what?"

"The Giants are scheduled to play in Pittsburgh tomorrow, and the Dodgers in Chicago and they *won't get on the plane.*"

"I certainly hope they won't," I said. "Those are our recommendations."

Feeney's face was flushed. "There are *games* tomorrow!" he shouted.

"Not without a settlement," I said as calmly as possible. Suddenly it dawned on me. Management still thought we were bluffing! They couldn't conceive of ballplayers making six- and seven-figure salaries walking out in midseason.

Later, I realized that Phil Niekro had expressed it best when he said: "Until you go to some of the meetings, you have no idea what goes on in these negotiations. The day before the strike, Ray Grebey's first question to Marvin Miller was, 'Are you really going to strike?' Where had he been all those months? I couldn't believe it."

No sooner had we walked out than the owners launched a campaign against the real source of their troubles. They issued statements to the press saying *I* was the real problem, that I had my own personal, sinister reasons for calling the strike. If they could only deal with the players directly, the owners said, they could hammer out a settlement. This is an age-old management line: "My 'boys' are reasonable; it is only the 'outside agitators' who cause trouble." Years later, referring to 1980 study committee members Bando and Boone, Bowie Kuhn wrote: "These were reasonable people who, *left to their own devices* [my italics], could have resolved the compensation issue."* The truth was that I'd told the rather unreasonable Ray Grebey many times that if I suddenly became feebleminded and flat-out *accepted* their compensation plan, there would *still* be no way to sell it to the players. He didn't believe me.

---

*Kuhn, *Hardball*, p. 341.

So I decided to call their bluff by removing myself from the bargaining table.

Donald Fehr represented the Association, but I asked him to say as little as possible and let the experienced players—Doug De-Cinces, Mark Belanger, Bob Boone, Steve Rogers, Don Baylor, Phil Garner, and others who might attend the sessions—run the show. George Steinbrenner said my walkout reminded him of a captain who has guided his ship across the ocean and, just at the crucial time, when the vessel is approaching harbor, turns command over to the crew. Another owner who wisely chose to remain anonymous was quoted as saying: "General Custer rides to the crest of a hill overlooking the Alamo and says, 'Well, boys, that's the entire Sioux nation. I quit.'" Not only had he violated Grebey's gag rule, he had butchered history.

I stayed away from the bargaining table for almost two weeks—no great sacrifice considering how many useless meetings we had had. Until the owners became convinced that the players weren't going to panic and fold, I knew there would be no progress anyway. Apparently the only thing I missed were some good old shouting matches. Some of the meetings nearly got out of hand. After one session, Doug DeCinces said, "As the strike goes on, I become more angry and hardline. We've done everything in our power to end the strike, and all they do is slap us in the face. Grebey tells one owner one thing and something entirely different to another." Tom Seaver, one of the more moderate player reps, said: "If they are trying to alienate the players, then they are doing a good job. The position Ray Grebey takes is absolutely destructive." Rusty Staub showed less restraint. "There were a lot of us who would have liked five minutes alone in a padded room with him."

My absence was turned into an issue. The same owners who two weeks earlier claimed that I had been an obstacle were now telling the press that my presence was necessary for a settlement. I put that issue to rest and returned, unannounced, near the end of June. I never thought I'd see the day, but when I walked into the room, Grebey & Co. were visibly relieved to see me. And with good reason: There was less risk in angering me than Willie Stargell, Steve Renko, or Dave Winfield, and at least Grebey knew there wouldn't be a settlement without my recommending it.

People have asked me why the players didn't lose their tempers more often during the strike. But after years of individual salary negotiation, players were used to being disparaged by their clubs come contract time. And this was less difficult to deal with. Players had leverage, they had the Association behind them; simply put, they weren't taking the slights personally.

I've said this many times: The 1981 strike was the most principled I've ever been associated with. Through the entire ordeal, the players remained united and strong. In 1981 scores of players had nothing to gain personally from the strike, but there were veterans on every team who remembered how it used to be and the role of union solidarity in changing things. Yankee player rep Rudy May put it, "Just seven years ago, having a big season got you a $5,000 raise...if you fought real hard." High-profile stars like Dave Winfield, who had just entered the first year of a ten-year, $20 million contract, and Reggie Jackson and Tom Seaver and Rod Carew (to name just a few), not only spoke out against the owners' compensation scheme, they got actively involved. In his autobiography, Don Baylor notes: "The fact that baseball 'super-stars' have always been out front separates the MLBPA from the NFL Players Association, a union that has consistently struggled to make gains." (I wish Joe Montana would have thought of that when he wrote in his 1986 autobiography, "I thought we should have fought to dump [Ed] Garvey and put in someone with guts— a guy like Marvin Miller." Thanks, Joe, but even a strong union leader still needs a resolute rank and file.) Because the stars spoke up, younger players recognized how damaging compensation paid to a club for a free agent would be.

Top to bottom, star to sub, liberal to conservative, the players stood firm. I was sixty-four years old at the time. I had been involved with labor for over forty years, the last fifteen with the Players Association. I was thinking seriously about retirement, but in the midst of this terribly stressful strike I found it tremendously uplifting to watch the players stand their ground. Rereading the press clippings ten years later, I'm reminded of how strong and effective and militant the Players Association had become. I'll say it again: It was the most principled strike I'd ever been associated with; it was the Association's finest hour.

If there is future trouble between the owners and the Players Association, I'd like to think that the players could take inspiration from some of these remarks that were widely quoted in the press:

Rusty Staub: "This is the easiest issue we've ever had to vote on. We recognize the gravity of the situation, but we know we're right and what they are asking is so easy to say no to."

Ferguson Jenkins: "Of course, I support the strike. We would be lost without the Association. We're like a bunch of foundering idiots without it."

Ex-Yankee Jim Bouton: "When I was winning twenty-one games, they paid me $10,500. I had to hold out the following year for an $8,000 raise. They abused players; they told us that if we didn't like the contract, we could go become a plumber or a gardener. Now I see the owners squawking about selling their ball clubs. Well, if they don't like it, they can go into the gardening or plumbing business."

Sparky Lyle: "We have a hundred years of catching up to do."

Ted Simmons: "All I need to know is what he [Marvin] wants done." (Ted's remark was really geared for the press; he was always one of the more skeptical players and questioned every proposal and position carefully, a trait I admired.)

Richie Zisk: "Everything I have and everything my family has is due to the Association. One thing I'm not is a hypocrite."

And Mike Marshall (the relief pitcher): "We have to protect younger players, and in my opinion we will. I think the stars understand that they have to pay back in some measure what others have won for them. I don't think they'll sell out, even though the sacrifice is going to be big."

Marshall's comments carried added weight and need to be placed in context. One year earlier, the Twins had waived him, claiming he was finished as a pitcher. Marshall was not nearly as effective as he had been in the midseventies, but that's not why they let him go. Historically, the Twins had a habit of getting rid of players who articulated union support or talked about Griffith's penny-pinching ways. Just before Marshall arrived, Minnesota had had five different player reps in five years, all of whom were eventually traded or released. Minnesota Manager Gene Mauch hated the Players Association, and he hated me. (So did Leo

Durocher. Though he profited from the ever-increasing pension benefits he received, the Lip never missed an opportunity to bad-mouth the union. Mauch, at least, paid union dues; Durocher never did.) During my annual spring training visits, most field managers would say hello and (unless we were discussing strategy during a dispute) sit in on our meetings. Not Mauch. Whenever I visited a team he managed—whether it was in Philadelphia, Montreal, Minnesota, or California—he made himself scarce.

When the Twins signed Marshall as a free agent in 1978, Mauch said: "Of course, you're not going to do any of that Players Association stuff, are you? These people aren't very big on player reps." (Nothing like starting off with a little attempted coercion.) According to Marshall, Mauch would rant, much in the same tone as his bosses, about how I was "ruining baseball," and he wasn't above using anti-Semitic epithets.

Marshall and Mauch had a handful of union-related conflicts in the ensuing years. After one of Mauch's typical tirades against the Association, Marshall said, "Oh, yes, Gene, I have this check for you from the union." Marshall expected an explosion. But Mauch took it, folded it, and stuffed it into his pocket.* I take some comfort in the knowledge that I didn't entirely ruin baseball for Gene Mauch.

When the players voted to strike the last week of spring training in 1980, Mauch reportedly told Marshall, "You've chosen to walk with Marvin Miller instead of me. I told you not to get involved with the Players Association."

Marshall saw few save opportunities after that. He claimed Mauch was trying to bury him. In June, after allowing *one run* in his last *11²/₃ innings* over five consecutive appearances, Marshall was released, supposedly for lack of ability. We filed a grievance alleging a discharge based on union activity and a charge with the NLRB because such a dismissal is illegal. Minnesota settled, agreeing to pay his contract in full, which meant the remainder of 1980 and all of 1981. The Mets picked him up in 1981. He appeared in twenty games and retired at the end of the season.

Anyone attempting to evaluate Gene Mauch's behavior should

---

*A by-product of the Association's licensing program, a pro rata share was distributed each spring to players, managers, coaches, and trainers. Started in 1966, the program expanded and eventually produced *tremendous* dividends.

consider the frustrations he must have endured during his twenty-six-year career. Whether he managed in the National League or the American League, in the East, Midwest, or Far West, in the United States or Canada, Mauch was the perennial loser, third on the all-time list. He set negative records, including the longest losing streak in modern times. And *no one* has ever managed as long without winning a pennant. He lost a pennant by blowing a phenomenal lead in the closing weeks of the 1964 season. And Mauch's Angels blew the 1986 league championship series when his club couldn't hold a three-games-to-one lead.

After all that, it must have been difficult to stay on an even keel. Some writers and even some players think Mauch had ability. Perhaps. But the fact that he talked so much about the "art" of managing probably explained why reporters often wrote about his baseball acumen and blamed losses on his players, not on his tendency to overmanage. Conversely, Yogi Berra—the king of the malapropism—managed seven seasons, had a winning percentage of .522, produced pennant winners in both leagues, and came within two games of winning two World Series (with the 1964 Yanks and the 1973 Mets) and was never considered in Mauch's league as a skipper. But by the standards of the world, and even by the standards of baseball, the many times Mauch was fired seemed to have been merited by his consistent losing record (.483 lifetime). He was called "Gentleman Gene" by many writers; I always wondered if it was meant facetiously, like calling an overweight person "Slim."

Most unions with fewer than a thousand members would feel fortunate to receive attention in the local newspaper. Not the Players Association. The media barrage prompted Grebey to say, "We have to stop pissing on each other in public." Which I took to mean that he felt uncomfortable when the winds of public opinion shifted and he started to get some on his own trousers. Presumably this led him in 1980 to adopt his stance against bargaining in the press.

The media coverage in 1981 was even more intense. Prior to the walkout, most of the sports reporters cast the players as uncompromising and greedy. Which, of course, was what Grebey—despite his antimedia posture—had planned. He would say something to the press like: "Is a guy who gets eight hundred or nine hundred thousand dollars instead of a million dollars a year damaged if compensation affects salaries?" Or he would insist that compensation affected only a handful of "premium" free agents. If that were the case, as Kuhn and Grebey chorused, and only "two or three players a year" would be affected, what owner, commissioner, or league president would be willing to take out $50 million in strike insurance and endure a fifty-day shutdown to put their plan into effect? That would be sheer insanity. And management wasn't *insane*. They were *lying*.

Few reporters challenged Grebey's claims, although it was clear that they perceived him as discredited. No matter how often I explained it, some writers never even tried to articulate the union's position. To be fair, the issues were complex, particularly to sportswriters who knew nothing about labor relations. As one writer quipped, assigning a sportswriter to cover baseball's hassles was "like sending the food editor to cover Vietnam."

One writer from a Cleveland newspaper, who specialized in trivia, typified the "logic" of an owner's flack. When I said that much more than salary reduction of two or three players a year was involved in the owners' plan, he wrote, in effect: "Ha! If only a few players are affected, how come Miller is willing to strike!" Clearly, I was saying the opposite: The compensation proposal *would affect the entire salary structure* and all the players, and therefore had to be resisted. But he was unable to discern the hole in his "logic." It was the *owners* who claimed it would have only a trifling impact and illogically insisted that it was worth the loss of the season and tens of millions of dollars to affect the salaries of a few. The players, at least, saw through the propaganda. Doug DeCinces said: "Obviously, they're trying to undo everything we've gained."

The inevitable and distressing result was that a lot of fans believed that player demands had created the strike. The mayor of Cincinnati threatened to file a suit against *us* for losses sustained during the strike, as did eighteen members of the grounds crew at Tigers Stadium. And even in blue-collar cities like Pittsburgh or Chicago, places where many fans come to the ballpark with a beer in one hand and a union card in their pocket, the public sided with management. And why not? The press was constantly spouting the owners' line about "greedy" players (when there were *no* player demands).

Whenever I saw a public opinion poll which was anti-Association, I was reminded of Gene Hermanski, an outfielder with the Brooklyn Dodgers during the 1940s. He stomped into Branch Rickey's office after a good season hell-bent on asking for a raise. When he emerged, he was asked if he had gotten his raise. "No," he said, "but at least I didn't take a pay cut." Thirty years later, fans were shouting that the present-day players should take a cut in pay. In their minds, these overgrown kids were getting big bucks to play a boy's game.

The fans had been carefully taught not to think, not to understand that, for example, if an arbitrator awards a player $100,000 a year more than the owner offered, the disputed money goes to the player instead of being pocketed by the multi-millionaire owner. That's all it means. No one else is affected— and I mean *no one*. If ballplayers got paid less, teachers and nurses and postmen and anyone else wouldn't get raises—the baseball owners would. What's more, the price of admission or of a hot dog or parking wouldn't change, because the relationship between players' salaries and ballpark prices is *nil*. The responsibility of a businessman includes maximizing his revenue and profits. If he can sell his hot dogs at $3.50 per, instead of at a lesser price, he charges $3.50, whether the minimum salary is $6,000 or $100,000 a year. The same principle applies to ticket prices. The fans didn't want to hear about the players' struggle to save free agency; they wanted baseball, and most of them blamed us for their not getting it. A poll in the *Cleveland Plain Dealer* said 67 percent of the fans felt the owners shouldn't have relented on their position on salary scales.

Roger Angell pointed out in the *New Yorker* that few fans resent a boxer earning $2 million for a single fight (now $20 or even $30 million), and they don't mind actors or rock singers raking in gigantic sums for a few weeks (or a few hours) of work. They do, however, resent a baseball player's being paid, say, $700,000 over a period of seven months. (Call it the Sinatra-Seaver schism.) Many fans think that it's only an accident that *they* are not out on the field playing ball; after all, most people (or at least most men) have played some form of ball, be it softball, stickball, or even Whiffleball, in their lifetimes. There's an identification, beginning in childhood, that doesn't have a counterpart in music or film.

And though it's not a pleasant subject, I also believe that racism was (and is) a factor in fan and press resentment of player salaries. If there was adverse criticism of Babe Ruth's peak salary of $80,000 a year (worth about $1 million a year at today's price and tax level), it was buried beneath the favorable publicity he received. In fact, when the Yankees signed the Babe to ever-higher contracts, they staged press conferences to publicize them, feeling that this helped make the Yankees the biggest draw in baseball. It was also the occasion for one of baseball's most famous quotes. When it was pointed out to Ruth that he earned more money than President Hoover, he said, referring to the Depression then underway, "I had a better year than he did." It could easily be argued that Hank Aaron and Willie Mays had *many* years that were better than most American Presidents', but the astonishing fact is that the two greatest black players of all time were not unanimous Hall of Fame choices.

Generally speaking, fans and writers seem to begrudge blacks and Latins the recognition and the big bucks more than they do whites. Dick Allen, the flamboyant slugger, used to tell me about the racist hate mail he received during the season. He was called an "overpriced hotdog" and worse. Much worse. Even Roberto Clemente, one of the classiest players in the game, had to change his unlisted phone number several times a season. And when Hank Aaron, as polite and dignified a man as I knew in baseball, made his run on Ruth's career home-run record in 1974, he received so much hate mail and even death threats that he had to travel with a bodyguard. Nothing of the kind happened in 1961 when Roger Maris broke the Babe's single-season home-run record. (Maris's troubles were with the handful of New York sportswriters, not the fans.)

The same feelings persist today. Fans in New York complained bitterly when Daryl Strawberry negotiated his 1990 contract but seemed pleased when George Steinbrenner paid Don Mattingly $3 million per season. And when Pete Rose hung around baseball for several years for the sole purpose of breaking Ty Cobb's hit record, he was applauded by press and public alike. More power to Pete, but I can't help wondering what the reaction would have been to a cocky, aggressive black player who sprinted to first on walks and spiked baseballs and broke a legend's sacred record.

In 1981, the public failed to realize—and the press failed to make clear—that the strike grew out of conflicts among the owners. Theoretically, these high-powered entrepreneurs believed in, or at least gave lip service to, the virtues of individualism and competition. But some of them—hard-liners like Calvin Griffith, Gussie Busch, and Ruly Carpenter—were outraged by the free-spending, high-profile owners like George Steinbrenner, Ted Turner, and Gene Autry. As Oakland owner Roy Eisenhardt phrased it: "People always ridicule the owners because they never have been able to stay together and the players always do. But it's not that simple. The players are a monolithic group with one apparent interest. The owners are twenty-six monolithic groups, with distinctly different financial interests. It's practically impossible for George Steinbrenner and Calvin Griffith to view overall industry economic issues in the same terms." With all due respect to Eisenhardt, what I think he was groping toward was a realization that the owners were, finally, as they always should have been, in competition with each other because of free agency. And Eisenhardt (and others) aren't terribly fond of competition. Understandably, but not admirably, they prefer monopoly.

The Player Relations Committee wanted the players to protect the owners from themselves. The union—no matter what Ray Grebey said—was not making demands. None. The basic agreement was not open and would not be until 1984. The same was true of the benefit plan agreement. We struck because the *owners* had a demand—compensation for the loss of a free agent—and were doing everything in their power to wrest back what we had won at the bargaining table in 1976. Namely, free agency.

As the strike wore on, the press—at least a small but vocal minority—began to articulate, and in some cases come around to, our position. The players were losing money; the owners were losing face. *Sports Illustrated* ran a cover story that read: "Strike! The Walkout the Owners Provoked." Red Smith (who called Kuhn "the owners' hatchet man"), Dave Anderson, and Murray Chass of the *New York Times* and Mike Lupica of the *Daily News* blasted

Bowie, Grebey, and the owners. Even the *Wall Street Journal* sided with us, running an editorial entitled "Baseball Owners Want Something for Nothing." (When the *Wall Street Journal* supports a union, that's news!) Cartoonists around the country got into the act. One pictured two cigar-smoking executives standing outside the negotiating room. One says: "Remember when you could own a player body and soul?" The other replies: "Yeah. If he gave you any trouble, you could crush his spirit like a paper cup and drive him out of the game." The first fellow sighs nostalgically and says: "Baseball was fun then." Maybe some writers came over to our side simply because it gave them a whole new mine of material to tap at a time when filling column space was tough. Whatever, the change was refreshing.

By July 12, the strike had caused the cancellation of 392 games and the All-Star Game. Many if not most of the owners began to realize that they had misjudged the players' solidarity and resolve. However, Grebey continued his attempts to divide the union. At this point I think it could honestly be said that he was no longer pursuing the best interests of his bosses, but the dictates of his own ego. (Of course, his job was also at stake.) First, he offered players with twelve or more years of major league service exemption from the free-agency compensation scheme. This included scores of prominent players like Tom Seaver, Don Baylor, Johnny Bench, Ferguson Jenkins, Phil and Joe Niekro, to name just a few. He let that percolate for a while, and when no one bit, he offered the same deal to players who declared free agency for a *second* time— most notably, Reggie Jackson, who would be eligible for free agency a second time at the end of the season, but including perhaps another *two hundred* active players. Finally, he appealed to those players with long-term deals who, most likely, would retire when their contracts expired so that the compensation scheme would never affect them. Winfield, for example, was in the first year of a ten-year guaranteed contract. And in order to divide the younger players from the others, Grebey pointed out that those with just a few years of big-league service would not be affected because they weren't eligible to be free agents during the life of the basic agreement, which would expire in two years. When you tallied all the players in these categories, you had a majority of players who would be exempt from or unaffected by free-agent compensation—and therefore no longer had any personal incentive to resist the owners' compensation demand.

The players saw what Grebey was doing and, in essence, said, "No way, Ray!" From that point on, one didn't have to be prounion to recognize and respect the players' principled position. They remained united, willing to make sacrifices to protect the rights and interests of younger players and players yet to come.

Federal mediator Ken Moffett had presented proposals for ending the dispute, but never got past first base. That's not a knock on Moffett. It takes an unusually skilled mediator to bring two parties together in a one-issue strike because each side has little maneuverability. Moffett told me that U.S. Secretary of Labor Raymond J. Donovan wanted to intercede in the dispute. Despite President Reagan's stance that neither he nor the Labor Department should "interject" themselves into union-management negotiations, Donovan called Grebey and me down to Washington and met with us separately for roughly an hour. A few days later, on July 15, with mammoth media coverage, he visited New York to urge both sides to reach an agreement. It was more a public relations move than anything else. Donovan meant well, but he didn't really know what was going on. And he couldn't offer anything but platitudes: "My aim is to use this office as a vehicle to get the voice of the people into the talks."

Some reporters wondered why the labor secretary was taking such an interest in baseball at a time when coal operators, air-traffic controllers, and postal employees were heading toward strikes. The reason was simple. The cities with major league franchises were complaining bitterly about lost revenue. By lending his prestige to the more glamorous dispute, he could, if successful, win the administration some acclaim. (Later, former union member Reagan made another exception about intervening in union-management disputes: His principles went down the drain as he busted the air-traffic controllers union.)

Two days after his trip to New York, Donovan summoned both negotiating teams to Washington to continue talks. It had been ten years since manager Ted Williams and the Senators played in Washington, but on July 17, 1981—more than a month into the strike—baseball returned, as it were, to the nation's capital.

When we arrived, Donovan asked for a pledge to refrain from

speaking to the press. He believed that airing our views publicly only made a bad situation worse. The reporters hated that; they had been covering the story for five weeks, and now they had to content themselves with bland statements issued between sessions by Donovan or Ken Moffett. One reporter said: "If they really wanted to avoid the press, they could have gone to Newark."

Now, with Donovan in attendance, the Players Association and the Player Relations Committee faced off each day in a conference room in the offices of the Federal Mediation Service. But as the days dragged on and Donovan became acquainted with the personalities and issues involved in the strike, he grew increasingly frustrated. It wasn't unusual to see him emerge from a closed-door caucus with management, red in the face and muttering audibly, "Those no-good SOBs."

Before long I realized that agreeing to a media blackout was a tactical error on my part. I had cut myself off from the players. The easiest, fastest way to communicate with the 650 players spread out across the country was through the media. The Players Association had a staff of four or five (depending on whether we had one or two secretaries working at the time); the owners had hundreds of people, including twenty-six public relations departments, at their disposal, plus PR people in the offices of the leagues and the commissioner, working the phones and sending out press releases. Due to the blackout, the players had lost touch with what was going on.

This became painfully apparent when Davey Lopes of the Dodgers told a reporter from the *Los Angeles Times* that contract negotiations had become a "circus." He vented his frustrations by saying: "What the hell is the players' executive board doing in negotiations?...The last thing I want to do is pick up a paper and read Doug DeCinces' synopsis about the players' feelings, because he is not qualified, and he doesn't know what he's talking about." There were also grumblings by Boston's Dennis Eckersley ("Screw the strike, let's play ball") and Champ Summers and Dan Schatzeder of Detroit. Too bad we couldn't have arranged for Eckersley to play *and* be bound to accept whatever salary the owners decided to pay him forevermore—without any union interference. (His salary in 1991 is $3 million.)

That was enough for me. I called the players who had been

quoted, reached some, and filled them in on what was happening. Once they had the facts, they seemed satisfied. Next I spoke to Secretary Donovan and explained that I could no longer abide by the blackout. At the same time, I decided to recess the fruitless negotiations and hold a series of regional meetings across the country to update the players on the strike, now beginning its seventh week.

Management leaped to the conclusion that there was dissension in the ranks. Orioles owner Edward Bennett Williams said: "I think Miller has lost control of his union." This was self-delusion. (Williams was miffed because he had no control over his own fate. He had a lot of his money invested in his club and opposed the owners' position and the strike it had caused. His efforts to move MacPhail or Grebey or Kuhn or a sufficient number of owners to avoid a strike had obviously failed.) As events would prove, he couldn't have been more wrong about the solidarity of the union. The players had not drawn salaries during the past weeks. Four objectionable comments during that time hardly constituted a mutiny. The only thing I had lost control of was my tennis game. Besides, it was not "my" union; it had always belonged to the players.

The first regional meeting was held in Los Angeles. When I set the date for recessing negotiations so that I could meet with the players, the PRC reacted by considering our "pool" proposal for the first time, and we had two days of productive bargaining sessions before I left for California. Seventy-five players attended the meeting in Los Angeles, including Davey Lopes. Afterward, Lopes told the press: "There were some misconceptions that myself and some other players who spoke up were not behind the Players Association. . . . We are strong collectively." Schatzeder, who attended the regional meeting in Chicago with sixty other players, stated, "All I said was that I wished we were better informed. I'm in full support of the union, and I'm upset that in every story I read there's a reference to me as being opposed."

In retrospect, it might have been these demonstrations of solidarity at the players' meetings that broke the owners' resolve. But there was another, more tangible reason as well. The owners had been collecting roughly $100,000 for each canceled game from the $50 million insurance policy held with the underwriter,

Lloyd's of London. The policy expired on August 8. What Lloyd's of London hadn't seemed to realize was that this was not a typical strike situation—the owners essentially *called* the strike. The union *could not* strike unless the owners unilaterally imposed their compensation plan, which they did, having first prudently taken out strike insurance. This meant that Lloyd's had boxed themselves into a corner in a manner entirely inconsistent with the principle of insurance. They had to pay strike benefits to those who had caused the strike—the owners. (The local agent for placing the insurance, by the way, was Alphonse D'Amato, later the Republican senator from New York.)

Late in the negotiations rumors surfaced about Grebey's being replaced as the owners' spokesman. In the midst of the denials by the PRC, I received a call from Lee MacPhail: Would I meet with him alone? Normally, I would have declined, but I was too curious to say no. We met at a hotel in midtown and accomplished very little, but the rumor was confirmed: MacPhail was now the chief negotiator for the owners.

Shortly before a meeting with the Association's executive board, I decided to sound out MacPhail on the possibility of a settlement. I sensed that the owners were falling apart. The newspapers had reported that some owners were angry over the handling of the negotiations and looking to axe Grebey. Kuhn, too, had been threatened with loss of support. My feeling was that the time had come to take the initiative, and that unless I did, the entire 1981 season could be lost. I mapped out a proposal, based on the Association's position in the Washington meetings, for modest compensation for a club losing a free agent. Not *direct* compensation, but from a "pool" of players. In principle, the plan was similar to the one I had offered before the strike started, although in some ways not as favorable to the owners. I called Lee and read to him all the terms of the proposal, stressing that this was meant to be the basis for settlement and could not be modified. I told him, truthfully, that the proposal had not been cleared with the players, but if the owners accepted it, I would commit to fight for its approval. It turned out to be perhaps the single most important conversation of the crisis.

At the executive board meeting in Chicago, the board members reiterated their desire to continue striking until the owners' compensation scheme was off the table. After the meeting, I informed MacPhail of the Association's position.

"I understand," he said, sounding like a man who knew his options were few.

When I got off the phone, I felt that a settlement was only days away. If not, I thought, the season that never really began was over, and we would begin planning to continue this struggle into the 1982 season.

On the flight from Chicago to New York the next morning, Arthur Ashe, a fellow passenger, politely asked the question millions of Americans—myself included—were dying to have answered. "Is there going to be a settlement?"

I said, "Yeah, I don't know when, but it's going to happen."

Ashe had heard that I was a tennis enthusiast and asked if I'd like tickets to the next U.S. Open. It was the best offer I'd heard in seven weeks.

I received another offer on that flight. Reggie Jackson, sitting across the aisle, told me that George Steinbrenner was playing hardball with him. There was little chance he'd be playing with the Yankees in 1982. I had heard this, but found it hard to believe. Why would Steinbrenner give up a player of Reggie's ability and drawing power?

"How would you like to represent me as a free agent?" he asked.

"Reggie," I said, "I don't think it would be appropriate. It would be a conflict of interest." I had publicly criticized union reps in hockey and basketball for acting as agents for selected individual players when their responsibility was to represent the interests of all the players as a group.

"Thought so," he said. "Just figured I'd ask." I didn't tell Reggie, but over the years literally dozens of the best-known players had asked me to serve as their agent, and I had declined each request for the same reason.

Reggie's request reminded me, once again, of the unbalanced, derivative role players' agents played in the free-agency equation. Agents played no part in building the union or in achieving any of the gains in the bargaining power of their clients. In fact, without the union there would be no agents in baseball at all, for their very existence was forbidden until the Players Association won for players the right to have agents. Nevertheless, players proceeded to pay a handful of agents enormous sums of money each year for minimal services. And so, as we closed in on the fiftieth day of a strike—payless days for us all—the job was to continue the fight on behalf of all 650 major leaguers. And when the strike was over, Reggie's agent, assisted further by the union, would "negotiate" Jackson's new contract, and for that he would receive a fee which would surpass the combined annual salaries of the entire staff of the Association, the organization that produced the remarkable salary structure for the players in the first place. Surely an unhealthy state of affairs, but also a prime example of players' waste and carelessness.

I returned to New York on Sunday. On Monday, MacPhail called. That afternoon—Day Fifty—Don Fehr and I met Ray Grebey and Lee MacPhail at the National League office in midtown. It went as I had hoped and expected. Grebey sat there solemnly and said very little. And MacPhail, who acted as spokesman, made no bones about it. "We're here," he said, "to make a settlement."

They tried, without much force, to amend parts of the settlement proposal I had given them. But my response each time was a firm no. I have always subscribed to the philosophy that one should allow a vanquished opponent an alley by which to escape. As the Chinese philosopher Sun-tzu said, "If you corner an opponent, his only response must be to fight." But the hardline owners in baseball had brought us to a situation that allowed no room for maneuver. Time was of the essence. If I had had to reconvene the executive board yet again to consider amendments on compensation, it would have jeopardized what little was left of the season. And we had reached a point where my credibility was at stake, too. I had told MacPhail, "This is it," and after fifty days and countless hours of dialogue, I wasn't about to budge. In the past, I had always been careful not to use the word "victory" in dealing with baseball's management. For one thing, it created bad feeling; for another, I hadn't been after "victory" over the owners but for justice for the players. This time was somewhat different: this time I was angry, and I wanted my opponents to know it. I wanted nothing less than "complete and unconditional surrender." When I got it, I was willing to consider, jointly, how best to deal with the period ahead.

Grebey and Kuhn had made the 1981 strike almost a sure thing by falsely asserting in 1980 that the owners' compensation scheme was "in place" and a part of the basic agreement. That was not so. In order to put it into effect, the owners had to have the union's agreement—either before or after a strike. Since they failed to get our agreement, their plan could not be implemented. My proposed memorandum of settlement addressed this point by mandating that the owners' compensation scheme, which never went into effect, now be stricken from the basic agreement. And so it was, in clear and unmistakable language. Bowie's baloney about having "won free-agent compensation" was now buried once and for all.

Aside from covering this matter and the "pooled" compensation settlement, the memorandum also dealt with the credited service of all the strikers. As was the case in the 1972 strike, the owners had foolishly added a disputed issue during the strike. They had stated publicly that they *never* would agree to crediting the players with service time for the days they had been on strike. "Never" proved to be slightly inaccurate. At our insistence, all players were credited with service for the fifty days of the strike for pensions and all other purposes involving service requirements under the contract.

When the memorandum of settlement had been agreed upon, MacPhail said, "You know, we have one more thing to ask. The 1981 season is a wreck, almost lost. The basic agreement and pension agreement are going to expire in 1983, just two years from now. We'd like you to extend both agreements one year, through 1984."

MacPhail's request made sense. The stress and strain of the strike was great. The prospect of another year of stability was appealing. Before I could state the obvious, Lee said they would be willing to agree now on increases in the players' minimum salary and on various economic benefits which would become effective for the 1984 season, and they would be willing to adjust the owners' contribution to the pension plan for 1984.

Don and I returned to the office and reviewed the plan with the executive committee. I lobbied for them to accept the proposal, which they did after much discussion, and we all returned to hammer out the details with the PRC. The basic agreement was extended one year, to December 31, 1984, and the pension plan was also extended one year, until March 31, 1985. Finally, around two A.M.—eleven hours after we had begun these latest talks—the settlement was complete.

I was in no mood to smile and pose for "We're one big happy family again" pictures with Ray Grebey or Bowie Kuhn. I wondered if either of them knew their days on the job were numbered. They had painted their bosses inextricably into a corner, and they had no one to blame but themselves.

The owners' direct losses from the strike were said to exceed $72 million after insurance payments. The actual dollar losses were probably considerably higher—and none of the loss was recoverable. They failed to win *any* restraints on the free-agent system, which had been their objective. Salaries skyrocketed in the years that followed, which is what they had worked so hard to avoid. And instead of cracking the players' union, their assault had made it much stronger. In short, *nothing* management had set out to do had come to pass.

Salary losses for the players during the strike averaged about $52,000 and totaled almost $34 million, a fraction of the loss the owners had intended to inflict on them by stifling free agency. The players' successful resistance led to a phenomenal growth of their salaries, starting the very next year. The average prestrike salary of almost $186,000 increased by $56,000 in 1982; by 1985 it had doubled to $371,000; and by 1990 it had more than tripled to over $597,000 a year. The player payroll of less than $121 million in 1981 exceeded $388 million in 1990!* (This should give pause to the pundits who assert that wages and salaries lost in a strike are never recovered.)

At the press conference following the settlement I didn't wave a flag or pound my chest. But I did say, in salute to the players, "It was a victory for the spirit of the players."

Several owners, like Eddie Chiles of the Rangers and John

---

*On April 10, 1991, the *New York Times* reported that Opening Day salaries of major league players in 1991 averaged more than $890,000 a year. For a full year this would translate into a player payroll of over $579 million.

McMullen of Houston, realized right away that they had struck out. Chiles, who had pressured Kuhn throughout the strike to talk some sense into management, was quoted by several different sources as saying essentially: "*This* is what we struck fifty days for? *This* is what we won? I can still lose a player off my roster without getting one myself?" Grebey said, "It was a million-dollar strike over a ten-cent issue." (Some ten-cent issue. Because of their successful resistance to that issue of free-agent compensation, players' salaries have climbed by tens of millions of dollars each year since then.)

Management's final assessment of the 1981 experience became obvious when, after a suitable interval, Grebey and then Kuhn were fired and when, in 1985, the owners began the negotiations by asking to remove the pooled compensation clause they had "won" in 1981!

What history should record is that the strike was planned by the owners, articulated by Bowie Kuhn, orchestrated by Ray Grebey (who wanted to replace Kuhn as commissioner, though Bowie didn't seem to realize it), run according to management's timetable, and concluded only when baseball's brass realized that the union couldn't be split and free agency was not going away.

Someone once said that history doesn't repeat itself. But human nature does. Nothing brought that home to me as clearly as the nine years that followed the 1981 strike. I don't think the owners even waited for the abbreviated season to resume before laying the groundwork for their future disasters.

16 ...

Take Me Out of the Ball Game

THE PHONE RANG AT TEN P.M., somewhat later than usual at our home, later still considering that Terry and I had just returned from a month-long vacation in Europe, our first real vacation since my retirement ten and a half months earlier. I certainly wasn't expecting a call about Players Association business. Most, if not all, of my ties to the Association had been cut. When I was in France, Don Fehr called with the sad news that Peter Seitz had died, but other than that, I hadn't given union matters much thought.

The voice on the other end changed everything. It was Steve Renko, the American League player rep and a member of an eight-man executive subcommittee. Brief and to the point, Steve sounded somber. "We've made a decision to fire Ken Moffett."

Moffett had been executive director only since January 1, 1983. It was now November. While I was still groggy from jet lag, I was sure I had heard him correctly.

Renko said, "The executive board is being polled. Some of the

• 320 •

player reps want to meet with you as quickly as possible. We need advice."

I was of two minds. The player reps Renko named had, I believed, acted in a very disappointing fashion the prior March by failing to take action against some really outlandish behavior by Moffett. I had tried to alert them, but my words fell on deaf ears. Now it was November, and the board had all but kicked their newly elected executive director out the door and they wanted my help. While I wasn't feeling particularly charitable, I didn't want the players to think that I had turned my back on them.

"When?" I asked.

"Now," Renko replied. "We're at the Hyatt Regency."

Terry was preparing for bed; I was wearing my bathrobe. "I'm retired," I muttered under my breath. "What the hell," I said. "C'mon over."

Twenty minutes later, four members of the executive subcommittee—Renko, Bob Boone (National League player rep), Steve Rogers, and Kent Tekulve—and Mark Belanger were sitting in my living room. (Mark was no longer a player, but for the past few months he had been on the Association's staff as Moffett's full-time administrative aide.)

As we settled down to business, I thought back to that less-than-cordial conference call I had had with several of these players eight months earlier. At the time, I was acting as a consultant to the Association, mostly to make Moffett's transition into office as smooth as possible. But in March these players had let pass a memo from Moffett that, in essence, suggested I mind my own business—which I had done from that moment. When the players on the executive subcommittee learned about my reaction, they set up a conference call, telling me that "we don't want any hurt feelings."

Feelings? There were serious issues involved, including the future course of the union. They didn't see it then. Now, after many months, apparently a light had dawned. At least, I thought, they had the good sense to set the union back on course.

First they wanted to talk about mechanics: How should Moffett be told of the board's decision? What, if any, severance payments should be made? And so on.

"Then what?" I asked. They were unsure.

I reminded them that the executive board's winter meeting was two weeks away. "Make a list of your options and have the board determine what it wants done." My reluctance to make recommendations was uncharacteristic of me, and obvious to everyone in my living room.

Finally, someone—Boone, I think—broke the awkward silence. "Look, it's November already, and there'll be major negotiations on a new basic agreement and pension plan next year. Would you consider coming back?"

"Come back?" I asked. "As what?"

"Executive director?" one player said hesitantly.

This wasn't something I felt I had to think about or discuss with Terry. "No," I said. "I decided to retire when I did because the timing was right, and that hasn't changed. I didn't alert you to Moffett's behavior last March because I wanted my old job back. I told you because, at your request, I was serving as an advisor to the organization, and it was my responsibility to do so."

Boone broke the silence again. "Would you be willing to serve as chairman of the negotiating committee during the upcoming negotiations?"

"Bad idea," I said. "That's more work than I care to take on. It's *more* than a full-time job, and since I expect you'll have a new executive director in place by then, we'd be asking for trouble if I, instead of the director, were the chief negotiator. He should do that."

"No one else has ever led the negotiations," Rogers said. "The new director, whoever he is, will need assistance." Renko seconded Rogers. So did Boone, Tekulve, and Belanger.

It was late, and I was groggy from lack of sleep. "I'll think about providing some help," I said, "but only in a limited role during the negotiations...if the circumstances seem right."

We then turned our attention to possible replacements, including several candidates from the prior year. Naturally, Don Fehr's name came up. Several players said they would feel much more comfortable selecting Don if I was retained as an active consultant throughout the negotiations.

"Well, it's a possibility," I said, thinking that coming back was a foolish, thankless task, an opinion that my sleeping wife would no doubt second in the morning. Her reaction to the players' indifferent behavior in March had been even more negative than mine.

After Steve Renko called, but before the players arrived, Terry had said, "You owe them nothing. It's totally the other way around, and I hope you don't forget it."

Some time around two A.M. the players asked if I would return as executive director *until* a replacement was found.

"Okay," I said, proving that one says things in a somnambulant state that one might not say at another time. "But only until the end of your winter meetings in December. If you don't find anyone by then, you're on your own."

Finally, as the players were leaving, someone asked, "As the interim executive director, will you be on hand when we give Moffett the bad news and handle the termination of the two attorneys [Nancy Broff and David Vaughan]?"

"Why not?" I said wearily before closing the door.

The dismissals occurred a few days later. A barrage of phone calls from the media followed, as did a lawsuit filed by Moffett and his two associates. I skipped the players' executive board meeting in Hawaii, tending instead to Association matters in New York. I suppose it was fitting, as my three-week stint as interim director came to a close, that I finished my first year of retirement back in office, thinking about upcoming negotiations. Whatever misgivings I had had about the events in the early part of my retirement, it had been undeniably satisfying to be asked to return during the players' time of need.

But Terry had the final word. "Marvin," she said, "you've flunked retirement."

Planning to retire had seemed easy. I had intended to leave the Association in 1981 after giving the players ample time to find a capable replacement. But the unmistakable portents of a crisis in 1981—almost certainly a strike—changed that. Once we had reached a settlement of that dispute, I told the players I would step aside at the end of 1982. At my suggestion, they set up a search committee, interviewed a series of candidates, and finally selected Ken Moffett. Even though he was not a trade unionist, Moffett had several things going for him. He had been the federal mediator during the 1980–81 baseball negotiations. He was amiable and had become friendly with some of the players—notably Mark Belanger and Doug DeCinces.

I invited Moffett, as the only candidate recommended by the committee, to the board's winter meeting in Hawaii so that the player reps who hadn't met him could do so. I also set up a cocktail party so that the player reps could talk to him in an informal setting before voting on his candidacy as executive director. At the end of the fourth and final session, after Moffett had been elected, I invited him to say a few words to the board. His remarks could have been written by management's public relations staff. When he repeated the owners' old line that "no one ever wins a strike," I pinched myself to make sure I had heard him correctly. Here was someone about to head the most successful union in the nation, the man who had mediated the longest strike in the history of sports, who had seen us beat back the owners' attempts to smash free agency and reduce salaries and emerge in the very next season with a $56,000-a-year *increase* in the average salary level—and his opening gambit was the brainless cliché that everyone loses in a strike! The rest of his remarks sounded like the neutral he had been at the Federal Mediation and Conciliation Service rather than the partisan he was expected to be as director of the Players Association.

We adjourned the meeting—my last, after almost seventeen years—shook hands all around, and wished each other well. Several players commented on how much they would miss me, what my leadership had meant, things like that. Later, relaxing with a drink after a few sets of tennis, I reflected on the day's events and thought of those old sentimental films in which the skinflint employer rewards his loyal retiring employee, who had endured decades of drudgery, with a pocket watch. At least I was spared that. In fact, the players, under Don Fehr's leadership, each time the players' pension plan has been improved, have supplemented my pension payments to keep them on par with the players' benefits.

Ken Moffett started on the job on January 2, 1983. Let me correct that: He started on the payroll on that date. He never really started on the job. Before he had any idea of the Association's needs, and without consulting general counsel Don Fehr, he hired two former associates, both attorneys, Nancy Broff* and David

---

*A few weeks after she reported to the Players Association, Broff took off on a vacation to Europe. Moffett had no time to be briefed about his first spring training meetings because he went on a vacation before the end of February. (Vacation first, earn it later?)

Vaughan. Don almost quit. I dissuaded him, as he was the only person left on the staff who could provide continuity.

Though I was supposed to ease Moffett into his new position, he didn't want any help from me. That is, when I could find him. Since he was commuting from his home in Maryland, Mondays and Fridays, and sometimes Thursdays, were travel days. On the three days he *was* in the New York office, he never seemed to have time to get together with me. Nor to read important material I left for him: the basic agreement, the pension agreement, parts of the Major League Rules, the union's bylaws, and previous decisions of arbitrators. At least, he never had questions about them.

The players thought that I had been briefing Moffett and had no idea that they had hired someone who had no stomach for meeting the owners' challenges head-on, someone who hoped that he might be able to slide by without a lot of work if he could just maintain the status quo. One incident after another revealed his approach to the job. Finally, after one of his particularly egregious goofs I decided that I had to alert the players.

The gaffe involved his uninformed public comments on a new television package. The Players Association had filed a countersuit against the owners which claimed, in part, that the players had a basic right to participate in the negotiation of television and cable contracts. In the past, the owners had always negotiated them. I didn't know whether Ken remembered that the lawsuit was pending. He was publicly heaping praise on the owners after they had approved a poor TV contract. I wanted to tell him that his public comments might be damaging to our case. I was concerned, too, about a related matter: Moffett was showing a distinct failure to understand that extending the League Championship Series to seven games (from five) would generate a considerable amount of new television revenue—and that it should be shared with the players.

Moffett was down in the spring training camps at the time, and I tried to reach him there. When he didn't return my phone calls, I wrote a memo to the players advising them of what was at stake.

The next few days were a circus.

I had dictated the memo over the phone from my home to my former secretary (now Moffett's secretary), and she was to type it and mail it from the Players Association office. That never happened. The memo disappeared—pocketed or destroyed by Moffett's right-hand man, David Vaughan.

To add insult to injury, the locks to the office were changed, and my former secretary told me that she couldn't find any of the five sets of keys that she was sure she had had. Vaughan, who had been on the staff for roughly a month, refused to return my memo, and he did not have any explanation for what had happened to the new office keys. It was like a scene from a Marx Brothers movie: Vaughan following me around the office trying desperately to justify purloining the memo. I ignored him, rewrote it at home and mailed copies to the board on my own. (When the task of firing Vaughan and Broff fell to me eight months later, I said: "You can take a reasonable time to clean out your desks, but you are to leave your office keys with me when you leave today. If you need to return, call for an appointment." I had tried hard not to be vindictive, but I did enjoy delivering those lines.)

After reconstructing the first memo, I wrote a second one to the players describing this brazen bit of censorship. Within a few days, several players called with questions. Some, like Reggie Jackson and Joe Morgan, were furious with Moffett and Co. If others called, I missed them because Terry and I left soon after for a stay at a favorite haunt of ours in Sarasota. It wasn't much of a vacation. Don Fehr was also there—he had been there all week, and our schedules overlapped by one day—and though I didn't know it, Moffett, too.

As I was to find out, Moffett had been getting feedback on my memos, and much of it was hostile to him. His response was to call a meeting in Tampa of the executive subcommittee, which at the time consisted of Don Baylor, Phil Garner, Bob Boone, Ted Simmons, Doug DeCinces, Steve Rogers, and Steve Renko. (Mark Belanger was also present.)

To this day I've not gotten a coherent report on what went on at the meeting—not from Don Fehr, not from anyone. The Moffett memo that was so offensive, Don told me, was composed by Broff and Vaughn. I never learned whether it was written before or after the meeting in Tampa. I'll also never know (nor do I need to) whether that memo represented the committee members' views. I *do* know that it was disturbing, especially in the sense that it seemed to indicate that the players had no understanding that the path of their union had been altered without their knowing it—to a path that, if followed, would have been quite damaging.

Before I saw the memo in print, Don Fehr called from Tampa and read it over the phone. It was a slap in the face. Upon the players' request a year before, I was supposed to serve as a consultant to the *organization*. This new arrangement asked that I give *Moffett* the benefit of my experience, but only when *he* requested it. (He was more likely to ask me to recommend a local lunch spot than to explain the pension plan.) Don then asked if we could get together to discuss what he had just read me. I had already decided to wash my hands of any further dealings with the players or the Association, but I agreed.

Don tried to downplay the whole thing later that afternoon, saying, "Look, this memo really doesn't convey a sense of what went on at the meeting, but there was nothing I could do about all of this." I was astonished. Don had been my general counsel since 1977—hell, he was *still* general counsel—and he was telling me that he couldn't have done anything to protest such foolishness. I sighed inwardly and let it pass. There was no point in my pressing Don for an explanation. (I did not know until I saw the memo that Don had initialed it also.) I wanted nothing more to do with Moffett and his crew.

Later that night, Don set up the conference call—the one I mentioned earlier in the chapter—with Steve Renko, Steve Rogers, and Phil Garner. I thought: "Why does everyone want to talk about this *now,* when they could have called me before to get the facts? Why didn't they confront Moffett when he was giving them the snow job at the meeting?" Perhaps the players felt the memo hadn't really represented what they said at the meeting. Maybe it had been written in a way that distorted the tenor of what really was said. But, as I said, to this day no one has told me what *did* happen there, so I don't know.

While we waited for the call, Don repeated what he had told me earlier: I shouldn't have sent my memo to the players alerting them to Moffett's behavior. It only made me feel more weary and disgusted. "Don," I said, "I didn't want to go off half-cocked, so I didn't say this before, when I was angry. I'll say it now that I've had a chance to think it over: I want nothing more to do with the Players Association." (Eight months later Don and Mark finally alerted the player reps about Moffett's failures, and that led to his discharge.)

Years later, while gathering material for this book, Allen Barra asked Don for his view of the events leading up to and following my retirement. Here's what he said: "The players, you must remember, knew Ken Moffett from the bargaining history, and for whatever reason I think it's fair to say that Marvin chose not to attempt to influence the ultimate selection. . . . In retrospect, [I see] this was a disaster, because the people who were in the best position to know what the day-to-day job requirements were were not making evaluations and recommendations. I think this led to an even worse situation with the ballplayers' union than it would have with other unions, because Marvin, for all intents and purposes, *created* the union. In a sense, he was the only one justified to say precisely what the job involved. . . . It wasn't like a situation where you changed heads every four years.

"The thing that comes across to me most vividly now is this: I sat with Marvin in what was essentially a two-man office day after day from August 1, 1977, to December 31, 1982, which was a time of incredible growth in the industry, including negotiations, a fifty-day strike, and so on. In other words, I was closer to him in a professional sense than anyone else in that period. I thought I knew what his job involved. It turns out that I didn't. Everybody, I think, tends to view what an organization does in terms of what their own responsibilities are, but I really had no idea of what he did in terms of what was really important until I had the job. And then I looked at things altogether differently.

"You sit there as legal counsel doing all the paperwork and all the things necessary to run the office, and you think you know the job. What Marvin was doing was making sure that the positions were well thought out, that they were well taken, that we had a player consensus behind us, that we could educate the players, either directly or through the press. *That's* the job: The organization cannot be effective at all without that. That and being able to supply leadership. I'm not denigrating the job of legal counsel, because Dick Moss and I had tremendous freedom of action under Marvin. But being legal counsel and thinking you understand the executive director's job is like being a staff officer and thinking you know what a general's job is. We all erred in thinking we understood what Marvin had been doing for years; I believe he erred in thinking that a suitable replacement could be found if he didn't take a hand in it."

Don's perception of the executive director's job from his vantage point of having been in the job for about seven years is interesting and mostly accurate. There is, indeed, a wide gap between having the primary responsibility for policy decisions as the chief executive of an organization and the duties of any other job.

Don Fehr's analysis of the job could not have been made had he not become the director, no matter how long he might have been general counsel. It has seemed to me that the organization's first general counsel, Richard Moss, not having had the responsibility of the top job, never has understood what it entails, any more than I comprehended accurately at the time the role of the union presidents under whom I served when my responsibilities were quite secondary. Don, with more balanced experience at this point, apparently understands clearly the significant differences between his responsibilities as director and those of his staff, that the leadership role is indispensable if progress is to be achieved. Supporting roles of the staff are precisely that.

My reluctance to influence the choice of my successor clearly was a mistake, but I feel even today I was in a no-win situation. How was I to start an organization on the road to self-sufficiency if I had to choose a leader for the members? I felt this all the more because, seventeen years before, the players had proved themselves perfectly capable of electing their first executive director. But, on balance, Don's conclusion seems correct. I made a major error in not providing firm leadership in the selection of a new director. The result was a grand mess.

At the time, in April 1983, I felt a mixture of relief and sadness—relief at *not* being involved (when a messenger dropped off a new set of keys to the offices of the Association, I sent them back) and sadness that much of my seventeen years of work was in danger of being undone. But making a clean break seemed like the best move for everyone. And with all the extra time, my tennis game improved.

Soon afterward, a group of steelworkers from Weirton Steel

asked me to be their advisor and serve on the corporate board of directors. Under an Employees' Stock Option Plan (ESOP), the workers were buying an interest in the plant. Their request reminded me of some of the other odd offers I had received. During my seventeen years at the Players Association, I had been asked to represent such disparate groups as the Northeast Conference of Rabbis, thoroughbred racehorse jockeys, distributors of General Motors cars and trucks, major league umpires, and Playboy Bunnies. Each group had serious gripes about their economic conditions and wanted me to help them organize. While I tried to offer helpful advice now and then, I never had the time to get involved. (If I had assisted the Bunnies, I suppose the photo section of this book would have become a more attractive feature. Representing the umpires would have involved a conflict of interest.) For a while, I seriously considered the Weirton proposal, then decided that I didn't want to play the role of helping workers cut costs by firing other workers. Instead I turned my attention to more appropriate retirement matters: a month's vacation in the south of France.

A month-long vacation was a novelty to me, a certified workaholic. But after a time, I began to enjoy it. Which, unfortunately, was when Don Fehr called me with the news that Peter Seitz, the arbitrator of the Messersmith-McNally case, had died. After the owners fired him, Peter and I became good friends. He was wise and literate and adept at writing acerbic letters. In fact, I had brought a few of his letters along so that I could answer them while I was away. When I learned of his death, I read them to Terry and the friends with whom we were vacationing as my own kind of memorial service.

Here, for instance, is a copy of a letter he had written to the *New York Times* roughly a month before his death:

MILLER AND KUHN:
NEW FREE AGENTS

To the Sports Editor:
  Sportcasters and sportswriters have made their annual report on the most significant sports events of 1982. Intent,

as they seem to be, on reporting "Who won?" they failed to note two historic occasions in baseball.

The old reserve system went out in December 1975. Since then, in amended form, it has resulted in the emergence of a considerable number of free agents, many of whom were pursued frantically and recklessly (and sometimes improvidently) by franchise owners. The millions of dollars provided for as compensation in their multiyear contracts was big news and generated more discussion among fans and others than the subject of supply-side economics or the dense-pack basing plan for MX missiles in Wyoming.

The annual sports roundups made little mention of two of the most important free agency developments of all. Bowie Kuhn and Marvin Miller have become free agents. In 1982 it developed that Kuhn was departing from his long-held job as commissioner of baseball; and that Miller, the Moses who had led Baseball's Children of Israel out of the land of bondage, was resigning his position.

Both have made great contributions to the National Pastime (the demise of which as a result of the Andy Messersmith case decision seems to have been exaggerated by some sportswriters).

I know nothing of the arrangements made by their respective principals in connection with their departures. It is to be hoped, however, (1) that their rich experience will continue to be available to players and clubs, for guidance in the future, in some appropriate capacity; and, (2) that they will enjoy some of the extraordinary monetary benefactions that have been made available to other free agents during their incumbency of the top positions in baseball.

PETER SEITZ
New York

The reference to "Baseball's Children of Israel" and his suggestion that the demise of baseball had been "exaggerated by some sportswriters" were typical of Peter's wit, but there was also a remarkable subtlety to his writing that often escaped a reader who glanced over his letters for the first time. The hidden joke in the *Times* letter, of course, is that Bowie Kuhn, who was now free to "enjoy some of the extraordinary monetary benefactions that have been made available to other free agents," had to be dragged kicking and screaming into a system that allowed free agency.

To get the full flavor of what was behind that letter it's necessary to look at a letter Seitz had written to Kuhn the year before, when it became public that the owners were not going to renew Kuhn's contract. Some excerpts follow:

Dear Mr. Kuhn,

In time, as it happened to Cardinal Wolsey, Sir Thomas More, Archbishop Cranmer, Billy Martin (the itinerant and ubiquitous manager) and to Seitz (your one-time quondam arbitrator) destiny has finally overtaken Bowie Kuhn. I take no pleasure in welcoming you into the company of the erstwhile makers and shakers. Indeed, I feel some remorse, despite the fact that there were some rather important occasions when your convictions were at odds with my own. The Messersmith Case, by now, is as ancient history as the Carthaginian Wars. I bear no discernible scars and I am wholly free of feelings of animosity.... In my case, I was cast out by the Major Leagues with the same grace and empathy as John Milton's Jehovah when he cast out Satan from Heaven in *Paradise Lost*. The fact that I did make some small contribution to dispute settlement in Baseball (it is my impression that aside from the Catfish Hunter and Reserve System cases, the clubs benefited more from my decisions than the Players' Association) was utterly ignored. I was dismissed unceremoniously with the conventional pink slip without a word of kindness except from John Gaherin, who, being a gentleman, could not act otherwise.... At the age of seventy-seven my indignation at the crude, vulgar and offensive manner in which the owners saw fit to disparage my professionalism and integrity is considerably mellowed by time.... The fact that we had strongly contradictory views on the Messersmith Case, however, does not dissuade me from hoping that your departure from your post as Commissioner will not be characterized by the meanness and rudeness which accompanied my dismissal....

Very truly yours,
Peter Seitz

Peter was a student of history and literature as well as baseball; it's doubtful that anyone else could have brought Sir Thomas More and Billy Martin into the same discussion (or at least doubtful that anyone else could have done it and still have kept his sense of humor about it).

In another letter, as gracious as it is barbed, he says, "Perhaps the manner of [my] dismissal told the public more about the character of those who ran the Major Leagues of Baseball than it told them of my competence and integrity." Surely Seitz knew—and Kuhn knew he knew—that Kuhn had had a hand in firing him. And it should also be mentioned that he was absolutely correct in his contention that "aside from the Catfish Hunter and Reserve System cases, the clubs benefited more from my decisions than the Players' Association." (Of course, the clubs also benefited from the long-term effects of the Reserve System cases, though they were too shortsighted to realize it.)

Looking through Peter's letters again, I'm only sorry that I can't devote an entire chapter to them. One of my personal favorites was a letter he dashed off during the 1981 strike that helped relieve some tension at a crucial period. (One of the delights of his letters was that you never knew when they would arrive or quite what he was going to say):

June 15, 1981

Marvin J. Miller
Major League Baseball Players Association
1370 Avenue of the Americas
New York City, New York

Dear Mr. Miller,

In the last two weeks, both in and out of town, I have been summoned to the telephone on, it seems, scores of occasions by media (if you will forgive the expression) persons, asking me to express myself on the baseball dispute. I have been asked to go live on a radio interview with a sports broadcaster, to appear on TV, to give my views to sports writers, et cetera. Whenever the telephone bell tolls, it tolls for me! Uniformly, I have refused all requests to appear or to comment on two grounds: a) I know absolutely nothing about the current dispute excepting what I read in the papers and hear broadcast;

and I have not spoken about baseball to any of the principals in the dispute for some time; and b) I regard it to be a breach of the Code of Professional Responsibility for Labor-Management Arbitrators to discuss my decision or its relationship to the current dispute with them at this time. In each case I have referred my caller to the text of the Messersmith Decision printed in the arbitration services (LA) of the Bureau of National Affairs, Inc. So far, none of my callers has responded affirmatively to my question whether he has read my decision. Red Smith was not one of those who has phoned.

The point of this letter, Mr. Miller, is that I am just about fed up! Your baseball dispute is making it impossible for me to devote myself to my professional affairs. It results in multiple trespasses and intrusions on my privacy; and it is interfering with my marital felicity and domestic tranquility!

If the baseball brouhaha is not settled promptly, so that I can live in peace, I shall have to place this matter in the hands of an attorney—probably Louis L. Hoynes, Jr., or Richard Moss.

Very truly yours,
Peter Seitz

So, as I explained earlier, after my return from Europe, my retirement was short-lived. At the board's winter meeting, Don was elected acting director, and it was decided that in lieu of defending a lawsuit, the Association would pay off Moffett and his two associates. It should come as no surprise that I was against handing over "severance." I felt Moffett & Co. had been irresponsible during the ten months they were on the payroll—what with the amazing number of personal long-distance phone calls, taking vacations in advance of having earned them (Moffett and Broff)— to say nothing of the generally lousy job they had done. While I was against rewarding poor performance even with a relatively small cash settlement, the players wanted to put this unfortunate chapter behind them.

Don was elected executive director on an interim basis. The board was taking a wait-and-see attitude until completion of the basic agreement negotiations in 1984–85. In April 1984, four months after Don was elected, I agreed to act as consultant to the organization. Why? Well, I felt comfortable working with Don, and I had a clearly defined role. More important, in the wake of the recent turmoil at the Association I felt a protective urge to watch over what I had worked so hard to build. But if the truth be told, had it not been for that midnight vigil in my living room with Renko and the other player reps when I committed myself to assisting in the negotiations, I wouldn't have participated.

FROM A PERSONAL STANDPOINT the 1985 negotiations were unsatisfactory. Instead of being seen as an advisor, I was perceived as a puppeteer pulling the Association's strings. Perhaps that was inevitable. The fact is, I didn't make decisions or even initiate strategy. No matter. These rumors worked against us. Don overcompensated, even excluding me at a critical point from a subcommittee meeting (apparently at the urging of Commissioner Peter Ueberroth and a few others). Hearing the events secondhand was like playing high-stakes poker by phone. For a while I considered packing it in. I was there at the players' request to help Don, but providing that help was becoming impossible. As the negotiations drew to a close, Don met with Barry Rona alone at a key point. Past experience had shown it was a mistake to meet with someone you did not trust, without a witness. To do so again was to set yourself up for trouble. But I had come to appreciate the difference between being first in command and serving as an advisor. I let it go.

For the first time in its almost twenty years of existence, the Players Association took backward steps. Going into the negotiations, I wasn't involved enough to notice that there wasn't the support among the players that there should have been. It was a miscalculation on my part, something I hadn't considered. I hadn't been to spring training meetings since 1982, I hadn't attended most board meetings, I wasn't talking to player reps and other players on a daily basis. There were cracks, and they became apparent as the negotiations went on.

There was no real reason for the change in the players' attitudes. We were dealing from a position of strength. In 1981 we had faced off against management—and their $50 million worth of strike insurance, and an additional war chest—and held them off for fifty days. We had forced them to abandon their plan for free-agent compensation and to accept a pool proposal that gave them less than had been offered the day before we walked out.

What had happened? For one thing, ironically, the dramatic increase in salaries over the years was eroding one of the bonds that had traditionally held the players tightly together: the pension plan. When I became executive director of the Players Association, a player earning $19,000 per year (the average major league salary), or less, was continually forced to ask himself, "What the hell am I going to do when my three or four or five years in the majors are over?" (Even top players, those making $100,000 a year, considered the pension vital.) Nineteen years later, a player earning, say, $350,000 had very different views. The pension plan was important, but it didn't grab the modern players as it once had.

More important, there was a diminished concern for the younger players among their older, established teammates. Milt Wilcox, for example, when discussing the owners' demand that a player with less than three years of major league service should be forced to accept whatever his owner wanted to pay him, said: "We want them [the union] to know that we don't want to...lose a lot of money over something like the arbitration thing [salary arbitration] that would only affect a few players." This was the same guy who, as a result of the determined struggle of the veterans when he was a young player, had received important rights, including salary arbitration. Now, in effect, he was saying, "Screw 'em. I've got mine."

Wilcox was not alone. The grumblings of high-profile players like Reggie Jackson, Bob Boone, and Mike Schmidt highlighted the shift in attitudes since the strike in 1981. These players, no doubt, had "paid their dues," but they also had benefited beyond their wildest expectations, and their bellyaching didn't seem to take into account that there were stars before them—Willie Mays, for example—who had made similar sacrifices without ever having reaped anywhere near the same rewards.

Player turnover had a lot to do with the change in attitude. By 1985, roughly 50 percent of the players hadn't experienced the 1981 strike, the unity it forged, or what it had actually achieved. If they had read anything about it, it was probably something along the lines of "God, country, motherhood, and baseball have been besmirched."

It's important to note that there have been only three significant work stoppages in baseball. The first, a strike in 1972, lasted thirteen days, only nine of them during the season. The next, the owners' lockout in 1976, took place entirely in spring training. The third, the big one, lasted fifty days. In addition, in 1985, a walkout lasted two days. The total was sixty-one days during the season over a period of twenty years. In 1990, five years later, the owners' second lockout also took place entirely during spring training. In any other industry—steel, auto, or coal—scholars would have remarked on the peaceful management-union relationship that involved an average of less than two and a half missed working days a year due to disputes over a period of twenty-five years.

Not baseball. Of course, it must be remembered that in no other industry would a writer covering a labor dispute be penalized by a strike. Without baseball, baseball writers had nothing to write about. In 1985, several writers complained to me, "What the hell are you doing? I had my late winter all planned. My wife and kids were flying down to Florida, I had rented a house, now I'm going to have to cancel everything." The networks were even worse. Tons of equipment transported down south had to be shipped back; scores of sponsors had to be reimbursed. (When the NFL players walked out in 1987, the networks would not allow announcers to refer to their scab replacements as scabs; they wanted the public to think it was business as usual, and considering that they continued to broadcast "games," it was.)

Still, these reasons don't fully explain why, in 1985, the players were willing to compromise on two important issues like salary arbitration and the owners' pension contributions. People used to tell me, "No matter what the issue, you always had the support of the players." While that's true, it didn't happen of itself. I worked at it. I made sure that the players understood what I was doing, that they had input into decisions, that their reactions and ideas were seriously considered, that the information they needed to make intelligent decisions was theirs for the asking (and even when they didn't ask). Most important of all, I made sure that they understood the struggle involved in getting what they had. I used to stress that there was more to be had, but it, too, would require a struggle. The minute we relaxed, we were greasing the skids for failure. I tried to pound this message home to the players each spring. If one side becomes complacent, the other side becomes bolder. Either you push forward or you're going to get pushed back. In the type of labor-management situation in baseball, attempting to hold your ground, marking time, is an invitation to being shoved backward.

When I joined the Steelworkers staff in 1950, many workers had already forgotten that just a few years before there had been no such things as paid holidays or vacations or pension plans or health-care insurance. When I first met the ballplayers in 1966, nobody knew the derivation of the term "Murphy money" (the expense allowance given to players in spring training) or that in 1947 Robert Murphy had fought for the allowance as well as the first minimum salary of $5,000 a year. Paraphrasing the philosopher George Santayana, I used to say: "The man who forgets or does not know his own history is doomed to repeat it."

By 1985 the players had lost touch with their own history. This was the union's fault—Don Fehr's fault. Which is not to say that Don didn't negotiate a good agreement. He did, given the decline in the players' understanding and in their solidarity. The owners tried to do away with salary arbitration altogether, made motions toward weakening free agency, tried to implement a salary structure. Don stood firm. But he couldn't hold out for something more with half-assed support. His error was not at the bargaining table, but in the clubhouses and elsewhere, in not instilling in the players the determination to fight the good fight. This error had its origin in 1983, when Moffett was the director and there was *no* leadership, and in 1984 and 1985, when the leadership was still inexperienced. Trying to instill morale in troops after a battle has started is foredoomed. Once negotiations are underway, it is too late.

When the 1985 negotiations ended, the players accepted the defeat; eligibility for salary arbitration was increased from two years to three years of service (something which was a direct cause of the lockout in 1990, as the union attempted to get back this 1985 concession). And for the first time, the union agreed to accept less than one-third of the national television and radio revenue for the pension plan. Management agreed to contribute $33 million in 1985, 1986, 1987, and 1988 and $39 million in 1989—a healthy increase, but many millions less than the players would have gotten had they maintained the one-third formula we had established in each pension agreement until then.

I'm a realist, a pragmatist. I was always aware of the possibility that the union's progress would one day be interrupted. What happened under Don could have happened under me. But I had not expected the union to lose ground while the owners were making such fabulous sums of money.

Some time before the negotiations really heated up in 1985, I got a phone call from James St. Clair, a senior law partner with Hale & Dorr, a prestigious Boston firm. Both his name and the name of his firm seemed familiar, but I couldn't at first remember why. St. Clair was representing a group of limited partners of the Boston Red Sox. They had been involved in litigation with the general partners—primarily Mrs. Tom Yawkey, widow of the longtime owner of the club, and Heywood Sullivan. Buddy LeRoux, a former trainer for the Sox and owner of physical therapy facilities, was a third general partner, but he was at odds with the other two.

As a result of the litigation, the Yawkey-Sullivan duo was forcing a buyout of St. Clair's clients, who were the primary limited partners. (There were other limited partners, including LeRoux, who were not represented by St. Clair.) The charter and the bylaws of the partnership provided that the general partners could buy out the limited partners without their consent under certain circumstances. And in the event of a buyout, if a price couldn't be agreed upon, there would be an arbitration proceeding to decide it. Each side was to select an arbitrator, and those two would agree on a third. St. Clair said that he and his clients were convinced that I would be the best person to represent them in the arbitration proceeding.

As James St. Clair was describing the case, the name Hale & Dorr rang a bell. In the 1950s, I recalled, I had been riveted to the television screen during the Army-McCarthy hearings when an attorney named Joseph Welch had delivered a stunning rebuke: "At long last, Senator McCarthy, have you no shame?" Joe Welch, a senior partner at Hale & Dorr, castigated McCarthy for his calculated smear of a young assistant of Welch's. The assistant, McCarthy implied, was a Communist because he was a member of the American Lawyers Guild, and the guild, McCarthy falsely alleged, was a subversive organization. Then the connection dawned on me: St. Clair had been an attorney for Richard Nixon in some of the federal court proceedings which grew out of the Watergate hearings. Of course, Nixon had been one of McCarthy's allies, which made the connection more interesting.

Not long after our conversation, St. Clair and I had dinner at the Regency Hotel in New York. I said that in order to determine an appropriate price for the limited partners' equity in the franchise, the three arbitrators would need to have access to detailed financial data from the Boston club as well as from other major league clubs. Given the paranoia of baseball owners about shielding this information from the Players Association, they would, no doubt, moan and groan if I were appointed by the limited partners. St. Clair said not to worry. "We'll deal with that when we come to it."

The case interested me. Though I was still involved with the Players Association negotiations, I believed (incorrectly) that the Red Sox arbitration procedure could be dealt with quickly and be over before the baseball negotiations heated up. In addition, there was a personal connection. In 1972, when my son, Peter, then a graduate student in Berkeley, California, was struck by an out-of-control car and pinned against a brick wall, LeRoux was one of the few baseball people who noticed the item in the newspaper. He gave us the names of physical therapists in California and continued to offer encouragement throughout Peter's ordeal. He never contacted me about the arbitration, but his predicament of being constantly outvoted by Yawkey-Sullivan was covered in numerous news stories.

I decided to take the assignment. Right off the bat, the lawyers for the general partners tried to have me barred from the proceedings. Finally, after a time-consuming court case, the judge threw out the Yawkey-Sullivan complaint, including the demand that I sign a form agreeing to pay $50,000 if financial information about the team leaked to others. (I had agreed from the start that I wouldn't disclose information made available during the arbitration proceedings.)

We got started. As their representative, the general partners selected Tal Smith, a former general manager at Houston, then an independent businessman working for the owners. (Smith was another management man who benefited from the union's achievements. For substantial fees he represented owners against players in salary arbitrations. Without the union there would be no salary arbitration.) Smith and I had trouble agreeing on a third arbitrator. Finally, I suggested we select a salary arbitrator from baseball, someone who had previously been agreed to by both sides. That succeeded.

Working with Tal Smith was like banging my head on the Astrodome. He had the creativity of a file clerk and little or no understanding of the meaning of rational discussion. Hour after hour, day after day, like a broken record, he stuck to the lines given him by the Red Sox attorneys, even after his arguments had been demolished. The neutral arbitrator, Robert Stutz, seemed lost. He tried to find a middle ground, but he had no theory on which to base the value of the club. His figure was ludicrously low. The value of the real estate under Fenway Park, which is owned by the Red Sox, was astronomically higher than the value Stutz placed on the club. And Tal Smith's proposed value was way below anything Stutz could agree to.

I was outraged, and I said so to the representatives of the limited partners. At the end of a long meeting, they said that they agreed with my position that Stutz's figure was miserably low in relation to the real value of the franchise, but, they added, "Believe it or not, we're happy with the figure you've gotten him up to." It wasn't a figure I recommended, but it did represent a tremendous profit over what they had paid. I told them that Stutz was unable to justify his figures and was showing signs of discomfort at the thought of having to write an opinion in support of them. I felt that I should insist on a written opinion even though Stutz was making noises about his schedule and how long it would delay things if he had to do that.

My problem was that time was on the side of Yawkey-Sullivan. The agreement signed by the limited partners had a serious hitch.

The general partners were not required to pay interest on the money owed to the limited partners. Thus, the longer the case dragged on, the happier Yawkey-Sullivan and their attorneys were. With no agreement among the three arbitrators, the necessary two votes to make the final decision were not there. A new arbitrator might have to be found, and we would have to start the case all over again.

I arranged a conference call with Smith and Stutz.

"I have a proposition," I said to Stutz. "I'd like to suggest, rather than do this all over again, that Tal give you a figure and I give you a figure and you have to pick one or the other like a salary arbitrator."

Neither liked the idea, but they said they'd think about it for forty-eight hours. More important, *we agreed to make a final decision, one way or the other, during this next conference call.* When we spoke again, Smith and Stutz said that they couldn't abide by the proposed either-or procedure.

I said, "Okay, then I formally advise both of you that I am now accepting Stutz's figure. The case is over."

Smith was stunned. He was so sure I wouldn't accept Stutz's figure and was confident that the whole procedure would start again. Of course, he didn't know that my party was happy with arbitrator Stutz's figure.

Smith said, "I demand a meeting."

I said, "No, we agreed that a final decision would be made. You can record your dissent. The vote is two to one."

And that was it.

One postscript. On behalf of the Red Sox, Tal Smith presented "evidence" to Stutz that the most recent sale of a baseball franchise, that of the Detroit Tigers, was the highest price that would be seen in the foreseeable future* (newspapers quoted the figure as $55 million); after that, he said, baseball franchise prices would decline for years to come. This was supposed to be persuasive that the Boston franchise should be valued at much less

---

*The price of recent sales of baseball franchises is one important indication of the value of other baseball franchises, although appropriate adjustments—up or down—may be indicated.

than any franchise sold in the past. (The documentation, exhibits, and arguments were prepared by a well-known appraiser who had been used frequently as a consultant to buyers and sellers of baseball franchises.) The information was self-serving balderdash and easily refuted, but somehow Stutz swallowed it hook, line, and sinker. Stutz's gullibility about Smith's forecast of doom and gloom is readily apparent. Every franchise in baseball that has been sold since then has far exceeded the sales price reported for the Tigers franchise—even when the club that has been sold has been a perennial cellar dweller. In fact, the next *expansion* franchises are priced at $95 million each, about twice the reported sales figure of the then champion Detroit Tigers! You don't have to be an economist to know that that's not a declining market.

The bargaining in baseball ended in August, and Tal Smith, Bob Stutz, and I battled until Labor Day. While both negotiations were at their most intense, I found myself flying back and forth from New York to Boston, meeting all day and half the night. I was drinking too much coffee, not sleeping enough, not eating right, and by this time, smoking as many as three packs of cigarettes a day. (I'd been a steady smoker for fifty years and always smoked more during times of tension and stress.)

I was heading for trouble. Ironically, it didn't hit while I was working, but after I stopped. I had been so geared up, working through the stress, coasting along on adrenaline for weeks on end. Then, bingo, the baseball fight was over. The Red Sox negotiations continued for a short while, and suddenly, boom, that was over, too. I was a free man. The letdown was enormous.

Right after Labor Day, I was playing tennis with a friend. Normally we played an hour or more of singles, but after thirty minutes I didn't feel right. On a court change, I sat down heavily and said, "I hate to quit in the middle, but I don't think I should finish." I smoked a cigarette, as was my custom, talked a while, and soon I felt better.

Several weeks later, on a cloudy, chilly October afternoon, I was hitting with a pro from the tennis club. He ran me nonstop. It was always a tougher workout than an actual match, but I felt fine. Afterward, I sat down, lit a cigarette, and felt a terrible tightness in my chest. Breathing was difficult; my arms tingled. I extinguished the cigarette and looked around in case I might need help. The pro had gone inside, and no one else was out on the courts. I pulled myself to my feet and went inside where several people were lounging around drinking coffee.

I thought about calling Terry to come to the club to drive me home, but after sitting for several minutes the pain subsided. Stupidly, I said nothing to Terry when I returned home. I knew something was wrong—this was warning number two—but I rationalized the fatigue as a residue of overwork.

A classic case of denial. I'd never been seriously ill, never been admitted to a hospital (I wasn't even born in a hospital); I'd been athletic my entire life and had always worked like a mule.

The third strike came after dinner in early October. Terry and I were watching Kansas City play Toronto in the American League Championship Series. This time I was unable to catch my breath, and it owed nothing to the excitement of the game. I tried to conceal the discomfort from Terry—until the pain shot down both arms and I lost feeling in my fingers.

"I'm not feeling well," I announced sheepishly.

Terry took one look at me and dialed 911.

A half century of smoking had finally caught up with me.

The ambulance arrived within minutes. The medics placed nitroglycerin under my tongue, put me on a stretcher, and raced me to the emergency room at New York Hospital. (Luckily for me, rush hour had passed, and traffic was light.)

The first electrocardiogram was negative, indicating I had *not* had a heart attack. The second said the same. Perhaps I'd imagined the whole thing. Suddenly, I felt really foolish. The third EKG contradicted the first two. And the doctor said the words I had feared: "Heart attack under way." The brief moment of relief I had experienced turned quickly to fear. I had to decide whether or not to undergo a slew of treatments, each with possibly perilous side effects like paralysis, blindness, brain damage, or, according to the release which had to be signed, death.

I agreed to a catheterization, in which a tubular device is inserted into an artery in the groin and snaked up to the heart. The device, I was told, enabled the doctors to get a picture of the blood flow. It was well past midnight when I was wheeled into the operating room. (Needless to say, I had missed the rest of the game.) A curious sense of detachment replaced the feeling of fear. Lying on my back on a moving stretcher, I stared intently at the ceiling, at the light fixtures, at the pipes. Voices swirled around me. As the nurses prepped me for the procedure, the doctors started talking baseball. What were the players really like? Who did I predict to win the World Series? Who would I rather have on a team, Valenzuela or Koufax? I knew what they were doing, but when someone with a surgical mask is about to insert a catheter in your groin, any distraction is welcome.

The procedure indicated that the trauma was relatively minor. Thankfully, no bypass surgery was necessary.

I was hospitalized for two weeks. Two days before my release, I passed a series of stress tests. I was put on a steady diet of medication—beta blockers mostly—and given a clean bill of health.

With the doctor's permission, I was back on the tennis court less than two weeks after my release. And from the third inning of the Royals game to this day, I haven't taken a puff on a cigarette.

Two months after my heart attack, the executive board of the Players Association had their winter meeting in Hawaii. I declined the trip and formally ended the consulting agreement that we had begun the year before. The negotiations with the industry were over. When Don returned, he told me he had let it be known that he had been thinking about his future—he had three children and expected to have a fourth—and was considering returning to the practice of law. Whether he will admit it or not, I think he was campaigning for a higher salary, saying, in effect, I can make a lot more money elsewhere. Evidently, the executive board agreed. It responded by offering him a long-term contract with a salary rising to $500,000 a year.*

When Don finished telling me about his new contract, he asked me if I would be interested in writing a book about the history of the Players Association. It might be particularly helpful to the young players who knew nothing of the Association's past, he felt. No one else would be able to recreate this history, he said, and

---

*Salaries of union officials are public information under the provisions of the Landrum-Griffin Act.

unless I were to do it, a lot of valuable information about the beginning of the union would be lost.* His offer included a back office at the Association and a retainer of one to two thousand dollars a month. I was taken aback. That was probably less than the compensation paid to secretaries and perhaps a tenth of the market value of a book contract available from publishers. I have no doubt that Don was trying to act in the best interests of the Association, but the suggestion, considering the timing, struck me as incongruous. Unlike the proverbial offer from the Godfather, this one I found quite easy to refuse. I didn't ask whether the idea was his or the executive board's, and I still don't want to know.

But there were far more important goings-on in December 1985. There was convincing evidence that the officials of organized baseball—from the commissioner to the league presidents on down to the general managers—were acting in concert to destroy the free-agent market. In fact, the first act of what would eventually be revealed as the greatest scandal in baseball history was already underway. Since the inception of the free-agent market in 1976, the owners had apparently complied, for the most part, with the contractual prohibition against collusion. The language in the 1976 basic agreement was duplicated in the 1980 and 1985 agreements, and its meaning was and is crystal clear: No club shall act in concert with any other club with respect to free agents.

The opening of the free-agent period in 1985 was marked by a resounding silence. Just as suddenly, I was a retired executive director with a lot to do. The Players Association, of course, moved to expose the owners' conspiracy, and as the union's negotiator of the anticollusion language in the basic agreement, I would become one of the lead witnesses in the first grievance, known as "Collusion I."

This scenario was repeated during various situations and cases in the years to come: retirement followed by unretirement when there was anything I could do to assist the union and its members.

---

*The beginning of the Players Association as a legitimate union dates to July 1, 1966. An earlier organization—a company union dominated and financially supported (illegally) by the owners—began in 1954.

BASEBALL PLAYERS are always writing books about their careers. Many make the claim that their aim is to "set the record straight." Most of these books, however, are written with ghostwriters, so it is hard to say who is at fault when such works fictionalize actual events. No matter. During my retirement I've read innumerable books that either twist the facts or leave them out. Jim Hunter's 1988 autobiography, *Catfish,* for example.

Either Hunter or Armen Keteyian, the writer working with him, or a source supplying Keteyian, would have readers believe that the chief executive of the Association (yours truly) somehow vanished during two of the most important arbitrations in the union's history. A nifty feat, considering that nothing of significance occurred without my direct involvement in the entire seventeen years of my tenure. I was very much a "hands on" administrator. How could it have been otherwise in what was essentially a two-man office all those years? There was no grievance of significance settled without consultation with me. There was no grievance that went to arbitration without my okay. I was involved in the preparation of every arbitration case, in helping to develop the theory of the case, in the presentation of the case to be made, and in the arbitration panel's decision in each case. As a member of the panel, I cast one of the two votes needed to decide each case and had the responsibility in executive sessions of the three panel members of informing, educating, reasoning with, and persuading the chairman to cast the necessary second vote to sustain the union's grievance. It was also my responsibility to rebut misstatements and faulty arguments of the owners' appointee. During hearings I served often as the union's lead witness and, as a member of the panel, examined witnesses and challenged testimony and arguments of the opposing side. Whether the union counsel was Dick Moss or, later, Don Fehr, the union never rested its case without counsel's obtaining a recess to consult with me about what remained to be added or clarified before concluding presentation of the case. Yet, according to the fanciful account of Hunter or Keteyian, the second in command, Dick Moss (a.k.a. "a one-man gang"), took over. Moss "quickly challenged the commissioner," who then withdrew from his attempt to mediate the Hunter dispute with Finley; then Moss "won the Hunter case." The authors also say: "Moss...would turn baseball upside down in

1976 when *he* won the landmark Andy Messersmith free-agent case" (my italics). I'll have to check my dates. I thought I retired at the end of 1982, but according to *Catfish* I must have packed it in before the Hunter case in 1974, since none of the events occurred while I was the executive director.

The absurdity of Hunter's view of the events is obvious to any student of the case. A moment's thought (or a little research) would have told the writer that a union's great victories are brought about by the union and its members and not by a "one-man gang" in the form of a staff lawyer in a strictly secondary role, no matter how capable he was in that role. Hunter and Messersmith were freed from the constrictions of the reserve rules *only* because of the accumulated gains of the union over the years, only because the players had been organized into a union. Then again, Hunter's version fits with his fairy-tale belief that George Steinbrenner made him a free agent, and hence wealthy, out of the goodness of his heart—a sentiment he actually expressed at his induction into the Hall of Fame.

Another book astonished me even more, *Reggie*, a 1989 title by Reggie Jackson and Mike Lupica. Reggie was an active, devoted, and effective player rep for many years. Mike Lupica is a bright and well-informed reporter. That is why I'm at a loss to explain the single passage in their book that purports to deal with the real-life struggle to bring about free-agent rights for players—without ever mentioning the union! In fact, unless I accidentally missed it, there is not a single mention of the Players Association in the book—odd, when you consider that Reggie played the game in three different decades, was twice a free agent, served as an active member of the executive board for many years, and was a veteran of strikes in 1972, 1980, 1981, and 1985. How is it that Reggie chose to say nothing about those significant events in his career? And how is it that Mike Lupica, a reporter who supported the union with his straight shooting over the years, didn't think to nudge him to give a more complete picture of his baseball life?

I don't mean to single out Hunter and Jackson—it has been the mode of scores of former players' books, as if the profound economic change in their lives was somehow achieved magically. (Three notable exceptions were books by Don Baylor, Keith Hernandez, and Dave Winfield.) But even Tim McCarver, currently an articulate, intelligent baseball broadcaster, authorized a book about his playing days that had not a single reference to the Players Association. Tim was in the first group of player reps who reorganized the union in 1966. As the Cardinals' player rep, he helped elect me executive director. He was on the first negotiating committee to obtain a basic collective bargaining agreement and the first negotiated increase in the major league minimum salary.

In any event, if the players who were involved in the actions that changed the entire course of the game can't remember them clearly, what hope is there that the players who weren't there—a Darryl Strawberry, Jose Canseco, Will Clark, Dwight Gooden, or Roger Clemens—and their successors—are going to keep the Players Association strong?

17 . . .

Lockout, 1990

A MORE FUTILE and incompetent strategy for collective bargaining probably has never been concocted than the plotting and planning of the baseball owners and their officials in the period leading up to the 1989–90 negotiations. It's as if the owners had been infiltrated by a fifth column that tried to figure the best way to halt and reverse major league baseball's astonishing growth in popularity and prosperity.

In the negotiations in 1985, the Players Association had made some modest advances at minimal cost, but it had made two significant concessions. First, a player with less than three full years of major league service (in place of two years) would be required to accept whatever salary the clubs' owners offered, and he would have no recourse to impartial salary arbitration. Second, for the first time in more than three decades the union accepted less than the traditional percentage (one-third) of the national TV-radio revenues to finance the benefit plan that provides pensions, disability benefits, widows' benefits, allowances for minor depen-

• 350 •

dents, life insurance, and health care to active and former players, coaches, managers, and trainers. These two concessions, which saved the owners tens of millions of dollars each year, were responses to the owners' vociferous claims of poverty—claims that proved to be as counterfeit as a three-dollar bill.

Following the union's good-faith action in the 1985 negotiations, perhaps within days, all owners, general managers, league and club officials, their labor relations people, and the commissioner embarked on a program of collusion to drive down the salaries of players by abolishing the market for free agents. The key word here is "all," because without the compliance of each and every one of the twenty-six clubs and all of their supporting cast who had any role in trying to build winning teams or in preserving the "integrity of the game," the collusion effort necessarily would have failed.

It did not fail. It was a smashing success. The owners' disgraceful disregard for their written contractual commitment ("clubs shall not act in concert with other clubs [with respect to free agents]") directly dried up the free-agent market, prevented players from obtaining offers from other clubs, resulted in a shifting of at least a third of a billion dollars out of players' salaries into the owners' coffers, and prematurely ended the careers of a number of players. The collusion scheme of 1985 continued into 1986, 1987, and 1988, at the very least. (Its impact of course continues further). For a long period, even though the collusion was obvious, most of the sporting press and the media at large ignored it, or approved of it, or pretended that it was simply an allegation of the Players Association not supported by the evidence. Commissioners of baseball professed not to see it. Bart Giamatti, now deceased—he had been part of the conspiracy as a league president—denied that anything untoward had happened even after two impartial arbitrators made official findings of the existence of collusion for (at that time) two years or more by all of major league baseball.

But then, the spirit that produced collusion was nothing new. George Steinbrenner and Ted Turner and the burger and beer barons who run major league baseball love to go on the rubber-chicken circuit and tell America's young idealists about the glories of the free-enterprise system, but the truth is that they have spent their entire baseball lives trying to avoid it. For roughly three quarters of a century, the owners had it pretty much their own way. But all that changed in the 1970s, when the players finally won the right to salary arbitration and then free agency, that is, the basic right to change employers—hardly a revolutionary notion. For the first time, free enterprise became an element in the dealings in big-time professional sports.

And it worked. In fact, it worked spectacularly well. The primary objection to free agency—that is, the owners' primary objection, which was picked up and echoed in the press—was that free agency would guarantee that teams with the most money would buy up the best players and destroy competition. Of course, as anyone who has a modicum of knowledge of baseball history could see, this was nonsense. The teams in the biggest population areas had enjoyed something of an advantage under the previous system, during the 1950s, for instance, the Yankees won eight pennants and the Dodgers won five, totals that seem unmatchable in today's game.

In the eighties, at a time when the teams with the most fans and the largest revenue were supposed to dominate, teams from smaller locations—Kansas City (twice), St. Louis (three times), Milwaukee, and Minnesota—played for the championship. Some baseball experts used to argue that the San Francisco Bay area couldn't support one major league team; in 1989 it supported two teams, and both played in the World Series.

What happened with free agency turned out to be exactly the opposite of what the owners said: Teams could no longer stockpile talent, perennial cellar dwellers could improve themselves. Competition became keener, pennant races became more exciting, attendance increased, TV revenues went up, players were finally rewarded as the professionals they were, and everyone was happy. Everyone, that is except the owners.

It wasn't because their profits weren't greater than ever—they were, and no amount of propaganda or creative bookkeeping could disguise that fact. (To the owners' credit, they didn't try to insult everyone's intelligence in 1990 by screaming poverty).* The combined salaries for major league ballplayers in 1990 amounted

---

*They waited until 1991, when their anticipated revenue will hit a new high.

to about $388 million. Does that sound like a lot of money? It certainly should, but it doesn't look like nearly as much when placed alongside the owners' revenue of $1.5 *billion.*

What upset the owners was that they felt their profits could be greater still if only the players could be pushed back into their former exploited condition. And at least some of the owners lusted for the full control of the players that they had enjoyed in all the years before the union. Having been dragged kicking and screaming into a system that brought them more revenue than they had ever dreamed possible, the owners banded together and have ever since been trying to destroy the very thing that was making them richer: free agency. That's what baseball's labor disputes were about, as well as the owners' collusive attempts to avoid the free-agent market entirely. And that's also what the lockout of 1990 was all about.

Initially the owners and their reps told us that the lockout was to bring about a new form of revenue sharing that would eliminate the need for individual contracts. Now, it isn't out of the realm of possibility that some kind of real revenue-sharing plan would be feasible, but that would have to involve something the owners don't want to touch: a real partnership. No legitimate union representing the interests of its members could agree to accept a fixed percentage of revenues without having a significant voice in all the decisions that affect revenue. Needless to say, this isn't what the owners had in mind. What they wanted was for the players to give up a one-hundred-year-old right to negotiate their own contracts at a time when that system was at last working for them—and accept a fixed share of the revenue, the level of which would be dependent on the owners' competence (or lack of it).

Where did the owners come up with such a radical plan? Largely, I would guess, from the National Football League and the National Basketball Association, sports leagues in which there have been only unsuccessful or compliant player organizations. Most of the NFL's income, for example, comes from a national television contract, the proceeds of which are divided evenly among twenty-eight teams, guaranteeing each team a profit before the season begins. It also, incidentally, eliminates competition among the teams: The Jets and the Giants, for instance, are not in any meaningful competition for the fan dollar the way the

Yankees and the Mets are, so there is little economic incentive for NFL teams to bid for the better players and coaches—and little reason to share the wealth with the men who produce it by bidding for their services.

The structure in baseball is somewhat different, since local radio and television revenues are not shared. It is this disparity that the owners and their spokesmen were concerned about. The sharing of such money among owners, at least more equitable sharing, could have met that problem. But the haves are not about to share their local bonanzas with the other clubs. They wanted the players to make up the difference between the haves and the have-nots, and in order to get this, they risked punishing the players and the fans with a lockout.

Luckily for everyone, much of the press had, by 1990, reached a point where it could distinguish between a strike and a lockout. After taking constant hammering from the local TV and print media and some accurate salvos from the new sports daily *The National,* the owners realized that, for the first time, they weren't even close to winning the public relations battle. So they backed down. Unfortunately, that didn't mean that they changed the error of their ways; it only meant that they changed the way of their errors.

They dropped their revenue-sharing plan and their ridiculous idea of pay based on an unintelligible performance formula, and they withdrew their demands for caps on salaries and an end to all salary arbitration. For all intents and purposes, this was an admission that the lockout had been an ill-conceived mistake. But instead of admitting as much by ending the lockout and negotiating with a union that on the whole had not attempted to plow any new ground in the 1990 negotiations, the owners then said, Well, okay, the lockout wasn't really about all that other stuff, it was really about salary arbitration eligibility—three years as opposed to two.

This ploy should have been seen as the owners' most transparent move up to that point, but, instead, something strange happened: Just as it appeared that the owners' stand was about to collapse and spring training might begin, a segment of the press and then the public began to buy the new line. As a result, the lockout was extended for several weeks. Actually, what happened is not so strange in retrospect. The owners sensed a general exasperation with the slowness of the negotiations and gambled that at least a handful of writers was ready to write something along the lines of, Well, the owners have given in to all the other players' demands, why shouldn't the players compromise on this one issue and let the owners have the right to dictate the salaries of players who have not completed three years?

Of course, the players had made no strike threat, and they were being locked out, but after weeks of writing the same thing, a few writers were grateful for the chance to have a new slant on the baseball stoppage. And so a lockout that seemed to be on the verge of ending as a failure was given new life when Commissioner Fay Vincent called a press conference and there made a dramatic but phoney settlement proposal to "both sides" that was treated as a legitimate attempt at a solution by a portion of the media.

As late as 1990, quite a few sportswriters still saw the commissioner as a neutral, not as a spokesperson for management, and cheered his "plan," in which the players would agree not to strike if the owners ended the lockout. Vincent's proposal, if accepted, would have destroyed the union's bargaining power: it gave the union precisely nothing. The promise to "continue" the negotiations would have been meaningless from the union's point of view if it had to forego the possibility of a strike and be left at the mercy of the owners. I'm amazed to hear myself saying this, but Bowie Kuhn actually showed more initiative in 1976 than Vincent did in 1990. Kuhn ordered the 1976 lockout lifted, unconditionally, on March 17 (though he may have been "persuaded" by Walter O'Malley, who considered the lockout futile at that point).

So, then, what is the verdict on the settlement that ended the lockout, and what does it portend for the future of the Players Association and major league baseball? One of the first things we heard was Milwaukee Brewers owner Bud Selig saying that "though the lockout did not achieve its purpose, that doesn't mean it was a failure." It amazes me that someone could say publicly something so meaningless and not have it challenged. How could something that failed to achieve its expressed purposes, or anything else, not be a failure? This is a little like a politician saying that the purpose of a long war was to produce peace, and even though it didn't achieve peace, that doesn't mean the war was a failure.

The owners said they were locking the players out in an attempt to force a revenue-sharing plan on them. They soon dropped that goal, but the lockout continued. They said they wanted to implement a pay-for-performance plan; that, too, was dropped, but the lockout continued. Finally, they said they wouldn't compromise on giving back any of the requirements for salary arbitration eligibility they had been given as a concession in 1985. In the end, they compromised on that. If the lockout achieved none of the things it was supposed to achieve, how did it succeed?

But, of course, the lockout wasn't about those issues at all. What it was really about was power. There are still quite a few baseball executives who dream of the good old days when the Players Association was a company union and the players had no leverage. The 1990 lockout was their latest attempt to roll back the advances the union had made over the last twenty-odd years, and it failed.

Though the final settlement, on the whole, was a good one for the players, there were some developments toward the end that keep me from being overly optimistic about the union and big league baseball.

I started to get uneasy a week or so before the settlement when I read and heard about the activities and public comments of two men who really should have known better, Paul Molitor and Bob Boone. Both have benefited spectacularly from the salary structure brought about by arbitration and free agency, rights created by the union. Each enjoyed a multimillion-dollar contract. Each was paid from twenty-five to thirty times more than Babe Ruth, Mickey Mantle, Joe DiMaggio, Brooks Robinson, or Bill Dickey. Boone almost certainly will receive a large damage award won by the union's successful fight against the owners' collusion since 1985.

Despite this, I wasn't surprised at Boone's public statements that he didn't want to lose one day's pay, since he had been known to have a bad attitude back during the 1985 negotiations. I was more disappointed by the remarks of Molitor, who, I'm pretty sure, didn't realize the damage he was doing. By joining Boone and giving the owners reason to hope that the players would fold, he was helping to extend the lockout.

Bud Selig of the Brewers had been one of the owners' genuine hardliners all along. During the negotiations, Molitor had succeeded in obtaining a fine contract. His relationship with his owner, Selig, is apparently a good one, but what Molitor failed to remember was that bargaining for your contract and bargaining for a collective agreement are totally different processes and have different responsibilities.

It was obvious that Boone's and Molitor's statements indicating that an earlier owners' offer was acceptable (no part of the union's demand on salary arbitration was even addressed in the offer) were undermining the efforts of the union. It was just as obvious that, if Boone's and Molitor's activities went unchecked, the lockout would be extended. Union members who grumble publicly, even when they are few in number, accomplish the opposite of what they intend. They want a stoppage to end rapidly. They get, instead, a longer stoppage. Such things, of course, are an inevitable part of work stoppages in baseball, since the players, unlike the owners, have no self-imposed gag order and are free to speak their minds in any and all situations.

The owners then take the players' words as a sign of dissension in the ranks and are encouraged to believe that the union is about to fold. In this case, there was no chance of a reversal of position by the leadership of the players' union. This was not a strike, which sometimes can be undermined by a minority of members. It was a lockout. Literally, the owners locked the gates. Even if a few players wanted to play, they couldn't unlock the gates. There would have to be an overwhelming majority of players who wanted to accept the owners' proposals, and a leadership that agreed, before baseball could resume. And that was most unlikely. But Boone's and Molitor's remarks in support of the owners were extremely counterproductive.

The Players Association head, Donald Fehr, called me on Thursday morning, March 15, 1990, and told me he thought there was insufficient understanding by a couple of the player reps as to the significance of the dispute. Although he thought a settlement was near, any statements that undermined union solidarity would prolong the stoppage. Would I, he asked, come to the board meeting on Saturday and talk to the player reps, perhaps give some of the younger ones a quick historical perspective on the issue of salary arbitration and on what it took to achieve progress in collective bargaining? I told him I would do it, but privately I felt some reluctance.

One of the owners' tactics in the previous two weeks had been to spread the rumor that I had been secretly "leading" the negotiations for the union—the Godfather, as it were, of the Players Association. That was rather easy to do, since Don Fehr and I are friends and talk fairly regularly, but the truth is that I sweated out this lockout as any fan would, and often had nothing to go by except what I read in the papers.

I talked to the players' negotiating committee on Friday, the day before the executive board was scheduled to meet. One of the things I tried to get across to the players was that the issue of salary arbitration was not a new issue. In fact, it was the cornerstone of the prosperity that players had enjoyed since salary arbitration was introduced in 1973. It had been a major subject in every contract negotiation in the prior seventeen years. They shouldn't panic, I said, if they noticed some players in the ranks or one or two of their fellow reps wavering. In such high-pressure situations there was always some wavering, but never more than a handful of waverers in major league baseball negotiations.

Present at the meeting on Friday, March 16, were most of the members of the union's negotiating committee (including Paul Molitor), Bob Boone, who had been invited to discuss his views and his recent activities, Don Fehr, and the staff. The previous evening, there had been a fanciful TV story by Peter Gammons, a sports reporter, to the effect that Molitor and Selig had reached a private agreement (without the union!). Gammons alleged that his sources were two players (unnamed), two owners (unnamed), and one agent (unnamed). Really great reporting. The story, either made up of whole cloth or planted by guess-who, was denied on television later that evening by Molitor.

At the meeting, Paul denied the entire story as baseless and disclaimed any improper conversations with Selig, but revealed he *had* joined with Boone in calling many players. It was apparent that he had been somewhat naive and had been used, without realizing it initially, by his owner and by Boone, a veteran of many prior negotiations. If Molitor had not understood the seriousness of his failure to discuss his activities with the union, Boone understood it thoroughly. I got the impression that Paul felt embarrassed and that he was now aware of the error of giving false encouragement to the owners and would solidly support the position of the union's negotiating committee and executive board from there on in.

With Boone, unfortunately, the problem was that he was making a conscious, active effort to undermine the union's position. He spoke freely about his aim and his methods. He had telephoned, and recruited others to telephone, hundreds of players, nominally to ask their views, but actually steering their responses by asking loaded and invalid questions like "Is one year of salary arbitration eligibility worth losing an entire year's salary over?"

This is patently a phoney question the way it's framed. It fails to address the complexities of the salary arbitration issue. It says nothing about the long-range consequences of undermining the union and forcing it to reverse itself and accept the owners' position. Additionally, Bob Boone certainly knew that the owners would not sacrifice $1.5 billion (the year's projected revenue) for any issue, let alone this one. The point was, Boone wasn't getting appeasement sentiments from players. He was helping to spread them. He had been quoted as saying that he did not think that it was worth losing even one day's pay to obtain salary arbitration rights for a relatively large group of younger players.

Boone was asked about this, and immediately became defensive. He said his actions had been "in the best interests of the union." I told him frankly that I was disappointed in his attitude. "In the 1981 strike," I told him, "you were magnificent. I have to conclude from your actions now that you aren't the same man I knew then." (I might well have added: "Bob, I knew Bob Boone in 1981, and you're no Bob Boone.") "I am," he replied. "It's the issue that's different here. We have free agency; we have salary arbitration. Why risk the season for a question of one year's salary arbitration eligibility?" I told him that, in my opinion, he had forgotten how important principle was in such cases. After all, 1981 had been a strike for principle by the overwhelming majority of players. The solidarity of the union astonished the owners, who didn't think the players would hold together "for five days," as one owner predicted, let alone fifty, on an issue that benefited the younger players and those to come after them.

In 1981, the owners had sought to change the basic agreement by demanding that a professional player on a major league roster and an amateur draft choice be the compensation for a lost free agent. Although the issue probably didn't directly and immediately affect 75 percent of the players, they rejected the owners' plan and struck in support of the minority.

They saw that the owners' proposal was a tactic designed to create divisions in the players' ranks. Superstars like Reggie Jackson had a chance to be heroes off the field, and they carried themselves with class and dignity. Bob Boone, who had been one of the players on the union's negotiating committee and on the executive board, had been another.

And finally, in March 1990, when the owners' "new" offer came down to the negotiating committee on Friday afternoon, the players held together. All the members voted to reject it, and Boone supported the decision. And with good reason: It was March 16, with spring training on hold, and the owners' "final" offer said absolutely nothing about salary arbitration. The only possible explanation is that the owners chose to interpret the few negative comments made by the players during the week as meaning that the vast majority of players were suddenly willing to concede salary arbitration eligibility as an issue. The arrogance and stupidity of such a move was astonishing. It was as if they had begun to believe their own propaganda.

On Saturday, players began to arrive early for the board meeting. The executive board consists of about thirty players; more than sixty flew in to attend the meeting. Many were there to show solidarity in the ranks and to prove that the few grumbles heard in the previous two weeks were aberrations. Dave Winfield, I recall, was particularly forceful: "What's all this stuff about Bob Boone, Paul Molitor, Bert Blyleven, and this poll of younger players?" he said when he first saw me. "Listen to them," I cautioned. "At least, hear what they have to say."

"I'll listen," he said, "and then I'm gonna talk."

The arrival of the players gave a morale boost to the union that the owners were deprived of, for their own gag rule kept them separate and anxious. They didn't know whether to trust one another. By Saturday afternoon, the mood of the players was terrific. I spoke to them, many of whom weren't in major league baseball in 1981, and reminded them that when we finally negotiated salary arbitration in 1973, it was the first big break-through for the players union. Prior to that time, baseball owners told the players what they would get. If a player didn't like that, his option was to find a new line of work.

I mentioned that before the union, it didn't matter whether you were a marginal player or a superstar like Joe DiMaggio, the owner dictated your salary. If you refused to accept it, you were subject to banishment from baseball. Even Jimmy Foxx, who won the American League triple crown, was actually forced to take a pay cut the following year. In 1976, the owners again tried to limit salary arbitration, and it had to be defended again. In 1980, the owners' attempt to limit salary arbitration was once again a backdrop for a work stoppage.

I closed by emphasizing that it wasn't my place to tell them what to do, but that it was clear to me that what had happened in the few days leading up to this point had hurt them. The dissenting remarks made by certain players had given new strength to the owners' resolve. The result was that a settlement had already been delayed, and the settlement they were going to get out of the negotiations would not be as good as it could have been. But, I said, whatever happens you'll get a better deal if you stay together. I told them what I had told the players from the beginning: Stay solid, because you are irreplaceable. Stay solid, and you can have anything that's reasonable and fair.

Finally, I reminded the players of a basic truth: Failure to support the democratically arrived-at decisions of their own negotiating committee, their executive director, and their staff could have only one result, a permanent loss of credibility. If there were any wavering, the players could count on the owners never again taking the player reps seriously. The issue was no longer just salary arbitration. It was the future effectiveness of their union.

I left the meeting before the executive board finished its discussion. Later I learned that it had unanimously rejected the owners' final offer. The next morning I watched David Brinkley's show on NBC. To my surprise, George Will seemed to be taking a very reasonable position on the lockout, or maybe I had just had a long day Saturday. Bud Selig was on the show. I didn't think he came off well. Around 10:30 that night Don Fehr called to say there had been a settlement. He was too tired to give me the details just then, but there had been a compromise on the salary arbitration issue.

As I said, I had mixed feelings about the settlement after it was reached. Some good things have come out of it. I was glad, for instance, to read that Fay Vincent said "collusion [in 1985–87] wouldn't have happened if I was commissioner" (whether or not that holds for the future remains to be seen, but it's certainly a good sign that he said it). And I was astonished and rather pleased to read these remarks from the owners' chief negotiator, Chuck O'Connor: "This might sound strange coming from my side of the table, but let's not forget that first of all baseball is part of the entertainment business. And second, what these players involved here have just gone through is a part of their career that I believe they should be every bit as proud of as anything they accomplish on the field. They have just taken part in one of the most important parts of our society, the right of self-negotiation, the union movement, and the collective-bargaining process. I hope that's viewed as a major accomplishment." A statement that intelligent has never before been uttered by baseball officialdom. I wish I had said it.

But while it's all well and good to say "We've learned a lesson from this," let's remember that the one lesson that we've learned up to now is that the owners *never* seem to learn their lesson. If nothing else, let's keep this in mind about the 1990 lockout: Labor disputes resulting in stoppages usually arise when an industry is in financial difficulty. Baseball has never been more prosperous. If you can have a dispute when profits are in the hundreds of millions of dollars and and at an all-time high, you can have a dispute *anytime*. Such as when the basic agreement comes up for negotiation again.

18...

Owners and Other Bosses

IN THE YEARS after I first became professionally involved in baseball, certain individuals stood out as characters of a different cut than the usual run of baseball executives. Some of them I have touched on in earlier chapters, and the flavor of their personalities, whether rogue or charmer, competent or treacherous, has, I hope, come through where they have figured in this account. Others, because of their complexity or their prominence or sheerly memorable qualities, for good and for bad, made lasting impressions on me. And here they are, as I saw them: Bill Veeck, George Steinbrenner, Charles O. Finley, and Commissioner Peter Ueberroth. (Commissioners A. Bartlett Giamatti and Fay Vincent I discuss in the final chapter.)

VEECK AS IN VEECK

DURING THE LOCKOUT in 1976, a disgruntled Hank Aaron said something to the effect, "What do we need owners for anyway?" If

I had had to reply to that, I would have said, "Bill Veeck would be an exception." Unlike many of the owners, who sat back and did little or nothing to create the wealth they raked in, Veeck regarded it as his job to put an entertaining product on the field. Veeck loved baseball, and he loved promoting the game. And like a poker player looking for the best possible combination of cards, he continually searched for new ways to sell baseball to the public. In his autobiography, *Veeck as in Wreck,* he explains his philosophy: "Baseball has sold itself as a civic monument for so long that it has come to believe its own propaganda. A baseball team is a commercial venture, operating for a profit. The idea that you don't have to package your product as attractively as General Motors packages its products, and hustle your product the way General Motors hustles its products, is baseball's most pernicious enemy." Of course, Veeck couldn't afford to be complacent. He had no source of income outside of baseball, and his creative promotions stemmed, to a large extent, from need.

Bill Veeck, Jr., owned his first ball club (a minor league team) when he was twenty-eight years old. He ran five teams—three in the majors and two in the minors—won three pennants, and set scores of attendance records. He also worked as a scout, an announcer, a newspaper columnist, and the list goes on.

In the rarefied, old-boy network inhabited by fabulously wealthy business magnates like Gene Autry, Gussie Busch, Bob Carpenter, Ray Kroc, Walter O'Malley, George Steinbrenner, Phil Wrigley, and Tom Yawkey, Veeck stood out as prominently as Eddie Gaedel, the midget whom Veeck sent to bat for the St. Louis Browns in 1951. But Veeck was a giant in a world of midgets. Outmuscled and outside the fold, Veeck was that rarest of breeds, a progressive-thinking baseball owner. And if that's not an oxymoron, nothing is. "It used to be fifteen to one against me," Veeck said late in his career. "And now it's twenty-three to one."

But Veeck was much more than a showman. Many people have forgotten that in 1947 Veeck signed a second baseman with the Newark Eagles named Larry Doby to play with Cleveland, making him the first black player in the American League, the same year Jackie Robinson joined the Dodgers. In fact, in 1944 Veeck made a serious bid to buy the Philadelphia Phillies and bring black players like Satchel Paige, Roy Campanella, and Monte Irvin into the major leagues. The CIO, which had started a campaign to organize black workers down south, was willing to finance the purchase. But National League president Ford Frick foiled the deal and saw that the floundering club was sold to a lumber dealer named William Cox for about half of what Veeck had been willing to pay. Later Veeck wrote, "Given the choice between doing something right or something wrong, Frick will usually begin by doing as little as possible. It is only when he is pushed to the wall for a decision that he will almost always, with sure instinct and unerring aim, make an unholy mess of things."

In 1948, Veeck signed Paige, that old barnstorming right-hander. Because of Paige's age—his program age was forty-two, but Veeck figured he was at least forty-eight—Veeck was accused of pulling another publicity stunt. Never mind that Cleveland needed a spot starter as well as a pitcher who could come on in relief, and never mind that Paige still had plenty left in that old arm of his. The forty-something rookie won six, lost one, *and* was a big box office hit. The Indians won ninety-seven games (Doby hit .301 for the season) and went on to win the World Series, downing the Boston Braves four games to two. Some publicity stunt.

But even when his club was out of contention, Veeck used entertainment to build interest in his ball club. Over the years Veeck's fans witnessed exploding scoreboards, belly dancers, and circus acts. He put a portable shower in the bleachers to cool fans off. And he even had a barber out there until a local union lodged a protest. There were Teen Nights, Family Nights, Senior Citizen Nights, and Shakespeare Night (featuring a performance by a local troupe). On Music Night at Comiskey Park, fans who came to the ballpark with a musical instrument entered at half price. Anybody without an instrument was handed a kazoo at the gate. During the seventh-inning stretch, the associate conductor of the Chicago Symphony Orchestra waltzed out onto the field in his white tie and tails and led the playing of "Take Me Out to the Ball Game."

My first contact with Veeck came in 1967, eight years before he purchased the White Sox for the second time. At the time he was writing a column for the *Chicago Tribune,* which he sent to me whenever he discussed something relevant to the Players Association. He called one day to say he was writing a column highly critical of baseball's owners and wanted some information. Talking to him was almost like speaking to an old friend. The year before, during my first spring training trip, I had read both of his books, *Veeck as in Wreck* and *Hustler's Handbook*. Judge Cannon and Co. were doing their best to bar me from baseball then, and Veeck's writing stood out as a beacon of hope. Over the next few years, we spoke frequently, always by phone.

During the Curt Flood ordeal, Veeck proved to be a valuable ally. When the case began, I sat down with our general counsel, Arthur Goldberg, to decide whom we would like to call as witnesses. Flood would testify, of course, and so would I. Who else? We went through a lot of names and settled on former players Jim Brosnan and Jackie Robinson, one former owner, Bill Veeck, and one former player and former owner, Hank Greenberg.

Brosnan, a reliever with four NL teams, was the author of *The Long Season*. Written in 1960, it was the first really hard look at baseball and its "heroes," the first articulation of discontent among the players. Jimmy Cannon, perhaps the most influential baseball writer of the day (and no relation to Judge C.) called it the best baseball book ever written.

When I contacted Robinson, he was working in Manhattan as an executive for the Chock Full o' Nuts Company. He had read about the case and was willing to testify. Putting Robinson on the stand, however, involved some risk. In the late 1950s, a Brooklyn congressman named Emanuel Cellar (an old Dodger fan who was infuriated when Walter O'Malley moved the club to Los Angeles) chaired a judiciary subcommittee to investigate baseball's status under the antitrust laws. Among the witnesses were manager Casey Stengel and Jackie Robinson, who, unfortunately, followed the owners party line about how essential the reserve rule system was. I pointed out to Robinson that his remarks at that hearing would be revived and could be embarrassing. He didn't bat an eye. "I was young and ignorant at the time," he said. "That is what they told me, and that is what I said. But I know differently now, and I won't hesitate to say so."

I called Veeck and asked him if he would testify. He had read a great deal about the case and was eager to hear some more. As it turned out, both of us were going to be in Washington at the same time, and we decided to meet for dinner. Veeck was a great storyteller. He loved to talk and drink and laugh, and over the next three hours we did quite a bit of all three. Before we parted, he said he'd be glad to testify on behalf of Flood, which was quite a gamble for a man hoping to get back into baseball's fold one day.

When Veeck showed up at the courthouse, the first thing I noticed was his casual attire. He wasn't wearing a tie, his shirt was open, and he didn't have a jacket. When we were seated at the counsel's table waiting for Judge Irving Ben Cooper to arrive, Veeck, a four-pack-a-day smoker, lit another cigarette. There were No Smoking signs posted throughout the courtroom, but I decided I wasn't going to say anything. Finally, as the federal judge was about to enter the courtroom, Arthur Goldberg leaned over and said, "Bill, you can't smoke in the courtroom." Veeck nodded, looked around for an ashtray, found none, hiked up his trousers, and without missing a beat extinguished his cigarette on his wooden leg.

All four men were excellent witnesses—honest, straightforward, unshakable—but Veeck was the best. And certainly the most entertaining, using his great sense of humor to make the cross-examiner look foolish.

Another outstanding memory I have of him occurred about a year later, in 1972. My son, Peter, had been in a terrible accident while he was a graduate student at Berkeley. He was walking on the sidewalk, just across from the campus, when a car backed out of an alley, then moved forward and jumped the curb, out of control. The car smashed him against a brick wall. He never lost consciousness; in fact, while he was lying on the ground, bleeding and fighting against falling into shock, he spotted someone with a camera and asked him to take pictures before the ambulance arrived. The tendons and muscles in one leg, from the calf down, had been ripped unmercifully, and the doctors had a devil of a time cleaning the wound. Infection was a big concern. For almost ten days we weren't sure whether he would lose the leg or not. Luckily he didn't. But several months later, he had to return for a second round of surgery. I mention all of this because I ran into Veeck in Washington around the same time. He had read about Peter's accident in the paper. When I mentioned the second surgery, his face turned solemn. Veeck had injured his right leg in the Marine Corps, and despite all medical advice refused for more than two years to have it amputated. In the interim, he endured a dozen operations. He said, "I'm not a doctor, and it's none of my business, but if I had to do it all over again, I wouldn't go through the poisonous process of one surgery after the other. I would have had an amputation. I wouldn't say this if the amputation had to be above the knee, but below the knee there's almost nothing you can't do with an artificial leg." I was struck by the sincerity and power of his speech. And in all the years that I knew Veeck, it was the first and only time he ever mentioned his leg. I never told Peter this because it wasn't necessary. He made a remarkable recovery. And after he earned his doctorate in sociology, he flew to Europe and bicycled hundreds of miles around France by himself as his way of sorting out his world and his feelings after the trauma.

Veeck remained the most progressive owner in baseball. But by the end of his run with the White Sox, just before the 1981 strike, he started sounding more and more like many of his brethren. "We'll go bankrupt if salaries keep skyrocketing," he said. It should be noted that he was quite ill and under a severe financial strain. And I think it honors his memory best to write off this reactionary period to ill health, financial trouble, and general crustiness.

The last time I saw Bill was during spring training in 1981, although I had telephone conversations with him after that. I was shocked at the change in his appearance. He had been hospitalized with a collapsed lung. He was legally blind; he was deaf in one ear and had a hearing aid in the other. "The good news is," he said of the aid, which tended to squeal "that with a little deft fingerwork on the adjustment, I can play a fair approximation of 'Yankee Doodle Dandy.' The bad news is that I can no longer creep up on mine enemies unawares." That was Bill Veeck, filled with hope and humor. He lived four more years and died in 1985 at the age of seventy-one.

I'm just one of the many who felt that Veeck belonged in the Hall of Fame and was delighted that he was elected to the Hall in 1991. He viewed the ballpark as his theater, and he had more schemes than P. T. Barnum. And when you contrast his schtick with what passes for entertainment today—especially the electronic scoreboards that transform a tranquil ballpark into a commercial for MTV—his promotional acumen seems that much greater. For my money, mascots like the Philly Fanatic and the San Diego Chicken don't seem nearly as inventive, charming, or witty as marauding Martians and pinch-hitting midgets.

That's the legacy Veeck left baseball: He wasn't afraid to take the solemnity out of the game—even (and perhaps especially) if it meant making fun of himself. During Opening Day festivities in 1976, he honored America's Bicentennial with a recreation of *The Three Minutemen*. Who was the peg-legged fife player, complete with a blood-soaked bandage around his wig? Bill Veeck. "If you've got the guy with the wooden leg," he said, "you've got the casting beat."

"CHARLIE O"

IF I HAD TO PICK a single man as representing the transition from the old "family" business baseball men to the newer corporate types who came into baseball after having made their fortunes elsewhere, that man would be Charles O. Finley. As I've said before, he was, without a doubt, the finest judge of baseball talent I ever saw at the head of a team. A Southerner, born and raised in Birmingham, Alabama, Finley made a sizable sum of money in insurance. A longtime baseball fan, he established that city's minor league connection when the legendary Barons, of the Negro League, went out of business in the early 1960s. He renamed the franchise the A's and filtered through it Reggie Jackson, Rollie Fingers, Dave Duncan, Bert Campaneris, and other mainstays of his remarkable three-straight World Series champions from 1972 through 1974.*

To the generation that has grown up since Finley left the game—and especially to fans who know the Oakland A's as a streamlined, relatively progressive franchise powered by Jose Canseco, Rickey Henderson, Dave Stewart, Bob Welsh, and Dennis Eckersley—Finley seems almost like something from the Stone Age. He is largely remembered now as a cranky, crafty tyrant, part

---

*After Finley left baseball the Birmingham franchise reverted to its old name, the Barons. It is now affiliated with the Chicago White Sox.

P. T. Barnum and part George Steinbrenner. He was all these things, though as a showman he was never quite in Bill Veeck's class (but there are quite a few big-league hitters who would like to see his idea of orange balls for night baseball implemented). And though he bullied his players as Steinbrenner later would, Steinbrenner could never begin to equal him as an architect of championship teams. For most of the years that Finley ran the A's, he was the team's chief talent scout. In fact, during some of the leaner years he was the team's *only* scout. If anyone had kept count, he would probably find that Finley came up with as many crackpot ideas as good ones. But I'll grant him this: He never stopped trying to think up ways to improve the game and bring out more fans. It's a shame, in a way, that baseball doesn't seem to be able to accommodate mavericks like Finley anymore. Catfish Hunter may have had the last word on him when he said, "I never appreciated Charlie until I played for George Steinbrenner."

In the wake of the Messersmith decision it dawned on me, as a terrifying possibility, that the owners might suddenly wake up one day and realize that yearly free agency was the best possible thing for them; that is, if all players became free agents at the end of each year, the market would be flooded, and salaries would be held down. It wouldn't so much be a matter of the teams bidding against one another for one player as of players competing against *each other.* I realized that it would be in the interests of the players to "stagger" free agency so that every year there would be, say, three or four players available at a particular position and many teams to compete for their services. What would we do, I wondered, if just *one* of the owners was smart enough to figure out the money they would save if all players became free agents every year? One owner *was* smart enough: Charlie Finley.

In the midst of all the panic in the owners' ranks after the arbitration decision requiring (basically) one year of service for eligibility for free-agent status, there was Finley, maybe the only original thinker in the group, saying, "Hey, what's the problem? *Let* them be free agents every year. It'll flood the market with players; it'll keep salaries down." It was so logical, so obvious, that to this day I can't understand why other owners didn't think of it. All I can imagine is that they had such a fixation on power, such an abhorrence of the idea of the players winning any kind of freedom, that they refused even to consider an idea that clearly was in their own economic interest. I think that if Walter O'Malley had realized what Finley realized, things might have turned out differently. Luckily, the only owner who advocated unlimited free agency was the man who had gone to bat for the designated runner, colored shirts with white shoes, and orange baseballs. He was anathema to Commissioner Kuhn and an irritant to most other owners. (I think it was Larry Bowa who looked out on a spring training practice field at Finley's new uniforms and muttered, "Is this fast or slow pitch?")

Finley was a one-man front office. In addition to being his own best scout, he was also his own general manager. He argued his own arbitration cases. (Poorly, I should add. His defense of the A's against Catfish Hunter's claim of free agency was so weak that the case was a shoo-in for the Association.) He was also, too often, his own manager.

And he was his own worst press agent. He humiliated second baseman Mike Andrews by maneuvering to replace him after he made an error in the 1973 World Series against the Mets. Replacing an eligible player in the World Series takes some doing. Finley tried to rise to the occasion by intimidating the team physician, Harry Walker, into writing a letter that said Andrews was in no condition to play. Then he bullied Andrews into signing Walker's "diagnosis" that he was unable to continue. Then Finley tried to follow though by replacing Andrews with rookie Manny Trillo, who was not eligible under the rules. (Trillo would later set a record for consecutive errorless chances.) Finley needed the Mets' approval for such a move, and when it wasn't forthcoming, he had the Oakland PA man announce that the Mets were forcing the A's to play shorthanded. Bowie Kuhn, to his credit, took action. He later fined Finley $5,000 for trying to force Andrews out and $1,000 for the announcement. (Mike did make it back into the lineup in Game Four.) It's hard to think of a single incident when another owner, even George Steinbrenner, behaved with more arrogance and insensitivity.

Still, though I'm almost ashamed to admit it, I was charmed by the man. He told stories well, he loved the game, there was always something interesting going on around him. He certainly was an individual—and he had some of the strangest idiosyncrasies I've ever seen. I recall once being in a seafood restaurant on New York's East Side with Dick Moss when Finley, who was already there with an A's club official, asked us to join them. So here we were seated in one of New York's finer fish houses, and the man is unwrapping and handing to the waiter a slab of snapper he had just bought at a fish market. (Though now that I think of it, I could be selling him short; he may have caught it himself.) Finley, we found out, didn't trust restaurants to serve him fresh fish, so he made special arrangements with restaurants in different coastal cities. Charlie selected his own fish at waterfront markets, carried it to the restaurant, and let them prepare it.

After we finished eating, Finley began to badger me a bit in a gruff, good-humored way. Why, he wanted to know, did we have to have a maximum cut rule—this was before free agency, and the rule at the time was that an owner couldn't cut a player's salary by more than 20 percent from the year before or more than 30 percent over a two-year period—when there was no limit on the amount salaries could be *raised?* "After all," he said, "there's no rule like that in private industry. Right? You can cut someone's salary as much as you want in private industry. You're always saying how baseball should be subject to antitrust laws because it's a business, so if you want it to be like a business, why not allow the employer the same right as the businessman to cut an employee's salary as much as he thinks is merited?"

There was a pause. Finley grinned, thinking he had us. I smiled at Dick, then turned to Finley. "Charlie," I said, "I'll make you a deal. I'll agree to recommend to the player reps that we remove the maximum salary cut provision."

There was another pause. "Okay," he said, "what's the catch?"

"The catch," I said, "is that baseball owners make another concession to private industry and free enterprise: If the player whose salary you want to cut doesn't like the deal, he's free to go where he wants and make another deal with another team."

This time the pause was a gasp. "Come on now," he finally sputtered. "That's too much!"

"Too much," I said, laughing. "You're the one who offered the comparison to private industry. So, okay, we'll grant your wish: You baseball employers can have the same freedoms as those in other private industries if you'll grant the players the same freedoms as *workers* in other industries. Okay?"

Finley laughed and changed the subject.

Charlie never really understood the new kind of baseball that free agency brought about. For that matter, he never really understood salary arbitration. In the beginning, the players and their agents didn't understand it very well either, and Dick Moss and I had to log a lot of days helping out in arbitration cases. The year that stands out the most in my mind is 1974, both because it was the first year of salary arbitration and because the A's had won their second straight World Series in 1973 (on the way to three in a row in 1974) and had the largest number of players unhappy with salary offers. I monitored the cases in Oakland and assisted the players and their agents in presenting the cases to the arbitrators. I had been in Oakland for the cases of six players and needed to get back to New York, but Reggie Jackson asked me to stick around a couple of more days to help him out. I was really anxious to get home to my family, and besides, Reggie's case seemed pretty clear-cut. "Please," Jackson said, "I just know that that tricky SOB is going to try *something*. Just stay two more days."

I relented and thus had a chance to see Finley at his best, or rather, his worst.

Sal Bando had asked for $100,000—up from $75,000—and the arbitrator picked Sal's figure. A hard-nosed third baseman and clutch performer, Bando in 1973 had led the American League in doubles (32), and batted .287 with 29 HR and 98 RBI. Jackson and his agent had planned on coming in with far too modest a figure, but at our urging asked for $135,000—a raise from $90,000. Reggie had hit .293 and led the league in home runs (32), RBIs (117), and runs (99). Given Bando's raise, I didn't see how Jackson could lose. He was a bigger star than Bando and one of the game's great gate attractions. Finley's salary figure for Jackson was just $100,000, so the arbitrator had to pick between Finley's figure and ours, and while you never know what might be going through an arbitrator's head, we didn't see how he could possibly rule that Jackson wasn't worth more than Bando. Bando was a fine ballplayer, but Jackson was clearly better—clearly, in fact, one of the best players in baseball.

As it turned out, we were right, but Finley made us work. Reggie brought his agent with him, an Arizona-based lawyer who had a fear of flying, the result of which was that we had to wait an extra two days for him to drive to the Bay area. Reggie's agent, unfortunately, didn't know a great deal about the arbitration process, so it was more or less a learning process for him, and I was the teacher. This cost yet another day. I was really anxious to get home by then, but Reggie was nervous and didn't trust his agent to make his case, so I stayed. For my trouble, I got quite a show. Finley cross-examined Reggie, and I, in turn, cross-examined Finley. This thoroughly exasperated Finley, who called time out and went into the hall for a private caucus with John Gaherin.

Shortly afterward, Gaherin returned, leaned over, and whispered in my ear. "You'll never guess what Finley wants me to do." I thought about it for a moment, and John was right; I had no idea what Finley wanted him to do. "He wants me to see that you're removed from this room." We both laughed; Gaherin had no illusions that the time when a baseball owner had the unrestricted power to demand such a thing was long gone. Finley seemed oblivious to the fact that times had changed.

Charlie's method of presenting an arbitration case was to act like a movie version of a small-town lawyer. He was a spectacle to behold. He used no notes. He never sat down; he strolled all over the room, gesturing with his hands and talking. While he acted antsy, his speech was slow and deliberate, as if he were Perry Mason delivering a big courtroom speech. He acted as if he were *above* the debate instead of an involved party; he didn't present his case, he expounded and pronounced. He was the God of Baseball, sent down from Olympus to set confused mortals straight on all questions pertaining to baseball. It was a stellar performance. I loved watching him.

He would say things like: "*Mister* Reggie Jackson and his representative maintain that he deserves this *princely* salary"—"princely" was delivered with scorn—"because he is"—he would pause deliberately—"a *superstar*." He'd pause again before looking around the room and say, "Gentlemen, I ask you, *what is a superstar?*" We waited with bated breath for him to tell us precisely what, in his evaluation, a superstar was and why Reggie Jackson failed to meet those standards. Of course, he was dissembling. No one in the room, not Finley, not Gaherin, not the arbitrator, and certainly not Reggie himself, put the slightest stock in what he was saying. Myself, I had to chuckle inwardly during the "What is a superstar?" speech. I wanted to reply: "Charlie, you know, maybe a superstar is someone who has averaged thirty home runs and seventeen stolen bases over the previous seven seasons, someone who, just two seasons ago, led the league in home runs, runs batted in, runs scored, and slugging, while stealing twenty-two bases; someone who despite injuries last year hit twenty-nine home runs and twenty-five doubles in just five hundred six at bats and who, in addition, walked eighty-six times and stole twenty-five bases. Maybe it's someone who was the primary force on a team that won two straight World Series and is favored to win another. Would that be a close definition?" But I decided I'd be doing Reggie more good by keeping quiet and letting Finley bury himself.

When our turn came, of course, I trotted out the figures, which made a case that couldn't be denied. Simply, I pointed out that there was absolutely no precedent in baseball history for the best players on the best team not receiving the highest salaries—and that there was absolutely no precedent for a team that had just won two straight World Series having the next-to-lowest payroll in the league. When I said this, Finley finally lost his pompous cool and flew into a rage, ranting that the numbers I had just used were "meaningless." They didn't take the "intangibles" into account.

It didn't seem possible, I replied, that a team which had just won two straight World Series could be so lacking in intangibles; or if they were, how intangibles could be all that important.

Then he would return to his "What is a superstar?" routine as if his argument hadn't jumped the track. "Babe Ruth," he would say, and then pause, "was a superstar. Ty Cobb"—pause again—"was a superstar. Mickey Mantle and Ted Williams"—a longer pause, presumably so we'd have time to remember them both—"were superstars. Is Reggie Jackson—*Mister* Reggie Jackson—a superstar? Who knows what he'll be hitting ten years from now? Who knows how many home runs he'll hit ten years from now?" As if this were relevant to what Jackson should have been paid *then*. (For the record, Jackson went on to lead the league in home runs in 1975 and hit 345 homers from 1974 to the end of his career.)

I didn't see much point in challenging this kind of rhetoric. Instead, I pointed out that "there's nothing in the rules for arbitration proceedings that says anyone has to top Babe Ruth to receive $135,000. Could we please get on with this?"

Well, the bottom line was that Reggie got the $135,000; Finley's oratory apparently had no effect on the arbitrator. What amazes me in retrospect is that Finley had been able to hoodwink Jackson and other A's for so long into believing that they didn't deserve substantial raises. This was not the brash, bold Reggie Jackson the public would later come to know, the one who refused to take abuse from George Steinbrenner—we practically had to bash *this* Reggie over the head to get him to try for $135,000! It was a chore to convince him that by *not* asking for that much he'd be hurting not just himself but his fellow players: *His* salary would help raise *theirs* in salary arbitration cases.

Besides the no-superstar route, Finley's other basic approach at these arbitration cases was the "con" game. The latter was the more comical. Take the cases of Ken Holtzman, the A's standout southpaw starter, and Rollie Fingers, one of the best relievers in the game. First, Finley tried to convince the arbitrator that the reason for Holtzman's winning record (he won twenty-one games in 1973) was the brilliant performance of his bullpen ace, Rollie Fingers. The *next* day, Fingers's case was heard by the same arbitrator. At one point, Finley turned to the arbitrator and said, "Mr. Arbitrator, Fingers here is a good enough reliever, but you must not be misled by all the saves he had. Without the great staff of starting pitchers I have, who day after day keep the runs scored against us down so that we remain ahead in the late innings, Mr. Fingers's saves total would be quite modest!" It was vintage Finley: Don't let the left hand know what the right is doing. But it didn't work. Left-handed Holtzman and right-handed Fingers both won their arbitration cases.

Finley did the jobs of four men—unfortunately, three of them were named Groucho, Chico, and Harpo. It was as a talent scout that he helped his team the most, but in the age of free agency he didn't know how to hold on to the talent he had discovered. Probably it wasn't in his nature to compete for a player after he had brought him up through his system and regarded him as "his." No one made better use of the amateur free-agent draft that went into effect in 1965. It was designed to help second-division teams improve *if* they had an eye for baseball talent. Finley had it. Like Walter O'Malley, as a baseball owner, Finley was a baseball man first, a businessman second. If I had to single out the one big difference between Finley and O'Malley, it would be stubbornness. On most labor relations issues that affected baseball from the sixties to the late seventies, O'Malley could see the train coming and knew when to move, whereas Finley stood squarely on the tracks and tried to block it.

It may seem strange that I haven't said anything about one of the most famous Finley incidents, his attempt in 1976 to sell Rollie Fingers and Joe Rudi to the Red Sox for $2 million and Vida Blue to the Yankees for $1.5 million. By then, Finley had lost Hunter to free agency and had traded Jackson because he would become a free agent at the end of the year. The deals were an attempt by Finley to get as much as he could before his three most valuable remaining properties also became free agents. With Fingers, Rudi, and Blue just a few months away from free agency, he didn't figure to get the kind of money he wanted for selling the A's franchise. Who would pay a premium price for a team that was soon to lose its best players, or at the least to have to shell out million-dollar contracts just to keep them? Finley felt he was fighting for his financial life. By stepping in to void the sale, Bowie Kuhn had found a way to avenge a decade's worth of insults and humiliations at the hands (and mouth) of the irascible Finley: He could keep his foot on Finley's economic windpipe. (It ought to be noted that Finley had already made his decision to sell the A's and get out of baseball. This was the principal difference between his action in 1976 and Connie Mack's sale of the A's stars in 1914 and in the 1930s; Mack sold players as a way of staying in baseball.) This was the incident which caused Finley to make his oft-quoted "village idiot" remark about Kuhn; it was a remark made in anger and without thought. Later, calmer, more reflective, Finley modified the remark: Kuhn was a *"global"* idiot."

The Players Association didn't file a grievance against Kuhn's move to block the sale. I talked to the players, and while they were ready to leave Oakland, each understood the advantages of waiting until the end of the season and leaving via free agency. In a *trade*, the team Rudi or Blue went to had to pay "compensation"—the purchase price—to Oakland. In simplest terms, the $2 million Boston had agreed to pay for Rudi and the $1.5 million the Yankees had agreed to pay for Blue was "compensation" to Finley. Once they became free agents at the end of the season, the team interested in signing Rudi and Blue had *no* cash obligation to Finley or to anyone else—except, of course, the players involved.

This is exactly what happened at the end of the 1976 season. Instead of Finley receiving $1 million from the Red Sox for signing Rudi, Joe became a free agent, signed with the California Angels, and received a bonus of $1 million just for signing. It was such an obvious and important difference that I will never know why, five years later, so many people didn't understand what the owners were up to in the 1981 strike by demanding *direct compensation* so that free agency would be hobbled.

One thing that Finley's foiled deal did do, however, was to jolt everyone who followed baseball into realizing what the services of All-Star players were worth. If Fingers and Rudi were not worth a million apiece and Blue a million and a half, why would clubs be so eager to sign them up? And if they *were* worth that kind of money, why should Charles Finley or any owner have a right to the money? Once figures like that were bandied about for the sale of players, then with free agency beginning at the end of that season, the money representing the value of the player would be going from owner to player, instead of owner to owner (as in a trade). Finley's sales were voided, but the cat was out of the bag.

I was invited to the hearing which Kuhn called on the matter. The others there, as I recall, were George Steinbrenner and his lawyer, Bill Shea, and Sandy Hadden, Dick O'Connell, the Red Sox general manager, as well as Finley, Kuhn, and Dick Moss. I didn't feel that the issue was one on which the Players Association needed to take a stand, but I directed some criticism toward Kuhn. Why, in this particular case, I asked, did the commissioner have the right to block a sale of players when no commissioner had ever claimed the power before? Wasn't this simply an arbitrary action on Kuhn's part? Would the next step be voiding the trades of players, and if so, on what basis? Did Bowie believe he had the right to affect pennant races? I reminded him that if any such actions affected players adversely, the Players Association would become involved. I'm sure Charlie Finley had always viewed me as his enemy, and I can appreciate his point of view. It must have seemed strange to him, in his last great baseball controversy, to hear me taking a position more or less close to his own. After I finished speaking, he looked over at me and said, "Where have you been all my life?"

By 1980, Finley was out of baseball. My life became a little easier, and, in truth, a little duller. Years later, Bowie Kuhn was quoted as saying about Finley: "One more like him and I would have gone to work for Marvin Miller." So he says. Given a choice between the two of them, I'd have hired Charles Finley.

GEORGE STEINBRENNER: THE BOSS

THE TELEPHONE CALLS began one night in the early evening in the summer of 1981. Then, over the next several days the calls came in the late evening hours, from ten to eleven P.M. My work hours at the office stretched into the late evening hours almost every night, so my wife, Terry, took the messages. The persistent caller, Richie Phillips, said he was acting on behalf of George Steinbrenner. Mr. Steinbrenner wanted to talk with me about some ideas for settling the 1981 baseball strike, which we were well into. The negotiations were going nowhere; they were nerve-wracking and time-consuming. Terry suggested that Mr. Steinbrenner could reach me through the Players Association office.

Impossible, Phillips said. Any conversation with me had to be kept confidential. Under the owners' self-imposed gag rule, George could be fined up to half a million dollars for talking to me. George didn't want to call me at the office, Phillips said, because that would involve going through a switchboard or a secretary, who would then know he was calling for me.

I had never met Richie Phillips, a Philadelphia lawyer who acted as an agent for the major league umpires, but I had spoken to him on the phone several times over the years. After a number of his calls, Terry became annoyed. She told him that she couldn't understand such scared behavior on the part of Steinbrenner. As for Phillips's continued reference to the potential fine, Terry responded that George probably lost more than that each weekend the strike continued. If he really had ideas which could bring about a settlement, she said, Steinbrenner's delays would cost him more than any fine.

Terry's remarks about Steinbrenner's timidity coaxed a chuckle out of Phillips. Would she, he asked, be willing to tell him that directly? Phillips didn't know Terry. She sure would. A few minutes later Steinbrenner called and received my wife's criticism point-blank. They talked for a while. He wasn't scared, George protested, but he had to be realistic. He told her that he would find a way to meet with me.

The next night I was home when Phillips telephoned again. What the hell, I thought. We began a discussion of the sole issue in the strike, the owners' demand for direct compensation of a club that lost a free agent to another team. After a series of phone conversations about the issue, its ramifications, and possible solutions—with Phillips relaying my thoughts to Steinbrenner and his to me—I told Richie that this form of communication was inadequate for dealing with the problem. He agreed. A short time later he called back and asked if I would meet with Steinbrenner if he, Phillips, arranged a meeting in a New York hotel the next day during lunchtime. What the hell, I thought again. I agreed.

I arrived at the Hyatt Regency Hotel on East Forty-second Street at the appointed time. The arrangement was that there would be a suite in Phillips's name. I didn't see the house phones, so I walked to the bell captain's booth for directions. He looked up and apparently recognized me, because he said, "They're just around the corner to your left, Mr. Miller." So much for secrecy. I could picture Steinbrenner, whose face was infinitely more recognizable than mine, going through the same routine, being recognized, and one or more people drawing the correct conclusion that we were there to meet each other.

When I reached Phillips's suite, George was there already, chatting with Richie. We made some small talk about the ongoing NLRB hearings before a trial examiner, which I had just left. George said he understood that "we [the owners] were getting killed." I said, yes, that was my reading of the situation, too. I also affirmed that the owners and Ray Grebey were not holding up well under cross-examination: There was no credibility to their testimony that "compensation was not an economic issue" and that their poverty claims were unrelated to collective bargaining.

Steinbrenner and I had met a number of times in the past, and I had always been pleasantly surprised to find that his public persona was not the same in private. For one thing, he had a problem-solving attitude when the occasion called for it. Also, he had a practical side to him; he seemed to have a good feel for what was or was not feasible. And for a man who shamelessly bullied his employees, he understood better than any other owner the role of a union. When his club acted inappropriately toward a player and a grievance was filed, his reactions were businesslike and not overly defensive. On a one-to-one basis he never showed me the bully about whom so much has been written, but then again, I was never his employee or under his control in any way. On this day we explored the disputed issue frankly, including the possibility of the owners creating their own pooled compensation fund, with payments from that fund going to the clubs that lost free agents. George felt the idea had merit and said he would try to sound out a few key people and get reactions. Steinbrenner said he appreciated the meeting because he now felt that he had a better grasp of the issue in question than he had before. He was critical of what he described as sketchy and somewhat misleading reports of the negotiations that he had been getting.

Phillips had been present, but mostly silent. With the meeting about to end, Richie recommended that George and I leave separately. He left first, and after about ten minutes, I left. Phillips remained in the suite.

That evening Phillips surprised me with another call. He said that after I left, something happened which he felt would have been hilarious if it had occurred just a few minutes before. Laughing, Phillips told me that after I left he went into the bedroom of the suite to get his briefcase and a few belongings, when he heard a crashing sound from the room where we had been meeting. This was followed instantly by the sound of rushing water. He looked into the other room and saw that the water pipes had burst, causing the plaster to cover the two chairs where George and I had been sitting, and there was water gushing from the broken pipes. Within minutes the room was full of maintenance men attempting to deal with the problem. The hallway was full of hotel guests who had heard the noise and were trying to discover the cause.

Phillips, obviously enjoying the whole thing in retrospect, said, "All I could think of as I saw that mess was that if it had happened fifteen minutes earlier, you and George would have been covered with water and plaster, and there surely would have been a story about it, including pictures, on the evening news."

Very funny indeed, though the joke wouldn't have cost me half a million; I'd have gotten off with just a dry cleaning bill. But given the disparity in our income, that might have been fair.

Nothing came of our meeting. Lee MacPhail talked to me privately a few days later and said that the idea of a pooled compensation fund wouldn't "float." The strike continued until the owners folded. Eventually they got less in the settlement than the pooled fund would have provided. I think, though, that the Steinbrenner effort to bring about a strike settlement was a more meaningful action than had been undertaken by any other owner or official during that whole long, dreary period.

George Steinbrenner is an easy person to caricature, but a difficult one to characterize. As "the Boss," his excesses, his boorishness, his bullying of others, and his incessant desire for publicity are all well known. But some of the actions that led to his downfall (his banishment as general partner of the Yankees in 1990) did not deserve opprobrium. He was the first baseball owner to understand how free agency would change the game, and the first to utilize free agents to build winning teams. He saw the potential, calculated the costs, and determined, as a businessman, that he could maximize his income and the value of the New York Yankees franchise by spending freely for players. In that he succeeded. But one cost of his success was the enmity of many other owners who, though paying lip service to competition and free enterprise, shudder when they see it in action.

George Steinbrenner's behavior toward Dave Winfield was indefensible. Their feud had been going on for many years, and culminated in the allegation that Steinbrenner was making payments for information with which to damage and pressure Winfield. The weird saga of the star-chamber proceedings before Commissioner Fay Vincent, which ended in Steinbrenner's "permanent" banishment, may some day be explained.

Steinbrenner's behavior unquestionably merited discipline, but let no one doubt that when an owner is banished, he is sent away because a consensus of owners wants it that way. A commissioner has no power whatsoever to do what owners don't want him to do—not if he wants to retain his job. This being so, a moment's thought will reveal that the other owners did not give two hoots whether George's behavior toward Winfield was rotten or whether George fired and rehired managers to the point of absurdity. In fact, the owners cared not at all what Steinbrenner did or did not do, except for one thing. They heartily disliked his policy on players' salaries. It was here that they felt he was a loose cannon; it was this and only this that concerned them. They believed that, starting with the signing of free agent Catfish Hunter in 1975, Steinbrenner had provided impetus to players' rising salaries.

And they were right. In 1990 the owners' fears of Steinbrenner became more sharply focused than ever. The exposure of the owners' collusive actions against the players after 1985, and the ending of those endeavors, caused great owner trepidation about what Steinbrenner would do in the postcollusion period. His local television and cable revenue was said to be $50 million a year, and a new record-high network contract, beginning in 1990, would enrich all the clubs. With the competitive Steinbrenner aching to rebuild the lagging Yankees into pennant contenders, all the elements were in place for Yankee spending on players that would make prior spending sprees look miserly.

That, I think, sealed George's fate. The owners wanted George out in 1990, as they had in the past, but this time they were more determined. There is a naiveté about George Steinbrenner that doesn't seem to have been perceived by most observers; although the owners' long-held opposition to him was well known, he never seemed to realize it. In that, he was not helped by the sporting press, which, too often, accepts official handouts and leaked stories (if the source is a friendly commissioner or other official). To this day, I would wager, Steinbrenner and many sportswriters believe that he is out of the game because the institution of baseball rose up in its majesty to defend a player—Dave Winfield—from the machinations of an owner! This is a fairy tale for adults. If Winfield needed defending, the Players Association, not the commissioner's office, would have done it. He didn't ask anyone to defend him.

Steinbrenner's unwillingness or inability to recognize opposition to him first became apparent to me with the beginning of the owners' collusion in 1985. Although he was the first to utilize free agents, and the most successful in building winning teams, he became a coconspirator by depriving his club of the opportunity to sign free agents. I was astonished at the time because it was so obvious that *he* was the principal target (along with the players) of the owners' planned collusion in the first place, but apparently this thought had not occurred to him. Ted Turner, Gene Autry, and a few others were also targets, but George was the owner they most wanted to curb. Yet he seemed incapable of understanding that a club like the Yankees—one with no success (or talent) in building a team through effective trading, and without a record of effective player recruitment and development in the minors for some time—would certainly fall out of contention if it could not sign free agents. But he agreed and joined with his "brother" owners in a scheme aimed at himself.

Steinbrenner's failure to comprehend that he was the victim was accompanied by a more common failing: an inability to recognize injustice when it affects others. He was silent, as were others, as various commissioners violated the basic rights of players, a stray owner or two separated from the pack, a manager—Pete Rose—more recently. With such silence, acquiescence is assumed. When such assumptions pile up, the odds become heavy against having your basic rights respected when *you* are in the dock.

And so it was with George. He had never protested against the unfair disciplinary procedures of commissioners: the denial of the right of an accused to call witnesses on his own behalf; the denial of the right to confront and cross-examine witnesses against him; the concept of hearings conducted by prosecutor-judge-jury all embodied in one person; the presumption of guilt prior to any hearing; and the denial of any right to appeal a judgment, no matter how drastic it might be.

I will not say that George Steinbrenner deserved that same shabby treatment because he was not moved to protect others who experienced it before him, but I will argue that his indifference to earlier victims made his own fate more likely, as did his unwilling-ness to confront authority. My wife, Terry, who questioned Steinbrenner's courage because he accepted the owners' ban on speaking out during the 1981 strike, wrote a short piece after he was banned from baseball. It ended: "George, who was born on the Fourth of July, and bearer of the proud name of the father of his country, bore a closer resemblance to that other George of our nursery-rhyme days—the one who ran away."

PETER UEBERROTH

AS PRESIDENT of the 1984 Olympic Organizing Committee, Peter Ueberroth came into baseball riding the crest of his $225 million triumph in Los Angeles. The wave metaphor is apt. Ueberroth went to San Jose State on a water polo scholarship and reportedly is a dedicated skin diver. When Ueberroth, then forty-six years old, replaced Kuhn, *New York Times* columnist George Vecsey wrote: "Ueberroth knew he would be entering murky waters with the 26 assorted sharks, whales, sting rays, sea turtles and barnacled mossbunkers in baseball's sea of ownership." "Swamp" might have been more appropriate, but either way he wasn't in over his head.

Soon after Ueberroth moved into the commissioner's office in October 1984, he made some intriguing moves. He called Donald Fehr and asked to get together to become acquainted and to discuss ways to head off future problems. He then asked Don if he would object to his getting together with me. Don said, "Good idea."

Our first meeting, over lunch, was a long and candid one. Ueberroth encouraged me to talk—something that takes very little encouragement—and he listened intently. He asked, among other things, what my view would be if he removed Bowie Kuhn's "ban" on Willie Mays and Mickey Mantle. Kuhn's edict had required that first Mays and then several years later Mantle, the premier center fielders of their day, either resign from jobs as customer relations people for (entirely legal) gambling casinos or be banished from any connection with baseball: Mays as a batting coach for the Mets and Mantle as a batting instructor in spring training for the Yankees. Of course, Kuhn had had a chance to withdraw Mays's ban when Mantle accepted a similar casino job, but as usual, he did the wrong thing, banning both. (What was there about center fielders and Kuhn? Considering his actions against them and Curt Flood, how did Joe DiMaggio and Duke Snider escape his wrath?)

Surprisingly, only a few writers condemned Kuhn's arbitrary action. These all-time greats of the game, blatantly underpaid and exploited during their playing careers, now became victims of Bowie's hypocritical stance in retirement. (If that sounds like an overstatement, consider what Mantle and Mays would have earned if their primes had come *after* the Messersmith and McNally decision.) Their ties to gambling, which mostly consisted of shaking hands with customers or perhaps playing golf with high-rollers, were no more real than the connections of club owners like Ewing Kauffman, George Steinbrenner, or Dan Galbreath, racehorse breeders who rubbed elbows with touts, bookies, odds makers and, as it later developed, gamblers. (In a 1979 interview with *Penthouse,* Pete Rose revealed that Galbreath had actually dangled a couple of horses in front of him as an added incentive to play for the Pirates.)

I expressed enthusiasm about reversing Kuhn's sanctions. Ueberroth made no bones about how foolish and damaging Kuhn's actions were against Mays and Mantle, idols to millions of fans. Peter followed through on lifting the ban in a public ceremony, and the repudiation seemed to please everyone except Kuhn.

Fay Vincent reached out to Don and me in a similar fashion when he became commissioner after Bart Giamatti's death, but the difference was that Ueberroth was really looking for an education in the business of baseball. His critics probably were, on the whole, correct in their assessment that he knew very little about the game, but oddly enough, I don't think that really hurt Ueberroth. He was a pragmatist, not an ideologue like Kuhn (about whose capabilities, in private, he had a low estimate) or a pseudophilosopher like Giamatti, and he was smart enough to admit to himself that he had a lot to learn and to know where to go to find out.

Ueberroth was a businessman. He had built the nation's second-largest travel agency from scratch, selling it in 1984 for $10 million. At the 1984 Olympics, he used his entrepreneurial talents to turn a tidy profit—for the games, Los Angeles, and himself. He did this, in part, by appealing to the community's civic pride and patriotic spirit and by enlisting thousands of people to work for free. He prudently used existing stadiums to stage events and was able to cajole corporations into building velodromes and swimming pools in exchange for blocks of tickets. This was all done, I must stress, on the up and up. Throughout the ordeal, however, Ueberroth maintained (inaccurately) that the games were losing millions. When it was all over, the media praised him to the sky. "Such financial gymnastics," one reporter wrote, "should earn him a seat in the White House." In fact, his financial gymnastics were not unlike those being used by the man *in* the White House.

There was, however, a nonideological shrewdness in the way Ueberroth viewed the Association. When he came to baseball, he was smart enough to see what Kuhn and most of the owners could not, which was that the success of the Players Association, although achieved against the opposition of the owners, nevertheless was a victory for big-league baseball in general. To a degree, at least, Ueberroth understood, as no previous commissioner had, that warfare between the owners and players was bad for business. I don't want to give him too much credit in this area, but there's something to be said about a commissioner who understands that the game of baseball is also a business run for profit.

Quite simply, I think Ueberroth came to the Association to talk things over because he realized that no one on management's side was really capable of putting the changes of the previous eighteen years into perspective. Ueberroth seemed genuinely interested in what had gone on before he came into the game: What had impelled the players to organize? Why had I become interested? What was Ray Grebey like? Why had the owners fired him? What were the prime causes of the 1980–81 strike? What was Kuhn's role in the strike? (He paid particular attention to the answer to that question.) I'm not saying he accepted all that I said or that he even understood it all, but he certainly *started* his term in office knowing more about the history of baseball's labor-management relations than Bowie Kuhn did when he *left*. Ueberroth may not have been able to tell baseball writers who caught for the 1945 St. Louis Browns (or, for that matter, the 1985 Cardinals), but he became well versed in the most important legal decisions in the history of baseball. My guess is that by the time he left office he knew more about the business than any commissioner before or since.

All this being said, it's time to balance out Ueberroth's record. Prior to the 1985 negotiations, Ueberroth privately told Don Fehr and me that the owners' books were a farce—we already knew that, of course, but it was refreshing to hear a baseball commissioner *say* it. He had seen the data that the clubs had furnished to the leagues and to the commissioner and suspected that there must be two sets of books. Basically, he was saying, "I don't believe these figures about poverty, and you shouldn't be bothered by them." He repeated the same thing to Don and to the players' executive board in December 1984. It seemed to me that he believed this, though it's also possible that he was simply trying to impress us with his independence—again, the fiction that the commissioner represented "all of baseball" and that he wasn't just the "owners' house man." In fact, before taking the job Ueberroth stressed that he wanted baseball's bylaws changed in order to strengthen the commissioner's authority. Among these so-called powers was the ability to increase the amount of fines he could impose on a club—from $5,000 to $250,000. This provided the illusion of autonomy and strength, but what it really said was that the majority of the owners didn't trust their more dissident members. Considering what we now know about collusion, it's fair to say that the dramatic jump in the fine had something to do with the "do-not-leak" discussions the owners were conducting about the coming collusion.

By the time negotiations got started in 1985, the owners were taking the ludicrous line that at least eighteen of the twenty-six teams were losing money and that their books could verify this. Sure enough, the man who expressed such contempt for Kuhn was quick to do a great impression of him in front of the television cameras when it came to selling the owners' propaganda. And Peter Ueberroth was a much more persuasive salesman than Bowie Kuhn.

Then, when it looked as if a real deadlock was developing, he played the neutral and came out with written "suggestions" for a settlement that were almost as absurd as Fay Vincent's declaration during the 1990 lockout that the union should pledge not to use its only weapon—a strike—even if a settlement was never reached. I wasn't surprised at a commissioner returning to form, but I was surprised that a man as intelligent as Peter couldn't see that he had screwed up the negotiations at a critical point. His "ideas," several of them anyway, amounted to asking the union to make concessions on demands the owners had already dropped, then he did the same by reintroducing an issue which *we* had dropped. (They didn't even out—the edge would have gone to the owners.) The result was that negotiations didn't just stall, they were actually set back several days. All I could think of was that he must have been grandstanding for the cameras. Ueberroth's biggest flaw as a commissioner was that he came from outside collective bargaining, and the 1985 negotiations showed him at his most amateurish.

On the last day, when it appeared we were going to settle things, all the relevant parties were together at Lee MacPhail's apartment. We took a breather before trying to tackle some minor points. Just then, in walked Ueberroth with his entourage from the commissioner's office, obviously anxious to make it appear before the press, due any second, that he had been part of the final settlement. I had to laugh. He was an actor (not unlike Ronald Reagan, although he was smarter and smoother and not nearly as controlled), and he had a certain style and flair. After the settlement he had a large bouquet of flowers sent to Terry. I remember looking at the flowers and feeling sorry for whoever he ran against when he finally decided to go into politics.

Upon assuming office, Ueberroth announced that one of his first priorities was to stamp out drug use in professional baseball. Drugs (cocaine in particular) were a hot topic. Publicized cases involved four Kansas City Royals—Willie Wilson, Willie Aiken, Jerry Martin, and Vida Blue—in 1983; Pascual Perez in 1984; and Keith Hernandez, Dave Parker, and Dale Berra, among others, in 1985. Ueberroth had read the tea leaves of publicity. He started talking about wiping out drugs well before he had a coherent plan. When asked how drugs could be eliminated, he said, "It's built on trust and players helping players."

Ueberroth's drug "policy" was all for the camera. He was like George Bush over the last two years, still out there running for office after the election was over. In point of fact, a jointly negotiated drug program had been in existence since 1984. It was a humane and largely successful program, one that *did not* include mandatory and random drug testing. So you can imagine my astonishment one afternoon in 1985 when Ueberroth came on the tube during the Game of the Week and announced that the existing drug program was no good because it didn't have *mandatory* testing. Ueberroth said he had a new antidrug program which would clean up baseball once and for all. Essentially, he had declared war and claimed victory without ever having fired a shot.

Don Fehr told him to take a hike.

In 1986, he took another approach, again without consulting the Players Association. He sent a letter to every major leaguer, *urging* him to submit to voluntary drug tests during the season. The tests would be "totally confidential," he said, and free of penalties. Noble, but completely outside the framework of collective bargaining. Again, he was playing to the camera.

Don, in turn, urged the players to toss the letter in the garbage. When the two met, Ueberroth asked if Don would agree to testing, "even if it was just for the sake of public relations."

Whose PR? Don asked. No one recalls Ueberroth's reply, but the matter was dropped.

Ueberroth went ahead and imposed mandatory testing in the minor leagues—there was no union to do anything about it. But if the program was successful, we have certainly never heard about it. Ueberroth ducked almost every question reporters asked about how the program was working out. "How many tests have been given?" He couldn't say. "We don't want names, just numbers." Sorry, can't talk about it. "How many positive tests had there been?" No comment.

"Peter the Arrogant," as one reporter dubbed him, was less interested in eliminating drug use from baseball than he was in benefiting from the perception that something was being done.

In November 1990, *Sports Illustrated* ran a front-of-the-book item which read, in part, "When he left office in the spring of 1989, following the signing of lucrative TV contracts with CBS and ESPN,* Ueberroth was almost universally hailed as the financial savior of baseball. Much of the reason for the improved bottom line was that Ueberroth had cajoled the owners into keeping players' salaries down and ignoring free agents. But by doing that, the

---

*For $1.1 billion and $400 million, respectively.

owners were practicing collusion, in violation of baseball's labor agreement."

This is as accurate and concise a paragraph on the subject as I recall having seen. More interesting is that it was, three years after his term, the *first* time Ueberroth's participation in the conspiracy had been clearly stated in print.

Looking back at the negotiations of 1984–85, what strikes me most is the incredible bad faith shown. By midsummer 1985, Lee MacPhail, the chairman of the PRC, was pressing for a peaceful settlement. The Player Relations Committee had dropped its outlandish proposal that the union accept a salary cap or a freeze in benefits and pensions and—after a two-day walkout—we reached a settlement on August 8. At the very time that MacPhail, Ueberroth, and Barry Rona were supposedly trying to find a compromise, they were organizing a scheme to sabotage the contract.

MacPhail and Barry Rona worked hand in glove with Ueberroth. Lee MacPhail was the insider. A former deputy commissioner, general manager, and American League president, MacPhail was born and bred an owners' man. His father, Larry, had been a part owner of the Yankees and Brooklyn Dodgers and his son, Andy, is currently the general manager of the Minnesota Twins.* When Lee was general manager of the Yankees, a twenty-game winner made $20,000, sometimes *less.* He couldn't stomach the fact that players in 1985 were making as much as $2 million a season; moreover, he hated the idea of players not being controlled. When the union wouldn't agree with him about the "drastic" need to hold down salaries, he ultimately decided to take matters into his own hands.

Barry Rona, a legal counsel for the PRC, was the so-called technician. He told the powers that be—and I know this because he told us the same thing—that the language in the contract didn't prevent the owners from meeting and exchanging information about free agents. In effect, he said that as long as the owners didn't sit down and say, "We're going to take concerted action against free agents," they were safe from any repercussions. After

---

*An arbitrator in the collusion cases made a finding that Andy MacPhail's testimony—that there was no collusion because he had made a bona fide offer to Jack Morris, a free agent with Detroit in 1986–87—was not supported by the facts.

all, he reasoned, the owners are allowed to be "fiscally cautious" and "financially prudent." Apparently it was just a coincidence that they all became cautious and prudent in exactly the same way and at the same time.

Ueberroth provided the leadership. But unlike most of management's power brokers, he didn't bemoan the Association's success, the players' high salaries, or management's loss of control. That wasn't his bag. Ueberroth had a straightforward approach: "This is a business. I'm a businessman. You hired me to help improve profits, and I'm telling you how." He advised them against "spending themselves into the ground" and offered such helpful suggestions as "It's not smart to sign long-term contracts." As George Steinbrenner said, "Peter Ueberroth . . . got us together on numerous occasions—always with four lawyers in the room to guard against anything that might be construed as collusion—and made us tell each other how stupid we'd been in the past." In other words, he taught them how to collude without saying "collusion." (He was, however, unable to teach them how not to get caught.)

Peter Ueberroth left baseball in December 1989, hoping to scale greater heights through the purchase of Eastern Airlines, a company that had provoked a bitter strike by its employees. The deal was to be financed, in part, by his longtime friend, Kirk Kerkorian, the Beverly Hills financier. The purchase was never completed. When Commissioner Ueberroth stepped down, he was widely hailed as the savior of baseball, a myth he perpetuated. But in 1990 the third of three arbitration decisions finding the owners and officials guilty of violation of the basic agreement was issued. This induced the owners to settle by agreeing to pay $280 million (plus interest) for distribution to players disadvantaged by the owners' collusion. Additionally, a number of players were offered, as part of the settlement, the option of again becoming free agents. As *Sports Illustrated* put it: "The time has come to reassess the Ueberroth era. He was, in many ways, the Teflon commissioner." Baseball is paying the price for that part of his phoney prosperity, which was based on collusion, just as the country is paying for Reagan's.

19...

White Collars and Black Sox: Giamatti and Vincent

Or, "Say It Ain't So, Peter, Lee, Bart, Bobby, Hank, Tom, George, Haywood, Peter O', Bob, Al, Bud, Marge, Jean Joan, Jerry, Gene, Eddie, Jim, Bill, Ewing, Roy, Sandy, Andy, Charles, Fred, et al."

so, 2 weeks in a row bart captures the headlines. the week before it was his decision to ban pete rose from b.b. for life. whose life? m is unforgiving, death notwithstanding. he abhors all the hypocrisy that has surrounded the commissioner, the unified voice of the media to label him a god and rose a villain. well, god heard, and he, you may remember, is a jealous god. thou shalt have no other gods before me. giamatti was like a biblical character as he announced his punishment of rose. he was angry, cold, severe, flag-waving, pennant-waving. he was the savior of the national pastime, of the nation itself. he had saved the nation from pete rose, the gambler, while handing it over to ron peters, the drug dealer, whose sentence he sought to have reduced. he died a hero.

driving the money changers from the temple. employed by bigger money changers, he was looked upon as the great hope for the future of the game. not, mind you, to restore its integrity, but rather to rebuild its appearance *of integrity. appearance is all. who better than a renaissance scholar to shield the lords of baseball from exposure to the light of honesty and fair play. with bart to charm the public, the owners would be able to get away with anything. his death is a big blow to twenty-six owners and ten times that many reporters and commentators who will no longer have their biased propaganda sugar coated for them.*

here lies a smooth talking casuist, a union-busting conservative, a simple fan who was in over his head.

he did look a bit satanic, didn't he? had he perhaps signed a pact with the devil to gain the post of commissioner of all the baseballs? and failed to pay up? gambled and lost, you might say, or is it truman capote's "more tears are shed over prayers that are answered?"

i'm sorry i never met the man.

You may have noticed that the above paragraphs have a slightly different style—they were written on a Sunday afternoon in September 1989 by my wife, Terry. I would have changed a few things: calling me "m" makes me sound like a character out of a Kafka novel, and "bart," "rose," and "god" probably should be capitalized, but on the whole, it's also my evaluation of A. Bartlett Giamatti.

Like a Pope who died after just a few weeks in office, Giamatti has almost taken on the aura of sainthood; a philosophic scholar who descended on baseball from some higher level—or at least a higher level than most of the newspaper and magazine writers who quoted his pretentious, overripe prose with awe, without bothering to figure out the content of his precious emissions.

It all began when Giamatti became National League president at the end of 1986. His record in that office is most notable for his peculiar disciplinary actions, the harshest of sentences for Phillies pitcher Kevin Gross allegedly because his use of sandpaper was *premeditated,* followed by a harsh sentence for the *spontaneous, unpremeditated* action by Pete Rose when he shoved umpire Dave Pallone (in response to Pallone's hitting Rose under the eye, perhaps accidentally, according to the filmed record).

Once again it was disciplinary action that stood out as Giamatti's claim to fame after he became commissioner, and once again it was Pete Rose who was his target. It is ironic that Giamatti will be best remembered for his decision to ban Rose from baseball for life, that his major contribution to the game is his attempt to erase the contribution of one of its outstanding performers. (An attempt followed up on by Fay Vincent, Bowie Kuhn, Lee MacPhail, Chub Feeney, John McHale, Bud Selig, and other baseball management people connected with the Hall of Fame. I'm sad to say that their actions met with approval by others on the Hall of Fame Committees such as Bob Broeg of the *St. Louis Post-Dispatch*, long a management apologist, and, saddest of all, Robin Roberts.) This was accomplished by ruling in 1991 that Rose's name may not appear on the writers' ballots for Hall of Fame selection, no matter what the "independent" judgment of the writers may be.

Giamatti's action against Rose was a classic case of the punishment not fitting the crime. The Black Sox players who allegedly threw games for money in 1919—considered baseball's worst offense—received the stiffest penalty possible, banishment from the game for life. Rose, of course, was not even charged with such an offense or anything resembling it.

Until the Rose case, Giamatti, like other league presidents, wasn't called up to do much more than serve in a ceremonial capacity. Suddenly there entered his paradise of pure baseball a man by the name of John Dowd. Dowd had been gathering information about Pete Rose (as an impartial investigator? a detective? or a prosecutor?). His principal informants were two convicted felons, a shocking reliance that mostly escaped criticism. One of them, Ron Peters, was the subject of a letter Giamatti wrote to Judge Carl Rubin, asking that the judge be lenient in his sentencing of this drug dealer because he had been *truthful* when he presented evidence against Rose. How did Giamatti *know* that Peters had been truthful since Giamatti had not met the man and, more important, since Peters had *not* been subject to cross-examination?

Peters was the primary witness against Rose. Clearly, he was promised that Giamatti would intervene with the federal judge on his behalf if he, Peters, would "cooperate" with Dowd. For such a promise of help, it is hardly unknown for a convicted felon awaiting sentencing to say what his interrogator wants him to say. Giamatti, carrying out his end of the bargain, then injected himself into the pending sentencing of a convicted cocaine dealer. If Rose's effort to disqualify Giamatti from sitting in judgment on the grounds of bias had gone to trial, I believe that Giamatti's letter to the judge alone would have been found reason enough to disqualify him. The federal judge who had been about to sentence Peters said publicly that he was offended by Giamatti's letter and that he felt that Giamatti was engaged in a personal vendetta against Rose. (This was the judge's observation *before* the commissioner barred Rose from baseball for *life* without findings on "the allegation that Peter Edward Rose bet on any Major League Baseball game." If the judge thought there was a vendetta before, I wonder what he thought afterward.)

Pressing for the disqualification of Giamatti through a regular judicial process was not available to Rose in any practical terms. The protracted litigation forced on him by Giamatti would have cost Pete more money than he probably had.* (I'm still asked why the matter wasn't taken out of the commissioner's hands and referred to impartial arbitration by the Players Association. But by 1989 Rose was no longer a player; he was a member of management and thus deprived of recourse to the grievance and arbitration procedures and due process provided by the basic agreement.) Without the funds to sustain a continuing legal battle on the issue of the commissioner's bias—a battle costing Giamatti not a cent of his own money—Rose was forced to settle with the very individual who had pronounced him guilty *before* a hearing, *before* witnesses' accusations had been subject to cross-examination, and without normal prehearing procedures. Had Giamatti been sensitive to the fact that he had written a biased letter to Judge Rubin, he would have removed himself from the Rose case,

---

*The disciplinary action taken against Rose would have been even more severe and unjust had it not been for Pete's union. The original pension plan had a provision terminating all benefits of anyone declared permanently ineligible under Professional Baseball Rule 21. In 1976 I negotiated the deletion of this provision. So, regardless of Giamatti's actions against him, Rose and his family retain numerous benefits under the pension plan, including a retirement pension (worth in Pete's case, assuming normal life expectancy, millions of dollars) and a widow's benefit equal to 100 percent of the retirement benefit.

just as Rubin removed himself from the sentencing of Ron Peters after he expressed his anger at the Giamatti letter.

The settlement Rose and Giamatti signed (witnessed by his deputy, Fay Vincent) specifically called attention to the fact that *no finding had been made that Rose bet on a baseball game. The same document also recorded the commissioner's declaration that he would make no public statement which said anything to the contrary.* But within the next few hours, Giamatti held a televised press conference and announced his conclusion that Rose *had bet on baseball games.* Had the settlement been made under the jurisdiction of a court, Giamatti's violation almost certainly would have exposed him to contempt of court charges.

The Bill James Baseball Book 1990 contains a long, detailed study of the flaws and contradictions of the Dowd report on Rose. It is easily the best analysis and commentary on the subject, but the truth is that James only did what any writer who had the patience and objectivity to get through the document should have done before the rush to judge Pete Rose.

I would disagree with James on one point. He suggests that all the stress surrounding the Rose decision might have been a primary contributor to Giamatti's heart attack (overlooking his addiction to smoking). Well, we'll never know the answer, but I'd like to suggest another cause. I think Giamatti was an excessively prideful man, and I think that he recognized that he looked foolish and less than honorable when the letter to Judge Rubin became known, and when he was criticized publicly by the judge. (The fact that Giamatti knew he was doing something questionable in writing to Rubin is apparent from his request to the judge that the letter be kept confidential—"under the Court's seal"— until the Rose case was over.) The "vendetta" accusation may also have wounded him, because it did seem that Rose's basic offense was his vulgar (to Giamatti) working-class persona, his being a man of action rather than ideas. Pete Rose, we may assume, was not Bart Giamatti's idea of what the classic American baseball hero should be. Giamatti spoke of baseball in Olympian tones; gods don't get dirt all over their togas.

What the writers have never put together is Giamatti's gross inconsistency. He presented himself as someone devoted to the game, dedicated to upholding its values, purity, integrity. Yet in stark contrast to his management of the Rose case there was his manner of dealing with the far more serious threat to baseball, the collusion case. It seems odd that Giamatti convicted Pete Rose on the basis of testimony offered by a convicted felon yet refused to accept the judgment of two independent, professional arbitrators, who said, quite plainly, that all twenty-six owners and their officials had colluded in an effort to deprive their clubs of the best possible teams. To save money, the owners had agreed not to bid on one another's free agents *for three successive years.* During that time the players were trying their best to win games, but the owners were not. By any definition, the owners' actions badly scarred the "integrity of the game"—a fact that has never been fully explained to the fans.

Wasn't the Black Sox scandal of 1919 a case of players taking money for playing not to win? It's worth noting that the Black Sox were largely uneducated, miserably paid, working-class men. (The great "Shoeless" Joe Jackson was illiterate and signed his name with an X.) After the imposition of a lifetime ban, they were deprived of the chance to make a living using their only known skills.

The same cannot be said about the modern-day baseball establishment. This scandal was not about just eight men on one club over an eight-game series; it involved all the owners, all the general managers, all the club officials, both league presidents, and two baseball commissioners—over *three seasons.* And unlike the 1919 Sox, who were cleared in court of any wrongdoing, these were educated, affluent, and privileged owners, and they were found *guilty,* in two separate series of hearings, of colluding not to sign free agents from other clubs, no matter how much those free agents would improve their team. It was, undeniably, an agreement *not to field the best team possible*—which is tantamount to fixing, not just games, but entire pennant races, including all postseason series. (If players had been found guilty of making agreements not to compete, the commissioner would have banned them for life— and justifiably.) The fact that *not* signing free agents meant *not* fielding the best teams was revealed graphically when the conspiracy ended. Clubs again vied with each other to sign free agents, at record salaries, in order to become more competitive on the field. Just one of many possible examples is enlightening. After the Giants spent well over $30 million to sign three free agents, the

Dodgers spent over $36 million on three other free agents prior to the 1991 season. Los Angeles general manager Fred Clair said, "The motivation for us is to improve our ball club. It's not a reaction [to the Giants' signing of free agents] *but a dedication to try to be better."*

After the owners, commissioners, league presidents, and general managers had been found guilty of collusion, Giamatti had the gall to say that he saw no evidence of collusion among the owners and that the entire matter was a nonissue. It can be said with certainty that he was lying about not having seen evidence of collusion (the arbitration record of the collusion cases places him *on the scene* at meetings when collusive plans were made). I find it astonishing that he claimed that, as the National League president, he could be completely unaware that all twelve owners in his league were conspiring to violate the basic agreement by agreeing in unison to terminate the market for free agents. In fact, all owners *were* involved in this collusive conspiracy to hold down salaries. It was perhaps the most serious violation of a contract and disregard of players' rights that the owners as a group have engaged in since the pre-Jackie Robinson conspiracy against all nonwhite players. When the arbitrator's decision in the 1987 collusion case came down in 1988, making it clear that *all* officials were involved in collusion, I didn't see a single mention in the press that Giamatti had been league president during that period or that the arbitrator had found he was directly involved, along with other baseball officials. In that decision, the arbitrator, George Nicolau, stressed that the collusion could only have been accomplished with the help of everyone on management's side. The arbitrator cited as important evidence of collusion a letter which Dallas Green had written to Bart Giamatti, Bobby Brown, and Barry Rona which set forth Green's efforts to comply with the collusion policy.

The $280 million settlement which arose out of the arbitrator's awards involved not one penny of *penalty.* The payment was designed simply to "make whole" those players who were damaged by the owners' collusion. (However, since this was a negotiated settlement, the actual loss to the affected players was certainly greater than the amount agreed to in the settlement.) So, on a net basis, the twenty-six offending owners came out with a profit. The fans and writers who seem worried about the poor owners who have to pay out this large sum seem conveniently unaware that this award represents only a return to players of money which they would have had earlier if the owners had not colluded. When a reporter asked Commissioner Fay Vincent why he didn't take any disciplinary action against the guilty owners (as was done with Pete Rose and George Steinbrenner for clearly lesser offenses), Vincent said that since the owners had to pay (back) $280 million, any further discipline would be "double jeopardy"! Imagine that a bank robber was caught red-handed, convicted and forced to return the loot—and then claimed that going to jail constituted double jeopardy! Vincent can't be that uninformed. Rather, I think he was trying to con the reporter by pretending that the $280 million was a disciplinary fine instead of a return of money—the ill-gotten booty of the collusion conspiracy.

As the reader is no doubt well aware, the commissioner who is unable to finesse fact with fiction will no doubt find himself in a lot of hot water with his employers. Like Bowie Kuhn before him and Fay Vincent after, Bart Giamatti let the rhetoric about the "sanctity of baseball" steer him away from the far less idealistic truth that his job, as the owners' appointee, was to stick to representing *their* interests. And like Kuhn and Vincent, he began to see the vagueness of "the best interests of baseball" as blanket permission for him to play prosecutor, judge, and jury when he chose.

Another of Giamatti's judicial decisions was the dismissal of Dave Pallone, the very umpire who had been the source of his first confrontation with Pete Rose. Giamatti threw Pallone out because of a sex scandal. Once again Giamatti deprived a man of his livelihood even though he was not found guilty of any charges in a court of law. Pallone's sexuality is his own business. What is offensive is the way he uses his persecution as a gay in baseball to set himself up as a role model. I think young gay men and women can find better role models among those who don't try to steal other people's jobs. Pallone entered the major leagues as a scab during the 1979 umpires' strike, and his rationalizations for doing so are hypocritical and self-serving (as you would expect any scab's to be: minor league conditions were rough, he hadn't gotten into baseball to spend his life in the minors, etc., as if the same couldn't be said for any of his colleagues.) When Pallone crossed the picket line he forfeited his right to sympathy.

But the point isn't really Pallone, it's Giamatti. Giamatti didn't dismiss Pallone because he was a scab, and he didn't dismiss him because of any allegation of criminal behavior. He dismissed him because his name had been brought up in a sex scandal, and Giamatti saw himself as a man on a moral crusade—due process be damned. I believed that in his short baseball career Giamatti created more problems for the game than he resolved. Already the action against Rose has led directly to the debasement of the Hall of Fame voting procedures and of the Hall of Fame itself. It threatens the very integrity of the writers who, we were told up to now, were free to exercise independent judgment as to selection of inductees. Now they must decide whether to submit to the contamination introduced into the system of determining eligibility.

Like Terry, I never met the man. In 1981, during the strike, Giamatti, then the president of Yale University, wrote an op-ed piece for the *New York Times,* which, in effect called for strike-breaking by the players. He wrote that the players were really so well paid compared to the past, the wrongs of the past toward them had been righted, there was really no issue here worth striking about, there was never an excuse for a strike when reasonable men were involved—crap like that, all swathed in the poetic goo of baseball-ought-to-be-above-such-sordid-money-matters that owners love to see in print because it works on the fans' resentment of the wages of their heroes. In retrospect, I can see that Giamatti was sucking up to the owners even then. He wanted to get into baseball, and this kind of "neutrality" was exactly the kind of partisanship major league management was looking for.

Writers, too. The *Washington Post*'s Tom Boswell once wrote: "The sport's owners hired him in 1986 [to be president of the National League] because he had brains and energy. Now they want him to be the boss because they sense he has fallen in love with their game. Giamatti's long affair with baseball has turned into a marriage." This, from a "tough" writer! It doesn't seem to occur to Boswell that if "brains and energy" were the primary qualifications for the job of league president and commissioner, a great many men who held the posts would never have made it, or that many of those "love affairs" which led to "marriages" later ended in divorce. You'd think an insightful writer like Boswell would understand that what the owners are looking for first, last, and always is someone who they think can best represent their interests. I see absolutely nothing wrong with that, but I'm disgusted that the press allows such blatant self-interest to be served with such a sugar coating.

Anyway, I wrote a reply to the *Times* (with a copy to Giamatti) saying that I was disappointed that a strikebreaking letter had been written by a university president. After all, he ought to know better, since the "nonissue" he was referring to was the players' hard-won right to free agency. To them that was the most important issue of their professional lives. In reply, Giamatti said he couldn't understand why I was so upset about his piece. To this I wrote a detailed letter, restating the union's case and saying that I hoped he'd get his facts straight before once again straying from the groves of academe to the field of labor relations. He wrote me again, saying that we shouldn't waste our time like this; since he came to New York frequently, we should get together and have a drink or lunch and discuss these things.

I said fine, but we never followed up. Not long after Giamatti's piece in the *Times,* Yale's nonfaculty employees—secretaries, clerical and administrative staff, maintenance workers—went on strike. I was tempted to write a letter to Yale's president and governing board of directors reminding them that, according to Giamatti, where there are reasonable men, strikes are not needed. But I had too much on my mind at the time and dropped the idea.

Everyone was shocked at Giamatti's sudden and premature death. But the play must go on, and I recall watching George Steinbrenner on television, emotionally delivering a sort of eulogy and recommending that Giamatti's trusted assistant, Fay Vincent, be named to take his place. Little did Steinbrenner know that scarcely a year after Vincent's ascendancy to the position of commissioner, the favor would not only not be returned, but Steinbrenner would receive the most severe punishment meted out to an owner in recent years. Steinbrenner, after all, had not endeared himself to fellow owners by bidding up the price of free agents. Therefore, it was easy to cast him as the sacrificial lamb and to reinforce the fantasy that the commissioner was evenhanded in his discipline of players and owners alike, when in fact no commissioner can punish all of the owners (even for the most serious offense of collusion) and still remain in office.

Shortly after Fay Vincent replaced Giamatti as commissioner, he invited me to lunch with him. I thought he had the potential to become the best commissioner since I had started with the Players Association. He was more intelligent than Bowie Kuhn, more interested in the game and the problems of the industry than Peter Ueberroth (who often looked like he was counting the house when speaking at baseball functions), and far less pompous and righteous and less of a dilettante than A. Bartlett Giamatti. At that time he displayed a fine sense of humor about himself, a wry recognition of the "figurehead" aspects of his new post, and an eagerness to learn the labor relations history of the baseball business. He knew the difference between management and labor and didn't seem about to fall into the role his predecessors had accepted so avidly, the *deus ex machina*.

Then came the earthquake—literally. The dramatic disruption of the 1989 World Series by the California quake caused members of the press and television to seek a savior. Who should they turn to but the new commissioner? The buildings had scarcely stopped trembling when the reporters began shoving microphones in his face and asking him about all the "decisions" he was going to have to make. Now, precisely which "decisions" was the commissioner of baseball required to make in the midst of earthquake rubble? That the game be played? That decision was made for him by the engineers and city officials and the police, who were in the process of evacuating people even as the reporters were speaking. The decision about what to do next? Well, there was the question about possible aftershocks and their consequences, the structural damage to the ballpark, the facilities at the park, and the ability of Bay area transit to accommodate more than fifty thousand fans. And all the decisions to be made concerning these questions had at least one thing in common: They had absolutely nothing to do with the commissioner of baseball. You might have wondered, listening to the questions, whether the most serious consequence of the earthquake was its effect on major league baseball.

The funny thing is that most of the people asking Vincent the questions seemed unaware of how little say he had about *baseball* matters. Postponing or perhaps canceling the Series? Assuming that it was safe to continue—because if it wasn't safe, the decision would have been taken out of Vincent's and everyone else's hands. It wasn't up to the commissioner of baseball to decide that a Series worth *many* millions of dollars in contractual obligations was going to be scrapped. It's not the commissioner's job to *make* such decisions; it's his job to announce *that they've been made.*

In fact, it's not even clear that Vincent would have had any input into minor decisions, like whether the Series could be played entirely in one ballpark in the area or in a completely different area or even whether the games would be played by day or by night. The owners of the affected franchises just might have something to say about those decisions, to say nothing of NBC-TV's contractual rights in the matter. There were even contractual provisions in the stadium leases that affected such decisions. Yet all the while the sporting media turned only to Fay Vincent for the *answer to it all.*

It's possible that the most unfortunate result of the quake, after the toll in life and property, was that it turned Fay Vincent from such an ordinary man with some sense of balance and humor about his situation into someone who actually began to take seriously the role the media assigned him. I really think he came out of the Bay area a different person. And who can blame him? I still remember the scene on television, not many minutes after the quake had hit. Vincent was on the field surrounded by media people. It seemed fairly dark, with perhaps some emergency lighting. The stands were mostly empty. There were no reports yet on the damage to the stadium, on its structural soundness. Chaos ruled in Candlestick, and this man, shaken and troubled, was being told, in solemn tones, that he had momentous decisions to make, almost as if he could decide whether there should be aftershocks or not. This was the point, I believe, at which the job took possession of Fay Vincent.

Earlier, I mentioned the discrepancy between Pete Rose's "crimes" and those of the 1919 Black Sox. I don't want to rehash the 1919 scandal, nor will I deny that there was evidence that gambling interests were a danger to baseball before the 1920s. But we'll never know how many of the Sox were punished unjustly when they were banned from baseball for life *after* being *cleared* of charges in a court—Shoeless Joe Jackson and Buck Weaver, two of the "eight men out," batted .375 and .324 during the Series, respectively—nor will we know to what degree the tightfisted, meanspirited and questionable tactics of the Chicago owner, Charles Comiskey, contributed to the condition that made the players susceptible to gamblers. But I've always maintained that the question "Why isn't Joe Jackson in the Hall of Fame?" should be supplemented with "Why isn't Charles Comiskey *out?*"

The point, though, is that when Judge Kenesaw Mountain Landis was made commissioner, he was given wide powers by the owners to "clean up" baseball, and that meant, in that context, policing the players. It didn't mean the commissioner had the power to open the gates to black and Hispanic players, who were discriminated against for another quarter century, and more. It simply meant that the owners had selected a person to act in their best interests, a man who could brandish over the players the weapon called "the best interests of baseball," and do so in almost any manner he chose, without fear that the courts would interfere.

To maintain the fiction that baseball was a game, not a business—it is, of course, both—the owners were forced to pretend that they had given the commissioner unlimited power over them as well. But the commissioner's power over the players was real, while his power over the owners was only theoretical. He served for a specified term and could be replaced when his term was over, and his contract could be bought out at any time. In other words, whatever power a commissioner thought he had over the owners, the truth was that he was their man and was chosen to represent their interests, and if he ever became forgetful of this, he could be quickly reminded. Landis and Giamatti died in office. Every single commissioner between them was decisively reminded where the real power was situated.

The commissioner's relationship to the owners is neither secret nor complex. Although nominally authorized to enforce the rules and to use wide discretionary powers—even against owners—his discretion, in practice, is confined to what the owners as a group deem appropriate. There is a vast difference between acting against a maverick owner who is disliked, or distrusted, by the more powerful owners and disciplining one of the more popular, powerful owners. It's no coincidence that over the last seventeen years all the owners who have been penalized by the commissioner—Steinbrenner, by suspension in 1974 and permanent ineligibility in 1990; Ted Turner, by suspension in 1977; Charles Finley, by the $400,000 rule in 1976 and the vetoing of his profitable sale of players; Ray Kroc, by a fine—were relatively new kids on the block and considered expendable by establishment owners. It's always amazed me that so few baseball writers have grasped this obvious fact, opting instead for a romantic view of the commissioner as some kind of Socrates or Solomon whom baseball people flock to for an objective view of a current crisis. The owners select the commissioner and pay his salary, and they do not pay him to be objective. If Fay Vincent or any other commissioner ever attempted to act "in the best interests of baseball" *but* against the best interests of a significant group of owners, the press's illusions about the commissioner's power would be quickly shattered.

In February 1991, Vincent initiated himself into the "Illusion of the Commissioner Having Real Power Club" when, returning to his office after recovering from an illness, he held a press conference and announced, among other things, that ten clubs lost money in 1990. Some lost "substantial" amounts, he said, and other clubs were certain to suffer the same fate in 1991. (He declined to identify any of the clubs.) Either the assembled press didn't ask, or didn't get answers to, such questions as: Had Vincent seen audited financial reports? How much of the so-called losses was due to creative accounting? How much was due to tax gimmicks, such as depreciation of players (a tax break not found in other industries)? How many of the clubs were charging the payback of their three-year collusion gains to a single year's operations? How was this alleged poverty possible, given the latest $1-billion-plus TV-radio contract? And did anyone get an answer to the most obvious questions of all: With so many established clubs losing money in 1990 (and others supposedly headed for losses in 1991), why is it that when a club is sold it brings a record-high price? And why are the latest expansion franchises drawing astronomical prices ($95 million) from businessmen across the country who are competing for the privilege of buying into this "losing" proposition of baseball?

At the same press conference, Vincent responded to earlier stories claiming that unnamed owners were predicting that he would be out of office in a year. In what can be termed the fantasy of the year, Vincent was quoted as saying, "I'm not going to resign. . . . The decision whether I stay or go is mine. . . . That's the way it is. Whoever said it obviously doesn't understand how the constitution works."

Huh? Vincent also reportedly said that he was "immune" to any attempt to remove him from office before he completed his term. I know Vincent is an attorney, but he ought to consult one if he really believes those two statements. The hard facts are that he is an employee, and he has a personal-service contract. If the owners want to terminate him before his contract expires (and if they pay him the full amount called for in his contract), it would be Adios Fay—as in So-long Happy (Chandler), Sayonara Spike (Eckert), and Bye-bye Bowie. Despite these shortcomings, I don't wish Fay Vincent any bad luck. He may be the best baseball commissioner of the last quarter century.

The fantasy life of a commissioner has always been a problem. When the Players Association began to gain some leverage at the bargaining table, the commissioner's power over the players was seriously curtailed. Recognition that this was so took time to sink in. Ironically, the commissioner's real power isn't over the players, who are protected by the Players Association, but over owners like Steinbrenner, who are subjected to arbitrary punishment without the protection of due process.

I followed the events of 1990, and I think fans either misunderstood or completely ignored a number of important points, starting with the $225,000 fine levied on Steinbrenner by Vincent for "tampering"* during the Dave Winfield—Mike Witt deal. Although it was called a "trade," the deal wasn't completed in the usual way. The Angels assigned Witt to the Yankees, which officially made him a Yankee; Winfield's contract was "assigned" to the Angels in exchange, but because he was a "ten and five player" (ten years in the majors, the last five with the same team), he had a right to veto a trade, and he did so.

I don't think Dave was seriously considering remaining a Yankee at that point, partly because of near-constant harassment by

---

*Tampering means dealing with another club's player.

Steinbrenner, but also because the Yankees simply weren't playing him and the Angels obviously wanted to. But Dave also was prepared to oppose the "trade" on principle. A trade without his consent was a violation of the basic agreement. Until he gave his consent, Winfield was never off New York's roster.

During this period, while Winfield was still a Yankee, he and Steinbrenner had some discussion, presumably about terms. California protested, and their trusty agent, Commissioner Vincent, injected himself into the situation and found Steinbrenner guilty of "tampering." Simply put, the decision was asinine. It probably was the first time—and I hope the last—that a club was found guilty of tampering with its own player! Vincent even showed a lack of understanding of his own decision, making another ruling that the Yankees were responsible for Winfield's salary during the period in question, including the day George allegedly "tampered" by talking with Winfield. How you can be responsible for paying a player's salary while "tampering" with him is a mystery worthy of Sherlock Holmes. Winfield, finally, was able to make a better deal for himself and consented to the trade. But what if he hadn't? What if Vincent's meddling had resulted in Winfield's *not* getting the offer he wanted? I think Vincent is fortunate that Winfield was able to make a better deal with the Angels and therefore had no interest in filing a grievance.

Looked at separately or altogether, I can't see any *logic* to Giamatti's and Vincent's decisions. But I can see a *pattern,* namely, once they committed themselves to an investigation, they immediately abandoned such cumbersome devices as due process and precedent and tried to obscure the issue by talking about the "best interests of baseball." The Vincent action barring Steinbrenner did have some unique aspects. For one thing it gave the appearance of a commissioner taking drastic action against an owner (Steinbrenner) because of the owner's mistreatment of a player (Winfield). This turned out not to be the case. To me, the most curious fact about the infamous Steinbrenner-Vincent transcripts is that Vincent admits that the commissioner's office had known about Steinbrenner's "association" with Howard Spira since 1987 and did nothing. According to the hearing transcript, Steinbrenner at one point asked: "Why didn't somebody come to me in September of '87 and say 'Keep us [the Commissioner's office] posted,' instead of the PRC [Player Relations Committee] supposedly telling Spira, 'Continue dealing with the Yankees. We're aware of what's going on'?" And Vincent's answer was "Among the things that didn't happen is your own advisors didn't tell you in a way that persuaded you not to do what you were doing during '87 and '89. . . . I'm just focusing on right now because I happen to have been commissioner on the very day you paid this gambler, former gambler. . . . Why didn't you call, get help from other people. . . . ?" Get help from "other people"? That statement is ridiculous; if the commissioner's office wasn't going to help, then who was supposed to? Just how exactly was it in "the best interests of baseball" for *three* commissioners to know about an owner's "involvement" with a known gambler and not pick up the phone and warn him of the consequences?

If you read of such a thing in a detective novel, it would seem an awful lot like someone wanted George Steinbrenner to walk into a trap—one he had set for himself, to be sure, but a trap nonetheless. Steinbrenner was railroaded out of baseball on charges so flimsy that it's impossible to imagine his being taken to court on them. What was his "crime"? That he paid $40,000 to a "known" gambler? (What, I wonder, is an "unknown gambler"?) Let's disregard the cloud of excuses he made for paying the money—surely it should come as no surprise to find that Steinbrenner at times bends a long bow. If he paid the money to get dirt on Winfield, was he doing anything different than other owners have done over the years? Not that I can see. Why the sudden move by the commissioner's office to regulate the actions of one owner?

Don't misunderstand me. I'm not minimizing the possible damage that could come from paying money to gamblers, and I'm delighted to see an owner who was trying to besmirch the reputation of a player walk into his own booby trap. But if Dave Winfield felt his rights in this matter were violated, the case would come under the jurisdiction of the Players Association, *not* the commissioner's office; Donald Fehr and not Fay Vincent would take up Winfield's case. But Vincent's office didn't claim to represent Winfield, and Winfield never filed a grievance. So what is Steinbrenner guilty of? "Association" with a gambler. Okay. But no one implied that Steinbrenner's connection with Spira involved gambling. Why not brush aside the misdemeanor with a brief suspension or a fine or both?

I believe that's what would have happened if it had been almost any other owner but George. But of course, we all know that Steinbrenner was on trial for a multitude of sins that were more despicable than the $40,000 payment to Spira. The thing is that the press was condemning Steinbrenner for one set of crimes, namely, his treatment of his players, coaches, and managers and the destruction of the Yankee organization as a whole, and what really did Steinbrenner in was something quite different. In the end, Steinbrenner was gone because the other owners wanted him gone. Not so much out of personal dislike—it's not inconceivable that a few of the many owners who were reportedly anti-George might have been his friends—but because George Steinbrenner had been a loose cannon on the owners' ship for a long time. (As I said in the Steinbrenner chapter, it was his spending that the owners, by colluding, aimed at curbing in the first place.) A prime example is the $2.5 million he was all set to offer outfielder/defensive back Deion Sanders: I don't think we need to consult the Elias Sports Bureau to determine that this would have made Deion the first .160-hitting multimillionaire in baseball. And I think it was no coincidence that the offer was withdrawn at the time Steinbrenner met with Vincent.

Months after he was banned, George petitioned Vincent for permission to negotiate with free agents on behalf of the Yankees. Steinbrenner, to no one's surprise, was turned down; the very last thing that Vincent and the other owners wanted was for George to deal with free agents even though the Steinbrenner-Vincent agreement indicates that doing so might be permissible. (This raises an interesting question: If Vincent, either on behalf of the owners, or in connection with some or all of them, extends the ban on Steinbrenner's activities to prevent him from dealing with free agents, is that "concerted activity with respect to free agents"—an act that violates the basic agreement?)

It would take quite a leap to believe that Fay Vincent (with some important help from Steinbrenner) forced George out of baseball on his own. As is so often the case, the record simply does not come close to providing a rationale for permanent banishment from the game. Once again, the punishment does not fit the crime.

Once again, the victim's lack of popularity with much of the media guaranteed that there would be few, if any, close looks at what was done allegedly "in the best interests of the game."

One very important fact the press managed to overlook during the Steinbrenner circus was the arbitrator's decision on the 1987 collusion, which proved conclusively that for the third consecutive year *every* owner and his officials were guilty of acting against baseball's best interests. I'm not saying that the Steinbrenner mess was arranged to push the collusion decision to the back pages, but if it had been, I don't know how it could have been done more effectively. (Fay Vincent has never said a word about fining or otherwise punishing the owners for conspiracy to undermine their own agreement with the players. I very much doubt that he ever will. If he does, the question of whether he is immune from discharge will become academic.)

Shortly before Steinbrenner was to meet with Vincent, George complained to the press, "If [the commissioner] can't get the guy on this rule or that rule, [he] can always get him on 'the best interests of baseball.' " And he said: "The rule's too hard. It places the commissioner above the law and baseball above the law of the land." Steinbrenner's remarks were self-serving, but for once he was right. Not, of course, that he had rushed to Pete Rose's defense when the same assertion of "best interests" was involved. The problem for Vincent may be that he perceives his powers to be unlimited in *fact,* not in *theory.* For instance, if he had simply ruled that Steinbrenner had to sell the Yankees, he would have quickly found that his employers, the owners, were not granting him the power to make such arbitrary decisions with their property. He would also have found, if it came to that, that no court would have allowed a so-called "self-governing body" to take away a $200 million property; courts are often fuzzy about civil rights, but seldom about property rights. On second thought, make that *never* about property.

Finally, although the salaries of free agents signed after the 1989 and 1990 seasons indicate that collusion is (for the time being) not in operation, there is already some evidence that the owners are still looking for ways to violate the basic agreement without getting caught. A case in point may well be the jockeying that surrounded the selection of Robert Nederlander as the Yankees' managing partner. In order to become managing partner, Nederlander had to secure the approval of the commissioner and the other owners in the American League. He did both. After the American League meeting, Nederlander stressed that he would operate the Yankees with "fiscal responsibility." Several months later, he and Yankee general manager Gene Michael were quoted in the *New York Times* as disparaging George's "outlandish" spending on free agents. They said, "The new direction in the post-George Steinbrenner era is *fiscal responsibility,* free spending [on] free agents . . . [is] apparently gone forever." Fiscal responsibility was the phrase the owners used at the collusion hearings: We hadn't "colluded," they swore under oath; we were simply exercising "fiscal responsibility." (It reminded me of another code word, "states' rights," that bigoted Southern congressmen used years ago when they tried to shoot down federal civil rights legislation.)

Perhaps it's just a coincidence that the phrase "fiscal responsibility" resurfaced after Vincent handed Steinbrenner his walking papers. And perhaps it's just coincidence that unlike, say, the Dodgers, who recently signed talented free agents like Brett Butler and Darryl Strawberry, or the Giants, who signed Willie McGee and Dave Righetti (a Yankee mainstay) during the off-season in order to compete with Cincinnati for the pennant, the Yankees—a last-place club and one of the wealthiest in baseball—have shown a conspicuous reluctance to make meaningful moves in the free-agent market since Nederlander's ascension.

During the first collusion hearings the arbitrator asked for the minutes of the owners' meetings where collusion was discussed. The owners' story was that none were kept for those meetings. (We can only assume that Rosemary Woods didn't show up for work that week.) I wonder what the minutes would reveal about the league meeting at which Nederlander related his fondness for the phrase "fiscal responsibility"; that is, unless it was decided not to keep the minutes of that meeting.

I love baseball as it is, and I don't harbor sentimental illusions about it. I'm constantly amazed at the softheadedness of even the best baseball writers, who yearn for some remote past where "money wasn't so much a part of the game." When, I wonder, was that time? Does anyone who thinks about it for one minute believe that ballplayers voluntarily played for less than they were worth, or that owners fought for one hundred years to keep the reserve rule because of idealism and not because of a profit motive? Is there something romantic in seeing former ballplayers, the heroes of the writers' childhoods, pumping gas or tending bar (both honorable occupations) when they could have been living in relative comfort? Why did the issue of greed only enter the picture when the players finally got a fairer slice of the pie? Lest we forget, that pie became much bigger *because* of the players' unionizing efforts.

I read sportswriters who lament the players' "decline of loyalty" to teams, fans, and cities, but I never read accusations of disloyalty against the owners when they trade a team's favorite players (or for that matter move entire, long-established teams to bigger markets). Loyalty, as conceived by many writers, is a one-way street; players apparently owe loyalty to their clubs, but when their clubs trade them or sell them for cash, or simply fire them, that's okay— because it's business. And as we all know, loyalty has no place in business.

Given the consistent record of collusion, contract violations, hypocrisy, and just plain bad faith by the owners and their officials, and their seeming immunity from legislative or judicial oversight, and little or no tradition of investigative reporting in the sports field to educate the fans and public, the union—the Major League Baseball Players Association—may well be the only counter to a return to collusion and a pronounced unconcern for the *real* integrity of the game.

It has been twenty-five years since the baseball players came of age by moving to protect their real interests with a legitimate union. I doubt there'll be much media recognition when the silver anniversary comes, July 1, 1991, but it is important for players and the public alike to realize the source of the wealth and dignity of the players. It's a tough job for the Players Association—being the only force serving as a bulwark against an unregulated monopoly with antisocial tendencies—but somebody's got to do it.

INDEX